The Egan Irish Harps

To Alex —
a rebel for life_

Love,
Nancy Hurrell
July 19, 2019

THE EGAN IRISH HARPS

Tradition, patrons and players

Nancy Hurrell

FOUR COURTS PRESS

Set in 11.5pt on 13.5pt Centaur by
Carrigboy Typesetting Services for
FOUR COURTS PRESS LTD
7 Malpas Street, Dublin 8, Ireland
www.fourcourtspress.ie
and in North America for
FOUR COURTS PRESS
c/o IPG, 814 N Franklin St, Chicago, IL 60622.

A catalogue record for this title is available
from the British Library.

ISBN 978-1-84682-759-4

Printed in England
by CPI Antony Rowe, Chippenham, Wilts.

Contents

List of illustrations

FIGURES

PLATES

(between pages 128 and 129)

Acknowledgments

I was first introduced to a harp by John Egan in 2002, when the owner of a Royal Portable Irish Harp asked for my assistance in finding a suitable home for the historic instrument, where it could be appreciated (the harp is now on view at the John J. Burns Library, Boston College). At the time, there seemed to be very little written information on the Irish maker, and I began to examine Egan harps in various collections, with the generous assistance of curators, librarians and private collectors. I am deeply grateful to Darcy Kuronen, Pappalardo Curator of Musical Instruments at the Museum of Fine Arts, Boston, for his expertise and perspectives, and for putting me in touch with curators of musical instrument collections in museums in New England, the UK and continental Europe. Elizabeth Sweeney, librarian at the John J. Burns Library, Boston College, has also provided valuable assistance and access to important archival papers in the library's Irish Collection. I am indebted to Dr Jennifer Goff, curator of furniture, silver, metalware, music, science and the Eileen Gray Collection at the National Museum of Ireland, Collins Barracks, for allowing me to study the rare Egan harps in museum storage and for permission to use my photos in this book. I am grateful to Siobhán Fitzpatrick at the Royal Irish Academy for inviting me to lecture on Thomas Moore's Egan Irish harp in 2008; the numerous attendees who shared their historical harp anecdotes with me after the lecture influenced the writing of this book.

I owe special thanks to Nicholas Carolan, director emeritus, Irish Traditional Music Archive, for generously spending a morning with me contemplating answers to my questions, and to members of his helpful ITMA staff, Treasa Harkin and Maeve Gebruers. A collaboration with Una Hunt on an RTÉ Lyric FM programme on Sydney Owenson enlightened my research on this important literary figure, who played an Egan harp. Museum curators I wish to thank include Elaine Flanigan, Irish Linen Centre & Lisburn Museum; Annika McSeveny, Fermanagh County Museum; Linda Fairlie and Bruce Morgan, Dean Castle, Kilmarnock; Eamonn McEneaney and Rosemary Ryan, Waterford Treasures; Jennifer Nex, formerly at the Royal College of Music Museum, London; Margaret Birley and Mimi Waitzman, the Horniman Museum, London; Jayson Dobney and Dr Bradley Strauchen-Scherer, Metropolitan

Museum of Art, New York; David Mullin, Museum in the Park, Stroud; Kazuhiko Shima, Hamamatsu Museum of Musical Instruments, Japan; Evren Celimli, Harvard University. I wish to also thank Hans Zomer and John Grennan at Áras an Uachtaráin, the official residence of the president of Ireland, for allowing access to the historical Irish harp on display there, and for permission to use my photos of it in this book.

The earl and countess of Ross have my special gratitude for allowing me to perform a concert on Lady Alicia's splendid Portable Irish Harp and to study her harp music. Alec Cobbe has also generously assisted my research with information on his harpist ancestors and allowed me to study the three rare Egan harps at Hatchlands Park and one at Newbridge House in the Cobbe Collection. Siobhán Armstrong, Sarah Burn and Bonnie Shaljean all kindly arranged for me to examine Egan harps in private collections in Ireland, for which I am grateful. At the Royal Academy of Music Museum, for assistance in my research, I wish to thank Chris Nobbs, Janet Snowman, Barbara Meyer, Angela Doane, Gabrielle Gale and Ian Brearey. For photographs of Egan harps, thanks go to Robert and Audrey Gilmer and her father's legacy of the harp, Bill and Vicky Bodine, Ann Heymann, Linda P. Kaiser, Marilyn Rummel, Matthew Hurrell, Emily Laurance, Robert Adelson, Conall Ó Catháin, Hayato Sugimoto and Jim Dunne. Thanks also to Roberta Scarzello of Museo dell'Arpa Victor Salvi, Italy, for allowing me to include images of the beautiful Egan harp in the collection. I am indebted to several harp restorers, particularly Michael Parfett in London, who has continually answered my questions over the years and has faithfully alerted me whenever an Egan harp crossed his path. Other historical harp experts and technicians who were extraordinarily helpful include Paul Knoke, Howard Bryan, Bart Bjorneberg, Robert Pacey, Simon Chadwick, Arsalaan Fay, Rainer Thurau, Dr Panagiotis Poulopoulos, Tim Hamilton and Sam Milligan.

The production of this book would not be possible without the generosity of my sponsors, and I wish to particularly thank John and Patricia O'Brien for their financial support (arranged by Marty Fahey of O'Brien International), and to Dr Christian Dupont for additional generous support from the Mary Stack McNiff Fund, John J. Burns Library, Boston College. The research would not have been possible without the Historical Harp Society of America, an organization that continues to stimulate my interest in historical harps, and heartfelt thanks go to the Boston Biographers Group, who informed and encouraged me throughout the entire process. Finally, I'm especially grateful to Philip and my family, which also includes my Scots-Irish great-grandmother whom I never met, Mary Lindsey, and to her daughter, Fanny Clark — my grandmother, whose dream it was for me to play the harp.

Introduction

Ireland's harp tradition is at the core of the country's national identity and rich musical heritage. An Ireland without harps is unimaginable, and yet by 1800, the Irish harp, played in the country for nearly a thousand years, had all but disappeared and the esteemed harping tradition suddenly faced an uncertain future. The native Gaelic harp, or *cláirseach*, had a distinctive form with a curved pillar and a chunky sound chamber hewn from a single log. Ireland's wire-strung harp was renowned for its bright metallic sound and a prolonged resonance. The modal tuning of the Gaelic harp was well-suited to the ancient airs, and the instrument and players were esteemed at medieval courts and later were welcomed as resident performers in the big houses. By the eighteenth century, musical tastes had changed, however, with a preference for the Italianate art music imported from the Continent, and the Gaelic harp's limited tonal range was not idiomatic to the new chromatic style. The hand-carved Gaelic harp became obsolete as it was superseded in the music room by modern, sophisticated instruments, such as the harpsichord, pianoforte and French pedal harp. These instruments not only possessed the preferred delicate sound qualities and requisite semitones for the new music, they also doubled as exquisitely ornate pieces of furniture. Recognizing the reasons for the abandonment of the native harp, a young harp maker, John Egan (*fl.* 1797–1829), perceived an opening for a modernized national instrument. Egan developed a new Irish harp – one with a lighter timbre suited to the classical style, and Regency elegance. The Portable Irish Harp, later renamed the Royal Portable Irish Harp, was handsomely decorated with neoclassical motifs in gold, and it was an up-to-date chromatic instrument with a modern sound. Extolled in advertisements for its 'great brilliancy and sweetness of tone', it was strung with gut strings and fitted with modern mechanisms to facilitate key changes. Constructed with thin pieces of wood joined together, its organology was entirely different from the Gaelic harp, and yet Egan desired a connection with Ireland's former instrument, if only a superficial one. With its bowed pillar shape and small size, the model visually paid homage to Ireland's oldest and most celebrated instrument, the iconic 'Brian Boru' harp.[1] The harp's contour

1 The Trinity College harp and the Portable Irish Harp are both about 3ft in height and have

14

was characterized in the *Morning Post* as 'being [in] the exact form as the beautiful antique Irish Harp in the Museum of Trinity College, Dublin'.[2] John Egan had effectively fused old with new for his Irish harp, and the patriotic messaging was further enhanced by golden shamrocks embellished on a painted body of either green, blue or black. Barely 3ft in height, the Portable Irish Harp's small size was perhaps its most appealing feature, for it not only rendered the instrument portable, but also made it affordable.

Egan's Portable Irish Harp was a significant invention. Introduced at a pivotal moment in Irish history, it would lead the country's harping tradition into the future. The new Irish harp entered the marketplace as a nationalistic product, alongside Thomas Moore's *Irish melodies* and Sydney Owenson's national tales, in the politically charged era following the enactment of the Act of Union with Britain in 1801. The national branding of the instrument led to its immediate success among Egan's Anglo-Irish clients, for a small, green shamrock-adorned harp had potent patriotic associations. Over time the popular model came to be regarded as the template for Irish harp manufacture. It is no accident that the Portable Irish Harp set the standard for others to emulate, for the Egan instruments were well-designed and finely crafted. Nearly a century later, in the early 1900s, several principal harp makers imitated the Portable Irish Harp model, with minor design modifications, for their own versions of Irish harps, and a new generation of instruments was essential to the continuance of an Irish harp tradition. The modern Irish harp or 'Celtic' harp is still prized two hundred years on for the same qualities of portable size, chromatic capabilities, bright tone and affordability.

In the centuries since the Portable Irish Harp's invention, the practices of societal music-making have changed significantly, and the cultural perceptions of the Irish harp have evolved. As the model's name suggests, the Portable Irish Harp was initially promoted in the early 1800s as a uniquely 'portable' instrument, a suitable travel harp for aristocratic ladies embarking on the grand tour of Europe. It was seen as a practical second instrument for upper-class harpists who owned a large French pedal harp, a static instrument that would have remained in the music room. The portable harp model, promoted as 'not one-third the price or size' of a pedal harp,[3] was also an affordable alternative for aspiring harpists in the emerging merchant classes. Later, in the 1880s, a revived interest in Irish harp production commenced outside of Ireland: Joseph George Morley (1847–1921) copied Egan's model in England, and American harp

bowed pillars. The similarity is in contour only, as the organology of the two instruments greatly differs. Whereas the soundbox of the Trinity College harp is rectangular and carved from a log of wood, the Portable Irish Harp has a conical shaped soundbox and is constructed from pieces of wood joined together.   2 *Morning Post*, 5 June 1821.   3 Ibid., 29 Dec. 1826.

maker Melville Clark (1883–1953), working in the early 1900s, introduced his
Clark Irish Harp model based on Egan's design.[4] The harp companies of
Morley, Clark and later Lyon & Healy stressed the Irish identity of the
shamrock-adorned instruments, and the symbolic harps were attractive to
consumers in the Irish diaspora. The companies also adopted a marketing
strategy to promote the small Irish harps as suitable teaching instruments for
children. The harp firms, primarily operating as pedal harp manufacturers,
skilfully created a perception of the Irish harp as a temporary 'stepping stone'
to the eventual purchase of a more expensive pedal harp. Viewed through the
subjective lens of the 'superior' pedal harp, for a time the nomenclature used for
the small gut-strung Irish harp was simply the '*non*-pedal harp' or the 'lever harp',
with levers as the recognized equivalent to pedals.

Another shift in the perception of the Irish harp occurred in the late
twentieth century, with the rise of a vibrant cottage industry of independent
harp workshops in Ireland, the United Kingdom and America. The small gut-
strung harp came to be recognized as an instrument in its own right, with its
own musical heritage (particularly Irish and Scottish), which was separate from
that of the pedal harp. The independent harp makers offered greater choice in
size, contours and woods used for harp models, making Irish harps attractive
to increasing numbers of players. Since its invention, Ireland's portable harp has
experienced a cultural metamorphosis from an elite instrument in the 1820s
drawing room, to the instrument of the modern harpist joining fiddlers and
pipers in traditional sessions at the local pub. Today all genres of music are
embraced on the modern chromatic Irish harp, from traditional to classical, with
popular trends moving towards contemporary jazz. The portable harps are
regarded as convenient for transporting to gatherings of amateur players referred
to as harp circles, harp ensembles or harp orchestras.

Although the Royal Portable Irish Harp is considered John Egan's seminal
achievement, it is just one of several innovative harp designs in his extraordinary
body of work. The maker's signature – *John Egan, Inventor* – as engraved on the
brass plate of his pioneering Portable Irish Harp model, offers an insight into
what he valued in the process of harp-making. Whether imaginative by nature
or influenced by the 'improving age' in which he lived, John Egan was interested
in turning his visionary mental images into functioning instruments. Egan's
experimental prototypes were produced in a range of sizes and unconventional
forms, and he invented several groundbreaking mechanisms to facilitate greater
chromaticism. His ingenious hand-operated dital mechanism for changing keys
on portable harps was revolutionary, and he advanced pedal harp technology by

4 Morley and Clark each owned examples of Egan's Portable Irish Harp.

successfully manufacturing a *triple*-action pedal harp, capable of producing extreme tonalities. Egan continually pushed the conventional boundaries of harp construction, housing several of his playable instruments inside unorthodox bodies. One example is an unusual pedal harp formed with a curved pillar cast in bronze, and another extraordinary harp has a sculpted pillar in the form of a winged-maiden or Hibernia, with her wings cast in brass to form the instrument's harmonic curve. In the context of early nineteenth-century harp-making, Egan stood apart from his counterparts abroad who produced more standardized pedal harp designs in established London factories. The self-taught Dublin harp maker, working on his own at a distance across the Irish Sea, not only had the freedom to experiment with new ideas, but he also had the advantage of Ireland's special relationship with the cherished national instrument. The socio-political environment of early 1800s Ireland elevated the importance of his work and played a crucial role in initiating the development of new forms of Irish harps.

An Egan harp is admired for its handsome decoration and interesting construction, but the ultimate function of an instrument is to produce musical sounds. Therefore, in this book each Egan model is placed in an historical setting of musical performance, with descriptions of the players, the repertoire performed and contemporary observations of the harp's sound. Several notable figures played Egan harps, for Egan's patrons hailed from the noble families of Ireland as well as the ruling British aristocracy. Skilfully negotiating the conflicting political loyalties of post-union Ireland, the resourceful entrepreneur seemingly played to 'both sides' by supporting nationalist efforts to revive the native instrument, while at the same time courting commissions for pedal harps from the wives of the British viceroys residing at Dublin Castle. Eventually the instruments of John Egan attracted the attention of the king, and remarkably, several harps of Irish manufacture were delivered to Windsor Castle to be played by members of the royal family. In 1821, Egan was bestowed the prestigious appointment of 'Harp Maker to George IV', an astounding achievement for an Irishman.

This book's prologue explores the harp as a symbol of national identity, and the pictorial representations on coins and official crests are compared to actual contemporary playable instruments in Ireland. The prologue also charts the cultural role of the Gaelic harp, from a high-status position at court in early times to eventual decline in late eighteenth-century society. The chapters that follow introduce Egan harp models in order of invention, starting with the earliest surviving examples of pedal harps detailed in chapter 1. In post-union Ireland the exodus of Irish peers to London created a cultural shift, enabling new opportunities for a rising merchant class, and the chapter recounts how a young John Egan abandoned his blacksmith apprenticeship to start a harp workshop on Dawson Street. Chapter 2 covers Egan's newly invented small Irish harp as played by the literary celebrity Sydney Owenson (Lady Morgan). Owenson, an acquaintance of Egan, was known for her effective use of harp metaphors in nationalistic works, and this chapter uncovers new information on her harp, the music she played and her performance style. Chapter 3 identifies the lasting impact of Egan's wire-strung Improved Irish Harp models made for the Irish Harp Society schools in Dublin and Belfast, detailing how the instrument enabled the continued transmission of Ireland's ancient harp music into the late nineteenth century. The chapter highlights the celebrated careers of Patrick Byrne and other wire harp players, and an overview of the few surviving wire-strung instruments is given. Chapter 4 tells of the invention and the introduction in 1819 of Egan's Portable Irish Harp model with ditals, which was played by Thomas Moore, another acquaintance of Egan. The remarkable events of George IV's historic visit to Ireland in 1821 are reconstructed in chapter 5, with vivid descriptions of a succession of royal harp performances, commencing with the harp maker's son, Charles, playing Irish airs at the viceroy's official residence at Phoenix Park upon the king's arrival. Noteworthy concerts on Egan harps were given by the famed harpist N.C. Bochsa at St Patrick's cathedral, and Egan wire-strung harps were also used in performance at a magnificent state banquet held at the Mansion House. Finally, this chapter reveals the untold story of Egan's prestigious appointment as harp maker to the king, and the part played by a spectacular harp presented to George IV.

Chapter 6 identifies Egan family members who carried on the legendary harp business as it was passed on to the next generation and uncovers new information on a contentious sibling rivalry of competing family harp businesses. The charmed career of John Egan's son Charles is brought to light, with insights into his work as a composer and harp professor to the king's sister, Princess Augusta, a position that proved to be advantageous for promoting his father's inventions. In chapter 7, the societal role of the harp as a female 'accomplishment' is investigated through the life experiences and surviving instruments of three women who played Egan harps: Lady Alicia Parsons (Birr Castle), Frances Power Cobbe (Newbridge House) and Isabella Kelly (Thurles), a convent student who became the wife of the Irish composer William Wallace. Chapter 8 charts the development of the gut-strung Irish harp from the first examples faithfully imitating Egan's Portable Irish Harp, as exemplified by the iconic Robinson & Bussell harp displayed in Áras an Uachtaráin, which is now the official residence of the president of Ireland, to later models based on aspects of Egan's design. Tracing the instruments produced by later generations of harp makers, the Egan legacy of harp design and the lasting influence on the

Irish harping tradition is realized. The epilogue establishes the value of antique Egan harps as prized historical artefacts conserved by museums and collectors worldwide. The catalogue of John Egan harps in appendix 3 provides information on extant instruments, including serial numbers, dates, measurements, inscriptions and decorative styles.

Finally, this book presents new research on the sounds produced by Egan harps, based on my experience of playing several surviving instruments. The correlation between an Egan harp's tonal qualities and aspects of its construction is explored, and nineteenth-century pedal harps are compared with modern instruments. I aim to inform readers of the exceptional sound of Egan harps and to dispel an ill-founded negative perception which has persisted for many years. In Joan Rimmer's *The Irish harp* (1969), the author scathingly portrays the wire-strung 'neo-Irish' harps made by John Egan and his nephew, Francis Hewson, as 'nightmare parodies of the old Irish harp'.[5] Rimmer condemns the harp's sound as 'peculiarly unattractive', likening it to a 'decrepit piano', and finishes her critique with a final complaint about the resonance as 'excessively long-lasting unless damped'.[6] Unfortunately, the author offers no information as to the exact harp she played, but it may have been an example held in the National Museum of Ireland (pictured next to her text), where strings are kept at a low pitch and old wire strings typically descend into a state of deadened overtones. It is important to regard Rimmer's observations as a subjective point of view reflecting her preference for the Gaelic harp over the revival harps of Egan and Hewson. Owing to a lack of published resources on the organology of historical Irish harps, these fleeting negative impressions of the Egan harp's sound have been perceived as definitive facts and as such have been quoted in articles and books for decades. One significant example is the article on John Egan written by Brian Boydell in the 1997 *New Grove dictionary of musical instruments* stating the tone of surviving Egan harps was judged to be 'poor'.[7] To complicate the issue, there is a general lack of understanding as to the different Egan harp models produced, with no distinction between wire-strung and gut-strung instruments, and the disparaging pronouncement by Rimmer has been hastily applied to *all* Egan harps. A decidedly different opinion was put forth by the

5 Joan Rimmer, *The Irish harp* (Cork, 1969; 2nd ed., 1977), p. 67.   6 Ibid. Rimmer's comment on the quality of resonance as 'excessively long-lasting unless damped' is puzzling, since lasting resonance is a desirable quality for a wire-strung harp. The corresponding photo in the book is not of an Egan harp, but of a Hewson wire-strung harp in the National Museum of Ireland. The instrument's soundboard is greatly damaged, with several horizontal sections coming apart and large gaps in the lower area, which would have affected the sound if indeed this was the instrument she played.   7 Brian Boydell, 'Egan, John' in Stanley Sadie (ed.), *New Grove dictionary of musical instruments* (London, 1997), p. 645.

eminent harp historian R.B. Armstrong, who owned and played an Egan wire-strung harp. He wrote, 'It is unlikely any harper would be dissatisfied with the tone of the specimen described.'[8]

The idea that Egan harps are inferior to the older Gaelic harps is a matter of opinion and preference. An older instrument is not automatically better, but harps of a great age are rare, as wooden stringed instruments tend to not survive. Similarly, a newer instrument model is not necessarily better than an older one, as musical instruments are not evolutionary in the same sense as plants and animals in nature. Changes in instrumental design, decoration, mechanisms and sound are driven by fashion and tastes in music at any given time. In the case of Ireland's national instrument, perceptions may be influenced by interpretations of political history, whereby Egan harps manufactured in post-union Ireland may be perceived as lacking the pure Irish authenticity of pre-1800 instruments. I take a broader view, encompassing the great span of harp history, whereby instruments are rarely created in a vacuum. A newly invented instrument usually combines elements borrowed from several others. On the 1734 Bunworth Irish *cláirseach* in the Boston Museum of Fine Arts, for example, a head carved on the finial resembles earlier figurative carvings on German hook harps from around 1700, which in turn may have been inspired by the female torsos on even earlier baroque *arpa doppias* in Italy. Similarly, for Egan's 'new' wire-strung harps for the society schools, the maker combined the elements of rounded-back pedal harp construction with a high-headed Gaelic harp shape. The Portable Irish Harp also draws inspiration from the Gaelic harp shape, as well as pedal harp soundbox construction and mechanisms from hybrid instruments, but the unique combination of all these various elements was truly groundbreaking. Ultimately, the success of an instrument is gauged by its use and the impact it has on a culture's music-making.

The innovative Irish harp of John Egan was conceived at a critical juncture in Irish harp history. The Gaelic harp was rarely played, Bunting's book of ancient Irish harp tunes had been relegated to the pianoforte, and the French pedal harp was the preferred model in the music room. One cannot discount the possibility that without the invention of the Portable Irish Harp, an Irish harping tradition may well have disappeared altogether from the culture. This book uncovers this important chapter in Irish harp history, illuminating the instruments, the players and the legacy of John Egan – inventor, king's harp maker and Irish patriot.

---

8 R.B. Armstrong, *Musical instruments*, i: *The Irish and the Highland harps* (Edinburgh, 1904), p. 107. Armstrong's harp is in the National Museum of Ireland.

Prologue / Instrument and icon

'Sing, sweet harp, oh sing to me some song of ancient days ...'
— Thomas Moore, *Moore's Irish melodies*, 1834

In 1813 a well-preserved ancient Irish harp was discovered in a peat bog near Castle Fogarty. Incidents of uncovering buried treasure were well-known at the time, for Ireland's bogs proved to be an ideal burial ground for preserving centuries-old artefacts. The rare historical harp was one of numerous archaeological objects found in fields, including Bronze Age weapons and early Christian jewellery. Gold brooches were excavated at Slane, Co. Meath, and an ancient bronze vessel was raised from a bog near Grey Abbey, Co. Down. An assortment of extraordinary relics from former civilizations, such as a bronze horn and gold ornaments, were on exhibit for public viewing at Dublin's Trinity College Museum.[1] The discovery of a harp in a bog seemed particularly remarkable, however, and the incident was recounted in *Ierne*, an anonymous traveller's journal, with the instrument's form described as 'precisely similar in all its parts' to the celebrated Brian Boru harp[2] on display at the Trinity College Museum.[3] The famous Trinity College harp, donated to the museum in 1782 by William Burton Conyngham, was 3ft in height and formed with a bowed pillar and a rectangular soundbox.[4] The harp unearthed near Castle Fogarty was presumably also of a great age, dating from medieval times.

Although a momentous find, this was not the first harp discovered in an Irish bog. Another ancient harp had been uncovered a few years earlier, in the bog of

---

1 Antiquities illustrated in Charles Vallancey's *Collectanea de rebus Hibernicis* (Dublin, 1786) were exhibited at the Trinity College Museum according to the catalogue in the National Library of Ireland. Drawings of a latchet (brooch) and bronze horn are attributed to the artist Gabriel Beranger (1729–1817). See catalogue.nli.ie. 2 The legend connecting the harp to the ancient king Brian Boru (d. 1014) is recounted in Vallancey's *Collectanea de rebus Hibernicis* and is generally discounted. The harp actually dates from the fourteenth or early fifteenth century. See Hurrell, 'The "Brian Boru" Harp', *History Ireland*, 22:2 (2014), 49. 3 Anonymous, *Ierne: or, anecdotes and incidents during a life chiefly in Ireland* (London, 1861), p. 11. The anecdote appears in Part 1 of the book dated 1813. 4 The three main parts of the harp are the pillar, the neck or harmonic curve and the soundbox. The soundboard is the flat top surface of the soundbox, into which the strings

Drawling in Limerick, on the estate of Sir Richard Harte. This small harp was raised from a depth of twelve 'spadings' and, incredibly, it still had three metal strings intact.[5] Referring later to these significant discoveries, the antiquarian Dr Petrie expressed delightful anticipation that other 'bogs ... may still conserve and present to us a specimen of our ancient harp'.[6] Initially, the harps and other relics were of interest mainly to antiquarians like Edward Ledwich, J.C. Walker and Charles Vallancey, who expounded on the historical significance of the country's artefacts in lectures and essays. Ledwich opined on the metals and craftsmanship of brass swords, such as those unearthed in a Tipperary bog, in his essay on military weapons in *The antiquities of Ireland* (1804).[7] In Walker's *Historical memoirs of the Irish bards* (1786), he discussed the possible use in battle of curious brass trumpets from a bog between Cork and Mallow.[8] And in Vallancey's *Collectanea de rebus Hibernicis* (1786), drawings by Gabriel Beranger portrayed an array of ancient gold amulets and bronze vessels, visible proof of the fine metalworking skills in early Irish cultures.[9] The scholarly publications and archaeological objects on display at Dublin's museum generated an interest in the Gaelic past and an awareness of a high level of sophisticated artistry and craftsmanship in former societies. The artefacts, many adorned with intricate Celtic designs, elicited admiration and came to be a new source of national pride. Just as the ancient mementoes, long since buried, were coming to light at the turn of the nineteenth century, so too, did a new cultural identity surface.[10] The collective knowledge of Ireland's rich cultural history had been obscured by the ravages of time, wars and politics.[11] Now, through the discoveries of manuscripts and archaeological artefacts, a lost Gaelic world was re-emerging as a glorious age of self-governance and cultural sophistication.

Pride in the Gaelic past came to be aligned with the patriotic movements that had recently emerged within the country. Inspired by the ideals of the French and American revolutions, a rebellious crusade in Ireland began to forge its own valiant struggle. In the 1790s the Society of United Irishmen led a movement whose objectives were reforms, religious freedom and independence from Britain. Although the 1798 Rising was unsuccessful, Britain's reaction to

are attached.   5 Edward Bunting, *The ancient music of Ireland* (Dublin, 1840), p. 20, n. a.   6 Dr Petrie quoted in Eugene O'Curry, *On the manners and customs of the ancient Irish* (London, 1873), iii, p. 290.   7 Edward Ledwich, *The antiquities of Ireland* (Dublin, 1804), p. 282.   8 Joseph Cooper Walker, *Historical memoirs of the Irish bards* (Dublin, 1786), pp 109–10.   9 Charles Vallancey, *Collectanea de rebus Hibernicis* (Dublin, 1786).   10 For further reading, see Jeanne Sheehy, *The rediscovery of Ireland's past: the Celtic revival, 1830–1930* (London, 1980).   11 After the Williamite wars in the late 1600s, the spoils of war for the conquerors included confiscated lands and also the winners' prerogative to rewrite the country's history. The Ascendancy successfully managed to obscure any recognition of Ireland's Gaelic culture and instead perpetuated the myth of a nation long

the recent tumultuous events was to make law and order a priority in an unruly country. The 1801 Act of Union officially joined Ireland to the United Kingdom, and Dublin's parliament was subsequently dissolved. Governmental rule was transferred to London, and future decisions on Ireland's destiny would now be made in Westminster. The new state of political subordination triggered a spirited resistance to British rule within the national psyche, and there was a potent urgency to maintain a culturally distinct nation.

People looked to the artefacts of Ireland's past, and through Irish antiquarianism a separate national identity emerged, with such objects as ancient harps found in bogs serving as tangible mementos of a lost Gaelic culture. Antiquarians studying ancient manuscripts such as the twelfth-century Book of Leinster, learned of the high status of the harper in the protocol of the medieval court.[12] The native harp had been the favoured instrument of chieftains, and each clan maintained its own prized harper. The shimmering harp sounds skilfully articulated by harpers captivated listeners in banquet halls, and Ireland's harps were widely esteemed within the country and beyond. In medieval times, harps were common throughout Ireland, but most of these instruments did not survive. Thus, the newly discovered Limerick harp was deemed a historical treasure, and as such, was sent to the eminent antiquarian Dr O'Halloran for study and safe-keeping. In the end, however, the harp suffered the unintended fate of many old instruments made of wood. After Dr O'Halloran's death, it was relegated to the lumber room and was inadvertently burned for firewood by the cook.[13] Fortunately, an altogether different fate was in store for the harp found in the bog near Castle Fogarty. The ancient instrument was sent to Dublin to be examined by Ireland's leading harp maker, John Egan. The report in *Ierne* relayed that Egan, 'a man of singular ability in harp construction', proceeded to clean, restring and tune the harp and, 'now awaked [from] its slumbers', it produced 'marvelously quaint music'.[14]

The rare harp's distinctive voice, dormant for centuries, was reawakened by Egan's restorative work, which was also an important opportunity for the maker to closely examine the *cláirseach* in his workshop.[15] Egan was aware that Ireland's ancient harp was an entirely different type of instrument from the models he was producing. The maker was acquainted with the unique characteristics of the wire-strung Trinity College harp, with its soundbox adorned with incised lines

inhabited by barbarous savages.   12 The twelfth-century Book of Leinster is held by the Library of Trinity College, Dublin.   13 Edward Bunting, *A general collection of the ancient music of Ireland* (Dublin, 1809), p. 26, n. †.   14 Anonymous, *Ierne*, p. 11.   15 The terms 'early Irish harp', 'Gaelic harp' and *cláirseach* all refer to the same form of metal-strung early harp in Ireland, as distinct from the gut-strung medieval and renaissance Gothic harp played in Europe. For a discussion on terminology and surviving instruments see Simon Chadwick, 'The early Irish harp', *Early*

in geometric patterns and a pillar carved with zoomorphic figures, possibly eels. Egan manufactured the French empire pedal harp, a model dissimilar in almost every respect: size, shape, construction, stringing and decoration. The French harp was a taller, freestanding instrument about 5ft in height, with a slender conical soundbox, and the soundboard was painted with neoclassical figures in gold. Known as the 'pedal harp', the gut-strung instrument was equipped with pedals to operate a state-of-the-art mechanism for playing in different keys.[16] The French pedal harp had been developed in Paris in the late 1700s and was popularized by Queen Marie Antoinette, who was a harpist.[17] By the early 1800s, having an ornate gilded harp in one's salon had become the height of fashion in aristocratic circles.[18] As the growing demand for these sumptuously decorated instruments had spread to England, London became a bustling centre for pedal harp production. In Dublin, John Egan had seized the opportunity to open a pedal harp manufactory, and his successful business supplied the fashionable instruments to a steady stream of clients from the Anglo-Irish aristocracy.[19]

Although Egan was engaged in a flourishing trade of elite French harps, the young harp maker understood the country's increasingly nationalist mood, which championed native Irish products and held Ireland's ancient harp in high regard. However, the national instrument, the wire-strung *cláirseach*, was no longer widely played. It was generally perceived more as a relic from the past. The obvious question was: why had the wire-strung *cláirseach*, which had been played in Ireland for over a thousand years, disappeared from general use?

THE NATIONAL INSTRUMENT

In Ireland, the choice of a harp as a national emblem reflects the highly revered status of the instrument in Gaelic culture and the widespread renown of harpers and their instruments throughout Europe in early times. Over the centuries the pictorial symbol has evolved and changed, but in its many guises, the harp

Music, 36:4 (2008), 521–31.   **16** The term 'gut' refers to strings made from the guts of sheep. Although predominantly strung with gut strings, both pedal and the smaller Irish harps have strings of wound wire in the lower bass. For further reading see Jennifer Nex, 'Gut string makers in nineteenth-century London', *Galpin Society Journal*, 65 (Mar. 2012), 131–60.   **17** The form of pedal harp played by Marie Antoinette and the French aristocracy in the late eighteenth century was a slightly earlier model, with a scroll-top pillar, stave-back soundbox and earlier types of mechanisms. However, the aristocratic associations of the pedal harp as a feminine instrument are generally credited to Marie Antoinette.   **18** The French harp, its music and virtuoso players are explored in Hans Joachim Zingel, *Harp music in the nineteenth century*, trans. and ed. Mark Palkovic (Bloomington, IN, 1992).   **19** Recent publications with information on John Egan and his harp business include: Nancy Hurrell, 'Egan, John' in Lawrence Libin (ed.), *The Grove dictionary of musical instruments* (2nd ed., New York, 2014), p. 134; Catherine Foley, 'Egan, John' in Harry

P.1 (*left*) Trinity College harp in Bunting, *The ancient music of Ireland*, 1840.   P.2 (*right*) Silver groat coin issued by Henry VIII in 1534. Photo courtesy of AMR Coins.

continues to embody a collective national spirit and elicit a loyal response among the Irish and the Irish diaspora. Seán Farrell Moran, in his essay on images and icons states, 'The image has a power that succeeds where rational discourse fails; it persuades in ways that reason can not do; and it influences us in a manner that resists rational analysis.'[20] Instantly recognizable, with a triangular frame and linear strings, over time the symbolic depictions of the harp alternated between portraying real, functioning instruments and other more fanciful *ideas* of a harps. Today's official symbol, seen on coins, government buildings and tourist souvenirs, is an accurate drawing of the Trinity College harp (figure P.1). In former centuries, the harp symbols chosen to represent Ireland often bore no resemblance to the actual form of harps played in the country.[21] For example, as part of the Tudor conquest of Ireland, Henry VIII

White and Barra Boydell (eds), *The encyclopaedia of music in Ireland* (Dublin, 2013), p. 346; Mary Louise O'Donnell, *Ireland's harp: the shaping of Ireland's identity*, c.1770–1880 (Dublin, 2014).   **20** Seán Farrell Moran, 'Images, icons and the practice of Irish history' in Lawrence W. McBride (ed.), *Images, icons and the Irish nationalist imagination, 1870–1925* (Dublin, 1999), p. 167.   **21** For information on the earliest use of the harp to represent Ireland in a French coat of arms from the thirteenth century, see Séamus Ó Brógáin, *The Wolfhound guide to the Irish harp emblem* (Dublin, 1998), p. 8.

issued his own coinage in 1534 and chose a harp image to appear on the Irish silver groat coins, appropriately nicknamed 'harps'.[22] Oddly, the harp pictured has a shallow soundbox and a pillar culminating in a point, similar to Gothic harps played in England and on the Continent, but unlike the robust Gaelic harps of Ireland (figure P.2). Boydell observes that this misrepresentation of the Irish harp is not unexpected since the coins were minted in London rather than Ireland.[23] However, as Tom Dunne points out, by representing Ireland on Tudor coinage with an English or Continental instrument, the harp emblem became 'complexly colonial' and signalled English control.[24] And to reinforce the concept of English dominance, a crown appears above the harp. Nonetheless, the choice of a harp shows the important role of the instrument in Ireland's culture from ancient times.

Visually and aurally, Ireland's early harp was a unique and impressive instrument. The Gaelic harp's large soundbox was hollowed out from a single log, in contrast to Continental instruments built of thin sections of wood. In sound, the wire-strung harp's timbre was strikingly different from that of gut-strung European harps. In 1581, Vincenzo Galilei, in his *Dialogo della musica antica et moderna*, observed, 'The harps used by the Irish people are a lot bigger than our ordinary ones, and they commonly have strings of brass with some steel in the higher pitches in the manner of the harpsichord.'[25] In the hands of a skilled player, the *cláirseach* created spellbinding musical textures with a complicated layering of sounds. The harp's wire strings were plucked with nails, creating a soundscape of gossamer filigree in the treble, drifting above deep, sustained notes in the bass. A great ruler understood the power of an expert harper and bard at his court, for they were also masterful communicators. Through the use of powerful melodies and verse, heroic tales of victorious battles were recounted, and sagas proclaiming noble lineage cleverly swayed eager listeners to greater devotion towards the clan. The harps themselves also excited wonder, for the finely carved instruments were crowned with precious jewels mounted on the harmonic curve. With its metal strings, perhaps of gold, the instrument glistened in the candlelight as the harper strummed, affording pre-eminence to the clan chief and honour to the harper. The harp's spellbinding nature was a frequent theme in ancient Irish lore, with the instrument assuming supernatural powers. In tales and myths, the fairy-like harp voice was regarded as being

---

22 See Barra Boydell, 'The iconography of the Irish harp as a national symbol' in Patrick Devine and Harry White (eds), *The Maynooth International Musicological Conference 1995: selected proceedings part III*, Irish Musical Studies 5 (Dublin, 1996), pp 131–45.   23 Ibid., p. 132.   24 Tom Dunne, 'The Irish harp: political symbolism and romantic revival, 1534–1854', *Irish Architectural & Decorative Studies: Journal of the Irish Georgian Society*, 17 (2014), 16.   25 Vincenzo Galilei, *Dialogo della musica antica et moderna* (Florence, 1581), trans. Claude V. Palisca (New Haven, 2003), p. 357.   26 See Ann Dooley

unworldly, and the instrument's irresistible sounds often lured an unsuspecting listener to his doom in dangerous 'underworlds' or lulled one to sleep as part of a sinister plot.[26] The powerful effect of the instrument, in both imagined stories and real performances, was intertwined in Irish cultural life from early times.

The harper's exalted societal role, however, was not to last, for as a new era dawned in the 1600s, the Gaelic order finally came to an end after a period of invasion. The Tudor conquest of Ireland resulted in the confiscation of Gaelic lands and the subsequent colonisation by the Protestant 'Ascendancy'. In the seventeenth century, the ruling Anglo-Irish aristocracy in the big houses offered a different form of patronage to professional harp players. Still highly regarded, they became resident musicians to the landed gentry, but the positions were largely temporary. Staying for a period of time as a guest performer, the travelling musicians had a precarious existence journeying from castle to country house along muddy roads, carrying their harps on horseback. Welcomed as guests, in addition to providing music, sometimes a harper instructed family members on how to play the instrument. The travelling harpers were regarded as the keepers of Ireland's heritage, for they alone possessed the historical harp tunes from the past. As was the custom, the ancient airs had been passed from one generation to another, from master to pupil, in an oral tradition. Many of the harpers had been blinded by smallpox and had turned to music as a suitable career. The harper's role was to entertain and to satisfy the patron, which meant catering to an employer's requests to hear the latest musical repertoire. As the seventeenth century advanced, Ireland's music was increasingly influenced by cross-cultural trends, particularly the new classical art music imported from the Continent. The aristocracy developed a taste for Italian composers such as Corelli and Vivaldi, whose compositions were frequently performed by touring artists from Italy in Dublin concert halls. As baroque music rapidly became the preferred genre in the music room, one of the blind harpers, the great Turlough Carolan (1670–1738) composed harp tunes in the new Italianate style.[27] The other travelling harpers soon learned his tunes by ear, emulating the fashionable style, and added Carolan tunes to their repertoire to please their patrons. The wire-strung *cláirseachs* played by Carolan and his contemporaries in the early 1700s were now taller and larger floor-standing instruments, which produced a greater volume than the smaller hand-held harps played in medieval times. The

and Harry Roe, *Tales of the elders of Ireland* (New York, 1999); Russell Walton, *A harp of fishbones* (Belfast, 1992); and Keith Sanger and Alison Kinnaird, *Tree of strings* (Midlothian, Scotland, 1992). **27** For further reading, see Colette Moloney, *The Irish music manuscripts of Edward Bunting (1773–1843): introduction and catalogue* (Dublin, 2000); and Donal O'Sullivan, *Carolan: the life times and music*

increased harp size and sound may have been prompted by an encroaching competitor in the music room: the harpsichord.

As Ireland's playable harp model underwent changes in its size and form, so too did the harp symbol evolve. Séamus Ó Brógáin attributes to James I the adoption of a harp for Ireland on the royal arms and standard in 1603, along with lions representing England and a unicorn for Scotland (figure P.3).[28] During this period the pictorial harp image for Ireland on coinage had various interpretations, but the lasting version of Ireland's symbol that survived into the 1700s was the 'winged-maiden' harp. The harp's female head and torso formed the pillar, and her angelic wings created the harmonic curve.[29] Unlike any known instrument played in Ireland, the winged-maiden symbol instead bears a strong resemblance to Italian baroque harps which were typically formed with sculpted female figures on the pillars. For example, a sixteenth-century *arpa doppia* (multi-row harp) with a female torso and wings survives in Bologna, Italy, and a similar harp with carved female on the finial is seen in the well-known painting *King David playing the harp* by Domenico Zampieri (1581–1641).[30] Ossian Ellis points out that the Italian harp was introduced in England during the reign of Charles I (1625–49), played at court by the French harpist, Jean le Flelle.[31] The selection of a winged-maiden harp image on the royal standard and crest very likely reflected the actual Italian instrument played at the English court, and the artists who replicated the image were simply unaware of (or not interested in) Irish harp organology. Nevertheless the winged-maiden harp symbol was accepted and lived on to become the people's own emblem as Hibernia or Erin, the female personification of Ireland. In the 1780s–'90s, the winged-maiden emblem increasingly assumed more of a political role. Barra Boydell cites its use by the Volunteers and the United Irishmen as important influences on the adoption and popularization of the harp image in nationalist political movements (figure P.4).[32] Co-opted by the Volunteers for the banner on their newspapers, the *Volunteers Journal* and the *Northern Star*, the winged-maiden harp also featured in the frontispiece of the movement's songbook, *Paddy's Resource*.[33] And on the membership cards of the United Irishmen, the harp design appeared with royal

---

of an Irish harper (London, 1958).   **28** Brógáin, *The Wolfhound guide to the Irish harp emblem*, p. 14. **29** See O'Donnell, *Ireland's harp*, pp 9–28.   **30** The harp is in the International Museum and Library of Music of Bologna. See museibologna.it/ musicaen/ documenti/ 65329. For further information on the harp see David Brown, 'Some notes on extant chromatic harps' in Heidrun Rosenzweig (ed.), *Historical harps* (Dornach, Switzerland, 1991), pp 165–76.   **31** Ossian Ellis, *The story of the harp in Wales* (Cardiff, Wales, 1991), p. 50.   **32** Barra Boydell, 'The female harp: the Irish harp in 18th- and early 19th-century romantic nationalism', *RIdIM/RCMI Newsletter*, 20:1 (1995), 11.   **33** Ibid. See also Mary Helen Thuente, *The harp restrung: the United Irishmen and the rise of literary nationalism* (Syracuse, 1994), p. 107.

Royal Standard

P.3 (*left*) Winged-maiden harp emblem for Ireland on the British royal standard, nineteenth century.   P.4 (*right*) Seal of the United Irishmen.

crown removed and replaced by the revolutionary cap of liberty, with the accompanying motto, 'It is new strung and shall be heard.'[34]

By the late 1700s, as influences from the outside world continued to guide Ireland's cultural trends, new musical styles confronted the old, with art songs and the latest opera themes generally preferred in music room performances over the ancient harp airs. Unfortunately, the new music was simply not idiomatic to the wire-strung Gaelic harp. More suited to the ancient music, the harp had a fixed tuning in modes. However, to play the new chromatic art music, a harp needed to access the passing accidentals (sharps and flats) and play in different keys, features not attainable on a wire-strung harp which lacked a pitch-raising mechanism. Unable to accommodate patrons' musical requests, the harpers found that invitations from patrons were no longer forthcoming, and consequently by the close of the eighteenth century, only a handful of players of Ireland's wire harp remained. The plight of the harpers was first described in Joseph Cooper Walker's *Historical memoirs of the Irish bards* in 1786 stating, 'In Ireland, the Harpers … have until lately, been uniformly cherished, and supported by the Nobility and Gentry … The taste for that style of

---

34 For a discussion on the transformation of the winged-maiden harp from Ascendancy icon to a nationalist image, see Barra Boydell, 'The United Irishmen, music, harps, and national identity', *Eighteenth-Century Ireland/Iris an dá chultúr*, 13 (1998), 44–51.

performance, seems now, however, to be declining. The native harpers are not much encouraged.'[35]

Times were changing, and instead of engaging a resident harper, the new custom was for ladies in aristocratic families to provide the evening's entertainment, playing the family's own French pedal harp. It was a chance to display female graces and musical accomplishments as well as magnificent harps, and more importantly, the instruments easily coped with the chromaticism in Italian airs. By simply moving a pedal, a mechanism on the neck stopped the pliable gut strings to raise the pitches for the semitones present in the music. Lords of manors, ever conscious of being perceived as staying abreast with the current cultural trends, now maintained a pedal harp and a pianoforte in the music room for performances of baroque and classical music. Patronage for the old harpers slowly came to an end, and Ireland's native wire-strung harp ceased to be made.

While the playable Irish harp was disappearing from the culture, the Irish harp symbol was ubiquitous in nationalist literature, popular songs and pictorial illustrations. At the turn of the nineteenth century the maiden harp Hibernia became ever more lifelike, with a realistic head and body, and even human emotions. The idealized harp icon still bore no relation to a functioning musical instrument, but it was clearly understood as a voice expressing Ireland's discontent in the post-union era. A weeping, 'dying harp' with broken strings in Thomas Moore's song collections, the *Irish melodies*, was a dramatic metaphor for the country's suppressed national spirit. A dying harp image was also poignantly applicable to the loss of the Gaelic harping tradition. It seemed as if the country's revered national instrument would become a silent emblem, no longer a living musical tradition. At this pivotal moment, concerned individuals formed a civic movement to revive Ireland's wire-strung harp and to save the ancient harp music for posterity. New instruments would be needed, and John Egan, as the country's foremost manufacturer of harps, became involved in the formidable challenge of reviving Ireland's harp. An ambitious, self-motivated artist, already he had rejected the career path chosen for him. He had experienced a remarkable ascent in society, rising from fairly humble beginnings to become Ireland's preeminent harp maker, operating at a well-appointed address on Dawson Street.

---

35 Walker, *Historical memoirs of the Irish bards*, p. 157. The observation is a quote from 'an ingenious Scottish writer', McDonald.

1 / Strike while the iron is hot

The young John Egan began his working life apprenticed to a blacksmith. Worlds away from gilded harps in drawing rooms, Egan spent his early days amid the deafening clang of hammer against anvil and showers of fiery sparks as he learned his trade. Only the strongest of lads were apprenticed to a blacksmith owing to the arduous physical labour required, for as the smith pounded hot lumps of metal into desired shapes, the apprentice was tasked with pumping bellows to fuel the flames and also thrusting heavy irons into the fire. The apprenticeship, lasting several years, was a path to a fairly respectable occupation for a young man like John Egan. In 1790s Ireland, the local smith provided the essential services of shoeing horses and producing tools, but was also a specialist artisan who skilfully crafted motifs and scrollwork on wrought-iron gates commissioned for the entrances to the demesnes of great houses. Observing the basic principles of the forge, John Egan acquired an early understanding of the creative process, namely to visualize a finished product and methodically follow a procedure of steps to produce it. The work required dexterity, timing and precision, in addition to an eye for artistic design.

Egan was engaged in training for his life's work as a smith when a different path unexpectedly opened before him. By chance, an encounter with a French pedal harp left the young man transfixed by its beauty and intrigued by its mechanism, as author Sydney Owenson writes:

> Brought up from his earliest youth to the labours of the anvil, Mr Egan was still serving his time to a smith, when chance threw in his way a French harp. A natural fondness for music, and the curiosity and admiration excited by a first view of the most beautiful and picturesque of all instruments, induced him to examine its machinery ...[1]

French pedal harps of the late eighteenth century were stunning art objects, with richly carved pillars and soundboards appearing like artists' canvases, finely

---

1 Sydney Owenson, *Patriotic sketches of Ireland* (London, 1807), i, pp 162–3.

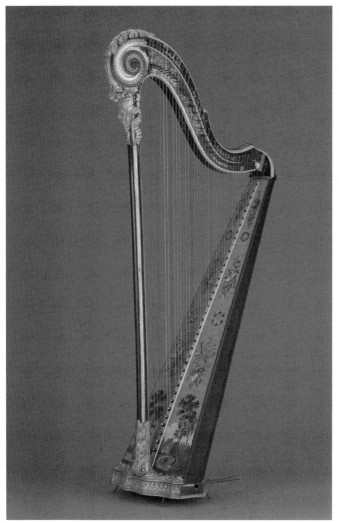

1.1 French pedal harp, about 1785, by Godefroi Holtzman. Photograph © 2019 Museum of Fine Arts, Boston.

painted with pastoral scenes (figure 1.1).[2] Egan studied the harp's mechanical workings of iron pedals and brass action, drawing insights from his experience in metalwork. Fascinated by the instrument's parts and structural form, he decided to make a copy:

2 The exact model of French pedal harp Egan encountered is unknown. In the 1790s two types of French pedal harps were in existence: the earlier scroll top rococo model and the newly invented empire model with a cylindrical capital and ram's head decoration. The developments in pedal harp designs and mechanisms are chronicled in Paul Knoke, 'An overview of the development of the pedal harp', *Historical Harp Society Bulletin*, 8:3 (Spring 1998), 2–11. For further reading on the French single-action harp, see Mike Parker, *Child of pure harmony: a sourcebook for the single-action harp* (lulu.com, 2005).

[A]ll the money he possessed in the world was shortly after laid out in the purchase of such materials as were requisite for the construction of a pedal harp, which he accomplished with so much success, as to find a high and immediate sale for it.[3]

It was a formidable achievement to construct a pedal harp and to also sell it, providing the needed impetus to abandon his apprenticeship and forge a new career as a harp maker in 1797.[4] Egan's ability to unlock the secrets of harp organology on his own was an early signifier of the maker's lifelong traits of self-reliance and inventiveness, characteristics of the age in which he lived. In an era of innovation, instrument makers were continually experimenting with new ideas, mechanisms and forms for their products. John Egan continued to indirectly refer to his early achievement in harp-making by marketing himself as 'Mr John Egan, a self-taught artist', in advertisements in the *Freeman's Journal*.[5]

According to Owenson's brief sketch, the harp maker had a 'natural fondness for music', a not uncommon trait at the time. Music-making was the customary evening entertainment throughout all strands of society, and singing, dancing and playing musical instruments were part of the fabric of daily life.[6] At one time it was believed that John Egan had belonged to an instrument-making family, since there was another well-known 'Egan' who made uilleann pipes in the late 1700s. In the National Museum of Ireland, a famous set of ivory pipes once owned by Lord Edward Fitzgerald has the name Egan stamped on the ivory cylinder, and the silver band is engraved with the date 1768. The set, formerly in the Royal Irish Academy, had been acquired in 1876 from George Tuke esq., who supplied the information, 'Manufactured by Egan of Dublin, a well-known maker of Bagpipes, father of the late eminent Harp-maker of the Same City.'[7] However tempting it might be to accept the familial connection as fact, it is most likely an assumption based on a shared name.[8]

In the period between 1780 and 1830, according to Hogan, aristocratic Anglo-Irish families usually owned several musical instruments and houses had

---

3 Owenson, *Patriotic sketches of Ireland*, i, pp 162–3.   4 The date is inferred from the phrase 'twenty-four years of study and application to improve the harps' in an advertisement in the *Freeman's Journal*, 31 Dec. 1821.   5 *Freeman's Journal*, 14 Oct. 1809.   6 See Ita Margaret Hogan, *Anglo-Irish music, 1780–1830* (Cork, 1966).   7 Seán Donnelly, 'Lord Edward Fitzgerald's pipes', *Ceol. A Journal of Irish Music* (Apr. 1983), p. 8. A coat of arms and crest of the MacEgans on the pipe set raises further questions as to the original owner and maker, and Donnelly argues it is unlikely the maker would stamp his own coat of arms on an instrument made for a client.   8 See Nicholas Carolan, 'Egan of Dublin, an 18th-century maker of Irish pipes', *An Piobaire*, 13:3 (Aug. 2017), 32–8. Carolan concludes from recent evidence that Egan of Dublin was active in the 1760s and did make the Lord Edward set of pipes, but a familial connection to the harp maker John Egan remains unconfirmed.

designated music rooms.[9] Owenson commented on the prevalence of part-time
musical instrument makers in many small towns who mended instruments for
respectable families, and she describes a 'hedge-carpenter' in Strabane making
violins and flutes as well as a Connaught carpenter building a small piano.[10] The
fact that there was a burgeoning community of instrument makers inhabiting
Dublin city no doubt influenced Egan's decision to change careers.[11] The 1804
Dublin Directory records five merchants listed in the general category of 'Musical-
instrument-maker': Power, Delany, Thompson, Lee and Perry.[12] Additionally,
there were merchants who specialised in instrument types, such as Pace, a 'Wind-
instrument-maker', and Bennet, a 'French-horn & Trumpet-maker'. Specialist
firms making harpsichords and pianofortes, deemed essential instruments for
the music room, were operated by the companies of McDonnell, Southwell,
Ryder and Woffington. Two additional workshops, Hull and Cornmell,
specialized in building organs. Instrument-making had transitioned from
primarily a rural craft of handmade products to a community of small urban
workshops where greater numbers of instruments were produced. With the
Industrial Revolution in the late 1700s came modern manufacturing techniques
that utilized more advanced machinery, and the parts and components for
instruments were becoming increasingly standardized. The brisk trade in musical
instruments additionally provided work for ancillary craftsmen to assist with
instrument decoration, like carvers and gilders, who were also numerous in
Dublin. A pedal harp builder valued the expertise of a carver for details such as
the pedal harp's fluted column, and a gilder was needed for applying gold-leaf
decoration to the instrument's column, soundboard and base. In 1804 there were
no less than eighteen specialist firms of carvers and gilders in Dublin.[13] These
artisans divided their time between creating exquisite gilt mirror frames with
the additional work of applying the finishing touches to fine musical
instruments, particularly harps and harpsichords. The music business was now
booming, and finely decorated instruments displayed in Dublin shop windows
attracted potential customers.

Angela Alexander comments that 'in historical terms, the picture presented
has been one of decline in artisan manufacture in the years following the
union'.[14] The negative assessment by historians can be traced to contemporary
complaints of manufacturers prior to 1801, as merchants feared a drop in the
sale of luxury goods in a post-union Dublin. According to David Dickson,

9 Hogan, *Anglo-Irish music, 1780–1830*, p. 86.   10 Owenson, *Patriotic sketches of Ireland*, i, p. 115.
11 See John Teahan, 'A list of Irish instrument makers', *Galpin Society Journal*, 16 (May 1963), 28–32.
12 The *Treble Almanack* containing *Wilson's Dublin Directory* (Dublin, 1804).   13 Ibid.   14 Angela
Alexander, 'The post-union cabinetmaking trade in Ireland, 1800–40: a time of transition', *Irish
Architectural & Decorative Studies: Journal of the Irish Georgian Society*, 17 (2014), 51.

immediately preceding the union, interest groups of professionals, lawyers, merchants and manufacturers published opposition pamphlets listing their arguments: the fear of a collapsed property market, a withering of luxury retail trade, and the loss of crucial import tariffs and support from a government removed to Westminster.[15] After the union, these negative assessments persisted for political reasons; however, Alexander's archival research demonstrates the continued manufacture of a considerable volume of upscale goods, such as silver plate and high-end furniture, in the early nineteenth century.[16] Cabinetmaking flourished as craftsmen supplied their wares to both town houses and country estates, and trades still looked to the landed gentry to buy the most expensive products, like furniture and musical instruments. A similar politically coloured attitude has been applied to early nineteenth-century harp production, viewing instruments made in this period as 'colonial' and not 'authentically Irish', whereas in reality, the union sparked a patriotic reaction in independent craftsmen like Egan and others, motivating them to produce and promote Irish-made products.[17]

In both appearance and sound, pedal harps were extremely desirable, and the prospects of establishing a successful harp business in Ireland appeared promising to Egan. At the time, the standard means of acquiring a pedal harp was to import an instrument from London or Paris, adding extra expense to the overall cost, and Egan cleverly foresaw an opening in the marketplace. The advantages of buying from a local pedal harp supplier were not only convenience and a competitive price, but also the avoidance of the risk of possible damage from shipping a delicate harp across the Irish Sea. Another selling point was to offer the option of harps made to order and decorated in one's personal taste. The greatest attraction of purchasing an Irish-made harp however was socio-political, for it demonstrated one's loyal support of local workers in post-union Ireland, and Egan effectively capitalized on the concept of Irishness as a central marketing strategy. In advertisements in the *Freeman's Journal*, he called for patrons to support a native harp business:

> For brilliancy of tone and classic finish, he betters himself that his Harps are excelled by none; and when the Native Instrument of Erin is presented to her Children by a Native Artist, employing Native Workmen, and at

15 David Dickson, 'Death of a capital? Dublin and the consequences of union' in Peter Clark and Raymond Gillespie (eds), *Two capitals: London and Dublin, 1500–1840* (Oxford, 2001), p. 114. 16 Alexander, 'The post-union cabinetmaking trade', p. 51. 17 Manufacturers in this period were aware of London competition and the attitudes of their aristocratic clients in the big houses expecting quality products styled in the latest fashion. Craftsmen walked a fine line between copying the newest patterns and motifs seen in decorative arts imported from London, while

nearly half the price imported, Egan feels confident of a continuance of that support which he has already experienced from a generous and discriminating Public.[18]

At once combining the attractive advantages of reduced prices with patriotism, it was an obvious choice for harpists to buy locally made Egan harps, with a clear conscience.

DAWSON STREET, DUBLIN

Six years after the sale of his first harp, Egan had successfully established a workshop in a prominent location on Dawson Street (figure 1.2). In *Wilson's Dublin Directory* (1804) the maker's entry appears as 'Egan (John), Pedal-harp-maker, 25 Dawson-Street', and he is the sole harp maker listed.[19] John Egan's new venture, like other similar small businesses, had benefitted from the upheaval indirectly caused by the Act of Union of 1801. Against the backdrop of a tumultuous political situation, a societal shift created advantageous circumstances for Egan to emerge as a harp maker. With the closing of the Irish parliament in Dublin, legislative members moved en masse to London to serve in Westminster's house of commons and house of lords. Following the exodus to England of around one hundred resident peers, many of the large houses in Dublin were vacant, and a cultural shift allowed a rising merchant class to emerge in a new age of opportunity. Desirable properties were snapped up as old businesses upgraded to new premises, and new commercial enterprises were now eagerly pursued. With the departure of Ireland's peerage, a new class of gentry was comprised of rising professionals such as physicians and lawyers, and in this fluid system, bankers, artisans and merchants likewise enjoyed greater social mobility. Social advancement for someone like Egan, formerly unattainable, was now possible in Irish society, and a smith's apprentice could realistically imagine the possibilities of a better life.

The new, unfamiliar landscape of Dublin's post-union society was described in Maria Edgeworth's novel, *The Absentee* (1812), by a character, Sir James:

> 'After the Union these [villas] were bought by citizens and tradesmen [...] Immediately, in Dublin, commerce rose into the vacated seats of rank; wealth rose into the place of birth [...] So that now,' concluded Sir James, 'you find a society in Dublin composed of a most agreeable and salutary

adding an Irish touch to appeal to the cultural patriotism of the age.   **18** *Freeman's Journal*, 2 Jan. 1817.   **19** *Wilson's Dublin Directory* (Dublin, 1804).

1.2 Dawson Street, Dublin. Photo by Nancy Hurrell.

mixture of birth and education, gentility and knowledge, manner and matter; and you see pervading the whole new life and energy, new talent, new ambition, a desire and a determination to improve and be improved – a perception that higher distinction can now be obtained in almost all company, by genius and merit, than by airs and dress [...]'[20]

In Dublin's post-union society, the emerging entrepreneur Egan acquired a prime location for his harp workshop. At one end, Dawson Street met Nassau Street across from Trinity College, and at the other end, where Egan resided, the street opened out onto the picturesque St Stephen's Green. Named for Joshua Dawson, who had developed the area in the early 1700s, the street was lined with fine Georgian houses. A prominent focal point was the affluent St Anne's church, also dating from the early eighteenth century. In a guide to Dublin in 1821 the Revd G.N. Wright wrote of the church, 'The parishioners of this church are rather the higher classes of society, as it is in a most respectable and fashionable neighbourhood.'[21]

The most prestigious presence on Dawson Street was the Mansion House, the official residence of the lord mayor of Dublin, located just down the street from Egan's shop. In use since 1715, it was described in Wright's travel guide as

20 Maria Edgeworth, *The Absentee* (London, 1812), p. 83.   21 Revd G.N. Wright, *An historical guide to ancient and modern Dublin* (London, 1821), p. 151.

'an excellent suite of apartments, capable of accommodating several hundred persons, which number is not unfrequently to be met at the convivial assemblies of his Lordship'.[22] Egan's shop windows displaying ornate harps were well placed to be noticed by the frequent noble visitors strolling past or peering out from their carriages on their way to attend the lord mayor's functions. Egan's immediate neighbours on Dawson Street were fairly utilitarian: John O'Neill, haberdasher (sewing notions); Judith Mathews, tallow-chandler (candle maker); and a grocer, William Watkins. Nearby was John McEnery, who sold perfume and hair powder – a useful commodity, since wigs had generally been discarded and the current fashion was to powder one's hair. With the new social mobility, aspiring merchant shops inhabited Dawson Street next to loftier firms, such as William Greene, secretary to the Grand Canal Company.

Musical instruments were also coveted by the middle classes as a social necessity, in imitation of the gentry. While noble families gathered for recitals in splendid music salons, the middle classes, in less grand lodgings above shops, rolled up their rugs for informal dancing and singing to a fiddle or keyboard. In the nightly drawing-room performances across Dublin, amateur and professional musicians mixed freely, with some of the performers using talent as a passport to gain entry in the grander Georgian houses.[23] With the prevalence of daily music-making within the culture, books of sheet music were in demand, and music companies rushed to publish the latest solos requested by customers. Supplemental to instrument shops selling music, six different merchants in the city sold only sheet music.[24] Irish music historian Grattan Flood made the observation, 'Probably one of the best evidences of the cultivation of music in Ireland in the latter half of the eighteenth century is the number of music publishers and musical instrument makers in Dublin at that period.'[25] The trend persisted well into the early nineteenth century as music-related businesses continued to thrive. It was also a busy time for music masters and teachers, who were called upon to assist pupils of all ages in the improvement of their musical skills, with an eye towards amateur performances. Advertisements for 'professor of music' and 'doctor of music' regularly appeared in newspapers and directories. Gentlemen in the upper classes considered it a necessity to engage a private music professor to instruct family members at home in preparation for informal evening drawing-room concerts. A slightly different form of musical tuition was available to those in the middle classes, whereby lessons took place in either the instructor's apartment or at one of many newly formed music schools.

---

22 Ibid., p. 206.   23 Ronan Kelly, *Bard of Erin: the life of Thomas Moore* (Dublin, 2008), p. 11.   24 Sheet-music merchants listed were: Rhames, Rice, McCalley, Southwell, Hime and Lee. *Wilson's Dublin Directory* (Dublin, 1804).   25 W.H. Grattan Flood, *A history of Irish music* (Dublin, 1906), p. 313.

Pedal harp teachers in Ireland broadcast their services by placing self-flattering ads in local newspapers. In an announcement by the Misses Cheese, an advert professes, 'in consequence of the approbation their style of playing has been met with' that they offer instruction on the harp and pianoforte to 'those who are pleased to employ them'.[26] Similarly, a newspaper piece submitted by Mr Poole says that the harpist 'late of London, from the flattering encouragement he has received in this City, will continue to give instructions on that beautiful and fashionable instrument, the pedal harp'.[27] Other harp instructors promoted themselves by naming their own renowned teachers. A notice in the *Hibernian Journal* in 1805 said,

> MISS C. COONEY respectfully informs the Nobility and Gentry, that she instructs young Ladies on the pedal harp and piano-forte, having been finished under Signors Corri and Clementi, in London, on the piano-forte, and Madame O'Haggerty, of Dublin, on the harp; – flatters herself to gain the approbation of those she may have the honour to attend.[28]

Madame O'Haggerty, a well-known Frenchwoman and harpist, had recently fled from Paris with her husband, Count O'Haggerty, due to the impending French Revolution. Formerly attached to the French court, the count had previously served as the master of the horse to the Comte d'Artois, and Madame O'Haggerty was known as a proficient harpist in royal circles. Having relocated to the safety of Ireland, the couple resided in a house in St Stephen's Green, where they held frequent musical evenings. A typical musical soirée one evening hosted by Madame O'Haggerty was recounted in a memoir recorded by Sydney Owenson, who had been a guest, along with her sister Olivia. Madame O'Haggerty played an impressive sonata by Krumpholtz on the harp and her pupils sang various duets, which was followed by a dramatic reading of Moliére. As the evening progressed, Sydney and her sister were persuaded to sing impromptu duets of French and English songs to the accompaniment of Madame O'Haggerty's arpeggios on the harp, to great appreciation and applause.[29]

Another celebrity harpist who offered lessons in Dublin was Madame Dussek, formerly Sophia Corri (1775–1847) from London. The wife of pianist and composer Jan Ladislav Dussek (1760–1812), Mme Dussek was on a concert tour in 1805 and, as was the practice for prominent visiting performers, she gave

26 *Hibernian Journal*, 24 May 1805.   27 Ibid., 19 June 1805.   28 Ibid., 11 Jan. 1805.   29 Hogan, *Anglo-Irish music, 1780–1830*, p. 87 and Lady Morgan, *Lady Morgan's memoirs: autobiography, diaries and correspondence*, ed. W. Hepworth Dixon, 2 vols (London, 1862), i, p. 143.

private lessons to aristocratic harp students. Mme Dussek informed 'the Nobility and Gentry' in a notice in the papers that she was available to instruct students in harp, pianoforte and singing.[30] Singing to the harp was a common practice for young ladies who played the instrument, and harpists were usually also proficient at the pianoforte, for much of the repertoire was idiomatic to both instruments.

Settled in his new location on fashionable Dawson Street, Egan was steadily gaining a reputation for manufacturing finely crafted pedal harps for his clients. Egan produced the standard model known as the 'empire' pedal harp, with a cylindrical capital and conical soundbox with a semi-circular curved back. The design is generally attributed to the French maker Sébastien Erard (1752–1831), who started a London harp factory with his nephew Pierre in Great Marlborough Street in the late eighteenth century.[31] Whereas Paris had been a Mecca for harp production in the 1770s, the turmoil of the revolution had caused harp makers like Sébastien Erard and others to flee the country in the 1790s, and the new centre for pedal harp production shifted to London. Erard set the trend in pedal harp design with his distinctive empire model, invented around 1789, with a column culminating in a rounded capital adorned in a neoclassical motif of ram's heads, and later, Grecian figures. The harp column cleverly imitated the architectural columns supporting ancient Greek temples, in both form and motifs.[32] Hilary Young of the Victoria & Albert Museum characterizes the neoclassical decorative arts style in the early nineteenth century as 'a result of a renewed passion for the remains of the classical past and a dissatisfaction with the rococo style'.[33] The rediscovery of antiquity was fuelled by archaeological discoveries in Italy, but also a search for the 'ideal' as opposed to the frivolous nature of the rococo. On harp column-tops, gone was the rococo scroll, a key element of the former style, and it was replaced by idealized two-dimensional Grecian figures. This motif was echoed on harp soundboards, with similarly sublime figurative images.[34] Neoclassicism, inspired by the arts of Greece and Rome, and also ancient Egypt, was universally embraced in the decorative arts in the period from the 1750s through the early 1800s. Published pattern books were sourced by craftspeople and designers, with the same motifs used in harp decoration by all the London makers and also Egan in Ireland.

30 *Hibernian Journal*, 22 Jan. 1805.   31 The changes in pedal harp design, construction and mechanism introduced by Erard are detailed in Pierre Erard, *The harp in its present improved state compared with the original pedal harp* (London, 1821). See also Robert Adelson et al. (eds), *The history of the Erard piano and harp in letters and documents, 1785–1959*, 2 vols (Cambridge, 2015).   32 Knoke categorizes the three Erard capital design stages as ram's head (1789), Grecian (1811) and Gothic (1834).   33 Hilary Young, 'Neoclassicism' in Michael Snodin and John Styles (eds), *Design & the decorative arts: Georgian Britain, 1714–1837* (London, 2004), p. 52.   34 Young attributes the popularity

EARLY EGAN PEDAL HARPS IN PRIVATE COLLECTIONS AND
AVONDALE HOUSE, CO. WICKLOW

The two oldest surviving Egan pedal harps that have come to light are currently in private collections, and both are fashioned in the empire style. One has a distinctive Egyptian-themed capital decoration of three stylized mummy figures, linked by palm leaves (see pp 218–19). The other rare harp has not survived intact, but both instruments are similar in their capital decorations made of composite material and gilded.[35] Both harps bear the inscription, '25 Dawson St. Dublin', reflecting Egan's initial business address, and one of the harps also has '1807' etched on a brass plate.[36] These early examples of Egan's work are equipped with *fourchette* or 'forked' mechanisms on the neck for sharpening the strings to play in different keys.[37] The mechanism is operated by pedals connected via rods inside the harp's hollow column. A harpist moves the pedals to set the key signature and to also play a passing accidental as it appears in the music.[38]

Although most surviving Egan pedal harps were made in the empire design with a rounded capital, one extant harp exemplifies the maker's penchant for experimenting with combining different forms. A rare harp on display at Avondale House in Co. Wicklow merges a rococo scroll top shape with neoclassical elements to create an unusual hybrid design (plate 1).[39] The rounded outline shape of the 'head' suggests a scroll, but the section is flat, with brass plates filling the area on both sides of the harp, and the column has banded sections, reflecting the empire style. The harp's applied decoration is even less

of two-dimensional classical figures in architecture, interior decoration and the applied arts to the parallel practice of English gentlemen at the time on the grand tour of Italy purchasing and sending home pieces of ancient sculpture. **35** The figurative ornaments on the harp capital and base were cast in a composite material, or plaster, using special moulds. The ornaments were then attached to the harp and gold leaf was applied. **36** The 1807 harp was dismantled by Howard Bryan in 2013, who discovered a striking feature of the mechanism: a simplified serpentine chain. Perhaps an effort to invent a new type of mechanical action, 'The first two spindles are conventional, with the brass arm riveted to two links making up the chain. After the first two spindles the chain is a single serpentine link, tapered toward the treble end, with the brass arms riveted to this single link.' Howard Bryan, personal communication, 17 Apr. 2013. **37** The *fourchette* disc was invented by Sébastien Erard and adopted by all the London harp makers and by John Egan in Dublin. The earlier scroll-top harps had different mechanisms, such as crochet hooks. **38** Egan's early pedal harps were 'single-action', meaning each pedal could move once. The strings were tuned in E-flat major, and when the pedals were moved down and hooked into the slots, the B, E and A became natural pitches. Similarly, all the other pitches could be sharpened. With various pedal settings, the harp could be pre-set to play in different key signatures. **39** The harp is currently on loan from the National Museum of Ireland. Dr Jennifer Goff kindly brought this instrument to my attention in 2009.

conventional. At first glance, the instrument appears to have the usual gold-leaf accents painted on the column and base. Upon closer inspection, however, the adornments are actually bronze appliqués. Handsomely formed Grecian figures, floral motifs and mythical beasts are all cast in bronze and attached to the harp. While most columns on harps from the period have moulded plaster decoration, here Egan displays skills acquired during his time at the forge, for the decorations are all cast in metal. Similarly, the harp's fluted pillar appears striped, an effect normally achieved with carved troughs painted in gold. Instead, the maker has inserted long thin strips of brass into the pillar's grooves. Similar thin brass strips also frame the edges of the soundboard and outline the back, instead of the more conventional painted borders seen on other harps.

Egan's sophisticated mastery of metal-casting is apparent in the harp's decorative appliqués, such as a small vignette of a bow and arrows on the instrument's head. The feathery texture of the arrows, the spiral threads of the bow's string and even the crinkle of the ribbon that binds them together are all finely detailed (plate 2). The stylish neoclassical themes continue with four robed Grecian figures playing cymbals as they dance their way around the pillar's lower area, while mythological winged griffins rest on the harp's base (plate 3). The beasts' tails morph into fanciful acanthus leaves which culminate in rosettes, but perhaps the most charming of all the harp's ornaments are the two trumpeting angels on either side of the column's top, in mirror image. Angel motifs often adorn the capitals and bases of pedal harps, but these unclothed cherubs are clearly Irish, for each angel rides on the back of an Irish wolfhound. A breed of hunting dogs peculiar to Ireland from early times, the wolfhound was mentioned in the ancient stories of Fionn and Oisín, and it became a national symbol of the Celtic past. The use of national symbols was a trademark of John Egan harps, distinguishing his instruments from those of London makers. The unique contour of the instrument, combined with its bronze appliqué ornaments, make this a one-of-a-kind instrument.[40]

In 1807, almost four years after the Egan harp manufactory was founded on Dawson Street, Sydney Owenson wrote favourably of the maker: 'He is now very extensively engaged in the business, and may be ranked among the first of the profession in Great Britain.'[41] Egan's new enterprise was flourishing as he fulfilled society's demand for the standard empire-style pedal harps, albeit

---

40 One cannot discount the possibility that John Egan knew of another harp decorated with bronze appliqués, as they did exist in France, but very few have survived. The most celebrated example is a harp once belonging to Empress Josephine. Made in 1805 by Cousineau & Sons, the harp has bronze appliqués of stars, honeybees and Grecian figures. It is currently housed in the Château de Malmaison, Paris.   41 Owenson, *Patriotic sketches of Ireland*, i, p. 163.

adorned with his own brand of symbolic Irish motifs. Having established himself in Anglo-Irish circles as an approved pedal harp maker, Egan began to explore the possibility of a new instrument designated as Irish not only in decoration but in its intrinsic form. A new type of Irish harp was introduced to the public by Owenson herself, who played Irish airs on her Egan harp to adoring audiences of *le bon ton* in London's elite salons.

2 / Lady Glorvina's harp

'Tell Egan all the world is running after his harps …'
— Lady Morgan

A few years into his career as a pedal harp maker, John Egan conceived a new model of Irish harp with a contour designed in homage to Ireland's iconic Brian Boru harp. The model was about 3ft in height with a distinctive bowed pillar, imitating the size and shape of the famous harp in Trinity College.[1] The model's appearance was instantly recognizable as Irish, in contrast to the larger, French-inspired pedal harp, the standard harp played at the time. Egan continued this messaging with delicate shamrocks richly painted in gold leaf over a lacquered background of either green, blue or black.[2] Although it resembled the ancient Brian Boru harp in size and shape, Egan's new harp was an entirely different instrument. Instead of a carved soundbox, the model was built of joined sections of wood using modern techniques. Primarily a scaled-down version of a pedal harp, the small soundbox was constructed with a semi-circular back of curved laminated wood, with three pairs of elongated oval-shaped soundholes, and the flat soundboard had horizontally grained sections of wood. Another crucial difference from the Brian Boru harp was in the stringing and sound, in that Egan's small Irish harp had gut strings that produced a warmer, rounder sound in contrast to the sharp metallic timbre of Gaelic harps strung with brass wire.[3] For tuning options, Egan's Irish harp with pliable gut strings had a pitch-raising mechanism for obtaining the semitones in music, in contrast to the fixed tuning of the Gaelic wire-strung harps.[4] John Egan, living in an era of 'new

1 The exact shape of Egan's first Irish harp model, and the harp owned by Sydney Owenson in 1805, is not known, and it is possible these early versions may have more closely resembled the Brian Boru harp contour rather than the later portable models with an extended 'head'. 2 Golden shamrocks became John Egan's signature decoration on his harps.   3 A description of an instrument's sound tends to be somewhat subjective. However, my observation of the tonal qualities is based on personal experience of performing on a gut-strung Egan harp as well as a wire-strung historically accurate replica of the Bunworth harp (1734) in the Museum of Fine Arts, Boston.   4 In her writings, Owenson does not mention a mechanism on her Egan harp. The earliest surviving portable harps by Egan all have various forms of ring stops fitted on the

improved' instruments, considered Gaelic harps to be relics of the past, to be preserved but not faithfully replicated. Instead, the maker saw himself as an innovator charged with designing a new Irish harp for a new century – a harp idiomatic to the contemporary music of the age.

One of the first people to own Egan's new Irish harp model was the novelist Sydney Owenson (1783?–1859), and passing references to her 'small Irish harp by Egan' are scattered throughout her memoirs. She often alludes to her 'small sweet harp', indicating a hand-held instrument rather than a larger floor-standing pedal harp. Affectionately referred to as her 'constant companion', the harp accompanied Sydney on her travels abroad, another indicator of its portable size, in contrast to the pedal harp, which was fairly cumbersome to move and generally considered a static piece of furniture in a music room. The convenient portability of Egan's small harp model was a selling point for the instrument, and eventually Egan named an improved model of similar dimensions the 'Portable Irish Harp' to emphasise this.[5] It was the custom for 'ladies of distinction' to embark on the grand tour of Europe for cultural enrichment and to take their instruments with them, and the Egan portable harps were accordingly supplied with fitted wooden travelling cases.[6] Sydney Owenson, later Lady Morgan,[7] ventured abroad on several occasions with her companion harp in tow, and her small wooden harp case is the subject of one of her amusing travel anecdotes. Having just arrived in Paris she writes,

> Dear friendly Mr Warden sent his *bonne* (maidservant) to inquire if we were arrived; and while I was writing him a note, I saw her eyes fixed on my little Irish harp case, with divers exclamations of 'Mon Dieu, est-il possible! Comment donc!' I looked up at her, and she answered my inquiry with '*C'est un petit mort, n'est-ce pas, Madame?*' She explained that she thought it was my dead child that I was travelling with, for the honour of entombment in Pére-la-Chaise! It was now *my* turn to exclaim, '*Mon Dieu et comment donc!*' and her answer was '*Mais, Madame, vous autres dames Anglaises, vous êtes si droles!*' The *drollery* of travelling with a dead child![8]

neck for changing keys. See pp 104–5, 108–11, 117–20 for descriptions of the Egan mechanisms on Portable Irish Harps.   5 Sydney referred to her Egan harp simply as an 'Irish harp'. The name 'Portable Irish Harp' first appeared in advertisements in 1819 with the invention of Egan's dital mechanism. Since the surviving small portable harps by Egan all have a similar organology, I use the term Portable Irish Harp as a classification of a particular model.   6 A handsome, fitted mahogany case with a brass handle made for a smaller Egan portable harp still survives in a private collection.   7 In 1812 Sydney Owenson married Sir Charles Morgan and became Lady Morgan.   8 Lady Morgan, *Passages from my autobiography* (London, 1859), p. 52.

Sydney Owenson became a modern, female version of an ancient bard, performing Irish airs for the Anglo-Irish gentry in the big houses in Ireland and in fashionable drawing rooms in London. Her dynamic performance style was vividly recounted by her biographer, W.J. Fitzpatrick:

> Her wit and vivacity, the nerve with which she swept the strings of her harp, and the exquisite modulations of her voice, in accompaniment, charmed widely, and bound captive many a heart long wrapped in apathy.[9]

The passage might equally pertain to one of Owenson's fictional characters, for the heroes and heroines in her novels all seem to bring forth music from their harps in the same dramatic, mesmerizing manner. For Sydney, Ireland's harp was of equal importance in both her real life and her imagined fictional world. In her novels, the sound of the harp is so heartrending, the instrument itself seems to be cast as a central figure in her romantic plots. Characters harbouring deep desires that cannot by convention be spoken of, instead convey their feelings through the playing of irresistible harp melodies. And in one haunting scene in Owenson's seminal work, *The wild Irish girl*, the Aeolian harp even plays itself, uttering a 'wild melody' produced by a sea breeze vibrating the strings from an open window.[10]

In these ever-present harp scenes in novels, much is revealed about actual music-making in the early nineteenth century, for Owenson is clearly writing from her personal experience as a harpist. She describes how characters pluck the strings for a desired effect, and the author occasionally names specific tunes performed. The harp-infused novels were enormously popular with the British public, becoming bestsellers, which enabled Owenson to ascend in society as a literary celebrity. She moved in London's elite circles, performing on her harp, and mingled with such famed poets as Lord Byron and Thomas Moore. Like Moore, Owenson gained entrance in London's upper classes through the novelty of her Irishness and her unusual musical talent, and both were in demand as party guests for telling witty stories and singing their native songs.[11]

Sydney's rapid rise to literary fame was somewhat of a Cinderella story. In her youth, having lost her English mother at an early age, she had to rely on her Irish father's rather precarious career in musical theatre, and Sydney yearned for a better life. She began working as a governess in 1801 and came to realize that one of the available avenues open to her for social advancement (other than

9 W.J. Fitzpatrick, *Lady Morgan, her career, literary and personal* (London, 1860), p. 91. 10 Sydney Owenson, *The wild Irish girl: a national tale*, 3 vols (London, 1806; repr. Oxford, 2008), p. 234. 11 For further discussion of Owenson's use of the harp in her life and works, see Una Hunt (producer), Nancy Hurrell, Claire Connolly and Julie Donovan, *The wild Irish girl and her harp* (RTÉ Radio

marriage) was to become a novelist. Full of ideas and driven by financial need, Owenson tried her hand at writing. Her first book, *St Clair*, was printed in Dublin in 1802. With her second novel, *The novice of St Dominick*, Sydney was eager to jump-start her fledgling career as a writer, and so she decided to submit the manuscript to a publisher in England. As she was new to the literary world 'without one friend' to recommend a London publisher, the enterprising young author found the name of a publisher in a newspaper, R. Phillips, and took a chance and wrote to him.[12] Phillips responded, expressing interest in her work, and encouraged her to go to London. In 1805 the young woman made the long, arduous trip on her own. Travelling as cheaply as possible, she first endured the frightening passage across the Irish Sea to Holyhead, and then she boarded a coach to the great city. It was her first visit to London, and with manuscript in hand, she eagerly anticipated her pre-arranged meeting with Phillips. The coach finally arrived at a London inn, the Swan with Two Necks in Lad Lane, and not knowing what to do next in unfamiliar surroundings, Sydney merely sat down on her small trunk, and greatly fatigued, fell asleep. Fortunately, a gentleman who had been a fellow passenger on the coach saw her and persuaded the owners of the establishment to take her in for the night.[13] The next morning, refreshed, Sydney found her way along the streets of the foreign city to the office of the publisher, who was charmed by the young writer. Accepting her manuscript on the spot, he immediately paid her for it but advised her to send a portion of the funds to her father for safe-keeping. With the remainder of the fee, Sydney relates, 'The first purchase she made for herself out of her literary earnings were an Irish harp, from Egan, and a black mode cloak! The harp was her companion wherever she went.'[14] Significant in both her professional and personal life, the emblematic harp was the perfect accessory for her image as an Irish author writing on Irish themes, and on a personal level, the Egan harp provided countless hours of pleasurable music-making.

It is no surprise that Owenson spent her precious earnings on a harp, for on the Irish side of her family there was a strong ancestral connection to the instrument. Her paternal grandmother, Sydney Bell, had been a well-known singer and harp player, and Sydney Owenson, the namesake of her grandmother, wrote of her:

> To derive an appellation from some eminent quality or talent, is still very common in the interior parts of Ireland. The Author's grandmother was

Lyric FM, Lyric Feature, 25 July 2014). **12** Lady Morgan, *Lady Morgan's memoirs*, i, p. 249. **13** Ibid., i, p. 251. **14** Ibid., i, p. 252. **15** Owenson, *The wild Irish girl*, p. 75. Little is known of the harp her grandmother played, but it may well have been strung with wire strings, as was the

known in the neighbourhood where she resided (in the county of Mayo), by the appellative of *Clarseach na Vallagh*, or the *Village Harp*; for the superiority of her musical abilities.[15]

Another primary influence was an inherited musical talent from her father, Robert Owenson, who sang professionally and for a time managed a musical theatre in Kilkenny. In their childhood, Sydney and her younger sister Olivia were surrounded by an extended family of actors, singers and instrumentalists. Sydney often sang at musical gatherings, and apparently emulated her father's characteristic robust vocal style, as chronicled in an account of a musical get-together in Tipperary:

> He [Counsellor Lysaght] stole into the drawing-room, which was full of company – not to interrupt a song which a young girl was singing to the harp; it was the Irish cronan of 'Emuck ac Nock-Ned of the Hill'; the air was scarce finished when he sprang forward and seized the harpist in his arms, exclaiming: – 'This must be Sydney Owenson – it is her father's voice – none but an Irish voice could have such a curve in it, and she is my godchild!'.[16]

It was a remarkable identification, considering the counsellor had not seen his godchild since the christening dinner.

Sydney's father not only influenced his daughter's particular manner of singing, he also passed on his musical preferences, including a particular fondness for the songs of the famed harper-composer, Turlough Carolan. They had a shared preference for Irish airs, and Sydney played Carolan's tunes on her Egan harp. Her next project was a unique song collection inspired by the Irish airs she heard her father sing and play on the violin. Sydney recounted, 'I was so enthusiastic in my passion for Irish music, and had obtained such a pretty little success by playing the airs of Carolan on my Irish harp, that I had actually engaged with Messrs Power and Golding, of London, to collect and arrange twelve Irish melodies …'[17] For the collection, titled *Twelve original Hibernian melodies, with English words, imitated and translated, from the works of the ancient Irish bards* (1805), Owenson described her method of arranging some of the neglected 'national airs' to also 'put English words of my own to their wild and plaintive strains'.[18] She believed her country's music to be 'more original, more purely its

tradition in the early 1700s.   16 Lady Morgan, *Lady Morgan's memoirs*, i, pp 14–15. Presumably the harp mentioned did not actually belong to Owenson, however it does suggest an early familiarity with the instrument.   17 Lady Morgan, *The book of the boudoir*, 2 vols (London, 1829), i, pp 70–1. 18 Lady Morgan, *Lady Morgan's memoirs*, i, p. 264.

own' and 'possessing more the soul of melody, than any other country in Europe'.[19] The collection presents her favourite, 'Ned of the hills', described in the preface as displaying 'characteristic wildness and melting pathos … an epitome of the ancient Irish style of composition'.[20] For the arrangement, Owenson honoured the original text and translated the Gaelic words into English. For various other songs in *Twelve original Hibernian melodies*, such as Carolan's 'Fanny Power', Owenson composed her own English lyrics to create a new song entitled 'Leave me not love'. Similarly, the traditional tune 'Open the door' was transformed into a vocal piece called 'Open the door 'tis your true love', and so on. The idea of furnishing new English lyrics to the ancient airs of Ireland was a novel concept, which originated with Owenson. The format was later copied by others, most notably the poet Thomas Moore, who achieved monumental success with his ten collections of the *Irish melodies* published between 1808 and 1834. Moore indirectly credited Sydney for her original idea, stating, 'the patriotic genius of Miss Owenson has been employed upon some of our finest airs'.[21] Although Sydney's song collection was initially inspired by ancient harp airs, the music was arranged and published for the pianoforte, a more widely played instrument. No stranger to the pianoforte, Owenson enjoyed playing the instrument and later in life is believed to have owned one.[22] An early training in keyboard skills was afforded her as a pupil at Miss Crowe's Academy in Dublin. In a letter to her father in 1794, Sydney recounts the 'delightful' evenings spent at Mrs Lynche's, where 'There is a very fine grand forte piano, and I am highly gratified with my favourite instrument.'[23]

After successfully publishing a songbook based on Irish harp airs, Owenson's next step was to 'play' the harp figuratively in her literary works through the use of a harp metaphor for Ireland. The symbolic harp was a powerful trope in post-union Ireland, and it was central in her volume of poems, *The lay of an Irish harp* (1807). However, another work she published around the same time, *The wild Irish girl: a national tale* (1806), caught the public's attention and was more widely read. This historical novel set in Gaelic Ireland incorporates the Irish harp on multiple thematic levels: as a symbolic metaphor, a playable instrument and an important cultural tradition in the country's history.[24] In *The wild Irish girl* the

19 Ibid., i, pp 264–5. 20 Sydney Owenson, *Twelve original Hibernian melodies* (London, 1805). 21 Thomas Moore, *Moore's Irish melodies: the illustrated 1846 edition* (New York, 2000), p. 222. 22 An early upright piano by Robert Woffington of Dublin, now in the musical instrument collection of the Museum of Fine Arts, Boston, had been exhibited in Dublin at an exhibition as the property of Lady Morgan, but more research on the provenance needs to be done. For further reading see Darcy Kuronen, 'The earliest upright piano? An instrument by Robert Woffington of Dublin', *Newsletter of the American Musical Instrument Society*, 37:3 (Fall 2008), 11–12. 23 Fitzpatrick, *Lady Morgan, her career, literary and personal*, p. 68. 24 The harp given a central role in *The wild Irish*

reader is introduced to an array of highly romanticized historical characters, including a Gaelic king, the prince of Inismore, his harp-playing daughter Glorvina, and an aged bard, who all live in a decayed ruin of a Gaelic castle. A passing reference is made by the prince to an old harper, O'Gallagher, who might be summoned to the hall to 'drive away sorrow with music', but it is Glorvina instead, who provides the evening entertainment.[25] English readers were eager to learn about the somewhat unknown Ireland of the past, and Owenson's brand of romantic cultural nationalism was enthusiastically consumed in Britain. Her publisher, R. Phillips, recognized the novelty of Irish-themed books and he professed to Sydney, 'The world is not informed about Ireland, and I am in the situation to command the *light* to shine!'[26] In the extraordinary novel, Owenson illuminates several facets of Gaelic Ireland, from historical accounts of battles to antiquities, ancient dress, jewellery and Gaelic harp history. The book's harp-playing heroine, the princess of Inismore, is in fact the 'wild Irish girl', with the term 'wild' meaning 'uncivilized'. Owenson's title infers a somewhat misguided prejudice held by the novel's English hero, Horatio, who soon discovers that the 'wild' princess is far from being uncultured in that she speaks several languages and is well-read in the classics. Her name comes from the Gaelic *Glor-bhin*, literally translated as 'sweet voice'. With the novel's immense success, Owenson shrewdly began to assume the name Glorvina for herself, and she was affectionately called Glorvina by her friends and also adopted it as her signature on letters. Both Glorvinas, author and fictional character, played the small Irish harp and no doubt the book's descriptions of harp-playing were drawn from Sydney's personal experiences, or highly romanticized versions of her experiences. In *The wild Irish girl*, quite by chance Horatio overhears Glorvina's harp-playing and is filled with 'undefinable emotion' as she sings with a low 'tremulous' voice and 'sweeps with a feathery touch the chords of her harp'.[27] The Gaelic princess Glorvina captivates Horatio through her irresistible singing to the harp, and we learn which piece she plays: an 'exquisite old Irish air called the "Dream of the Young Man"', which was also a favourite tune in Sydney's own repertoire.[28]

Glorvina was an imagined version of Sydney herself in Gaelic Ireland, and lines were suitably blurred between fact and fiction as Sydney increasingly took on Glorvina's persona by appearing publicly in the antique Irish dress of her fictional character. Known as the 'wild Irish girl', she donned a scarlet cloak and

girl is discussed in Barra Boydell, 'Constructs of nationality: the literary and visual politics of Irish music in the nineteenth century' in Michael Murphy and Jan Smaczny (eds), *Music in nineteenth-century Ireland*, Irish Musical Studies 9 (Dublin, 2007), pp 52–60.   **25** Owenson, *The wild Irish girl*, p. 59.   **26** Morgan, *Lady Morgan's memoirs*, i, p. 254.   **27** Owenson, *The wild Irish girl*, p. 52, 161. The term 'chords' refers to the strings on the harp.   **28** Ibid., p. 100.

fastened a golden bodkin in her upswept hair, and completed the picture with her Egan Irish harp. It was a masterful stroke of marketing by the author, and 'Glorvina cloaks' and Irish harps became fashion trends in England and also Ireland. Ladies in Dublin's viceregal court rearranged their hair to show off antique gold bodkins like Glorvina's, and the city's jewellers busily produced the hair ornaments to keep up with popular demand.[29]

At the height of its popularity, *The wild Irish girl* underwent seven reprintings in less than two years, elevating Sydney to a position of importance among London's literati. Unexpected doors opened for her in upper-class circles, and she wrote of her new status, 'In the process of time … when one "wild Irish girl" brought the other into notice – it became the fashion to ask that other and her Irish harp to Dublin parties.'[30] The fictional harpist Glorvina was now so well-known that it was expected of the author Glorvina to never fail to appear without her harp at social gatherings. A revealing memoir describes how, soon after arriving in London, flushed with success, Sydney was invited to a party given by the Countess Dowager of Cork. At the moment of Sydney's departure for the event, she received a note from the hostess: 'Everybody has been invited expressly to meet the Wild Irish Girl; so she must bring her Irish harp. M.C.O.'[31] Owenson arrived at the party (without her harp) and listened as the illustrious titles of guests were announced: princes, ambassadors, dukes and duchesses and luminaries such as Lord Byron, Lady Hamilton and the Irish playwright Richard Sheridan. Suddenly Lady Cork appeared, saying, 'What, no harp, Glorvina?' While one of the chairmen was sent to collect her harp from Stanhope Street, Sydney was pushed on towards the centre of the conservatory, and instead of a civilized sofa or chair, the 'wild Irish girl' was placed on 'a sort of rustic seat' by Lady Cork. Sydney described herself as being exhibited and shown off like 'the beautiful hyena that never was tamed', quite 'wild and savage'. The harp was eventually brought forth and Sydney made an attempt to play and sing but was emotionally overwhelmed and unaccustomed to the attention. She recalls, 'my howl was funereal; I was ready to cry in character, but endeavoured to laugh, and to cover out my real timidity by an affected ease, which was both awkward and impolitic'.[32] In time, Owenson overcame her initial shyness and began to relish being the centre of attention, capitalizing on her unusual status as an Irish female author and harpist.

Sydney became a sought-after guest in country houses, and it was a monumental change from her former days of working as a mere governess in such residences. In 1809, Sydney was offered a resident position by the marquis

29 Mary Campbell, *Lady Morgan, the life and times of Sydney Owenson* (London, 1988), pp 71–2. 30 Morgan, *The book of the boudoir*, i, pp 62–3.   31 Ibid., i, pp 101–2.   32 Ibid., i, p. 109.

2.1 Barons Court, seat of the dukes of Abercorn, where Sydney Owenson was a resident guest, from F.O. Morris, *A series of picturesque views of seats of the noblemen and gentlemen of Great Britain and Ireland*, 1840.

and the marchioness of Abercorn to be a companion at their country estate of Barons Court in Co. Tyrone (figure 2.1) and also Stanmore Priory near London. Her primary role was to be amusing at dinner parties and to entertain the guests with lively fictional tales and harp-playing. During her time with the Abercorns, she occasionally slipped away temporarily to visit her family in Dublin, and the ongoing correspondence between Lady Abercorn and Sydney reveals a request from the marchioness for Sydney to purchase for her an Egan harp. The marchioness, 'A.J.A.' (Lady Anne Jane Abercorn) writes, 'I should like to see a small ten guinea Irish harp,' and continues in the next letter: 'My harp will be beautiful, and of course I chose Hawk head, and should like the threefold honours as ornaments.'[33] Lady Abercorn's harp was ordered accordingly, and upon the delivery of the instrument to Stanmore Priory in England, she wrote to Sydney:

> Your harp is arrived, and *for the honour of Ireland, I must tell you*, it is very much admired and quite beautiful. Lady Aberdeen [her daughter] played on it for an hour, last night, and thought it very good, *almost* as good as a French harp, and perhaps will be quite as good when it has recovered the *fatigues* of the journey; pray tell poor Egan I shall show it off to the best

33 Morgan, *Lady Morgan's memoirs*, i, pp 409, 412.

advantage, and I sincerely hope he will have many orders in consequence. [...] The harp suffered a little in the journey; but I shall, I hope, be able to get it repaired.[34]

One can only imagine what 'fatigues of the journey' the little harp must have suffered as it was shipped across the notoriously turbulent Irish Sea in a wooden box. It is certain that the humidity and temperature changes would have resulted in the instrument being horribly out of tune, and strings on a new harp often take several days to settle into secure pitches. Despite the damage, the instrument fulfilled expectations in its 'quite beautiful' appearance.

TWO EARLY SMALL IRISH HARPS, SNOWSHILL MANOR, WORCESTERSHIRE, ENGLAND

Although the personal harps of Sydney Owenson and Lady Abercorn have yet to come to light in modern times, a few early extant harps suggest the types of instruments played. An early example of a green portable harp in the musical instrument collection at Snowshill Manor has a fierce hawk head painted in gold at the rounded end of the neck, with the fanciful bird morphing into strands of shamrocks.[35] The harp's neck extends dramatically in a vertical attitude. A second harp in the collection is blue with a wolfhound head painted in the same location on the neck, and is also adorned with a decorative three-dimensional piece meant to suggest classical acanthus leaves, attached to the top front of the pillar, formed in a composite material and gilded (figure 2.2).[36] Although no inscription or label has been found on either harp, they are identical in both construction and decoration to other portable harps by John Egan. On the early portable harps, it was the practice for the maker to attach a label with his signature inside the soundbox, as evidenced by another similar harp in a private collection in Northern Ireland (figure 2.3).[37] Other extant harps display the decoration mentioned in Lady Abercorn's request for 'threefold honours as ornaments'. The shamrock (Ireland), rose (England) and thistle (Scotland) were joined together in a stylish decorative theme to commemorate the Act of Union.

34 Ibid., i, pp 416–17.   35 The ornament may be a symbolic reference to the ancient mythological beasts depicted in the Celtic artwork of Irish antiquities such as the Book of Kells (Trinity College, Dublin).   36 The sculptural piece attached to the front pillar top is a decorative feature on fewer than ten surviving early Egan portable harps, and on a harp in the author's collection it is combined with a strip of six raised shamrocks on the curve of the head.   37 The label in ink on a cloth-like square reads, 'John Egan, Maker/ No. 30 Dawson Street/ Dublin'. The street numbers on Dawson Street changed periodically. See p. 218, n.56 for dating of street number changes for the Egan workshop.

2.2 (*top left*) Portable Irish Harp at Snowshill Manor, Worcestershire, England. Photo by Claire Reeves, courtesy of the National Trust.

2.3 (*top right*) Hand-written John Egan label inside a Portable Irish Harp. Photo by Nancy Hurrell, courtesy of Frances O'Kane.

2.4 (*bottom left*) Decorative theme of shamrocks, roses and thistles on an Egan harp. Photo by Nancy Hurrell, courtesy of Oxmantown Settlement Trust, Birr Castle.

An ornamental bouquet of these symbols (figure 2.4) would have appealed to members of the Anglo-Irish aristocracy and was used in the decorative arts from furniture to china.[38]

Upon her return from one family visit in Dublin, Sydney discovered that in her absence the marquis and marchioness had engaged a new guest, Thomas Charles Morgan, to join their ranks at Barons Court. A family physician, Morgan proved in time to be more to Sydney than just an interesting guest, for a love match between the two gradually ensued, craftily engineered behind the scenes by Lady Abercorn. The fiercely independent Sydney resisted marriage at first, but eventually accepted Dr Morgan's proposal after he was knighted by the duke of Richmond, all carefully arranged by the marchioness. Sydney was not averse to gaining the title of Lady Morgan, and the couple was married one ordinary day without fanfare at Barons Court in 1812. Lord and Lady Morgan soon left their positions at the house to begin a new life together in Dublin, residing at 35 Kildare Street. Between 1816 and 1833, Lady Morgan turned her literary talents to writing travel books, and with her amiable husband as companion, visited France, Switzerland and Belgium; the results of her research trips were published in the travelogues *France* (1817) and *Italy* (1821).

PORTRAITS WITH HARP

As the Irish harp was central to Sydney's public image, at least three portraits were made of her with the instrument.[39] One was painted during a trip to France while she was staying with one of her high-ranking hosts, General Lafayette, in 1818 at the Château de la Grange. While a guest at the château, Sydney came to know Ary Scheffer, a young Dutch artist who had been commissioned to paint a portrait of the general. Scheffer persuaded Sydney to sit for her own portrait in which the painter chose to include her Irish harp, as Sydney relates in a letter to her sister Olivia:

> It is done for the Exhibition here; but whether it is to fall to my lot afterwards I don't know. He has introduced the little harp into it. Tell Egan all the world is running after his harp, and that he will soon be as well known here as at Dublin.[40]

38 Egan portable harps displaying intertwined shamrocks, roses and thistles in gold survive in collections at Birr Castle in Ireland, the Victoria & Albert Museum (London) and the Museum of Fine Arts (Boston).   39 Only two are extant as original engravings in the National Library of Ireland.   40 Morgan, *Passages from my autobiography*, p. 147. The location of the Scheffer portrait of Lady Morgan is not known.

Through the exhibited portrait of the celebrated author with her harp, as well
as Lady Morgan's performances at musical evenings among the French elite,
Egan's small harp model gained invaluable exposure abroad.[41]

In addition to the Scheffer painting, two engraved images of Sydney playing
the harp appear in selected editions of her novels: *The missionary: an Indian tale*
(1811) and the 1846 edition of *The wild Irish girl: a national tale*. Both engraved
portraits capture a fairly accurate likeness of the author and the images correctly
imply that Sydney played the harp. Therefore it might be assumed that the
instruments pictured are faithful representations of Sydney's harp, but as is often
the case in harp iconography, the instruments in both engravings are not
consistent with the small harp she actually played. Instead, both engravings
suggest a large French pedal harp, or rather the idea of a French pedal harp as
the instruments are somewhat incorrectly drawn. The first engraved portrait
appears as the frontispiece in *The missionary: an Indian tale by Miss Owenson, with a
portrait of the author* (figure 2.5).[42] The stringing of the harp in the picture is
problematical in that the string knots are on the opposite side of the actual
plane of strings and do not logically connect. Also the strings themselves are at
an awkward angle unlike any true stringing, and the spacing is proportionally
too wide, all of which suggests that the artist did not have an instrument before
him. Sydney is rendered in a static pose with an angelic expression, and her
hands are shown in a fairly accurate curved-finger hand position for playing the
French harp. The harpist is fashionably dressed in a high-waisted Grecian gown
with a draped shawl, in the typical period style.

The second engraved portrait of Owenson playing a harp is the frontispiece
in the 1846 edition of *The wild Irish girl*, published in London by Henry Colburn
(figure 2.6).[43] Once again, although the person in the sketch has Owenson's
likeness, this time more animated, the harp pictured is unlike Sydney's own
instrument or indeed any actual functioning harp. The wide-spaced strings
appear at an unusual angle, and although the harp has realistic tuning pegs, the
attached knots are tied to the pegs on the wrong side of the neck. Sydney's
hands are more accurately drawn, with her left hand rendered in a typical string-
dampening position.[44] The mistaken form of the harp might be overlooked in

---

41 An 1821 advert states that orders for Egan harps were received from instrument sellers on the
Continent as well as in Holland, in addition to London, Liverpool and Bath. See *Dublin Evening
Post*, 22 Dec. 1821.   **42** Sydney Owenson, *The missionary: an Indian tale*, 3 vols (London, 1811). The
engraved print in the National Library of Ireland (EP MORG-SY (6) I) lists Robert Dighton,
painter and James Godby, engraver.   **43** The engraved print in the National Library of Ireland
(EP MORG-SY (5) II) lists John Comerford, painter, and Samuel Freeman, engraver.   **44** In
both engraved portraits, the harp is held on the left shoulder, opposite to the standard playing
position for French harps, but this was probably due to the engraving technique, which reversed

2.5 Portrait of Sydney
Owenson by James Godby,
reproduced courtesy of the
National Library of Ireland.

light of the print's subject matter, for the portrait is actually meant to be the
character Glorvina, again merging the identity of the author with that of her
imagined heroine. However, in the novel's text, Glorvina's harp mirrors Sydney's
own instrument in its small size, like the Brian Boru harp.[45] The costume,
however, is authentic to the heroine Glorvina, who wears ancient dress with
cloak, along with a golden armlet and a bodkin in her hair, as she dramatically
strikes the harp. The portrait cleverly represents a moment in the story when
Horatio drew the harpist's likeness as she played:

> Wrapt in her charming avocation [...] I took her likeness. Conceive for a
> moment a form full of character, and full of grace, bending over an
> instrument singularly picturesque – a profusion of auburn hair fastened
> up to the top of the finest formed head I ever beheld, with a golden
> bodkin – an armlet of curious workmanship glittering above a finely

the original drawing in the process of printing.   **45** Owenson, *The wild Irish girl*, p. 71.

2.6 Portrait of Sydney Owenson by Samuel Freeman, reproduced courtesy of the National Library of Ireland.

turned elbow, and the loose sleeves of a flowing robe drawn up unusually high, to prevent this drapery from sweeping the chords of the instrument.[46]

'SWEEPS WITH A FEATHERY TOUCH THE CHORDS OF HER HARP'

It is one thing to conjure up an image of Sydney playing her Egan harp and quite another to imagine the musical sounds of her performances.[47] To ascertain her particular style of singing to the harp, one has to look no further than her fictional harpists, for their performance practices are presented in great detail in the novels. The songs are invariably Irish, and the characters fervently discuss the merits of Ireland's music, in line with the author's own views. In her first novel, *St Clair*, the main character, Mr St Clair, prefers Irish music over 'foreign music', saying it is 'calculated to harmonize every feeling of the soul; it is the music of sentiment and passion; and that is the true music of the heart'.[48] The heroine, Olivia, obliges by singing '*Emuinch Ecnuic*' or 'Ned of the Hills' to her harp:

> Olivia tuned her harp; and, after a prelude, in which she displayed an execution bold, various, and correct, struck a few low chords, and sung the air, first to the original Irish words, and then to a translation of her own [...] the air, so wild, so plaintive; the melancholy simplicity of its expression [...] all powerfully affected me [...] Her last verse was the best; and her voice, as it died over the faint vibration of the chords, had all the heart-breaking melancholy softness of the Eolian lyre.[49]

The scene is realistically rendered, as it commences with tuning the harp, a necessity clearly understood by the author. Then a 'prelude' is played, which is consistent with harp method books from the late 1700s and early 1800s, wherein a short prelude is often included either before or after a piece. In the harp tutors of Cousineau, Mayer and Bochsa, preludes are typically followed by minuets, waltzes and other light classical pieces.[50] Composed in the same key signature as the adjoining piece, a standard prelude consisted of arpeggios and chords, or a specific rhythmic motif, but without any particular melody. It could function as a sort of 'tuning' prelude for checking and adjusting the strings, and it also

46 Ibid., pp 97–8.   47 The CD, *The Egan Irish harp* by Nancy Hurrell (2011), provides sound samples recorded on two extant Portable Irish Harps.   48 Sydney Owenson, *St Clair, or the heiress of Desmond* (Dublin, 1803) p. 122.   49 Ibid., pp 121–3.   50 See Jacques-Georges Cousineau fils, *Méthode de harpe* (Paris, 1772); J.B. Mayer, *Complete instructions for the harp* (London, 1800); and N.C. Bochsa, *A new and improved method of instruction for the harp* (London, 1819).

served as a warm-up for the fingers to familiarize intervallic note placements within a given key. The prelude was sometimes played as part of the performance, just as the character Olivia has demonstrated. The 'bold' and 'correct' execution of the prelude implies a certain technique learned from a harp teacher or a professional harpist.[51]

Olivia then begins to play her harp piece with introductory 'low chords', allowing the longer bass strings to resonate. Several verses, first in Irish and then in English, are sung with 'wild' and 'melancholy' expression, culminating in the final quiet, 'faint' conclusion for dramatic effect, ending in a *decrescendo*. Olivia's bold yet sensitive playing employs dynamic contrasts of loud and soft, and the listener is powerfully moved. In Sydney's romantic scenes, the recurring theme of singing to trembling harp sounds always manages to render the listener powerless to resist the harp's enchanting spell. Olivia's suitor St Clair was so moved that he interrupted her harp-playing and suddenly 'snatched her hand from the strings, and in a moment of delirium pressed it to [his] lips'.[52]

The hypnotic effect of harp music on a listener as presented in Sydney's novels may well have been an embellishment of reality by the youthful writer, although the scenes do bear some relation to the cultural practices of the time. In Sydney's day there were few outlets for entertainment, and a heartfelt song performed to the delicate, resonant strains of a harp was a powerful, emotive experience. Another example of music eliciting an exaggerated response from the listener is an anecdote from *The book of the boudoir* (1829), in which Sydney performs her favourite air for a visitor, Mr Richard Kirwan, a 'philosopher':

> While he was speaking, I had drawn my harp forward, and begged permission to sing to it the fine old cronan of *Emunch-a-Knuic*, or 'Ned of the Hills,' which dates back to the time of Henry VIII. He bowed his head in sullen assent; but before I had finished the first stanza, the tears gushed from his eyes, and seizing my hands, he said with vehemence, 'Madam, I won't hear you – 'tis terrible – it goes to the very soul! – it wrings every nerve in the body!'[53]

The scene might well be exaggerated for dramatic effect, but the story nonetheless touches on real themes of the emotive power of music. In Owenson's historical fiction, music often plays a pivotal part in the story, although each novel is set in a different period or country and the type of harp changes accordingly. In Owenson's second book, *The novice of Saint Dominick*, a

---

51 It is not known if Sydney Owenson had taken lessons from a harp professor.   52 Owenson, *St Clair*, p. 162.   53 Morgan, *The book of the boudoir*, i, pp 70–3.

medieval harp is played by a minstrel, Orlando. The book is set in France, and the harpist is a troubadour, with a small harp suspended from his neck by a scarlet ribbon. His manner of playing, however, still has the same familiar elements of harpist characters Olivia and Glorvina, for he commenced with low chords, rose to a 'rich, wild, and various' accompaniment to his singing, and as he finished, 'the harp's soft vibrations faded into silence'.[54] The troubadour's impassioned performance succeeds in luring the heroine, Imogen. When she later hears the sound of the minstrel's harp from a distance, she is filled with 'indescribable emotion'.[55]

In Lady Morgan's next to last novel, *The O'Briens and the O'Flahertys* (1827), she chose a French harp for a cameo appearance. The book is set in 1790s Ireland, at a time when the French pedal harp was society's favoured instrument, and the musical scene depicts the actual performance practices of the time. A touring Italian harpist performs in Dublin Castle's Throne Room, singing a fashionable Italian air to harp accompaniment.[56]

IRISH HARP SCHOLAR

A stereotypical image of Sydney Owenson is a passionate 'Glorvina' striking her harp to spirited vocal strains of 'Ned of the hills'. Another apt characterization of Lady Morgan is a successful Irish writer and witty storyteller, a sought-after guest who was courted by the social elite in Dublin, London and Paris. Still another, less well-known, role she fulfilled is that of an Irish harp scholar, who researched and recorded valuable information on Ireland's ancient Gaelic harping tradition, the harps and the players, leaving behind a considerable legacy for future generations. In preparation for *The wild Irish girl*, Owenson tenaciously sought answers to fundamental questions concerning Irish harp history, and she corresponded with an impressive list of historians and harpers including the respected antiquarian J.C. Walker, the Gaelic harper Arthur O'Neill and the Revd Mr Sampson. In the extensive footnotes in *The wild Irish girl*, gems of information from O'Neill range from his explanation of Gaelic harp stringing with four kinds of wire, to his enlightening statement that at one time fifteen ladies were proficient on the ancient Irish harp, contrary to the generally held perception of it being a predominantly male profession.[57] Notes abound on the harper Turlough Carolan, including information on him composing songs for his patrons Miss Power and Grace Nugent. The letter from Revd Sampson to Owenson chronicles the life and work of the legendary harper Dennis

54 Sydney Owenson, *The novice of Saint Dominick* (London, 1805), i, pp 126–7.   55 Ibid., p. 192.
56 Lady Morgan, *The O'Briens and the O'Flahertys* (London, 1827), pp 127–9.   57 Owenson, *The wild*

Hempson, with pages of precious details describing his harp and the tunes he played as well as anecdotes on his life and performances. Revd Sampson's letter printed in *The wild Irish girl* was deemed so significant in its historical details that it was later reprinted in Edward Bunting's landmark volume, the 1840 edition of *The ancient music of Ireland*.

'I'M GETTING DOWN MY OLD HARP'

Sydney's small Egan harp was not only instrumental in her career, it was also a beloved personal object enjoyed in family music-making. A typical family gathering was recalled in her memoirs:

> Hot cake ordered for tea, and a boiled chicken for supper. We tuned the harp and piano, and Clarke *would* play his flute in such *time* and *tune* as it pleased God! There was never such a family picture.[58]

A final mention of her harp states, 'I am getting down my old harp, which I had exiled to a lumber-room, and will have to put in order. I will then get up a song or two.'[59]

The fortuitous timing of John Egan's production of a small Irish harp model coincided with Sydney Owenson's debut as Ireland's contemporary female bard. The symbolic harp perfectly completed her nationalistic persona and also fulfilled her personal music-making needs. Egan and Owenson had a mutually beneficial relationship, for while Egan's harp enhanced Sydney's commercial capital, in return, Sydney used her high-profile status to launch Egan's new harp model to the wider world. In performances, portraits and even her bestselling novel *The wild Irish girl*, Owenson promoted Egan's new Irish harp concept. An indirect reference to Egan's instrument is inferred by Glorvina, when she is asked if her harp matched the 'original ancient Irish harp' and she replies,

> Not exactly, for I have strung it with gut instead of wire, merely for the gratification of my own ear; but it is however, precisely the same form as that preserved in the Irish university, which belonged to one of the most celebrated of our heroes, Brian Boru.[60]

In an instance of veiled product placement, Egan's harp model is not directly mentioned, but the meaning is clearly understood. Egan, like Owenson, also

---

Irish girl, p. 71.   58 Morgan, *Lady Morgan's memoirs*, i, p. 497. 'Clarke' was married to Sydney's sister Olivia.   59 Ibid., ii, p. 415.   60 Owenson, *The wild Irish girl*, pp 71–2.

made use of the public's eager consumption of ancient Irish culture in his Brian Boru-shaped gut-strung Irish harp. He transformed the iconic representation of national identity into a commercial product that ushered in a modern era of harp-playing. In the subsequent two decades, Egan would continually experiment with improvements made to the model's structural form, shape and mechanisms for further expanded chromatic capabilities.

3 / The patriotic present

In the first few years of harp-making at the Egan workshop, two instrument models were produced: the empire-style pedal harp and the small Irish harp of the type Sydney Owenson played. In terms of the history of harp-playing in Ireland, the early nineteenth century was an era of overlapping traditions, with aristocratic pedal harp-playing dominant in the music room, while efforts were also made to preserve Ireland's ancient Gaelic harp practices. In the socio-political climate of post-union Ireland, a patriotic revival of the 'national instrument' was seen as crucial to safeguarding the country's ancient cultural heritage. Revival efforts had begun in earnest in the late eighteenth century, with a series of harp festivals to rally the few remaining wire harp players, and in the early nineteenth century, dedicated harp societies in Belfast and Dublin decided to start special schools to teach the wire-strung *cláirseach* to the next generation. These ongoing activities were frequently chronicled in the press under the headline 'The Irish harp'. On 14 October 1809, one such column printed in the *Freeman's Journal* began with, 'A thousand years have nearly passed away without any improvement having been made upon this sweet instrument'.[1] It was observed that the Welsh had 'improved the Harp by adopting gut, instead of brass wire', and the French nation had further added 'machinery' to their harps, referring to the invention of the pedals. This curious article hinted at the idea of an 'improved' Irish harp, and went on to extol the pioneering work of Ireland's own harp maker, 'our ingenious countryman, Mr John Egan of this city, a self-taught artist, and the only Harp-maker in Ireland'. Although presented in the guise of a news article, it was clearly a promotional ad for Egan's enterprise, as we learn that an Egan pedal harp had been recently constructed for the duchess of Richmond, wife of the lord lieutenant of Ireland (1807–13),[2] and several harps by the maker had lately been imported to England. As the usual flow of trade was in the reverse direction, with British goods deemed superior to Irish-made products, this was fairly noteworthy, and the ad

---

1 *Freeman's Journal*, 14 Oct. 1809. 2 The 'lord lieutenant' or 'viceroy' was the highest-ranking British representative in Ireland, with administrative offices based in Dublin Castle. The lord lieutenant's residence was the Viceregal Lodge at Phoenix Park.

lightly alludes to an old adage: 'fortunately his [Egan's] great ingenuity has not been like too many of his countrymen, "born to blush unseen, and waste its sweetness on the desert air"'. The article concludes with an important announcement:

> We understand that Mr Egan has now finished an Irish Harp, which for ingenuity of construction, elegance of form, and sweetness of tone, is highly creditable to his talents. This Harp Mr Egan intends as a patriotic present to the Charitable Institution of the 'Irish Harp Society'.[3]

Egan's 'Irish Harp' for the harp society retained the wire strings and ancient shape, but was crafted in the modern form of several joined sections of wood.

With this publicized gift to the Irish Harp Society, Egan openly aligned himself to the strong cultural current of nationalism at a time when the Irish harp was still viewed as a somewhat politicized symbol with inherent overtones of republican sentiment. Throughout his career, Egan would straddle the diverging worlds of the Protestant Ascendancy and the native Irish, with their often contradictory political loyalties. For a tradesman like Egan to succeed, it was vital to attain the patronage of the English aristocracy, which he had achieved by supplying a pedal harp to the duchess of Richmond, the wife of the residing British viceroy, England's official representative in Ireland. At the same time, the public conversation had turned to the ancient Irish harp as a nationalist symbol, and as the country's primary harp maker, Egan wanted to be part of that national dialogue. This self-made man was driven by a desire to succeed in his profession as well as an attraction to challenging, new projects. The 'patriotic present' widened Egan's commercial horizons as he began to launch a new line of wire-strung harps at his workshop. With the gift, Egan forged a relationship with the Irish Harp Society in Dublin, which led to his appointment as harp maker to the society, and later he would receive further orders from the Irish Harp Society of Belfast for his 'Improved Irish Harp'. As harp maker to the society schools, Egan now made harps for poor, often blind, children – quite a different strata of the population from his usual well-heeled clients.

A PLAN FOR REVIVING THE ANCIENT MUSIC

By the late 1700s, only a few players of the wire-strung Irish harp remained, as patrons for their style of music were not easily found. Attempts had been made

3 *Freeman's Journal*, 14 Oct. 1809.

3.1 High-headed Irish harp
(*cláirseach*), 1734, by John Kelly.
Photograph © 2019 Museum
of Fine Arts, Boston.

to adapt to the new musical genres, and Gaelic harps were larger and louder than in former times, with more strings added for deeper resonance in the bass. Whereas the medieval Irish harps were small and low-headed, typically 3ft in height, now the taller harps stood at 5ft and were formed in a distinctive high-headed shape (figure 3.1).[4] The pillar was less curved and the neck swept up at an acute angle to meet a high head, taking on a shape somewhat like the Welsh triple harp played in Britain at the time. Irish harpers expanded their repertoires, but the art music style was not particularly idiomatic to the Irish harp's modal tuning. The quick-changing harmonic progressions were apt to cause clashing tonalities on a wire-strung instrument, and to play in different keys, the harp had to be retuned. In contrast, the harp of Wales was fully chromatic. The Welsh

4 Joan Rimmer identifies the three phases in early Irish harp development as low-headed, large low-headed and high-headed. Rimmer, *The Irish harp*, p. 2.

triple harp, as its name suggests, had three rows of gut strings with the two outer rows tuned to a diatonic scale (white notes on a keyboard) and a middle row in chromatic tuning (black notes). There is evidence of at least one early chromatic harp produced in Ireland in the seventeenth century. The Cloyne harp, also known as the Dalway or Fitzgerald harp, had an added row of seven strings, as seen on the fragments housed in the National Museum of Ireland.[5] Despite these attempts to adapt to the changes taking place in instruments and music, by the 1780s, it was becoming clear that it would take concerted efforts to rescue the dying harp tradition, and concerned citizens organized competitions with monetary enticements to encourage the harpers. Festivals were held at Granard, with society balls attached to the harp competitions to attract greater attendance from the gentry.

The last great gathering of harpers took place in Belfast in 1792. Similar to the Granard festivals, financial reward was offered to the harpers, as announced in a *Dublin Evening Post* article that said, 'Performers on the Irish harp are requested to assemble in this town on the 10th day of July next, when a considerable sum will be distributed in premiums, in proportion to their respective merits', and stated that each harper would be paid for a performance.[6] It was hoped that the public performance would be morale-boosting for the harp players and also generate more widespread appreciation for the ancient harp music. In addition, there was a growing concern for the possible impending loss of the orally transmitted music, for it only existed in the memories of the few surviving harpers. To save the harp tunes for future generations, a trained musician was needed to notate the pieces as they were performed at the festival. A 19-year-old organist, Edward Bunting, was engaged for this important task.[7] Word of the proposed Belfast meeting spread throughout the country, and the momentous three-day event was held in the ballroom of the Exchange Buildings. A painfully small number of harpers, only ten, sat upon the stage in their 'comfortable homely' suits of 'drab coloured grey cloth, of coarse manufacture', as described by Bunting.[8] The harper Arthur O'Neill had the addition of silver buttons the size of half a crown on his jacket, engraved with the O'Neill crest, setting him apart. Of the ten harpers, six were blind, one was female (Rose Mooney) and most were of an advanced age. These travelling musicians had arrived with guides to carry their harps, and some had horses. Only one, Denis Hempson, aged 97, still played using a fingernail technique in the old manner. Bunting wrote that Hempson 'played with long crooked nails' and described the

5 See Michael Billinge and Bonnie Shaljean, 'The Dalway or Fitzgerald harp (1621)', *Early Music*, 15:2 (May 1987), 175–87.   6 *Dublin Evening Post*, 8 May 1792.   7 For a detailed account of the Belfast Harp Festival of 1792, see Gráinne Yeats, *The harp of Ireland* (Belfast, 1992).   8 Bunting, *The ancient music of Ireland*, p. 65.

'tinkling of the small wires under the deep notes of the bass' as thrilling to hear.[9] Several ancient airs, such as 'The dawning of the day', 'Soft mild morning' and 'Molly Bheag O', were performed at the festival. With origins and dates unknown, these old tunes had been passed orally from master to pupil for generations. However the majority of the pieces played were actually the relatively modern compositions of Turlough Carolan from the early 1700s. Tunes like 'Fanny Power', 'Mrs Maxwell' and 'Thomas Burke' had been composed and named for Carolan's patrons, reflecting the working life of the itinerant harper. Many of Carolan's melodies were not written in the ancient Irish style but were instead influenced by the Italian baroque style, as Bunting observed: 'The taste for Italian music, introduced by Geminiani and Corelli, seems about this time to have largely infected the works of Irish composers, especially those of Carolan.'[10] During the Belfast festival, as the harpers played their pieces, both ancient and modern, Bunting quickly notated the melodies with dots and dashes in his notebooks, to be edited later, and the harp melodies were preserved.[11]

Following the Belfast meeting, Bunting continued his important work, touring the counties of Galway and Mayo to meet with individual harpers and collect their harp tunes and songs, and he devoted years to the project, making it his life's mission to record Ireland's music. In preparing the music for publication, however, rather than present the arrangements exactly as they were played on the Irish harp, Bunting added new accompaniments to the old melodies, and often changed the key signatures. On the Irish harp, with its very resonant brass strings, the bass harmony typically would have been single notes, two-note chords and octaves. Bunting, a keyboard player, added more active accompaniments, with Alberti bass, quick passing tones and three-note chords in a pianistic style, and the collection was published as arrangements for the pianoforte, the primary instrument in use at the time for amateur music-making.[12] In this format Bunting hoped the tunes would continue to be played.[13] Nonetheless he was genuinely devoted to preserving this rapidly disappearing

9 Ibid., p. 3.   10 Ibid., p. 9.   11 Bunting's original notebooks are held in the Edward Bunting Manuscript Collection 1773–1843 at Queen's University, Belfast. See also Moloney, *The Irish music manuscripts of Edward Bunting (1773–1843)*.   12 Bunting's arrangements are generally acknowledged as unsuitable for the wire-strung harp and also the modern gut-strung Celtic harp. However, I discovered they are quite idiomatic to Egan's Portable Irish Harp, with its bright timbre and short resonance, an instrument with tone qualities similar to the early piano.   13 Bunting's decision to arrange the harp tunes for the pianoforte continues to be lamented by harpists and historians. The original integrity was lost and changes in notes and keys were unfortunately made. In his defence, it could be argued that to publish the music for the wire-strung harp in 1796 would have been fruitless, since there were so few players, and they were orally taught and most were blind. Instead, Bunting chose to market these collections to the widest audience possible so the melodies would continue to be played, and their continued popularity in modern times reflects his foresight.

chapter in Ireland's musical history, and he painstakingly recorded details of the harpers' tunings, techniques and ornamentations, as well as interesting anecdotes of the players themselves. His first volume was published in 1796 as *A general collection of the ancient Irish music*, and this was followed by a further two volumes: *A general collection of the ancient music of Ireland* in 1809 and *The ancient music of Ireland* in 1840.

In 1808, Bunting embarked on another ambitious endeavour towards a harping revival. He assisted in the formation of a harp society in Belfast whose purpose was to start a school to teach Irish harp technique and music.[14] Respectful of Ireland's long-standing tradition of blind harpers, places at the school, including board and lodging, were offered to poor blind children; thus, admirable charitable work was combined with lofty patriotism. Funds were raised by subscriptions, and Arthur O'Neill, now aged 75, was engaged to be the teacher. There was a genuine belief that the skill of harp-playing would not only lead to useful employment for a blind person, but also afford them genuine comfort:

> The highest gratification which a blind man seems to derive from external causes, arises from musical sounds, and he flies himself to the practice of some musical instrument, as his prime source of consolation.[15]

Aiken McClelland writes that the harps for the society's school were supplied by Mr White, a local 'mechanic' in the town, who had previously built two organs.[16] By the next year, in 1809, there were twelve blind pupils at the school, and in November they performed at a special banquet to honour Bunting:

> After dinner, he [O'Neill] led into the room his twelve blind pupils, one of whom is a female, Miss O'Reilly. – Their entrance exhibited a scene peculiarly impressive; but when Miss O'Reilly and two of the youths strung their harps, and played some trios, duets, & c. they were followed by the most enthusiastic applause. Among other admired airs were the following: – *Patrick's Day* – *The Green Wood Truigha* – *Ulligun dulh O!* or the Song of Sorrow – *Bumper Squire Jones* – *Planxty Plunket* – *Planxty Reilley, &c.*[17]

The programme was a combination of ancient airs and Carolan tunes, similar to the music heard at the Belfast festival. Bunting, the hero of the evening, was

14 For further details see Aiken McClelland, 'The Irish harp society', *Ulster Folklife*, 21 (Belfast, 1975), 16. **15** John Warburton, Revd J. Whitelaw and Revd Robert Walsh, *History of the city of Dublin* (London, 1818), p. 765. **16** McClelland, 'The Irish harp society', p. 17. **17** *Chester Chronicle*, 12 Jan. 1810.

repeatedly toasted for his achievements: 'By the publication of the ancient melodies of Ireland, he has fixed an era in the history of its national music [...] he has also been the happy means of restoring the ancient mode of preserving it, by a succession of Irish Bards.'[18] In spite of the initial success of the society and its school, both came to an end a few years later, in 1813, due to lack of funds.

IRISH HARP SOCIETY OF DUBLIN, 1809–12

With great interest, citizens in Dublin had followed the founding of the Irish Harp Society of Belfast and its school. Not to be outdone by their northern counterparts, they formed their own society – the Irish Harp Society – on 13 July 1809, led by John Bernard Trotter. A *Dublin Evening Post* article outlined its goals:

> An institution, every day increasing in numbers and respect, is at length formed, under the name of the IRISH HARP SOCIETY; the funds, created by voluntary subscription, are applied to the support of *poor Irish children*, and their *Instruction in the Harp of Ireland*. Thus, Charity and Science, Benevolence and Taste, Humility and Patriotism, are joined hand in hand; while the IRISH HARP excites and cherishes affections worthy its celebration.[19]

Patrick Quin of Portadown, another blind harper from the Belfast festival, was brought to Dublin by Trotter to be the tutor for the school, and Quin also regularly performed at society meetings and various social events. Although the list of subscribers was made up mainly of middle-class professionals, it's notable that the duke of Bedford, former lord lieutenant of Ireland (1806–7) also joined the cause. Subscribers included respected gentlemen such as General Vallancey (who served as president), the well-known poets Thomas Moore and Sir Walter Scott, antiquarian J.C. Walker and the harp maker John Egan. At one of the early meetings, 'Ladies of rank and respectability crowded to hear the strains of the venerable harper, Quin', and it was apparent that Quin's young blind pupil, who also played, already showed promise on the national instrument.[20] In the press, flowery emotive language was used to describe the Irish harp, with lines blurred between an actual instrument and a symbol of an awakening. Under the title 'The harp of their native land', one author wrote: 'its plaintive tones again swelled forth, as if breathing thanks, and promising fresh efforts at new

18 Ibid.   19 *Dublin Evening Post*, 12 Jan. 1810.   20 Ibid., 25 July 1809.

excellence on a future day, to its patrons and friends'.[21] The patriotic call had stirred the communal conscience, and for native Dubliners it was important to be publicly seen to support the cause.

To raise additional funds for Dublin's harp school, a grand concert in honour of Ireland's native composer, a 'Commemoration of Carolan', was planned for the 20 September 1809. It was to be held at the theatre in Fishamble Street, and the public was invited 'to celebrate the memory of an Irish Bard, as well as to aid the funds of an institution which is about to revive the national music of Ireland'.[22] The concert was so successful that it was repeated a week later on 27 September at the Rotunda. As one would expect, the society's harper, Patrick Quin performed, but the headliners of the concert were actually Mrs Cooke, the Misses Cheese, Sir J. Stevenson, Mr Spray and a band led by Mr Cooke, a member of the Irish Harp Society's music committee. These well-known performers on modern instruments commanded a good audience, and for the concert, Tom Moore generously contributed a new song to be premiered. Incorporating Carolan's 'Fairy queen' melody, Moore added poetic lyrics to a pianoforte accompaniment by Stevenson.[23] It's clear that Quin's old Irish harp music was not particularly appreciated at the concert, nor even heard, for the band of modern instruments actually drowned out the harper's efforts on the wire-strung harp. A reviewer of the concert in the *Dublin Satirist* observed:

> It is much to be regretted that the melody of the Irish Harp, as called forth by the sharp nails of the *venerable* Paddy Quin, was in a great degree lost to the audience, whose auricular nerves had been so violently assailed, and stunned, by the drums, clarionets [*sic*], and horns of *Tommy Cooke*, that the vibratory sounds of the brass wire were scarcely heard.[24]

The reviewer went on to say, 'During his performance the audience were principally engaged in conversation and walking in groups!' Quin seemed to sense that he was being ignored and reacted accordingly: 'the minstrel himself was rather uncourteous to his admirers, expressing his reluctance to perform by several exclamations'.[25] A scathing review of Quin's playing at the second concert appeared in *Hibernia Magazine*:

> The performance of the second was (if possible) superior to the first, with the exception of the old drunken harper, who was most successful in murdering some of our most favourite national airs. The audience, although not crowded, was very respectful indeed.[26]

21 *Freeman's Journal*, 12 Aug. 1809.   22 Ibid., 11 Sept. 1809.   23 Ibid.   24 'Commemoration of Carolan', *Dublin Satirist* (Nov. 1809), p. 32.   25 Ibid., p. 33.   26 'Irish Harp Society', *Hibernia*

Evidently the public was more interested in a romanticized ideal of the Irish harp, rather than supporting a performance of the actual instrument. To be fair, the wire-strung Irish harp was never meant to be a concert hall instrument, for the large cavernous space was acoustically quite different from an intimate music room.

Increasingly, the harp and its music were seen as a sort of historical curiosity, not on an equal footing with the sophisticated music normally heard in concert hall productions. Gaelic harp playing was now relegated to a narrow segment of society of ancient bards and poor blind children, whereas in the previous century the wire-strung harp had also been the instrument of aristocratic patrons and 'gentlemen harpers' taught by their esteemed guest musicians.[27] Historian Sylvester O'Halloran wrote in 1792, 'In every house was one or two harps, free to all travellers, who were most caressed, the more they excelled in music; and it was a reproach to a gentleman to want this branch of education.'[28] Unfortunately, these practices were no longer part of the collective memory in the early 1800s, and perhaps the harp societies' charitable work may have inadvertently led to a somewhat condescending attitude towards the players of the instrument.

'INGENUITY OF CONSTRUCTION'

Following the enormous success of the 'Commemoration of Carolan' concerts, the public's enthusiasm for the charitable harp school had reached a high point. John Egan, capitalizing on the moment, presented his 'patriotic present' of an Irish harp to the society within a fortnight of the event, in early October. In this heady atmosphere of public-spirited patriotism, Egan had appropriately arranged for a poem to be inscribed on the instrument's soundboard. The verse by Matthew Weld Hartstonge esq. reflected the society's aspirations:[29]

> The Harp once more at your command
> With ancient song shall charm the land.
> While each poor blind, poor Orphan boy,
> From your high bounty finds employ.
> May Erin's Harp sweet peace prolong,
> And glad inspire the dance and song.

Magazine (Jan. 1810), p. 36.   **27** A portrait of a gentleman harper *c*.1750 in a private collection shows Cork merchant William Archdeacon playing an Irish harp. The painting was featured in 'Image from the Archive', *Journal of Music* (Apr. /May 2009). Nicholas Carolan brought the image to my attention.   **28** Sylvester O'Halloran, *An introduction to the history and antiquities of Ireland* (London, 1772), p. 75, cited in Nicholas Carolan, 'Two Irish harps in Co. Dublin', *Ceol* (Dec. 1984), p. 40.   **29** M.W. Hartstonge was a member of the Finance Committee of the Dublin

R.B. Armstrong saw this harp decades later, and in his 1904 book, *Musical instruments* wrote, 'Egan, when constructing this harp, must have had an ancient harp before him, the form of which he followed with slight variations.'[30] Armstrong described some of the aspects of the traditional Irish form Egan had incorporated, like the projecting block extending from the bottom of the soundbox (5½ in. long). When played, the harp was balanced on the projecting block as it was held between the feet. According to Armstrong, the soundbox also had similarities with the ancient harps such as, 'The lower portion of the box takes the form of semicircular curves at either side of the projecting block.'[31] It is not known which ancient harp(s) Egan had before him to inspire this copy, but there are existing *cláirseachs* such as the O'Fogarty harp and the Fitzgerald harp with projecting blocks and lower soundboxes shaped with semicircular curves.[32] Like the O'Fogarty harp, Egan's instrument had thirty-six wire strings, and both harps were about 4ft in height. Egan's harp, when Armstrong saw it, had an added eagle's head, a restoration, but he suggests that the pillar may have originally culminated in a carved scroll like the O'Fogarty harp. The main difference was the method of construction for the sound chambers.

The sturdy single-log soundboxes of Gaelic harps were well suited to withstand the enormous tension of taught brass strings. Willow, proven a strong wood for making cricket bats, was commonly used for *cláirseachs*. As Armstrong observed, willow was not conveniently available in all regions, and perhaps that would explain why one unusual specimen, the Hollybrook harp from 1720, had a soundbox of built-up of sections of wood.[33] Among the few surviving eighteenth-century harps, two other similar harps were noticed in the 1980s by Nicholas Carolan at an exhibition at Malahide Castle (figure 3.2). The harps, then owned by William Kearney, were described as high-headed, about 4½ft in height, with built-up soundboxes, one of beech and the other of pine and sycamore.[34] These important examples indicate that Egan was not the first to construct an Irish harp with a box made of pieced-together sections. Another

Society as listed in the *Rules and regulations of the Irish-harp society*.   30 Armstrong, *Musical instruments*, i, p. 100. Egan was familiar with Gaelic harps from the 'bog harps' brought to his workshop, and Bunting saw Patrick Quin's harp 'at Egan's, the late harp maker's, in Dublin' in the 1830s. Quin's harp, known as the Castle Otway harp, was a large low-headed *cláirseach* made by Cormac O'Kelly. See Bunting, *The ancient music of Ireland*, p. 76.   31 Ibid., p. 101.   32 The O'Fogarty harp is currently displayed at Tipperary Library, Thurles, and the Fitzgerald or Kildare harp is in storage at the National Museum of Ireland.   33 The Hollybrook harp is in the collection of the National Museum of Ireland. The early Gaelic harp construction employed mortise and tenon joints that were held together solely by the tension of the strings.   34 Carolan, 'Two Irish harps in Co. Dublin', pp 40–5. The Malahide 2 harp strongly resembles Egan's presentation harp in shape, measurements, number of strings and shamrock decoration. If it wasn't made by Egan, perhaps Egan knew of this harp and copied it. The Malahide harps were auctioned in 2000 and are in private collections.

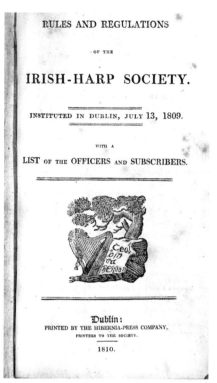

RULES AND REGULATIONS

OF THE

IRISH-HARP SOCIETY.

INSTITUTED IN DUBLIN, JULY 13, 1809.

WITH A

LIST OF THE OFFICERS AND SUBSCRIBERS.

Dublin:
PRINTED BY THE HIBERNIA-PRESS COMPANY,
PRINTERS TO THE SOCIETY.
1810.

3.2 Malahide harp. Photo by Liam McNulty, courtesy of the Irish Traditional Music Archive, Dublin.

3.3 Title page of *Rules and regulations of the Irish-Harp Society*, 1810. Courtesy of the Irish Collection, John J. Burns Library, Boston College.

modern design aspect of Egan's first Irish harp – his 'presentation harp' – was the neck, which curved to the player's right towards the pillar. Similar to pedal harp construction, the elegant neck shaping suited a playing position of the harp held on the right shoulder, giving more space for the player's head. But the Irish harp was traditionally played on the left shoulder, raising an interesting question as to whether Egan was in fact aware of this aspect of the Gaelic harp tradition.

By December of 1809, the goals of the Irish Harp Society were being realized. A house in Glasnevin had been donated by the bishop of Kildare, who was now president of the society. It was painted and prepared for the new pupils, and there was a large reception room where performances were to be held. Appropriately, the room was newly decorated with panels painted in *basso-relievo* by Miss Trotter, incorporating themes of the harp revival.[35] In the *Dublin Evening Post* it was announced that 'There are now three blind pupils in the

35 *Dublin Evening Post*, 12 Dec. 1809.

establishment, supported at the Society's expense, and a housekeeper of high respectability is engaged.'[36] The *Rules and regulations of the Irish-Harp Society* (figure 3.3), which had been drafted the previous summer, were now published for public dissemination. An all-encompassing treatise, it ordained everything from the duties of the three society committees – on music, literature and finance – to the proposed annual concerts and even the students' clothing of 'a uniform of cheap cloth, of Irish manufacture'.

In the rules, the society's policy on harps showed a distinctly favourable attitude towards developing a new 'improved' model. In fact, the purpose of the society as stated on the first page was 'to revive the Native Music and Poetry of Ireland' and also 'to improve the Irish Harp'. One of the regulations even suggests possible areas where improvements might be made:

> XI. That as the Irish Harp attained its present state by progressive improvements from rude beginnings, it is not essential to its character that it should remain as it now is, but may be further improved, either in its size, shape, or the number and quality of its strings, consistently with the origin and principles of the Instrument.[37]

And the next regulation, no. XII, went even further, proposing 'That one of the Objects of the Irish-Harp Society, shall be the further Improvement of the Instrument.'[38] Egan, who had been appointed harp maker to the society, was now granted official permission to proceed with designs for an improved model. The society's objective towards the Irish harp was not to recreate historically accurate copies of ancient *cláirseachs*. The emphasis was rather more on reviving the national music and the tradition of playing, and the wire-strung Irish harp was seen as the vehicle for disseminating the music. Also, in this 'improving' age, Egan and his fellow subscribers believed that for the Irish harp to continue and thrive, its design must evolve.

The society's rules included a provision for new harps to be supplied to the pupils, who would in turn exhibit the improved harps around the country:

> XXV. That the Society shall supply such of their Pupils, as they are certified by the Council are unable to do it themselves, with an improved Irish Harp, as a means of future Support, and of diffusing the Improvement through the Country; and that a number of Harps shall be made for that purpose, with such Improvement as may be suggested, provided always that they be cheap and portable.[39]

36 Ibid. 37 Irish Harp Society, *Rules and regulations of the Irish-Harp Society* (Dublin, 1810), p. 5.
38 Ibid., p. 5. 39 Ibid., p. 8.

By 'diffusing the improvement through the country', it was hoped a new desirable model would become widespread and attract greater numbers of players.

The Dublin society planned to reinvigorate the harping tradition by introducing an 'improved' Irish harp, and records show that Egan successfully designed and supplied Improved Irish Harp models to the school. The society's published minutes in the *Freeman's Journal* in May of 1812 affirm the payment to Egan for harps delivered to the society. And perhaps of greater significance, he was also compensated for the all-important 'improvement', to the Irish harp model:

> RESOLVED – That the sum of £30 be given to Mr Egan, Harp Maker to the Society, for his Improved Irish Harp, and that in consideration of the ingenuity evinced by him in its construction; the Society do present him with the same, to exhibit as a specimen of the Improvement, and that a further sum of £10 be given to him, as a remuneration for the expense he has incurred in constructing Models for the use of the Society.[40]

Two days later in the same newspaper Egan thanked the gentlemen of the Irish Harp Society 'with warmest feelings of gratitude' for the handsome payment and for their 'encouraging approval of his exertions in the new improvement and construction of the HARP'.[41] The maker then took the opportunity to inform the public that he had 'ready for sale, a variety of Irish and Pedal Harps'. Egan may have been aware of the impending closure of the society, which occurred that same year due to financial problems. The Irish harps advertised as 'ready for sale', could well have been produced in anticipation of future commissions from the society, but as it was now closing, they were briefly marketed to the public.[42] None of the Dublin society school harps have come to light – the fate of these instruments is unknown. The few rare examples of Egan's Improved Irish Harp that survive were all manufactured at a later date, for a second Belfast society.

IRISH HARP SOCIETY OF BELFAST, 1819–39

For Irish exiles abroad, the harp has always had a special symbolic significance. The iconic harp represents the cherished homeland, and for a group of exiled Ulstermen in India in 1819, many serving as army officers, the reports in

40 *Freeman's Journal*, 26 May 1812.   41 Ibid., 28 May 1812.   42 This Egan ad in 1812 in the *Freeman's Journal* announcing Irish harps for sale is unique. Most of the maker's advertisements promote

Calcutta newspapers of the harp society's financial woes were troubling. Moved by patriotism and nostalgia for home, these gentlemen decided to show their communal support and managed to collect adequate funds for the re-establishment of the Irish Harp Society of Belfast. The considerable sum of £1,200 16s. 6d. was raised from 309 donors and sent to Belfast, where a committee to manage the fund was duly formed. Its first meeting was held on 16 April 1819 with the stated purpose, 'to revive the Harp and Ancient Music of Ireland'.[43] Edward Bunting was among the members present, many of whom had also belonged to the earlier charitable harp society at Belfast. The aim of the society was essentially the same as before: to establish a school for blind children to be taught the Irish harp. For the tutor, Bunting selected Edward McBride, who had been a student at the first Belfast School under Arthur O'Neill. In May the *Dublin Evening Post* reported that, 'As patterns, a small number of harps, on the most approved construction, were ordered through the intervention of that eminent Master in Irish Music, Mr Bunting.'[44] The harps for this second formation of the Belfast Harp Society were made by Egan, who by now had established a reputation for his wire-strung Irish harp models. At the annual meeting on 20 August 1821 McBride reported that there were four resident pupils and two day pupils, and the treasurer's report stated that £45 17s. 3d. had been spent on the purchase of three harps, with the projected year's expenses including a further £12 for 'Donation of Harps to Finished Pupils'.[45] The harp course generally lasted for two years, but if found to be proficient on the harp after just eighteen months, a student could leave the school, and upon graduation each student was presented with a harp. In 1823 Valentine Rainey, or Rennie, succeeded McBride as teacher, and upon his death in 1837, James Jackson, a pupil of Rainey's, became the last instructor. It is of significance that these teachers and their music were a direct link to the Belfast meeting of 1792 and the ancient harping tradition. At least for a time, the music had continued to be taught and played, and Egan's revival harps were vital to the process.

The second Belfast school proved to be fairly successful, lasting almost twenty years, closing in 1839 when funding became scarce. But in addition to financial problems, by this time the effectiveness of the scheme was beginning to be questioned. The original motives undoubtedly had been honourable and charitable, but a lack of appropriate employment for graduates seemed to prevent positive results. John McAdam, the society's secretary, wrote to Bunting candidly describing the seemingly hopeless situation:

only pedal harps and Portable Irish Harps. It would seem that generally Egan's wire-strung Irish harps were produced for the society schools and not for commercial sale.   43 McClelland, 'The Irish Harp Society', p. 19.   44 *Dublin Evening Post*, 6 May 1819.   45 McClelland, 'The Irish Harp

I mentioned to you that we might probably keep up the society for a few years longer by private subscription, but from the fact that the young harpers can only earn their bread by playing in hotels, where they are too liable to contract fatal habits, we think the money could be more usefully laid out in other charities. Our gentry in Ireland are too scarce, and too little national, to encourage itinerant harpers, as of old; besides, the taste and fashion of music no longer bears upon our national instrument; it had its day, but, like all other fashions, it must give way to novelty.[46]

In the letter, McAdam also mentioned that one of the last two pupils, William Murphy, had perfect eyesight and a 'natural taste for music' and that the society was 'most desirous' to have a sighted pupil who 'could read music and therefore keep alive' the national airs. With the perspectives gained over time and in hindsight, historians have questioned the validity of expecting the harp tradition to rest solely on the shoulders of the blind, and after all, four of the ten harpers at the Belfast meeting had normal eyesight. The idea of blind boys trying to earn their living playing the harp was called a 'delusion' by Dr Petrie in a published lecture:

> The selection of blind boys, without any greater regard for their musical capacities than the possession of hearing, for a calling which doomed them to a wandering life, depending for existence mainly, if not wholly, on the sympathies of the poorer classes, and necessarily conducive to the formation of intemperate habits, was not well-considered benevolence, and should never have had any fair hope of success.[47]

Although it has been generally accepted that blind people often have special musical gifts due to their acutely developed hearing, it also follows that not every blind person is suited to playing the harp.

Gaelic harp technique, not surprisingly, is based on an anchored hand position, in which one plays more by 'feel' than by sight. Simon Chadwick describes the fundamental technique of playing a wire-strung harp in *Progressive lessons for the early Gaelic harp*: 'A general rule is to keep as many fingers on strings as much of the time as possible', which provides the dual advantages of controlling the resonance as well as finding the correct notes to play.[48] Each finger should return to the string it has just played for damping, Chadwick writes. He also comments that the strings on old Gaelic harps were not colour-coded like modern strings, so this visual aid did not exist. The anchored hand

Society', pp 19–20.   **46** Bunting, pp 66–7.   **47** Dr Petrie in O'Curry, *On the manners and customs of the ancient Irish*, iii, p. 298.   **48** Simon Chadwick, *Progressive lessons for early Gaelic harp* (St Andrews,

position is crucial to mastering the intricate dampening techniques for long-sounding wire strings. Dissonant pitches are damped while other strings still ring out to create chordal harmonies, and an array of distinctive textures can be produced from the quick dampening of single notes. Bunting was astonished by the clarity and textural effects of the old harper Hempson's playing and described the technique: 'His fingers lay over the strings in such a manner, that when he struck them with one finger, the other was instantly ready to stop the vibration, so that the staccato passages were heard in full perfection.'[49] In contrast, gut-strung harps have a shorter resonance, and the fingers and hands frequently come off the strings and in many instances should not be replaced too soon. Each type of harp model has its own unique timbre and envelope of sound, appropriate to a particular genre of music. A perpetual question is whether instrumental design follows the changes taking place in music, or whether the music derives its character from the instruments available within the culture, with both scenarios arguably applicable to Irish harp history.

'THE LAST IRISH HARPER'

As the century progressed towards the Victorian Age, many of the former pupils from the Belfast society schools found work playing in village taverns and hotels and also performed in concerts. One young harper, employed as a side act with the touring company called the Tyrolese Minstrels, was billed as 'The young harper from the Belfast Harp Society' playing 'national airs on the Irish harp'.[50] Another harper, Samuel Patrick, who left the school in 1839 after five years of tuition, held several positions providing music at hotels in Dublin and Greenore, and finally at the Bridge restaurant in Belfast. This might have been a profitable working life, but the unfortunate reality was that Patrick 'died in very reduced circumstances', so much so, that his sister, who relied on him financially, was forced to raffle his harp upon his death.[51]

A few harpers from the Belfast harp school were offered opportunities abroad, travelling to England and even to North America. One blind harper, Matthew Wall, graduating in 1830, was offered patronage by a Mr McCannon in New Brunswick, who generously sponsored his passage by ship from Belfast.[52] Upon Wall's departure, the society equipped him with an Egan harp, spare wire

2009), p. 28. **49** Bunting, *The ancient music of Ireland*, p. 73. **50** *Dublin Morning Register*, 12 Dec. 1832. **51** *Belfast News-Letter*, 23 Mar. 1888. Patrick's harp, made by Egan fifty years previously, was advertised as having merits as a musical instrument and also being attractive to antiquarians as 'a relic of old times, only to be found now in museums and collections of antiquity'. **52** Ibid., 22 June 1830.

strings and appropriate clothing. Wall eventually made his way to Boston, where he regularly performed and also taught Irish music. An advertisement in the *Boston Evening Transcript* in 1832 announced evening performances by Mr Wall on the Irish harp:

> As this is the first instrument of this kind ever in this country, the lovers of music will do well to avail themselves of the opportunity to witness the sweetness of its tones. It is much more powerful and melodious than the pedal harp. This was the instrument used by the bards of olden times, and is well calculated to touch and arouse the feelings.[53]

The description of the harp's sound as 'more powerful and melodious than the pedal harp' gives a favourable impression of Egan's model, but stating that the harp was used by 'the bards of olden times' confuses Wall's modern instrument with the ancient Gaelic models. Naturally, the reviewer was writing in generic or even metaphorical terms, reflecting the style of writing in newspaper articles on the Irish harp, which was often bathed in a sort of 'Celtic twilight' of bardic imagery and yearning for the glorious past. The harpers and their music were increasingly seen as almost theatrical characters representing the Gaelic world of old, and in concert advertisements, the performer was often billed as 'the last Irish harper'. The image of a snowy bearded bard in a robe bent over his harp was ubiquitous in poetry and the visual arts, and some of the harpers were not opposed to assuming this role for their audiences.[54]

One such pupil who was known as the 'blind Irish harper' went on to have the most extraordinary career touring and performing throughout Ireland, England and Scotland. This popular entertainer delighted audiences for over forty years in a wide range of performances, from impromptu gatherings at holiday resorts, to public concerts, to illustrious royal recitals before Queen Victoria and Prince Albert at Buckingham Palace. Referred to in the press as an 'Irish harp celebrity', Patrick Byrne (*c*.1794–1863) (figure 3.4) performed widely on his Egan Irish harp and for a time seemed to revive the venerable tradition of patronage, for he was frequently in demand as a resident musician, with extended stays in the great houses of Ireland and Britain.

---

53 *Boston Evening Transcript*, 12 Oct. 1832 as cited in Michael Quinlin, 'Blind Irish harpist Matthew Wall performs and teaches in Boston in 1832', irishboston.blogspot.com/2012/10/blind-irish-harpist-matthew-wall.html, accessed 17 Mar. 2015.   54 The cult of the 'last bard' is examined in Joep Leerssen, 'Last bard or first virtuoso? Carolan, conviviality and the need for an audience' in Liam P. Ó Murchú (ed.), *Amhráin Chearbhalláin/ The poems of Carolan: reassessments* (London, 2007), pp 30–42. Leerssen argues that Carolan was inaccurately labelled as a 'last bard' in that his contemporary musical style and appreciative audiences made him more of a 'cutting-edge virtuoso'.

3.4 Patrick Byrne in Capt.
Francis O'Neill's *Irish minstrels
and musicians*, 1913. Courtesy of
the Irish Traditional Music
Archive, Dublin.

Byrne graduated from the Belfast school in 1822 after eighteen months of
instruction with Edward McBride, and as was the custom, he was presented with
a harp mounted with a brass plaque inscribed with his name and that of the
Irish Harp Society. An extraordinary success story for the Irish Harp Society,
Byrne played the national music on his wire-strung harp and was greeted by
enthusiastic audiences wherever he went. Endowed with a winning combination
of personal charisma and musical talent, Byrne was described as possessing a
'genial wit and good humour', and one correspondent commented that Byrne
'tells some of his country's stories with great glee'.[55] Storytelling as part of the
harp performance was a vestige of the old tradition of the travelling harper who
was welcomed as much for his news and anecdotes as for his harp tunes. One
personal remembrance had memorialized the itinerant harper as 'an honoured
guest, whose appearance never failed to produce much animated excitement
wherever he came, laden with the music, the provincial intelligence and the
family gossip, amassed during half a year or more of tuneful peregrination'.[56]
Although he made no pretence of possessing a fine voice, Byrne also sang Irish
ballads to the harp, 'with pleasing effect'. From contemporary accounts, one can
conjure up a vivid image of his manner of playing his Egan harp:

55 *Greenock Advertiser*, 24 June 1845.   56 *Dublin Penny Journal*, 20 Oct. 1832.

This instrument, it must be remembered, is of peculiar structure. It contains about thirty brass wires, the twang of which give the music a striking metallic brilliancy. The high notes are given with the left hand, reserving the more powerful member for the deep chords of the bass. There is moreover – at least so we found it in Mr Byrne's playing – a certain national accent, like the tone in speech, given to the music by the Irish performer [...][57]

As a celebrity, Byrne was often in the news, and notices of his upcoming tours and performances were frequently mentioned in the press.

Early in his career, Byrne's Irish patronage came mainly from the Shirley family, who resided at their main estate in Warwickshire, England.[58] Byrne was a regular performer at the nearby Leamington Spa resort, a fashionable vacation spot for England's distinguished families. After hearing a performance, the Shirleys issued several invitations to Byrne for extended stays at their mansion. As Byrne's notoriety spread amongst the nobility and gentry, further patrons included the duke of Buccleuch and the duke of Leeds; subsequent invitations came from the lord lieutenant at the Viceregal Lodge in Dublin. Eventually, this talented Irish harper gained royal patronage and played for the royal couple at Balmoral, Windsor Castle and Buckingham Palace. Prince Albert was so taken by Byrne's playing that in 1841 a royal warrant was issued for Byrne to become 'Irish Harper to His Royal Highness'. Byrne's playing of the ancient airs was often referred to as having a certain 'wild sweetness'. His repertoire included old harp airs like 'Brian Boru's march' and 'The Coolun', but he also performed Moore's popular songs, like 'The harp that once through Tara's Hall' and 'The minstrel boy'. Welsh and Scottish songs were also part of his repertoire, according to concert notices, and perhaps they were learned from other musicians along the way during his years of extensive travels.

It is remarkable to put into historical perspective the lives of the former itinerant harpers plodding along on horseback with a guide, and Byrne, the modern bard, travelling a century later from England to Scotland by train. Unfortunately, in 1856 the harper was the victim of a pickpocket on the railway to Peebles, and afterwards a sympathetic group of citizens organized a public concert to make up for this terrible and unexpected financial loss. The concert took place in the ballroom of the Tontine Hotel and it was crowded with a respectable audience who were captivated by Byrne's performance. The unusual nature of the event was remarked upon in the *Belfast News-Letter*: 'That a poor blind man, with a single instrument, should have sustained close attention and

---

57 A quote from *Chambers Journal* in *Greenock Advertiser*, 24 June 1845, p. 2.   58 Keith Sanger, 'Patrick Byrne', wirestrungharp.com, accessed 6 Mar. 2015.

3.5 Patrick Byrne calotype by David Octavius Hill and Robert Adamson, 1843–8. © National Portrait Gallery, London.

interest for nearly two hours, is indeed something remarkable.'[59] It's impossible to know if audiences were attracted by a fondness for Byrne's Irish tunes and stories or the unusual sight and sound of the Irish harp, or perhaps mostly by the novelty of the event.

Like the other Irish harpers, Byrne was known as the 'last blind harper', which was not far from the truth, and promoting his performances as 'rare' was an effective marketing device. A typical notice for a concert in Scotland in 1845 read:

> We strongly recommend all lovers of fine music, and all who have reverence for things of the olden times, to embrace an opportunity they will probably never again enjoy of hearing, splendidly played on, the veritable instrument, which, for probably a thousand years, comforted, amused, and delighted the inhabitants of the Green Isle.[60]

Byrne played along with the romantic notion that he was the last Irish harper, and that same year while in Scotland, he posed for photographs in the costume

---

59 *Belfast News-Letter*, 3 Oct. 1856.   60 *Greenock Advertiser*, 24 June 1845.

of an ancient bard (figure 3.5). At the Waverly Ball in Edinburgh, he was part of a *tableau vivant*, posing in bardic dress improvised from a blanket, as 'The Last Minstrel Striking the Harp', and his image was captured in seven calotypes produced by David Octavious Hill and Robert Adamson.[61] Additional surviving portraits show Byrne at the harp in his evening suit.

These history-making images are the only extant photographs of a Gaelic harper. Not only are they a record of Byrne's playing position, with the left hand in the treble and right hand in the bass, showing how his fingers actually touched the strings, but also his splendidly decorated Egan harp is clearly seen. The high-headed harp is elaborately adorned with gilt shamrocks on the pillar and neck, and the soundboard is filled with scrolls of ornate foliate designs. The royal crest and Egan's inscription is just visible in the lower soundboard area. In the colourless photos, the bright sheen of gold painted on the edges and central strip of the soundboard catches the light, and Byrne's Irish harp would no doubt have attracted as much interest as his the sound of his playing.

THE IMPROVED IRISH HARP

The Improved Irish Harp model that Byrne and the other Belfast school students played differed in form from Egan's earlier 1809 'presentation harp' for the Dublin society. In the ten years since constructing his first wire-strung harp, Egan had been exploring new shapes for necks and pillars on his small gut-strung Irish harps, adjusting thicknesses and curves to improve structural strength as well as visual aesthetics. With the Belfast society's order for Irish harps in 1819 came the opportunity to put into practice new ideas gleaned from his prototypes made in the intervening years. The rare surviving Belfast society harps show that the maker decided to replace the earlier rectangular soundbox with a rounded back construction, similar to his pedal and portable harps. Six wire-strung Improved Irish Harps have come to light and the examples uniformly display the same characteristic features of construction, although each one has its own unique painted decoration.

COMPARISON OF EGAN'S IMPROVED IRISH HARP WITH GAELIC
HARPS OF THE EIGHTEENTH CENTURY

Egan's model imitated the traditional high-headed Gaelic harps in shape, size and number of strings. Both harp types have a common height of about 5ft, a

61 For more details and links to the photos see Simon Chadwick's website, earlygaelicharp.info.

high head and slightly curved pillar, with typically thirty-seven wire strings. Although the Egan Irish harp somewhat reflected the frame shape of eighteenth-century instruments, in terms of construction it more closely resembled the pedal harp.

- SOUNDBOX. Gaelic harps had single-log carved construction in a rectangular shape. The greatest depth of the box was at the top, in the treble range. On Egan's harps the box was formed from pieced-together sections of wood in a conical shape, with the greatest depth at the bottom. A thin, flat soundboard of horizontal grain was attached to the semi-circular laminated back. The box had four oval soundholes at the back and an open bottom, with four feet attached. The advantage was a more lightweight instrument that was freestanding.[62]
- PILLAR. On the Gaelic harp, the pillar was carved in a 'T' formation culminating with a scroll or figurative carving. Egan's plain pillar was formed from two sections of wood, and the head was actually an extension of the neck. Whereas the structure of some eighteenth-century Gaelic harps utilized mortise and tenon joints, Egan's pillar was secured to the box by a large bolt that entered through the bottom front of the pillar through the soundbox and was screwed into a round wooden block inside the box.
- NECK or HARMONIC CURVE. The neck of the Gaelic harp was hewn from a single piece of wood and was inserted into the centre of the top termination of the box. As Rimmer notes, the resulting treble strings were at an angle and out of plane, 'splayed into a fan shape'.[63] The Egan harp neck was formed of several pieces of laminated wood and joined to a knee block section at the top of the soundbox.[64] Both the knee block and neck curved to the player's right, thus creating a uniform plane of strings. An iron band was attached by screws to the underside of the neck, extending the entire length as a reinforcement to prevent the neck from twisting due to string tension.

---

62 To reinforce the soundboard on the inside surface, two thin pieces of wood were attached vertically on either side of a centre string strip extending the entire length, and linen strips provided further support.   63 Joan Rimmer, 'The morphology of the Irish harp', *Galpin Society Journal*, 17 (Feb. 1964), 41. The angled strings were easily played by the left hand as the Gaelic harp was held on the left shoulder.   64 In Armstrong's *Musical instruments*, i, p. 106, the neck construction is described as, 'The harmonic curve is constructed out of a number of pieces of wood carefully joined. There are two complete pieces; one of these is in the centre and the other at the right side. Between these, and on the left side, are several pieces joined together.' The twisting of the neck from string tension was a constant concern and this was Egan's design

- STRINGS. On the Egan harp's neck, bridge pins were added to prevent the strings from touching the neck when wound several times around the tuning pins. Although bridge pins appeared on the Sirr harp, they were not a regular feature on Gaelic harps. To prevent sharp wire strings cutting into the wood, the sound chest of the Gaelic harp had a raised string band with brass 'shoes' or a brass strip pierced for the strings. Egan harps also had a raised wooden string band but with staples for string guards.

Egan's Improved Irish Harp was in many ways a unique harp model, distinctively different in its organology from both the Gaelic harp and also the pedal harp. It has been generally suggested that Egan simply used the same supply of soundboxes for pedal harps and Irish harps. However the measurements of extant instruments demonstrate the two models to be consistently different.

Table 3.1. A comparison of soundbox dimensions and stringing from surveying eleven Egan pedal harps and five examples of the Improved Irish Harp. The circumference measurements were taken from two Egan harps in the NMI collection.

EGAN MODEL	GREATEST WIDTH OF SOUNDBOARD	CIRCUMFERENCE OF SEMI-CIRCULAR BACK	NUMBER OF STRINGS
Pedal harp	13.5–14in	22.5in	43
Improved Irish Harp	15.2–15.7in	24.5in	37

These dimensions reveal that the soundboxes on the Irish harps are slightly larger than on pedal harps. Although the pedal harps typically have six more strings, this can be explained by the placement of the pillar joined atop a pedal box instead of being attached to the lower section of the soundboard, enabling more space for additional strings. Also, almost all Egan pedal harps are fitted with shutter panels on the backs of the soundboxes requiring a different-shaped resonator, one with a flattened central section reinforced on the inside for the shutter doors and mechanism.[65] The pedal harp boxes all have four perfectly rectangular openings on the back instead of the smaller oval soundholes seen on the wire-strung Irish harps. The evidence suggests that the Egan workshop continually manufactured at least three different sized soundboxes: for pedal harps, Portable Irish Harps and Improved Irish Harps.[66] The 'improvement' the

concept to stabilize this important component of the harp frame.   **65** Shutter panels are discussed in chapter 6, see p. 178, n. 64.   **66** Conclusion derived from measurements recorded in my catalogue of Egan harps (appendix 3).

maker introduced was the conical soundbox with an added knee block resulting in an instrument that was lighter in weight, and hence more portable. The new construction of the neck, composed of several pieces of wood with an iron band attached to the underside, was designed for strength. Thus Egan's Gaelic harp-sized model with wire strings was meant to be both durable and portable.

TUNING AND TIMBRE

For a viable transition of the ancient techniques and repertoire to students playing Egan's newly made instruments, it was important to tune the Egan revival harps in the traditional manner used on the Gaelic instruments. Bunting had observed an ancient tuning peculiar to the *cláirseach* called '*na comhluighe*', whereby there were two consecutive G strings just below middle C in the bass. Bunting writes:

> Called by the harpers 'the sisters' were two strings in unison, which were the first tuned to the proper pitch; they answered to the tenor G, fourth string on the violin, and nearly divided the instrument into bass and treble.[67]

Confirmation of Egan adopting this tuning is mentioned in a notebook by John Bell from July of 1849 in which a rare interview with the harper Patrick Byrne was recorded. Much valuable information was passed to Bell, including Byrne's method of tuning his Egan harp. Byrne's explanation echoes the information given in Bunting's work, with the harper saying that in ancient times the unison strings were called '*Ne cawlee* – or the companions', and then the remaining harp strings were tuned in 3rds, 5ths, 4ths and octaves.[68]

As to the timbre of Egan's Improved Irish Harp, unfortunately the surviving instruments are too fragile to be played, but there are several written references to the harp model's actual sound. R.B. Armstrong, who owned and played one of the Belfast society harps in the early 1900s, said of it, 'It is unlikely any harper would be dissatisfied with the tone of the specimen described.'[69] Dr Petrie also had a wire-strung Egan harp in his collection, and he commented that 'These harps were of good form and size, about the height of pedal harps, rich in tone, and of excellent workmanship.'[70] Perhaps the best commentary on the sound of

67 Bunting, *The ancient music of Ireland*, p. 21.   68 Henry George Farmer quoting John Bell in 'Some notes on the Irish harp', *Music & Letters*, 24:2 (Apr. 1943), 102.   69 Armstrong, *Musical instruments*, i, p. 107. Armstrong's harp was a bequest to the National Museum of Ireland in 1913.   70 Petrie in O'Curry, *On the manners and customs of the ancient Irish*, iii, p. 298. Petrie continued his description

Egan's large Irish harp is a review in *The Emerald* newspaper of Patrick Byrne's performance of 'Brian Boru's march'. A veritable soundscape of tone colours was enthusiastically described.[71] The extraordinary range of dynamics commenced with a 'whisper like the sigh of the rising wind on a summer eve', rising to a 'clang with a martial fierceness'. Impressive timbral contrasts were characterized as 'fairy music heard from a distance' then becoming stronger and louder with 'a deep rumbling in the bass', and then the sounds were 'hard and harsh – clang! clang! like the fall of a sword or axe on armour'.[72] Finally, the music 'assumes a merry, lightsome character', showcasing the vast array of textural sounds possible on the wire-strung harp in Byrne's skilful hands.

THE SURVIVING HARPS

Of the six extant Egan wire-strung Improved Irish Harps made for the society school, all have uniformly painted motifs on a naturally varnished wood surface, in contrast to the coloured japanned decoration seen on Egan's pedal and portable harps. The main ornament is in the form of shamrocks painted in green on the upper section and mid-section of the soundboard, with the royal crest (lion and unicorn) and inscription in red filling the lower sections. On some harps, strands of gold shamrocks still adorn the pillar, neck and back.

Egan harp with Gaelic inscriptions, c.1821, National Museum of Ireland, Dublin
This harp is exceptional for its painted nationalistic symbols and Gaelic inscriptions (plate 4). Vines of shamrocks are artistically presented in a figure eight pattern on the upper and middle areas of the soundboard (figure 3.6). Below are two antique crowns (symbols of independence) within wreaths of tiny shamrocks, in mirror image, on either side of the centre strip. Next are painted Gaelic inscriptions framed in rectangles: on the left side (facing) is *Ceol. bin. nA. Heirion* ('Sweet music of Ireland') and on the right side is *YeArc. Coel/Clan. MileAd.* ('Love Music/Clan Mileadh'). In the bottom left section is a small harp image inside an oval frame encircled with the phrase, *LAmb. DeArg. eiron.* ('The Red Hand of Ireland'). The harp pictured has a male head as a finial, and above it is the symbolic red hand of Ireland on a shield. A similar oval on the right

---

of the harp, 'But they were wholly without ornament, and had nothing about them to remind us of "the loved harp of other days"'. Presumably by 'ornament' he meant 'carving' which was a feature of the ancient *cláirseachs*, whereas the Egan harps only had painted decoration.   **71** From an article in *The Emerald* of New York City, 1870, quoted in Capt. Francis O'Neill, *Irish minstrels and musicians, with numerous dissertations on related subjects* ([1913]; Cork and Dublin, 1987), p. 81. **72** Ibid.

3.6 Egan Gaelic
harp postcard,
courtesy of the
National
Museum of
Ireland
collection.

Áṁo-ṁúṕéum na h-éiṕeann.   National Museum, Ireland.

DUBLIN HARP. EARLY 19th CENTURY

contains the badge of the Order of St Patrick, with a crowned shamrock on top
of the red saltire. The Latin inscription circling the badge reads *QUI.
SEPERABIT* ('Who will separate us?') along with the date *M.D.C.CLXXXIII.*
(1783), the year George III created the Order of St Patrick, an honour bestowed
upon Irish notables for services to Ireland. It is reasonable to assume that the
symbols on the harp represent the patron of the harper who played the
instrument, and evidence strongly suggests that this was Charles O'Neill, 1st Earl
O'Neill (1779–1841), the lord of Shane Castle in 1821, who had been knighted
earlier in the prestigious Order of St Patrick.[73]

Enniskillen Castle harp, c.1821, Fermanagh County Museum
Presented to the museum in 1977 by Revd Sean Cahill (figure 3.7), this harp is
similar to the others in that strands of shamrocks adorn the upper and middle
areas of the soundboard (plates 5–7). Although the shamrocks are now red in
colour, there are traces of green paint, suggesting that the red may have been an
under sketch. The most curious feature is the decoration on the lower section,
where two paper copies of a John Egan advertisement were attached and
varnished to the harp surface, on either side of the string strip. This fanciful
restoration to the harp was probably an attempt by a former owner to cover

73 This idea was suggested to me by Nicholas Carolan, and further research has confirmed the
theory and the patron's identity (see p. 156).

3.7 Revd Sean Cahill presents an Egan Irish harp to Helen Hickey, Fermanagh County Museum curator, 1977. Photo courtesy of Enniskillen Castle Museums, Northern Ireland.

worm damage at the harp's base. The ad, originally published in the 1824 *Pigot & Co.'s City of Dublin and Hibernian Provincial Directory*, incongruously promotes Egan's Portable Irish Harp with a lady in a Grecian gown pictured playing a portable harp.[74] Curiously the ad now decorating the wire-strung harp announces the Portable Irish Harp as 'strung with gut' and 'capable of key changes'.[75] Woodworm damage is a common cause of deterioration on many of the old harps, and the Enniskillen instrument experienced such a considerable amount of destruction from insects that the harp's pillar had to be entirely replaced in 1980. Despite these later alterations to the harp, the instrument remains a rare example of an Egan Irish harp linked to the historic Belfast society school.

74 *Pigot & Co.'s City of Dublin and Hibernian Provincial Directory* (Dublin, 1824).   **75** An email communication with Annika McSeveny from the Fermanagh County Museum in 2010 explained the provenance of the harp: 'After being handed down through the Maguire Family, the harp was left with the Sisters of Mercy, Enniskillen for safe-keeping by a Miss Margaret Maguire (*c.*1870–80). Later it went to the Diocesan Museum in St Macartan's College (now dismantled). It was donated to Fermanagh County Museum in 1977.' In a 1977 photograph of the harp, the paper advertisement is present, confirming that it was applied prior to the harp's donation to the Fermanagh County Museum.

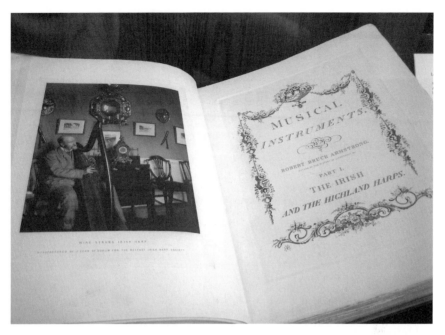

3.8 Title page and frontispiece with the author playing his Egan harp in R.B. Armstrong's *Musical instruments*, i, 1904. Courtesy of the Irish Collection, John J. Burns Library, Boston College.

J. Egan harp no. 1933, R.B. Armstrong bequest, c.1822–5, National Museum of Ireland, Dublin
A second society harp in the collection at the National Museum of Ireland, Dublin has a single clover spray motif more simply painted, obviously by a different artist. The coat of arms is present and the inscription on the left side reads, *MANUFACTURED FOR/ THE BELFAST/ IRISH-HARP/ SOCIETY./ No.1933* and on the right side, *By J. EGAN,/ DUBLIN./ HARP MAKER/ to His MAJESTY/ GEORGE IV/ AND THE ROYAL FAMILY.* In addition to its rarity, the harp is of historical significance due to its former owner, the eminent harp historian R.B. Armstrong, who is photographed playing it in the frontispiece of his landmark first volume of *Musical instruments* (figure 3.8). The harp is interesting also because it bears some unusual personal marks from a previous owner. As Armstrong observed, 'Upon the right-hand side of the sounding-board are deeply scratched letters and marks, indicating the notes to which the strings were tuned – perhaps to be fingered by a blind boy, as an early lesson, while the fingers of his left hand pulled the strings.'[76] The guiding letters and notches are still visible and provide a surprising intimate connection to an unknown blind student harper from the past (figure 3.9).

76 Armstrong, *Musical instruments*, i, p. 52, n. 3. Armstrong states there are twenty-one strings marked with letters, starting with B in the treble.

3.9 Scratched letters on soundboard of Egan wire-strung Irish harp no. 1933 as noted by R.B. Armstrong. Photo by Nancy Hurrell, courtesy of the National Museum of Ireland collection.

3.10 Egan wire-strung Irish harp attributed to Patrick Byrne. Photo by Ann Heymann, courtesy of the owner.

Belfast society school harp, c.1822, private collection, Ohio
An instrument identical to Patrick Byrne's harp in the Hill and Adamson calotypes of 1845 survives in a private collection in the US. Splendid foliate patterns fill the upper and middle areas of the soundboard and lower down is a royal crest and inscription, all in red (figure 3.10). Each spiralling vine of leafy shamrocks (or possibly clematis) culminates in a rosette.[77] The highly decorative instrument would have visually enhanced musical performances. On the surviving harp, the feet were removed and a modern base was added. The Byrne photo shows a polished brass strap attached to the upper back of the harp and the extant harp displays markings in this area confirming the former existence of a strap.[78]

J. Egan & Son harp no. 2044, c.1825–9, Fitzwilliam Museum, Cambridge
The best-preserved example of Egan's Improved Irish Harp is in the collection at the Fitzwilliam Museum in Cambridge, England (plates 8, 9). It bears the inscription, *J. EGAN & SON,/ 30 DAWSON ST./ DUBLIN./ HARPMAKERS/ TO HIS/ MAJESTY/ & the ROYAL FAMILY/ No. 2044.* Bright green shamrocks and the red royal crest fill the soundboard area, elegantly framed by the lustrous gold centre and side strips. The combination of these decorative elements of symbolic green, royal red and shimmering gold accents give the harp a stunning appearance. Gold sprays of shamrocks ornament the neck and all four sides of the pillar, with further golden bouquets adorning the knee block and the back of the harp between each of four soundholes, also outlined in gold. On the back, the gilt shamrock motif cascades down the sides and bottom edges, with an added gilt plaster moulded strip attached to the bottom edge in an egg-and-dart pattern. The feet on the harp are fairly detailed lions' paws (plaster on wood), a popular neoclassical theme also seen on pedal harps and furniture from the period. This rare instrument with much of its decoration intact, displays the impressive effect of delicate foliate designs combined with the royal stamp of approval.

J. Egan & Son harp, c.1825–9, private collection, France
This harp has undergone much restoration, including a new coat of varnish and the replacement of edging on the sides and bottom of the soundbox. The inscription, barely visible, is *J. EGAN & SON/ 30 DAWSON ST. DUBLIN/ HARPMAKERS TO HIS MAJESTY & the ROYAL FAMILY.* The royal crest is visible,

77 This was a decorative pattern adopted by Egan's nephew, Francis Hewson, who continued the business of producing wire-strung harps after Egan's death. Some of Egan's later pedal harps have this same pattern in gold.   78 Ann and Charlie Heymann brought this harp to my attention. It could well have been Patrick Byrne's harp.

but the serial number is illegible. Plump green shamrocks adorn the soundboard, and gold shamrocks outline the back and fill the neck and pillar areas in the signature Egan design.[79]

PATRIOTISM AND TEMPERANCE – THE DROGHEDA HARP SOCIETY

On 22 January 1842 in the *Dublin Weekly Register*, another newspaper article titled 'The Irish Harp' appeared, this time with an additional heading – 'Temperance':

> A delightful suggestion has been made, at a recent festival of the 'Drogheda New Total Abstinence Society,' by its president, the Revd T.V. Burke, to promote the revival of the Irish harp, by means of the musical bands established by the temperance societies. He stated that some young men in Drogheda had already succeeded in making a harp, which was considered a well-toned, excellent, instrument, and that he expected they would have at least a dozen ready before their next festival.[80]

It had been three years since the closing of the Irish Harp Society of Belfast, and the revival 'torch' was once again lit in the town of Drogheda. In January of 1842, Father Thomas Burke, OP, started the Drogheda Harp Society and appointed Hugh Frazer as teacher for the school. Frazer, who appears not to have been blind, had been a pupil of Edward McBride at the Belfast society's school in 1821. The Drogheda school, the last institution of its kind to teach the Irish harp, had the shared musical goals of the earlier harp societies, but it differed from the other organizations in several ways. Unlike its predecessors, the Drogheda society was aligned with the temperance movement and the Catholic faith, based on the belief that young boys pre-occupied with learning to play the harp would certainly reject the temptations of alcohol. The students' repertoire of traditional Irish airs also included 'vespers and other sacred melodies'. Another difference from the former society schools was that most of the sixteen pupils had normal eyesight, with blind boys in the minority (an article in 1844 included the statement, 'Among the pupils are two blind boys').[81]

At the school, Fr Burke reported that 'we have twelve excellent harps of Drogheda manufacture'.[82] This was another area in which the society differed from the previous schools, for the harps were not commissioned from a

79 Siobhán Armstrong, president of the Historical Harp Society of Ireland, brought this harp to my attention.   80 *Dublin Weekly Register*, 22 Jan. 1842.   81 *Drogheda Argus* quoted in *The Nation*, 2 Mar. 1844.   82 *The Nation*, 15 Apr. 1843.

3.11 Harp of William Griffith, of the Drogheda Harp Society, played at the Tara 'monster meeting' in 1843. Photo by Nancy Hurrell, courtesy of the family.

professional harp maker, but were constructed by the pupils themselves, supervised by a local craftsman, Francis Flood. It would seem that the stated goal of the Dublin society thirty years earlier, in its *Rules and regulations*, to 'diffuse the improvement throughout the country' had to some extent now been realized, for the form of the Irish harps made at Drogheda followed Egan's 'improved' design. Frazer, the Drogheda teacher, may well have played an Egan harp, for he had been a fellow pupil with Patrick Byrne at the Belfast society's school and presumably, like Byrne, would have been presented with a harp upon graduation.

One of the Drogheda harps, played by the student William Griffith, still survives (figure 3.11).[83] The extraordinary instrument has remained in the family for several generations. A first impression is one of amazement upon seeing the brightly coloured paintings on the harp's soundboard. Rather like an artist's canvas, a white background is filled with stirring images, including a portrait of Brian Boru and a landscape painting of Monasterboice. Like Egan's 'improved' model, the harp has a high-headed shape and a rounded back soundbox and is

---

83 Nancy Hurrell, 'A Drogheda harp: instrument and icon', *History Ireland*, 21:1 (Jan./Feb. 2013), 34–7.

about 5ft tall. It has more of a hand-crafted look than Egan's polished instruments. Some of the painted decoration may well have been inspired by the motifs on the Belfast society harps, namely the strands of (plump) shamrocks in a figure eight pattern and wreaths of shamrocks encircling patriotic inscriptions in Gaelic. On the left (facing) is the popular slogan *Eiren go-bragh* ('Ireland Forever') and on the right side is *Eire óg* ('Young Ireland'), paying homage to the nationalist movement of the time aligned with Ireland's campaign to repeal the Act of Union with Britain. Symbols of the Catholic faith also appear on the harp in the form of a papal crown and the crossed keys of St Peter, as well as an eagle bearing a shield with a Christian cross. Around both images are radiant brush strokes suggesting importance, and single roses in pink fill the spaces above and below.

In the 1840s, while Irish harps were being revived by the Drogheda Harp Society, the Irish harp symbol continued to endure in its role as an icon of independence from Britain. Stamped on the membership cards of Daniel O'Connell's Repeal Association was a harp logo. Harps — as well as round towers and wolfhounds — were common nationalist images on banners displayed at 'monster' meetings held by the Repeal Association at various sites around the country. Attended by hundreds of thousands of people, the most famous of these was held on 15 August 1843 at the Hill of Tara, a site of 'ancient importance' as the home of former Irish monarchs. Patrick Cooney relates that five students from the harp society played a welcome to Daniel O'Connell at the meeting, one of whom was William Griffith.[84] Cullen observes that the Drogheda Harp Society's use of the harp was as 'an instrument of political and social change as the society closely aligned the culture of the harp with the politics of repeal'.[85] Unfortunately, Fr Burke, who had been the primary driving force behind the society, died suddenly in 1844, and it ceased to exist the following year.

It is difficult to assess the impact of Egan's Improved Irish Harp on Ireland's attempted harp revival. The harper Patrick Byrne had succeeded for a time in reviving the practice of patronage, and he impressively brought the Irish harp back to the royal court, albeit an English one. While the harp societies' activities are well documented, less well known are the numbers of amateur players who may have learned to play the wire-strung harp during this period. Charlotte Milligan Fox, writing in 1912, relates a story of a cousin learning the harp:

---

84 Patrick L. Cooney, 'Drogheda Harp Society', *Journal of the Old Drogheda Society*, 1 (Drogheda, 1976), 39.   85 Emily Cullen, 'Tempering the stereotypes of Irishness abroad: the Irish harp as golden lever of temperance and respectability' in Joyce and Lawlor, *Harp studies* (2016), p. 113.

In the middle of life she opened a ladies' school at Drogheda, and was delighted on arriving in the town to hear of an old harper who rendered ancient Irish music in an exquisite fashion. She invited him to the school to play for her pleasure and for the pupils, and finally induced him to give her and her sister some lessons. This must have been one of the survivors of the Harp Society.[86]

Egan's Improved Irish Harp was not actively marketed to society in ads. Perhaps the stigma of being an instrument played by poor blind boys was a factor, and over time, the model's frame may have encountered structural difficulties due to the wire strings.[87]

A renewal of the Gaelic harping tradition was perhaps hindered by the widely accepted literary representation of 'the last harper' or 'the blind harper', relegating players and instruments to a place of antique oblivion, trapped in the past and unable to be revitalized in the present. An anecdote titled 'The Harper' in the *Dublin Penny Journal* in 1832 reinforces the stereotypical perception of the instrument. The writer recalls an old harper from his youth, Frene or Freney, aged about 90 and much bent by age, head crowned by white hair. His harp was described as a dark, antique-looking instrument, 'closely strung with thin brass wires, which produced that wild, low, ringing music' described as 'fairy chime'. The correspondent continues:

> The effect of this was heightened by the old man's peculiar expression of intense, and sometimes pleased attention to his own music, as he stooped forward, holding his head close to the wires, while he swept them over with a feeble, uncertain, and trembling hand. [...] He was a venerable ruin of those good old times [, ...] joyous and hospitable times.[88]

---

86 Charlotte Milligan Fox, *Annals of the Irish harpers* (New York, 1912), p. 59.   87 Egan may have found wire-strung harps problematical due to the extreme tension of wire strings. At least three of the surviving harps (Fitzwilliam Museum, NMI Gaelic harp and one in Ohio) show stress, with large vertical cracks on the back of the soundbox and brass bands were sometimes used as repairs. Some earlier *cláirseachs* also show signs of repair with brass bands, such as the Kildare harp in the NMI.   88 *Dublin Penny Journal*, 20 Oct. 1832.

4 / John Egan, inventor

> 'Egan, the harp-maker, most anxious that I should judge the power
> of his improved Irish harp – sent his son with one […]'
>
> – Thomas Moore

The most high-profile player of an Egan harp was undoubtedly the celebrated poet Thomas Moore (1779–1852), whose *Irish melodies* have continued to endure through the ages (figure 4.1).[1] The haunting airs and romanticized themes of shamrock, bard and harp have attained global recognition, and fragments of the stirring lyrics have slipped into language as colloquial phrases. For the Irish diaspora living abroad, the *Melodies* trigger an emotional longing for an idealized homeland, albeit set in Gaelic antiquity, and the fervent singing of harp-infused lyrics no doubt strengthens the sentimental bond with the national instrument. Moore's metaphorical harp, a personification of Ireland, is invariably ancient, singing heroic tales of 'vanished fame' from the noble past. Although at times the instrument seems fragile and dispirited, its strings unwaveringly sound a 'wild sweetness' as it yearns for liberty. Una Hunt observes that Moore's political harp, used as a trope, has the 'soft' and 'gentle' voice of a helpless victim.[2] The harp's broken strings are a metaphor for the country's spirit, broken by colonial rule. Moore's ancient harp is central to the *Melodies* on several levels, for the tunes themselves were drawn from the Gaelic harping tradition. Borrowing extensively from Edward Bunting's collection of airs, the poet Moore added his own words to the harp tunes, along with new pianoforte accompaniments provided mostly by Sir John Stevenson.[3] Using his astute musical intuition, Moore composed flowery phrases that perfectly fit the twists and turns in the ancient melodies, admitting, 'With respect to the verses which I have written for these melodies, as they are intended rather to be sung than read, I can answer for their sound with somewhat more confidence than their sense.'[4] The hazy, indistinct

1 The immensely popular song collections, comprising ten volumes spanning the years 1808 to 1834, were published simultaneously by brothers William and James Power, in Dublin and London, respectively.   2 Una Hunt, *Sources and style in Moore's Irish melodies* (London and New York, 2017), p. 20.   3 The accompaniments in the last three volumes were by Sir Henry Bishop (1786–1855).   4 Thomas Moore, 'Letter on music' prefixed to the third number of *Moore's Irish melodies*,

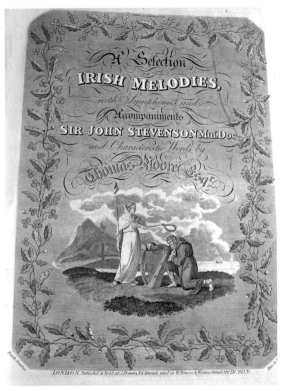

sentiments sung to lyrical tunes stir one's feelings and are satisfyingly open to individual interpretation. In the songs, Erin's harp-voice is awakened and silenced, in parallel to nationalist struggles for independence. At the same time, as noted by Ronan Kelly, the theme of longing is universal, and therein lies a key to the success of the *Melodies*.[5] With lines simultaneously relevant to political and personal themes, lyrics of faithfulness and desire are equally applicable to cultural crusades as well as romantic relationships. Moore recognized the complex blend of mirth and sadness in Irish music as relatable to the country's history, with 'the tone of defiance, succeeded by the languor of despondency – a burst of turbulence dying away into softness ...'[6]

A bevy of harp-themed songs in the *Melodies* includes: 'The harp that once through Tara's halls', 'Shall the harp then be silent', 'My gentle harp' and 'Sing, sweet harp'. In the celebrated song 'Dear harp of my country', the harp seems to be momentarily revived:

reprinted in Moore's Irish melodies: the illustrated 1846 edition (New York, 2000), p. 235.   **5** Ronan Kelly, *Bard of Erin: the life of Thomas Moore* (Dublin, 2008), pp 167–8.   **6** Moore, 'Letter on music', p. 227.

Dear harp of my country! In darkness I found thee,
The cold chain of silence had hung o'er thee long,
When proudly my own island harp, I unbound thee,
And gave all thy chords to light, freedom, and song![7]

If read in the poet's voice, he 'unbound' Ireland's harp – or rather the harp tunes that lay buried in Bunting's music books – and gave them 'light, freedom and song' by adding his own lyrics.

It displeased Bunting that Moore freely borrowed tunes from his antiquarian project for commercial gain, a case of what Joep Leerssen termed 'anthropological purism against commercial adaptation'.[8] Both Bunting and Moore aspired to the laurels of resurrecting authentic Irishness in their publications, and they each presented traditional melodies in contemporary music-making formats, altering the ancient material in different ways.[9] Moore seems to have had few qualms in the matter, stating that had he not taken liberties, the airs 'would have been still sleeping, with all their authentic dross about them, in Mr Bunting's first volume'.[10]

Another interpretation of the opening stanza of 'Dear harp of my country' is remarkably applicable to the culture's playable instrument of wood and strings, if read in the voice of the harp maker. Although clearly not the poet's intention, nonetheless the words are surprisingly relevant, for the Gaelic harp was indeed 'found' to be in a state of 'dark' neglect and an awakening, or a revival, did occur. John Egan enabled the ancient music to be brought back to life and once again transmitted via his new wire-strung harp, the Improved Irish Harp model created for the society schools. Then the maker 'unbound' the limited tonal range of the country's harp by inventing the Portable Irish Harp with mechanisms to enable new chromatic 'freedoms' for contemporary 'song'. If read in this manner, the dual meanings in 'Dear harp of my country' can equally relate to Egan's Portable Irish Harp and Moore's *Irish melodies*, two significant cultural products in a nationalistic post-union age. Both manufactured articles incorporated aspects of the ancient harping tradition in modern, commercially viable forms, and both concepts eventually transcended the period and politics of the age to later continue in revised formats and editions.[11] Moore and Egan were also connected personally, in that they knew

7 Thomas Moore, *A selection of Irish melodies*, vol. 6 (Dublin and London, 1815).   8 Joep Leerssen, *Remembrance and imagination: patterns in the historical and literary representation of Ireland in the nineteenth century* (Cork, 1996), p. 175.   9 Moore, 'Letter on music', p. 161. Bunting had altered the modal forms of the tunes by adding chromaticism and traditional key signatures. He also added pianistic accompaniments to the harp tunes.   10 Ibid.   11 Egan's harp concept and design was copied by subsequent makers (see chapter 8, pp 226–47) and similarly, Moore's *Melodies* were continually

one another, and in 1823 the harp maker presented a specially crafted vivid green, shamrock-covered Portable Irish Harp to the poet.[12]

A CHROMATIC PORTABLE IRISH HARP

The path leading to the development of Egan's chromatic Portable Irish Harp, capable of playing in every key, was shaped by favourable circumstances of time, place and need. Allegiance to the harp symbol in post-union Ireland logically transferred to public support for the tangible instrument, and Egan had capitalized on the national mood with his Brian Boru-shaped harp, an early version of which Sydney Owenson had played. The Regency period (1811–20) was an era of spirited innovation in instrument-making, and the maker eagerly participated in this invigorating environment. His workshop now manufactured an impressive range of instruments from pedal harps to Irish harps (wire-strung) and portable harps (gut-strung). Driven by a fascination for new mechanisms and 'improved' harp designs, Egan began to contemplate novel changes to his existing portable harp model. Like his London peers, the maker foresaw the growing commercial potential of new small instruments for accompanying the voice in amateur music-making, as singing was of central importance in domestic entertainment, especially for young women. In the Regency spheres of courtship, it was deemed desirable to be a proficient singer with a repertoire ranging from Irish airs to Italian art songs. To accompany a 'sweet' voice with the delicate touch of the strings on an instrument offered a chance to display one's alluring qualities of gracefulness and taste, and a sensitive performance was sure to excite corresponding emotions in the listener, preferably an unattached male (as so aptly described in Lady Morgan's novels).

With an increasing consumer demand for small, portable instruments that were both sweet-sounding and attractively finished, a variety of new products began to appear on the market. While the main accompanying instruments in music salons continued to be the larger pianoforte and pedal harp, the gentry and a new rising middle class were eager for smaller, more affordable parlour instruments. Certain attributes were particularly desirable: portability, pleasing tone and playable in every key. Of equal importance was the shape and decoration of an instrument, for the coveted pedal harp had set a high standard to emulate with its strikingly graceful form and sumptuous ornaments. Jennifer Nex observes that while musical instruments are objects for producing sounds, they are also visual representations of status, identity and taste:

transformed in new arrangements with stylistic alterations, but both are still perceived as intrinsically 'Irish'.   12 The harp survives as part of the Moore Library at the Royal Irish Academy in Dublin.

As well as contributing to the overall experience of an audience during performance, instruments remain visible when they are not being played. The presence of a silent musical instrument suggests not only a musical atmosphere, itself socially significant, but also a wider cultural context in terms of property, education and social standing.[13]

Ornamented in the same elegant style as the furniture and the other decorative arts in a room, the pedal harp was a conspicuous art object, with its tall sculptural frame adding a certain stature to the parlour environment.

Pedal harps were also exceedingly expensive and definitely not seen as 'portable', issues which came to preoccupy the thoughts of a contemporary London music professor and inventor, Edward Light (*c.*1747–1832).[14] In addition to the pedal harp's commanding appearance, Light was aware of society's particular fondness for the harp sound. The soundscape of the Regency music room was evolving, with a distinct preference for the new tonal qualities of recently developed instruments. A shift had occurred whereby the baroque-era harpsichord, with its crisp metallic tones, was being replaced by the richer, fuller pianoforte sound, capable of a wider range of expressive dynamics, as its name suggests.[15] In a survey of instrumental attributions on title pages of eighteenth-century keyboard music, David Cooper demonstrates that the pianoforte overtook the harpsichord as the primary instrument in the final two decades of the century.[16] Similarly, the silvery sharp timbre of the wire-strung Gaelic harp, admired in former centuries, was now superseded by the warmer-sounding gut-strung pedal harp. Edward Light saw an opening in the marketplace for a small hand-held instrument with a harp-like sound, a type of harp-guitar. He understood the basic concept of the pedal harp's timbre as attributed to gut strings resonating from a rounded back sound chamber. Incorporating these concepts, Light designed a guitar with a rounded stave back, resembling a lute, and he replaced the standard metal guitar strings with gut harp strings. The result was a hybrid instrument called the 'harp-lute', which quite convincingly replicated a harp sound.[17] The harp-lute was the first in a line of several subsequent similar

13 Jennifer Susan Nex, 'The business of musical instrument making in early industrial London' (PhD, Goldsmiths, University of London, 2013), pp 17–18.   14 See Hayato Sugimoto, 'The harp lute in Britain, 1800–30: a study of the inventor Edward Light and his instruments' (PhD, University of Edinburgh, 2014).   15 The strings of the harpsichord are plucked by a quill, whereas the pianoforte strings are struck by felt-covered hammers.   16 David Cooper, '"'Twas one of those dreams that by music are brought": the development of the piano and the preservation of Irish traditional music' in Michael Murphy and Jan Smaczny (eds), *Music in nineteenth-century Ireland*, Irish Musical Studies 9 (Dublin, 2007), pp 76–7. Cooper points to the increase in piano manufacture around 1800 as further evidence.   17 For further reading, see R.B. Armstrong, *Musical instruments*, ii: *English and Irish instruments* (Edinburgh, 1908).

4.2 Dital-harp, about 1820, by Edward Light. Photograph © 2019 Museum of Fine Arts, Boston.

instruments conceived by Light and others in the early 1800s, including the harp-guitar and harp-lute-guitar. An advert in the *Morning Post* in 1802 announced,

> The new-invented, fashionable, and much-admired Harp lute, an elegant little instrument, that sounds like the real harp, is exceedingly easy to play on, and a charming accompaniment to the voice, the pianoforte, &c. and very pleasing when played alone.[18]

Having replicated a harp sound, next Light set about to reproduce the harp's iconic shape. The harp-lute was given the visually striking addition of a tiny pillar and harp-like neck at the top of the instrument, while still maintaining a fretted fingerboard. It was a sort of miniature harp, with a tiny capital with gold foliate decoration, and the harp-lute's sound chambers were embellished with gilt neoclassical designs forged in the same style as those of its larger ancestor, the pedal harp (figure 4.2). However, the harp-lute, later named the 'dital-harp',

18 *Morning Post*, 21 Oct. 1802.

differed from the standard pedal harp in one important aspect. Due to the instrument's unusual organology, its plane of strings is actually angled back-to-front from normal harp stringing. In consequence, the fingers used and direction of playing harp-like sequences such as arpeggios and scales are backwards in relation to normal harp technique. Armstrong commented on the awkwardness of the instrument for experienced harpists: 'After a little practice, one or two interviews with a professional harpist will be of advantage, as, although unable to play the dital-harp, he could detect an incorrect method of playing in another.'[19]

In spite of this problematical aspect, the harp-lute achieved so much success that Edward Light soon discovered he had a steady stream of imitators, namely Ward, Clementi, Wheatsone and others. Light assured the public of the superior status of the harp-lute (over the low-class guitar), stating that his instruments were embraced by 'families of the most exalted rank and first musical taste' and that he had an ever-widening clientele of 'nobility and ladies in London, Bath, Dublin, &c'.[20] Members of Dublin society regularly took their cues from London for the latest fashionable trends, and in the active flow of music, artists and instruments across the Irish Sea, Light's unusual portable instruments began to appear in Ireland. In 1814 the *Freeman's Journal* advertised lessons taught in Dublin on the 'improved dytal [*sic*] harp lute', noting that 'This fascinating instrument, so much admired for its beauty, simplicity, and assistance to the voice, is taught by Mr Poole, professor of the pedal harp, 17 Westmoreland-street.'[21]

RING STOPS TO DITALS

John Egan was aware of this new product being sold in Dublin music shops, and he lost no time in pointing out the advantages of his portable harp model over the hybrid harp-lute. In numerous advertisements in the press he clarified the organological differences: 'As this instrument [portable harp] is not anything of the harp lute kind, it is not necessary the pedal harp player should take any lessons to be able to play on it, as the tuning and fingering is exactly the same as the pedal harp.'[22] It seems Egan's adverts were aimed at a slightly higher social class of patrons, for while Light promoted his harp-lute for playing by the fireside and taking on picnics, Egan's portable harp was touted as the perfect

19 Armstrong, *Musical instruments*, ii, p. 113.   20 *Norfolk Chronicle*, 18 Dec. 1813.   21 *Freeman's Journal*, 10 Mar. 1814.   22 Ibid., 8 Sept. 1819. The declaration became a standard marketing tool in Egan adverts from the time.

4.3 Ring stops on an Egan Royal Portable Irish Harp. Photo by Nancy Hurrell, Museum of Fine Arts, Boston (formerly in a private collection).

travel companion for the grand tour of Europe. The portable harp was meant to be a practical second instrument for the affluent lady who already possessed a pedal harp. However, a portable harp, held in the lap, obviously lacked a foot-operated pedal mechanism, the device for obtaining chromatic pitches. On a small portable harp, any pitch-raising mechanisms would need to be hand operated, and Egan's first portable harps were fitted with ring stops, a series of small brass loops on the neck, one at the top of each string (figure 4.3).[23] It was a workable solution for attaining limited chromaticism on the harp, but Egan desired a more efficient mechanism to expand the harp's tonal possibilities.

HOW RING STOPS WORK

A string is threaded through a brass loop, and with a simple twist, the loop turns and stops the string in two places, thus raising its pitch by a semitone. The portable harps were tuned in E-flat major, standard pedal harp tuning, and a variety of key signatures were attainable using various ring-stop settings. Earlier Egan portable harps have ring stops arranged in groups of twos in each octave: typically at E-flat, F and A-flat, B-flat. Thus, accessible keys included three flat keys, C major and G major. Ring stops in threes were placed at the strings B-flat, E-flat and A-flat. Later instruments, such as an example in the Museum of Fine Arts, Boston, were given a complete set, with a ring stop at each string.

23 The term 'loop-stops' was also used for ring stops. In eighteenth-century Germany, U-shaped

Edward Light's harp-lutes were also fitted with ring stops, mainly in the instrument's bass range. One cannot discount the possibility that these makers influenced each other's experimental designs, although sequential instrumental invention has yet to be established.[24] It is often the case that the originator of an instrument or mechanism goes unrecorded, and the system of patents in early times was at best only loosely enforced. Light continued to further 'harpanize' his instruments and on his next model, the 'British Lute Harp', the standard pedal harp tuning of E-flat major replaced the C major tuning of previous instruments. This meant that it was easier to play harp music on his instrument (although with opposite fingerings). The new tuning concept was put forth in Light's accompanying tutor published around 1819, *A new and complete directory to the art of playing on the patent British lute-harp, with suitable lessons &c*. He wrote that 'by a new method of stringing and tuning, the tone is greatly improved, being now more equal, much sweeter, and still nearer the quality of the real harp'.[25] In addition, the maker introduced 'ditals', an important new mechanism:

> Besides these advantages, it [the lute-harp] accompanies other instruments and the voice, with much greater ease and perfection, as by means of the new ditals it is now capable of modulation from one key to another, with the same facility as the Pedal Harp, for which it will be found an excellent substitute [...][26]

Light further explains that ditals function like pedals on the larger harp, except that they are moved by fingers instead of feet.[27] Light's ingenious ditals or 'thumb-keys' in the treble range were more sophisticated in design and operation than the ring stops in the bass.[28] Eventually, on later models, all the ring stops were discontinued in favour of ditals, and Light renamed his 'British lute-harp' as simply the 'dital-harp' in 1819. At the same time, Egan adopted ditals as the mechanism for his new Portable Irish Harp model, which he introduced that same year.

'hooks' were the earliest form of mechanism on the harp, as seen in an example of a hook harp from Bohemia in the MFA collection, Boston. Prior to this invention, chromaticism was obtained by pinching strings, retuning, *scordatura* tuning and the addition of a second rank of strings. For an in-depth discussion of lever mechanisms on harps, see Anne-Marie O'Farrell, 'The chromatic development of the lever harp: mechanism, resulting technique and repertoire' in Joyce and Lawlor, *Harp studies* (2016), pp 209–38.   **24** A form of ring stops was also in use on single-action pedal harps by Jacob Erat. An Erat harp *c*.1800 in the collection of Maria Christina Cleary has a ring-stop mechanism connected to the harp's action and pedals.   **25** Edward Light, *A new and complete directory to the art of playing on the patent British lute-harp, with suitable lessons, &c* (London, *c*.1819), p. 3.   **26** Ibid.   **27** The word 'dital' is derived from the Italian term 'dita' meaning 'finger'.   **28** For detailed information and diagrams of Light's dital mechanism, see Armstrong, *Musical instruments*, ii, pp 103–5.

> ### HOW LIGHT'S DITALS WORK
>
> When a brass dital knob on the back of the instrument is pressed, the corresponding stop on the front, threaded with a string, pulls it to the fret on the finger-board, raising the pitch by a semitone. The brass dital knob then hooks into a slot and is held by a small metal tooth. A spring inside the dital keeps it in place until it is released.

Although Edward Light was the mastermind behind these novel instruments, the harp-lutes were actually produced by a London harp maker, Alexander Barry (1777–1841). It seems reasonable to assume that Barry collaborated with Light on the harp-inspired ideas, but what remains unconfirmed is whether Egan had any sort of relationship with the Barry-Light firm. For many years, the address of Barry's harp workshop was listed in adverts as 18 Frith Street, Soho, and in 1820, Egan's portable-harp adverts listed a Soho trade address at 53 Frith Street, across the road.[29] A professional association or at least an exchange of ideas seems entirely possible, as they seem to have both simultaneously traded in this largely artisan neighbourhood, which was home to several harp makers at the time, including Jacob Erat at 100 Wardour Street, and Dodd at St Martin's Lane.[30] In any case, parallel use of mechanisms did take place in the Egan and Barry-Light workshops, and one possible scenario is that Egan was inspired by Light's invention and adapted the dital concept for his harps, only in a slightly different form.[31]

Egan may also have been aware of other types of dital devices on portable harps that were manufactured in France at the time. A few small French dital harps still survive, which may have been made as travel harps or instruments for children. In the collection at Dean Castle in Kilmarnock, Scotland, an attractive small French dital harp has a striking decoration of colourful floral bouquets on a black background. The instrument, fitted with an imaginative dital system on the neck for raising pitches, has an ivory dital placed at the top of each string (figures 4.4 and 4.5).[32] Another portable harp with a similar set of ivory ditals is part of the harp collection of the Metropolitan Museum of Art, New York.

29 In addition to several newspaper references to this address, Barry is listed at 18 Frith Street, Soho in *Kent's original London directory: 1823* (London, 1823), p. 25.   30 The addresses of harp makers typically appear in the engraved inscriptions on harps. The Soho area also included Erard's manufactory at 18 Great Marlborough Street, and it is believed that many workers who apprenticed at the Erard factory later started their own harp workshops.   31 In 1819 Egan also experimented with adding pedals to change the stops on a barrel organ. He was awarded a gold medal by the Committee of the London Society of Arts for 'having relinquished a patent' for his invention, presumably allowing London makers to freely copy the mechanism. *Dublin Weekly Register*, 17 Apr. 1819.   32 The harp is in the Charles van Raalte Collection at Dean Castle,

4.4 *(left)* French portable harp with ditals, early nineteenth century. Courtesy of Charles van Raalte Collection, Dean Castle, Scotland.

4.5 *(right)* Dital mechanism with metal crutches on French portable harp at Dean Castle. Photo by Nancy Hurrell.

Attributed to the French maker Domeny, the harp dates to 1814–30, and the shape of the soundbox and neck is remarkably similar to Egan's models.[33] The scarcity of nineteenth-century chromatic portable harps might be a reflection of the inherent fragility of small instruments fitted with sometimes weighty mechanisms.[34]

The French portable harps and Light's dital-harps similarly both use ditals as a smart, practical solution for obtaining chromatic pitches, one string at a time. Egan, however, envisioned a more efficient operation for his thumb keys. Rather than raising only a single string pitch, he imagined ditals sharpening several strings simultaneously, like pedals on a pedal harp.[35] The maker ingeniously

Kilmarnock. The ditals are located on the neck's brass plate. When moved into a slot, the dital activates a tiny metal crutch under the plate which pinches the string against a pin, thus sharpening it by a semitone. The harp is 66cm in height.   33 The similarity brings to mind Lady Morgan's quote that 'all the world is running after his [Egan's] harp', written in 1818 while on tour in France with her Egan portable harp, which may have inspired copies. Measurements of the Domeny harp show the height to be almost a foot shorter than Egan's Portable Irish Harp models. Similar to the French harp at Dean Castle, the pillar is formed with an inverted 'Y' at the base.   34 It highlights the significance of quality craftsmanship in that more than fifty Egan dital harps have survived intact.   35 Two extant portable harps with similar concepts include a small Erard harp in the Smithsonian Museum in Washington DC with oval shaped levers in brass on the neck to operate the mechanisms, and a French portable harp in a scroll-top design in the Cincinnati Art Museum that has brass levers on the pillar. The levers, connected to rods inside

4.6 Ivory ditals on harp by John Egan. Photo by Nancy Hurrell, courtesy of Oxmantown Settlement Trust, Birr Castle.

installed seven ivory ditals, one for each note in the scale, on the inner surface of the pillar (figure 4.6), and each dital was connected via rods to a *fourchette* disc mechanism on the neck. With this resourceful invention, a dital moved into a slot would change the pitch of the same note in each octave simultaneously, an infinitely quicker motion than operating ring stops individually. The harpist could simply move one or two ditals, and then the hand was free to resume playing.[36] In adverts Egan boasted that 'the keys can be changed quicker than on the pedal harp, by the slightest touch of the ivory stops'.[37] The addition of ditals

the pillar, activate the mechanism on the neck.   36 Although it is assumed that the ditals were operated by the player's left hand, the plane of strings is positioned slightly to the left of the pillar, making the ivory knobs more accessible to the right hand.   37 *Freeman's Journal*, 8 Sept. 1819. This may have been slightly misleading, in that the pedal harp still had the advantage of the hands being free to keep playing while the feet moved the pedals. However, a Royal Portable Irish Harp (no. 2098) in the collection of the Historical Harp Society of Ireland has ditals in working order and they are extremely easy to operate.

J. EGAN'S NEWLY INVENTED SMALL HARPS.—The Royal Portable **IRISH HARPS**, patronized by the King, capable of making as many Changes of Keys as the Pedal Harp.—The Royal Portable Irish Harps, (the most perfect Instruments of the kind ever invented) are capable of being played on in as many Keys as the Pedal Harp, and though possessing the general advantages of that Instrument, are not one-third the price or size ; they are most convenient for travelling or taking abroad, and a delightful accompaniment to the Voice, or Piano Forte.—Those instruments are particularly adapted for Proficients on the Pedal Harp, as it is not necessary to take additional lessons to play on them, the strings, tuning, and fingering being exactly similar. Their elegance of form, and superior advantages have obtained for them the distinguished honour of the Royal Patronage, also that of Ladies of the highest distinction, and the decided approbation of Professors of the first consideration in Europe. Those Harps, are beautifully ornamented, varnished, gilt, &c. packed up, in travelling wooden cases, and forwarded to any part of the Empire, at the shortest notice. Sold by the Inventor and Manufacturer, John Egan, (Harp Maker, by Authority of the Royal Warrant to his Majesty and the Royal Family), Dawson-street, Dublin ; and at No. 2, Wilton-street, Grosvenor Place, London ; where may be had every appendage of the Harp; also an Instruction Book for the Royal Portable Irish Harp, Price 8s. Fantasia on the ancient Irish Melody, "Aileen Aroone," 3s. 6d. And various other Compositions for the Harp. The Royal Portable Irish Harps are played on with both hands, and held in the same position as the Pedal Harp, they admit of the most graceful display of the Female figure, and are thereby free from the distate so justly felt for the Guitar and other ungraceful Instruments.

4.7 Egan advertisement in the *Morning Post*, 29 Dec. 1826 describing the 'newly invented small harps'. The Portable Irish Harp was renamed the 'Royal Irish Harp' in 1821.

meant that now a small harp, with the single-action harp tuning in E-flat major, was idiomatic to modern pedal harp repertoire. Its portable size effectively competed with Light's dital-harp as a popular instrument for accompanying the voice in art music. Egan's harp with ditals was introduced to the public in 1819, and at the same time he officially named his small harp model the 'Portable Irish Harp'. The name also applied to his small harps with ring stops, for the harp body was basically the same, but with a different mechanism.

Egan's pioneering chromatic Portable Irish Harp was touted in the press as a truly novel invention:

The defect, without the harp changing its ancient shape, without a second row of strings or pedals, but by means of seven ivory stops placed in the curve of the pillar, is remedied, and this instrument is now capable of making as many changes of key as the pedal harp; as those stops, when pressed down, have the same effect as the pedals have on the great harp – raising the flats to naturals, and the naturals to sharps. Thus this ingenious artist has added imperishable features of perfection to the Irish harp.[38]

Word of Egan's mechanical accomplishment spread and was deemed so momentous, it was mentioned in the *History of the city of Dublin* in 1818 as the longed-for improvement to the Irish harp made by an 'ingenious artist': 'He [Egan] has rendered the Irish harp capable of being played on in every key, and of introducing half tones in every tune without pedals [...]'[39] Throughout the subsequent decade, promotional ads for the newly invented harp regularly appeared in newspapers in both Dublin and London (figure 4.7).[40] The instrument was acclaimed as having 'great brilliancy of tone' and was a 'delightful accompaniment to the voice or pianoforte'. Additional irresistible attributes were touted: 'they stand in tune remarkably well, and seldom break a string'![41] However, the harp's main attraction was clearly that it could be played in various keys, like a pedal harp, but was only one-third the size and sold at one-third of the cost.

HOW EGAN'S DITALS WORK

Seven hand-operated ivory levers are attached to rods inside the pillar that activate *fourchette* discs on the neck. When a dital is moved down into a slot, the corresponding discs in each octave turn, and strings of that pitch are simultaneously stopped by the disc forks to raise pitches by a semitone. For example, when the F dital is engaged into a slot, the F strings in each octave became F-sharps. The seven ivory ditals functioned the same as pedals on a pedal harp, raising the pitches by a 'single-action' from flats to naturals and naturals to sharps. Tuned in E-flat major, the key signatures possible on the single-action dital harp were E-flat, B-flat, F and C major plus the sharp keys of G, D, A and E major.

38 *Saunders's Newsletter*, 21 July 1823.　39 Warburton, Whitelaw and Walsh, *History of the city of Dublin*, ii, p. 910.　40 Earlier portable harps, as mentioned in the chapter on Lady Morgan, may have been simply called 'Irish harps'. It is possible Egan may have been influenced to name his invention following Light's example. In particular, Light's 'British lute-harp' is somewhat similar to the 'Portable Irish Harp' in its attribution of nationality and form.　41 *The Times*, 21 Oct. 1820.

NOTABLE EXAMPLES OF EARLY PORTABLE IRISH HARPS

Although Egan harps are attributed to the maker himself, by 1818, John Egan would have been the master of a workshop with an established chain of specialist workers carrying out his designs. Helen Clifford described the practices in Georgian workshops: 'In most high-design trades it was not the creative work of an individual multi-skilled artisan who designed and made an object from start to finish.'[42] The design, invention of mechanisms, mode of construction and determination of painted decoration would have been directed by Egan, but the actual execution would have most certainly been done by craftsmen working for him. The painted gilt decoration on surviving Portable Irish Harps varies from instrument to instrument, displaying imaginative interpretations of shamrock patterns, from small leafy vines within lined borders to larger clusters filling the soundboard, pillar and back areas. Patterns of neoclassical swirling acanthus leaves on the harps also vary according to the artistic hand of the gilder, and several additional motifs are present on individual harps, including wolfhound heads, shells and feathers.[43]

Portable Irish Harp no. 1, Metropolitan Museum, New York
Egan's earliest Portable Irish Harp with ditals still survives in the instrument collection at the Metropolitan Museum (plates 10, 11). The engraved inscription on the brass plate is: *John Egan Inventer [sic] / 30 Dawson St. / Dublin / 1819 / No. 1*. The date and serial number provide valued information in light of a general absence of dates and numbers on other surviving harps. The 'no. 1' indicates the first successfully made Portable Irish Harp fitted with ditals, as opposed to ring stops. Another telling detail is the maker's signature with *Inventer* added, charmingly misspelled. This became the maker's trademark title in light of his recent innovation – *John Egan, Inventor* was inscribed on all subsequent Portable Irish Harps made in the next two years.[44] An overall first impression of this exceptionally rare instrument is of a 'work in progress', a prototype of a groundbreaking new model that would later evolve. Quite unconventionally, a

42 Helen Clifford, 'The printed illustrated catalogue' in Snodin and Styles (eds), *Design & the decorative arts* (London, 2004), p. 144.   43 One possible candidate for a gilder who adorned Egan harps is John Wilkinson, listed in several Dublin directories as 'carver and gilder', working at 19 Aungier street from 1820–2. In 1834, Wilkinson's address is 21 Aungier street, the same as Nicholas Read, pedal and portable harp maker, the firm John Egan Jnr joined at that time, suggesting Wilkinson was certainly known to the Egan firm and may have worked for them. Another possibility is Gervas Murray, who was a gilder working at 62 Dawson street in 1824, according to *Pigot & Co's* directory, later maintaining premises at 55 Great Britain Street.   44 The inscription *John Egan, Inventor* appeared on the brass plates of Portable Irish Harps with ditals, but was not inscribed on his pedal harps. The labelling can almost be viewed as a sort of

succession of joined brass plates extends from the neck downwards and continues around the harp's pillar, acting rather like a suit of armour to protect the fragile wooden frame underneath. This was an elaborate precaution to keep the frame from collapsing due to the weighty inner mechanism. The action on the neck is entirely encased in wood, leaving only the *fourchette* discs exposed. On later models, the underside of the neck is completely open. A practical aspect of the design is a removable brass plate on the pillar's inner surface, allowing access to the dital rods inside for adjustments.[45] Next to the dital slots are the delicately engraved symbols for sharp, flat and natural, a feature unique to this early harp. The small harp is constructed like a pedal harp, with a semi-circular curved back, and it has thirty-four strings, an increase from the twenty-nine strings seen on earlier ring-stop models.

Two distinctly different layers of painted decoration are visible: a base layer of gold leaf on gesso underneath a top layer of green japanned ground with sprays of gold shamrocks.[46] The lacquered green layer has largely flaked off, revealing the gold-leaf base layer. Inside the harp is a stabilizing rod, or 'slide', another of Egan's inventions. When extended to the floor, the apparatus steadied the harp while it was held in the lap.[47] The rod culminates with a metal foot (on some models the foot is of wood) and is held in place by a large decorative screw on the lower back of the soundbox. Another thoughtful accessory, although no longer present, was a carrying strap attached to the three small brass knobs on the harp. One knob is positioned on the lower front pillar and two more are on either side of the knee block, where the neck joins the soundbox. The harpist might choose to tie a colourful ribbon to the knobs, with the dual purpose of creating a visually pleasing decoration as well as a means to steady the harp in the lap, with the ribbon passed over the player's shoulder.

Fortunately, Egan's first Portable Irish Harp with ditals remained intact, and the maker felt confident enough to use fewer metal-plate supports on subsequent examples. The next phase of instrumental design was harps made with single brass plates formed in a 'T' shape with a small vertical extension down the pillar. Two portable harps made *c.*1819 exemplify this design stage, one

copyright for his invention of the dital mechanism.   **45** On subsequent models, the brass plate on the dital area was exchanged for a wooden panel. It was camouflaged and almost invisible, painted and adorned with gold shamrocks.   **46** The practice of using gold leaf as a base layer under green lacquer was thought to produce a more brilliant green finish. The no. 1 harp in the Metropolitan Museum was restored at some point in the late nineteenth century by the firm of J. George Morley, whose signature paper transfer label appears on top of the harmonic curve: *J. Geo. Morley/ HARP MAKER/ (From ERARD'S)/ 6, Sussex Place, South Kensington/ LONDON.* The same label was typically attached to the pillar on the Morley Irish harp model made at the turn of the twentieth century.   **47** The author can attest to the usefulness of the device having used a stabilizing rod in performances on a Portable Irish Harp in the Museum of Fine Arts, Boston.

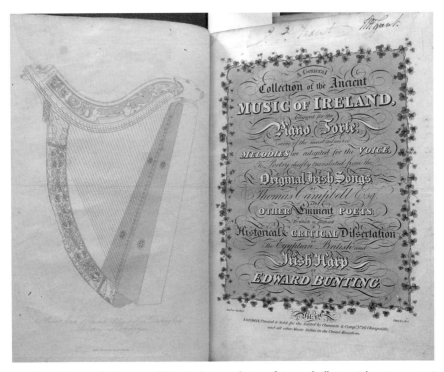

4.8 Frontispiece and title page of Bunting's 1809 edition of *A general collection of the ancient music of Ireland*. Courtesy of the Irish Collection, John J. Burns Library, Boston College.

in the Victoria & Albert Museum, London, and another in the Scenkonstmuseet (Swedish Museum Of Performing Arts), Stockholm. The harp contour in this next design phase is more daring, with a thinner pillar that is greatly bowed, somewhat like a belly, and a neck that juts dramatically into the air past the pillar, culminating in a high 'head'. Perhaps giving a nod to the ancient high-headed Gaelic harp shape of the seventeenth century, the portable harp profile echoes the outline of the Dalway harp in the frontispiece in Bunting's landmark volume of 1809, *A general collection of the ancient music of Ireland* (figure 4.8). Egan's shapely harp frames had strength due to a sophisticated construction technique of joining several sections of wood together for the neck and pillar. The laminated sections of the 'heads' were elegantly shaped and rounded, creating a highly sophisticated sculptural appearance.

Portable Irish Harp, Victoria & Albert Museum, London
The V&A's harp is a stunning example of floral themes painted in gold on a blue background, although due to oxidation it is now black in appearance (plate 12). Shamrocks are prettily joined together in bouquets with plump roses and thistles to commemorate the political union of Ireland, England and Scotland.

DECORATIVE MOTIFS ON PORTABLE IRISH HARPS

- *Shamrocks.* Egan's signature motif, strands of gilt shamrocks typically are depicted within lined borders framing the body, and on some examples continuous large bouquets of shamrocks fill the soundboard. A characteristic of the decoration on Egan harps is the detailed pen work on the gold motifs (figure 4.9). Shamrocks are vintage Egan, and the symbolic emblem, associated with St Patrick, gained increasing popularity in the late eighteenth century as a patriotic symbol adopted by the Volunteers and United Irishmen.
- *Shamrocks, roses and thistles.* The combination commemorates the political Act of Union in 1801, joining Ireland (shamrocks) with England (roses) and Scotland (thistles).
- *Ivy/acanthus/anthemion.* Classical foliate forms copied from the arts of ancient Greece and Rome were used in decorative arts in the Georgian period, from furniture and plasterwork to textiles. On a few rare Egan portable harps, the top front of the pillar is decorated with an attached sculptural form shaped like acanthus, made of a composite material and gilded (figure 4.10).
- *Oak leaves.* An indigenous tree in Ireland, also plentiful in the vast bog areas, oak had nationalistic symbolic meaning.
- *Feathers.* Egyptian themes such as eagle feathers became popular following Napoleon's campaign in Egypt (1798–1801).
- *Shells.* A common eighteenth-century rococo motif in furniture design (figure 4.11).
- *Wolfhound.* A nationalistic symbol of the Celtic past, the depiction of a fierce beast's head painted on the knee block morphs into swirling acanthus leaves (figure 4.12).

Near the uppermost edge of the head is a painted spiral or scroll, perhaps in tribute to the carved scrolls on the pillar tops of Gaelic harps like the O'Fogarty harp and the Rose Mooney harp (plate 13). The V&A harp also displays the neoclassical motifs synonymous with the Georgian period, inspired by ancient Greece and Rome: acanthus, anthemion and ivy, all swirling in luxuriant patterns. On the soundboard, rosettes fancifully sprout cornucopia-like acanthus leaves, which in turn spill out tiny bunches of grapes. And on the lower pillar are rows of Egyptian-inspired feathers.

Portable Irish Harp, Castle Leslie, Co. Monaghan
A visually striking Portable Irish Harp at Castle Leslie has ornate acanthus motifs adorning a dramatically extended head (plate 14). On the back is a finely painted anthemion design with strands of shamrocks (plate 15). The instrument came from the estate of the poet William Wordsworth, although a personal link to the poet has not been established.

4.9 (*left*) Shamrock decoration on a Portable Irish Harp by John Egan. Photo by Nancy Hurrell, courtesy of the Irish Collection, John J. Burns Library, Boston College.   4.10 (*right*) Gilt acanthus ornament on an Egan harp. Photo by Bernacki & Associates, Inc., courtesy of the O'Brien Collection.

4.11 (*left*) Shell motif on the back of Egan harp no. 1845. Photo by Bernacki & Associates, Inc., courtesy of the O'Brien Collection.   4.12 (*right*) Wolfhound on a Portable Irish Harp by John Egan. Photo by Nancy Hurrell, courtesy of Frances O'Kane.

Portable Irish Harp, Scenkonstmuseet (Swedish Museum of Performing Arts), Stockholm, Sweden
The Portable Irish Harp in the Scenkonstmuseet is also richly ornamented in gold on a deep blue background. A somewhat unusual inscription is engraved on the brass plate: *Manufactured by J. Egan Inventer. / 30 Dawson St. Dublin / For the Regent's Harmonic Institution Argyle Rooms, London.*[48] The Regent's Harmonic Institution was formed in 1818 by a group of professional musicians who aimed primarily to publish sheet music. Based in the Argyll Rooms on Regent Street, it sold music, pianos and harps in the lower saloon of the building. In 1820, a concert room was opened for performances and balls.[49] The premises, located near Regent's Park, were in an upscale planned development designed by the architect John Nash (1752–1835). To be invited to display harps at the Argyll Rooms was a feather in John Egan's cap, for only a select few firms were solicited by the Harmonic Institution to show their instruments. According to the aims of the establishment, outlined in an 1819 *English Musical Gazette*, musical instruments on view represented manufactories of only the 'esteemed makers'.[50] With his reputation ever growing in England, Egan further expanded his commercial presence by collaborating with London dealers Messrs Clementi & Co. and Messrs Chapper Co., while Mr Loder sold Egan's harps in Bath, and Messrs Yaniwitz and Weiss likewise in Liverpool.[51]

SINGLE-ACTION TO DOUBLE-ACTION

In Ireland, Egan's reputation was given a boost by lofty patronage from Dublin Castle, as the maker received prestigious commissions for pedal harps from the wives of lord lieutenants. Following a harp made for the duchess of Richmond, the practice continued for the succeeding viceroy's wife, the duchess of Dorset, Arabella Diana Cope. In 1816, newspaper articles headed 'Under the Patronage of Her Grace the Duchess of Dorset' announced Egan's momentous construction of a double-action pedal harp.[52] The new model was described in the *Freeman's Journal* as 'constructed on a principle entirely different from those

---

48 Although the inscription is 'Argyle' the correct spelling is 'Argyll'.   **49** See Donald William Krummel and Stanley Sadie, *Music printing and publishing* (New York, 1990), p. 387. In 1820 the firm became the 'Royal Harmonic Institution'. On the harp, plume-like forms painted on the back may be symbolic of triple feathers for the Prince of Wales, relating to the inscription 'Regent's'. **50** 'English literary intelligence', *English Musical Gazette*, Feb. 1819 in Leanne Langley, 'A place for music: John Nash, Regent Street and the Philharmonic Society of London', *Electronic British Library Journal* (2013), accessed online May 2015. One other Egan harp with a similar inscription, a double-action pedal harp, has come to light, so Egan apparently sold both portable and pedal harps at the RHI. **51** *Freeman's Journal*, 31 Dec. 1821. **52** *Freeman's Journal*, 2 Jan. 1817. The announcement reproduced in the newspaper is dated 30 Dec. 1816.

heretofore made', for as yet the double-action harp had not arrived in Ireland.[53] The first patent for the double-action harp had been granted to Sébastien Erard six years earlier in England, in 1810, and now Egan began to successfully produce double-action harps alongside his single-action instruments. The basic concept of the double-action pedal harp extended the chromatic capabilities of the single-action harp by adding an extra slot for each pedal, connected to a corresponding second row of *fourchette* discs. Pitches then could be raised an additional semitone. Tuned in C-flat major, each string could now play three different pitches according to the three pedal positions: flat, natural and sharp.

Having successfully made a double-action pedal harp, the next logical step was to attempt a double-action Portable Irish Harp. Using the same principle, an additional slot was added for the ditals, along with a second row of *fourchette* discs on the neck. The survival rate of these petite harps equipped with fairly heavy mechanisms seems to have been rather low, for only one double-action Portable Irish Harp with two rows of discs has come to light.[54] An Egan harp, no. 1885, held in storage at the Fitzwilliam Museum in Cambridge, displays an upper row of unusual discs in the bass with only a single prong on twenty-one strings (figures 4.13 and 4.14).[55] Egan continued to experiment with the concept of using a single prong to stop the strings on double-action portable harps. On a later, fully chromatic portable harp, no. 1898, which is now in the Munich Stadtmuseum, a unique mechanism has a single row of unusually shaped oblong *fourchette* discs at the bass strings (figure 4.15).[56] The extended disc length allows the prong at each end to function independently instead of the usual simultaneous stopping with both prongs. For example, when the dital moves down into the first slot, the disc rotates and a single upper prong stops the string (E-flat becomes E-natural). As the dital moves down into the second slot, the disc rotates further and the lower prong also stops the string (E-natural becomes E-sharp).[57] On a small portable harp with low-tension strings, the use of single prongs seemed to work, however double-pronged discs appear to be a more standard type of mechanism on Egan harps.

53 Ibid.   54 An Egan Portable Irish Harp exhibited in a 1902 Chickering & Sons exhibition held at Horticultural Hall in Boston was listed in the catalogue of the exhibition with the note: 'This instrument is also interesting from the fact that it is double action; a rare type of Irish harp.' The present location of the harp is unknown.   55 After the 21 bass strings with a single prong on the upper *fourchettes*, stringing continues with the usual double prongs on discs in both rows, then the five string discs in the treble have upper double prongs and lower single prongs.   56 The harp was examined in 2017 by Dr Maria Christina Cleary and Dr Panagiotis Poulopoulos, who brought the unusual double-action mechanism to my attention.   57 The oblong discs are in the lower two octaves of the bass; the remaining discs on the upper octaves are more rounded.

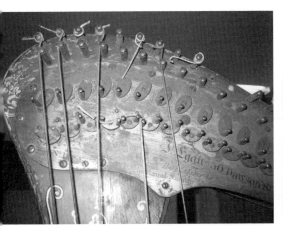

4.13 (*left*) Double-action *fourchette* discs on Royal Portable Irish Harp no. 1885 by John Egan. Photo by Nancy Hurrell, courtesy of the Fitzwilliam Museum.

4.14 (*right*) Detail of corresponding double-action slots on the inside pillar. Photo by Nancy Hurrell, courtesy of the Fitzwilliam Museum.

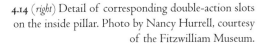

Double-action Portable Irish Harp no. 1885, Fitzwilliam Museum, Cambridge

The sole surviving example of this impressive technological feat, this harp's serial number dates it to *c.*1822–3. The basic dimensions of the harp match the earlier instruments in the V&A and Scenkonstmuseet, but its shape is noticeably different. The harp represents the third and final design phase of the Portable Irish Harp. The pillar is much thicker and straighter, and the head, no longer extending beyond the pillar, is now more rounded. The head merges with the thick pillar to create a broad area for greater stability. The dramatic shape of Egan's earlier portable harps, although aesthetically pleasing, was also structurally problematic.

On the earlier portable harps with extended 'heads', the tension of the bass wire strings almost invariably caused the neck to bend slightly to the left (from the player's perspective). On some examples, the longest bass strings are actually attached to the tip of a head, which extends beyond the pillar, putting strain on this top section of the harp. Consequently, Egan altered the design shape (starting with harps with serial numbers in the 1880s) by thickening the pillar where it joins the neck, and the head became more rounded, without an extension, to strengthen the frame (figure 4.16). The design change may have also been prompted by the portable harp's increased commercial success and a

4.15 Royal Portable Irish Harp no. 1898 by John Egan with extended stabilizing rod and a unique double-action dital mechanism. Photo courtesy of Munich Stadtmuseum, Germany.

4.16 (*right*) Rounded head and thicker pillar on Royal Portable Irish Harp, about 1823, by John Egan. Photograph © 2019 Museum of Fine Arts, Boston. **4.17** (*top left*) Sculpted and gilded base of an early Egan Portable Irish Harp. Photo by Nancy Hurrell, courtesy of the Irish Collection, John J. Burns Library, Boston College. **4.18** (*bottom left*) Simplified base construction of a later Royal Portable Irish Harp. Photo by Nancy Hurrell, courtesy of the Irish Collection, John J. Burns Library, Boston College.

need to streamline production. Evidence of this theory can be seen in the new style of head, composed of a large flat piece of wood instead of the earlier sculptural heads made of several pieces laminated together. Also, inside the base of the harp, whereas earlier instruments display beautifully hand carved and gilded oak base blocks (figure 4.17), the later harps have simple rectangular blocks of wood joined together (figure 4.18).

Each new mechanism devised for the Portable Irish Harp expanded the range of models available for purchase. The double-action portable harp was not viewed as an evolutionary replacement for the single-action model, for both

4.19 A promotional
advertisement for the
new Portable Irish Harp
in *Pigot and Co.'s Directory*,
1824. Courtesy of Janet
Snowman.

models continued to be produced and sold, as well as portables with ring stops.
A promotional ad in *Pigot and Co.'s Directory* of 1824 (figures 4.19 and 4.20) listed
the three models of Portable Irish Harps from which to choose.[58] Another
contemporary newspaper ad lists the price of a double-action portable harp,
ornamented and lacquered in a colour, as 24 guineas, whereas a varnished and

58 *Pigot and Co.'s* (Dublin, 1824). The ad was most likely composed for the earlier *Pigot's Commercial
Directory of Ireland* in 1820 and reprinted in 1824, for the model is advertised as a Portable Irish
Harp even though it became the Royal Portable Irish Harp in 1821. In Egan advertising 'ivory
stops' was the term used, whereas today the organological term 'ditals' is preferred.

4.20 Price list for the Portable Irish Harp in *Pigot and Co.'s Directory*, 1824. Courtesy of Janet Snowman.

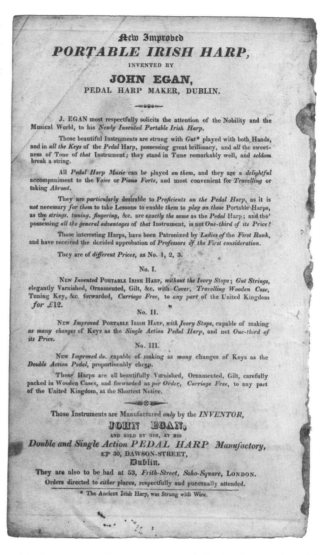

New Improved
PORTABLE IRISH HARP,
INVENTED BY
JOHN EGAN,
PEDAL HARP MAKER, DUBLIN.

J. EGAN most respectfully solicits the attention of the Nobility and the Musical World, to his *Newly Invented Portable Irish Harp.*

Those beautiful Instruments are strung with *Gut** played with both Hands, and in *all the Keys* of the *Pedal* Harp, possessing great brilliancy, and *all* the sweetness of Tone of *that* Instrument; they stand in Tune remarkably well, and *seldom* break a string.

All *Pedal Harp Music* can be played *on them*, and they are a *delightful* accompaniment to the *Voice* or *Piano Forte*, and most convenient for *Travelling* or taking *Abroad*.

They are *particularly* desirable to *Proficients on the Pedal Harp*, as it is *not necessary for them* to take Lessons to enable them *to play on those* Portable Harps, as the *strings, tuning, fingering*, &c. are *exactly the same* as the Pedal Harp; and tho' possessing *all the general advantages* of that Instrument, is not *One-third of its Price!*

Those interesting Harps, have been Patronized by *Ladies of* the *First Rank*, and have received the decided approbation of *Professors of the First consideration.*

They are of *different Prices*, as No. 1, 2, 3.

No. I.

NEW *Invented* PORTABLE IRISH HARP, *without the Ivory Stops*; Gut Strings, elegantly Varnished, Ornamented, Gilt, &c. with *Cover, Travelling Wooden Case*, Tuning Key, &c. forwarded, *Carriage Free*, to *any* part of the United Kingdom *for £12.*

No. II.

NEW *Improved* PORTABLE IRISH HARP, *with Ivory Stops*, capable of making *as many changes* of Keys as the *Single Action Pedal Harp*, and not *One-third of its Price.*

No. III.

NEW *Improved do.* capable of making as *many* changes of Keys as the *Double Action Pedal*, proportionably cheap.

Those Harps are all beautifully Varnished, Ornamented, Gilt, carefully packed in Wooden Cases, and forwarded as *per Order, Carriage Free*, to any part of the United Kingdom, at the Shortest Notice.

Those Instruments are Manufactured *only* by the *INVENTOR*,
JOHN EGAN,
AND SOLD BY HIM, AT HIS
Double and Single Action PEDAL HARP Manufactory,
☞ 30, DAWSON-STREET,
Dublin.
They are also to be had at 53, *Frith-Street, Soho-Square*, LONDON.
Orders directed to *either* places, respectfully and punctually attended.
* The Ancient Irish Harp, was Strung with Wire.

gilt single-action portable harp was only 8 guineas, and the high-priced pedal harps ranged from 40 to 65 guineas.[59]

In London and on the Continent, Portable Irish Harps, like other cultural products from Ireland, became highly fashionable. Without having to cross the Irish Sea, London society could experience Ireland's nationalistic pathos through the novels of Sydney Owenson and Maria Edgeworth or by singing deliciously romantic songs from *Irish melodies* around the pianoforte. So too, Egan's new

59 *Freeman's Journal*, 6 July 1822. The price of a pedal harp in the early 1800s was equal to a year's wages for a shopkeeper or a male servant.

shamrock-covered Irish harp was embraced as a novel Irish accessory for music-making, especially prized by the Irish residing abroad as a display of patriotism in the music saloon. Orders arrived from London for Egan's harp with ditals, and an advert in London's *Morning Post* in 1820 reported that 'as further proof of the increasing liberality of England towards Ireland that the orders are in general for the colour of the harps to be green, ornamented with shamrocks'.[60] Gentlemen, as well as ladies, performed on the instrument including the well-known Mr T. Cooke, who accompanied Miss Tree in a Dublin concert on 'that beautiful and interesting instrument … so much the fashion in London and on the Continent, the Portable Irish Harp'.[61] The harp became a fixture in Mr Cooke's musical shows, and six years on, Mr Cooke performed Irish airs on an Egan portable harp at Dublin's Theatre Royal following a production of the operas *Rob Roy* and *The son-in-law*.[62]

Egan, emboldened by all the attention his new harp model had garnered in society circles, decided to present one of his harps to the 'Bard of Erin' himself, Thomas Moore. Although Moore's literary works and song *Melodies* are quintessentially Irish, the poet actually lived most of his life abroad in England and France. Early in his career, Moore, like Owenson, had ventured to London for career advancement and had similarly experienced a meteoric rise in society despite his humble origins. Moore, the son of a Dublin grocer on Aungier Street, had achieved success at Trinity College, which propelled him to study law at the Middle Temple in London. With the publication in 1800 of his first book, *Odes of Anacreon*, a translation of the odes of a Greek poet, he abandoned his legal studies. A decade later the publication of the *Irish melodies* cinched Moore's celebrity status among London's upper-class drawing-room set. Although small in stature and delicate in appearance, Moore mesmerized audiences with his charismatic singing, sharp wit and clever conversation. His performance style was legendary, and many who witnessed his delivery of the *Melodies*, both women and men, were reduced to tears. In a memoir, Elizabeth Rennie recalled of his performances:

> When he commenced, every breath was almost hushed, lest a note should be lost. Yet his [voice] could scarcely be called singing – improvising describes it better. The soul felt intensity – the passionate earnestness with which every word and accent were intoned, I might say declaimed, were quite indescribable, and could only be conceived by those who heard him […][63]

60 *Morning Post*, 25 Sept. 1820.   61 Ibid.   62 *Dublin Evening Mail*, 31 July 1826.   63 Elizabeth Rennie, *Traits of character: being twenty-five years' literary and personal recollections*, 2 vols (London, 1860), i, p. 189.

Egan was anxious to place one of his new Irish harps in the hands of this gifted artist.

A TALE OF TWO HARPS: MOORE'S IRISH HARP AND 'A LITTLE ONE FOR ANASTASIA'

Egan wrote to Moore – with whom he had served a decade earlier in the Irish Harp Society in Dublin – in England in August of 1820, and Moore recorded in his *Journal*, 'Received a letter from Egan, the harp-maker in Dublin, very well & flatteringly indicted, telling me of the perfection to which he had at last brought the Irish harp, & begging me to allow him to present me one of his best, as a mark of admiration &c. &c.'[64] In October of the following year, Moore was in Dublin visiting his parents, and a meeting was arranged to show the new Irish harp model to the poet. Moore writes:

> Egan, the Harp-maker, most anxious that I should judge the power of his improved Irish harps – sent his son with one – the chaise at the door at ½ past three, and some beautiful Irish airs played to me during my last moments – Had wine in and all filled bumpers to the Irish harp and our next happy meeting – [65]

The instrument's debut entirely satisfactory, Egan proceeded to build a Portable Irish Harp especially for Moore, in a patriotic hue of green. The finished product was delivered to Moore in England in October of 1823, and he recorded in his journal, 'My Irish harp arrived from Ireland, and a little one of two octaves with it for Anastasia.'[66] It was a generous gesture to make a second, smaller harp for Moore's daughter, and it was also indicative of the maker's penchant for constructing harps of differing sizes and shapes. Anastasia, like other young ladies of a certain social standing, attended finishing school as a boarder at Mrs Foster's establishment in Bath. In his memoirs, Moore mentioned visiting the school with his wife Bessie to hear their daughter play the harp after only a fortnight of lessons, and remarked that she showed 'a very good promise'.[67] Beyond these somewhat sparse references, the instruments are not mentioned again in Moore's memoirs. His own proficiency on the instrument is somewhat unknown, and his harp-playing may well have been primarily a private pursuit.

64 Wilfred S. Dowden (ed.), *The journal of Thomas Moore* (East Brunswick, NJ, 1983), i, p. 334.
65 Ibid., ii, p. 495.   66 Ibid., ii, p. 683.   67 Thomas Moore, *Memoirs, journal, and correspondence* (London, 1854), iv, p. 57.

Casual references to Ireland's bard singing to his harp tend to be based on the ownership of the instrument and an assumed skill, rather than real, chronicled performances. A sort of bardic myth of Moore playing his Egan harp continued to be satisfyingly embellished in the decades following his death. Not unlike the merging of Owenson with Glorvina in the public's imagination, so too did Moore and his harp become like the mythical bardic harpers in his *Melodies*. Moore's two Egan harps are clearly visible among his belongings in a charming painting *Thomas Moore in his study at Sloperton Cottage*, in the National Gallery of Ireland (plate 17). Moore is pictured scribbling away at his desk. Anastasia's small harp rests upon a tall bookshelf and near the poet's chair is his own harp, lying on its rounded back and leaned up against the square pianoforte, convenient for playing, although it may have been a deliberate symbolic placement by the artist.

Moore's Royal Portable Irish Harp no. 1858, Royal Irish Academy, Dublin

Thomas Moore's harp survives in the collection at the Royal Irish Academy (plate 16). It is fitting that it has returned to Dawson Street, only a short distance away from the workshop where it was made. Upon Moore's death, his widow Elizabeth 'Bessie' Dyke (1796–1865) presented the harp and Moore's extensive personal library to the academy.[68] Carefully preserved inside a closed harp trunk for decades, it retains its original vibrant pea-green colour. A single vine of shamrocks within lined borders frames the soundboard and back, and there are additional strands of the leafy symbol on the pillar and neck. Shamrocks are the predominant theme on Moore's harp, with some swirling acanthus on the harp's head.

The harp delivered to Moore was one of several high-profile commissions in this time period, for Egan's harps had recently begun to also attract attention in royal circles. In 1820, London's *Morning Post* reported that Egan had lately received orders for harps from 'Ladies of the first rank in London, and even from the Royal Palaces of Carleton House and Hampton Court.'[69] The details of this royal reference are not known, but an extraordinary rise to the top of his profession did occur soon after. In 1821 Egan was appointed as harp maker to King George IV (see chapter 5, pp 145–8), and consequently his new harp model became the *Royal* Portable Irish Harp. With the award, all subsequent harps accordingly displayed the royal coat of arms (lion and unicorn), and the inscriptions reflected the lofty appointment. Thus, Thomas Moore's harp is inscribed on the brass plate: *J. Egan. 30 Dawson Street Dublin / Harp Maker by Special Appointment to His Most Gracious Majesty George IV & the Royal Family / No. 1858.*

---

68 Moore was elected a member to the Royal Irish Academy in 1846. See Siobhán Fitzpatrick (ed.), *My gentle harp: Moore's Irish melodies, 1808–2008* (Dublin, 2008).   69 *Morning Post*, 25 Sept. 1820.

Strangely, a description of the sound of Moore's harp did not appear until fifty years later, perhaps another indication that the poet rarely performed on it in public. Played by the Swedish harpist Adolf Sjoden in 1879, Moore's harp was centre-stage in a public concert held during the Moore centenary. The legacy of the *Irish melodies* had enhanced the reputation of the 'Bard of Erin' in the latter nineteenth century, prompting a grand commemoration of the hundredth anniversary of the poet's birth, held in the Exhibition Palace, Dublin. As part of several days of festivities, Moore's former childhood home on Aungier Street was opened to the public and various personal 'relics' were displayed: letters, manuscripts, portraits of Moore and his family, and his harp and piano.[70] In the evening, a grand concert showcased Moore's *Melodies* through performances by Dublin's prominent singers and instrumentalists, including harpists Herr Sjoden and Owen Lloyd, and a 'band of harps' joining a massive chorus in numbers such as a 'grand choral fantasia'.[71] The concert opened with 250 voices singing 'Oh the sight entrancing' to harp and organ accompaniment. Several soloists performed, including Mr Barton McGuckin, who sang 'The minstrel boy', 'Oft in the stilly night' and 'The meeting of the waters', followed by a horn quartet admirably playing 'Believe me if all'. But the highlight of the evening, according to the correspondent, was a rare chance to hear the sounds of Moore's small Royal Portable Irish Harp, lent by the Royal Irish Academy for the concert:

> Herr Sjoden played a fasticcio on Irish airs on the harp that belonged to and was so often used by Moore himself. The associations connected with the incident gave it a peculiar and melancholy interest – the clamouring crowd was stilled into silence for the few moments that it lasted, and the strains of 'Dear harp of my country' coming from that old harp stirred many a heart, and indeed made many an eye glisten, at the thoughts its tones recalled.[72]

This passage, typical of its day, underscores the blurring of myth and reality in regards to Moore playing his Irish harp.

Anastasia's small Egan harp no. 1864

Like Moore's harp, Anastasia's scaled-down model gained a certain notoriety decades after it was made. It is almost certainly the petite Egan harp with shamrock decoration pictured on a rare photocard from the 1880s (figure 4.21).[73]

70 *Freeman's Journal*, 29 May 1879.   71 Ibid., 28 May 1879.   72 Ibid., 29 May 1879.   73 Two photocards of the harp are known: one in the Mary Carroll Collection at the Corpus Christi Library, Texas, and another in the Annie Christitch Papers, John J. Burns Library, Boston College.

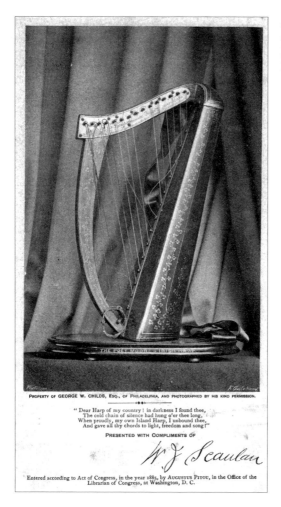

4.21 Photocard of small Egan harp owned by George W. Childs. Photo courtesy of Corpus Christi Library, Texas.

This instrument has the familiar rounded back soundbox, but the pillar and neck are joined together in a manner imitating the Trinity College harp, without a 'head'. The shamrock decoration within lined borders mirrors Moore's own portable harp, and the instrument's fifteen strings correspond to Moore's description of 'a harp of two octaves'. The inscription on the brass plate is identical to that on Moore's harp, *J. Egan – 30 Dawson Street Dublin/ Harp Maker by Special Appointment to His Most Gracious Majesty George IV & the Royal Family*, and the serial number, 1864, is fairly close in sequence to the poet's instrument, no. 1858. A thick satin ribbon hangs from a knob at the top of the soundbox as a decorative strap to steady the harp when held in the lap, as was the custom. The small harp rests on a stand labelled 'The Poet Moore's Irish Harp', a fairly common misattribution applied to Egan harps over the decades (and this was

1 John Egan single-action pedal harp at Avondale House. Photos by Nancy Hurrell, courtesy of the National Museum of Ireland collection.

2 (*above*) Bronze appliqué vignette of bow and arrows and an angel riding on an Irish wolfhound.

3 Winged griffin on the pedal box.

4 John Egan wire-strung Irish harp with Gaelic inscriptions. Photo by Nancy Hurrell, courtesy of the National Museum of Ireland collection.

5 (*left*) Egan wire-strung Irish harp in Fermanagh County Museum. Photos by Nancy Hurrell, courtesy of Enniskillen Castle Museums, Northern Ireland.

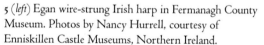

6 Tuning pins and an iron band attached to the underside of the neck for support.

8 Painted inscription and royal crest on Irish harp by J. Egan & Son no. 2044. Photo by Nancy Hurrell.

7 (*left*) Egan advertisement used as a decorative restoration on Fermanagh County Museum harp.

9 (*right*) J. Egan & Son no. 2044 wire-strung Irish harp. © The Fitzwilliam Museum, Cambridge.

10 John Egan
Portable Irish Harp
no. 1, with dital
mechanism.
Metropolitan
Museum of Art,
New York, Art
Resource.

11 The inscription
with no. 1 and the
date 1819. Photo by
Nancy Hurrell,
courtesy of the
Metropolitan
Museum of Art,
New York.

12 Portable Irish Harp
by John Egan.
© Victoria and Albert
Museum, London.

13 Detail of gilt decoration.
© Victoria and Albert
Museum, London.

14 Portable Irish Harp by John Egan. Photos by Nancy Hurrell, images reproduced courtesy of Castle Leslie Archives.

15 Anthemion and shamrock decoration on the back of the Portable Irish Harp at Castle Leslie.

16 Thomas Moore's Royal Portable Irish Harp no. 1858 by John Egan. Photo courtesy of the Royal Irish Academy collection, Dublin.

17 Portrait of Thomas Moore in his Study at Sloperton Cottage. © National Gallery of Ireland.

18, 19 Winged-maiden Portable Irish Harp by John Egan in the Royal Academy of Music Museum, London. Photos by Ian Brearey reproduced with permission.

20 Detail of winged-maiden figure and wing on Egan harp in the Royal Academy of Music Museum, London.

21, 22 Winged-maiden Portable Irish Harp by John
Egan and sons John and Charles Egan, 1820.
© Courtesy of Museo dell'Arpa Victor Salvi,
Piasco, Cuneo, Italy.

23 Portrait of Elizabeth
Conyngham playing an Egan
harp, 1824, by Sir Thomas
Lawrence (1769–1830).
© The Calouste Gulbenkian
Foundation/Scala/Art
Resource, New York.

24 (*left*) Grecian single-action pedal harp
by John Egan. Photos by Nancy Hurrell,
courtesy of Irish Linen Centre & Lisburn
Museum.

25 (*right*) Detail of angel on knee block.

26 Trumpeting angel on the base holding a sprig of shamrocks.

28 Capital with Grecian
figures playing lyres.

29 Mythological figures
painted on the back.

27 (*above*) John Egan Grecian single-action pedal harp,
courtesy of the Cobbe Collection, Newbridge House.
Photos by Nancy Hurrell.

30 Gothic music saloon at Birr Castle.

31 John Egan Portable Irish Harp owned by Lady Alicia Parsons. Photos by Nancy Hurrell, courtesy of Oxmantown Settlement Trust, Birr Castle.

32 Date 1821 inscribed on a small brass plate.

34 Pillar with pedestal, acanthus motifs and a spiralling garland of shamrocks.

33 John Egan single-action pedal harp with a curved bronze pillar. Photos by Nancy Hurrell, courtesy of Audrey Gilmer.

35 Pedal rods are inside the soundbox.

36, 37 Irish harp by Robinson & Bussell displayed in the Francini Corridor at the Áras an Uachtaráin. Photos by Nancy Hurrell, courtesy of Áras an Uachtaráin.

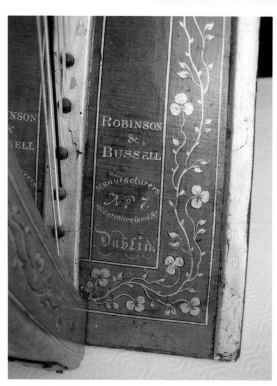

38 Inscription and shamrock border in the Egan decorative style.

39 (*right*) George Butler Irish harp with painted nationalistic motifs of Erin holding a harp, a wolfhound and shamrock vines. Photos by Nancy Hurrell, courtesy of the Horniman Museum and Gardens.

40 Round tower motifs decorate the mid-section of the soundboard.

42 John Egan Royal Portable Irish Harp no. 1845 in the O'Brien Collection is featured on the cover of the exhibition catalogue, *Ireland: crossroads of art and design, 1690–1840*, Art Institute of Chicago, 2015.

43 Egan harp in the O'Brien Collection. Photo courtesy of Bernacki & Associates, Inc.

41 John Egan Royal Portable Irish Harp no. 2036. Photo by Nancy Hurrell, courtesy of the John J. Burns Library, Boston College.

44 Europa musical instruments harp stamp issued 8 May 2014. Reproduced by kind permission of An Post.

in fact Anastasia's instrument), however, in this particular case it appears to be accurate in provenance, as it had belonged to the Moore family. The line under the photo, 'Property of George W. Childs, Esq., of Philadelphia', provides further clues to the harp's later ownership, and written accounts verify the harp was on display in a small museum exhibiting Child's personal collection at the Drexel Institute (now Drexel University) in the early 1900s.[74] According to a Philadelphia guide from 1937, Mr Childs had purchased the harp from Moore's family, and a fascinating trail of ownership can be traced to the events surrounding the Moore centenary in Dublin in 1879.

Initially, Moore's widow kept possession of Anastasia's small harp at the time of the transfer of the poet's library and larger Egan harp to the Royal Irish Academy. Elizabeth Moore retained a few personal belongings, including the Moore family Bible and the smaller harp, and shortly before her death the items were sent to her nephew, Charles Murray.[75] With his aunt's passing, Murray arranged for a special commemorative east window to be constructed in her honour in the Bromham church, where Bessie, Thomas and two of the children are buried. Murray also initiated plans for another projected west window to be added in memory of the poet. The funding for the west window by public subscription was organized by Samuel Carter Hall (1800–89), a former friend and admirer of Moore. Murray failed to live long enough to see the completion of the west window, but his widow, Mrs Murray, in appreciation of Hall's fundraising efforts, passed on to him the small harp, family Bible and other relics.[76] Hall was a journalist and editor of the London *Art Journal*, and as an additional fundraiser for the window he authored (with his wife) a small biographical pamphlet, *A memory of Thomas Moore*, which was sold during the centenary year. The major contributor to the Moore commemorative window was an American, George W. Childs (1829–94) of Philadelphia, a journalist acquaintance of Hall's, who owned the *Ledger* newspaper. Typical of gentlemen of his stature and wealth, Childs was also a collector of rare books and historical objects, and in 1884 Hall sent the Moore relics and harp to Childs

74 Federal Writers' Project, *Philadelphia: a guide to the nation's birthplace* (Harrisburg, 1937), p. 501. George W. Childs (1829–94) was a newspaper publisher and friend to the banker A.J. Drexel, who founded the institute in 1891. The museum displayed Childs' collection of coins, as well as the Moore harp, Lord Byron's (allegedly) desk and Napoleon Bonaparte's chess table from his exile on the island of St Helena.   75 Samuel Carter Hall, *A memory of Thomas Moore* (Dublin, 1879), p. 30.   76 A reference to a description of Moore performing on the small harp at parties recalled by S.C. Hall appears in Margaret M. Halvey, 'American reliques of Tom Moore', *Donahoe's Magazine*, 34:5 (Nov. 1895), 1185. It is possibly an imagined retelling, along the lines of an additional myth presented whereby the harp was given to Moore by friends in Limerick to urge him to enter politics and represent them in parliament.

with a view towards securing their long-term preservation.[77] And the financial contribution from Childs, combined with the aid of 200 subscribers, resulted in the completion of the Moore memorial window in Bromham church, which was unveiled by Mrs Anna Maria Hall on 13 September 1879.[78]

PLAYERS OF ANASTASIA'S SMALL HARP

Once in America, Anastasia's harp gained widespread attention, for Childs was not averse to putting it on public view, and in 1889 he lent the instrument to Governor Robert Taylor of Tennessee to be exhibited at the Scotch-Irish Congress held in Columbia.[79] A few years earlier, in 1885, the harp had been played in a performance in New York's Steinway Hall by Miss Maud Morgan, who wrote, 'It was very small, but of sweet tone, [it] had about two octaves of strings, and is about fifteen inches high.'[80] Confirmation of another performer who possibly played the harp is suggested in a personal signature reproduced

4.22 Irish tenor in New York, W.J. Scanlan (1856–98), who performed on a small Irish harp. Library of Congress Prints and Photographs Division.

77 S.C. Hall, letter repr. in *American Bookseller*, 15:5 (Mar. 1884), 227.   78 S.C. Hall (ed.), *Art Journal*, 18 (1879), 255. The memorial window to Moore was designed by W.H. Constable, a glass painter in Cambridge, and the subject represents the Last Judgment.   79 *New York Times*, 30 Apr. 1889.   80 Maud Morgan, 'The harp: historical paper', *Brainard's Musical World* (1885), 366.

on the aforementioned photocard. Near the bottom of the card, the familiar lines of 'Dear harp of my country' are printed, along with a salutation, 'Presented with compliments of *W.J. Scanlan*'. In the 1880s, the popular actor-singer W.J. Scanlan (1856–98) was a star of the New York musical stage, appearing in the Irish plays 'The Irish Minstrel' and 'Mavourneen' (figure 4.22). His stage persona was that of a rollicking Irish minstrel, known for getting into scrapes, wooing a sweetheart and singing Irish airs to his harp accompaniments, and Scanlan performed with a small 'floral harp which some admirers had given him'.[81] One cannot discount the possibility that Childs was the 'admirer' who loaned the small Egan harp to Scanlan for performances. It does appear that the actor and his agent, Mr Pitou, were in fact the persons responsible for the historic harp being photographed for the photocard, according to an article in the *Cork Constitution*.[82] The press clipping reveals that it was Mr Pitou who arranged the photo session, and the harp is described as being a 'dark green' in colour, with a faded green ribbon attached.

Although the present location of Anastasia Moore's instrument is unknown, Egan produced at least two of these tiny harps, for another similar harp with fifteen strings survives in a private collection (figure 4.23). The harp, just 40.6cm tall, is identical in form to the instrument in the photocard, but its original painted decoration has been removed. Now with a plain wood finish, only traces of blue paint remain, and slight remnants of gilding appear on the central string strip. There is no brass plate, and the inscription is instead written in black ink on the lower soundboard: *JOHN EGAN HARP MAKER / TO THE KING / AND ROYAL FAMILY / No 30 DAWSON ST DUBLIN / 1823*. Although possibly not the harp's original inscription, it does furnish the date of 1823 which corresponds with the delivery date of Anastasia's harp to Moore. S.C. Hall referred to 'Moore's harp in a time-worn ebony case',[83] and this extant harp also has a fitted mahogany case. It is lined in a red felt-like material, and a lidded compartment in the centre provides storage for strings and a tuning key. Presumably this is a smaller version of the wooden travelling cases normally supplied with Egan Portable Irish Harps.

INSTRUCTIONS FOR THE ROYAL PORTABLE IRISH HARP

Although Egan's Portable Irish Harp was advertised as idiomatic to playing pedal harp music, the Egan firm supplied books specially designated for the instrument. In 1822, John Egan's son Charles, who was a harpist, published an

---

81 William Ellis Horton, *Driftwood of the stage* (Detroit, 1904), p. 219.   82 *Cork Constitution*, 11 May 1889.   83 Hall, *American Bookseller*, 15:5 (1884), 227.

4.23 Small harp in travelling case by Egan. Photo by Nancy Hurrell, courtesy of private owner.

instruction booklet for the new harp model: *A new series of instructions arranged expressly for the Royal Portable Irish Harp invented by Mr John Egan.* In the booklet, the novice harpist finds useful sections on tuning and on how to obtain different key signatures on both the single-action and double-action Royal Portable Irish Harp, as well as exercises, preludes and pieces. Charles' introduction is primarily a grandiose commercial for his father's new invention, but it does offer a window into contemporary attitudes towards music-making:

> Of all the pleasures we enjoy from the exercise of our senses, there is none more delightful, more delicate, or capable of higher improvement than that which we perceive from the connection and complication of sweet sounds. The influence of melody over the feelings is too well known to be dwelt upon – it is innate in the constitution of man.[84]

84 Charles Egan, *A new series of instructions arranged expressly for the Royal Portable Irish Harp invented by*

4.24 Charles Egan, *A selection of ancient Irish melodies arranged for J. Egan's newly invented Royal Portable Irish Harp*, *c*.1822. Courtesy of the Irish Traditional Music Archive, Dublin.

He goes on to state that in no other period has musical industry and manufacture of musical instruments made such rapid strides towards 'improvement', and a brief summary of harp history steers the hypothesis towards his father's crowning invention. The Irish harp had advanced from its 'imperfect state' to its present capability without sacrificing its ancient shape and glorious nationality.[85] Charles Egan then quotes Moore's 'triumphant effusion' of 'Dear harp of my country' as an appropriate parallel to the work of the harp maker. In the music section of the book, a variety of Continental favourites such as 'French air' and 'Sul margine d'un Rio' are presented alongside national music like 'Irish melody', in the tune of 'Last rose of summer'. Charles Egan published another collection of Irish music in the same year, *A selection of ancient Irish melodies arranged for J. Egan's newly invented Royal Portable Irish Harp* featuring the favourites 'The young man's dream', 'Garry Owen', 'Langolee', 'Edmund of the hills', Carolan's 'Planxty Kelly' and others (figure 4.24). The style of the arrangements is generally a treble melody with simple chordal accompaniments in the bass and the use of occasional harmonics, a pedal harp technique for obtaining bell-like tones.[86]

Mr John Egan (Dublin, 1822), p. 3. **85** Ibid., p. 7. **86** Harmonics were championed by Charles Egan's teacher, N.C. Bochsa, who described them in his method book as produced by the 'fingers

The 1820s harpist now had an instructional tutor and music specifically arranged for the Royal Portable Irish Harp, and at the Egan manufactory on Dawson Street, every required harp appendage imaginable was sold: strings, tuning forks, harp keys, string gauges, music stools and sounding-boards to place underneath the harp for amplification. Egan, the inventor, also designed and produced special music desks that could 'turn over the leaves of music or other books, by the slightest touch of the pedal, without the assistance of the hand, or interruption to the performer'.[87] Another available accessory was the 'harp rest', designed to counteract the perceived grave, injurious effects on the female form resulting from playing the harp at an early age. (Sydney Owenson stated in her memoirs that as a young girl her figure was graceful and without the curvature that later developed from playing the harp.[88]) This perceived hazard of harp-playing could be easily prevented with Egan's device, which sustained 'the entire weight of the harp from off the performer' by holding the instrument in an upright position and could be 'attached to any harp or taken off it in a few seconds'.[89]

While the page-turner and harp rest attracted attention as temporary novelties, Egan's enduring invention was clearly the Royal Portable Irish Harp, with its chromatic capabilities. He was lauded for his technological innovation by London's premier harpist, N.C. Bochsa, who wrote to the maker:

> I have the pleasure in informing you, the Royal Portable Irish Harp invented by you has my decided approbation. Its peculiar sweetness of tone, so admirably adapted for accompanying the voice; the great facility of changing keys, and its portability, make it a desirable Instrument to proficients on the pedal Harp.[90]

The improving age of the early nineteenth century caused a flurry of new commercially opportunistic instruments to be invented by Edward Light and others, influencing the invention of Egan's novel dital mechanism at a time of

held vertically and lying almost against the strings, the fleshy part of the hand – just below the thumb – is pressed against the centre of the string, and the string is plucked by the thumb'. Bochsa's *Nouvelle méthode de harpe* [Paris, 1814], ed. and trans. Patricia John (Houston, 1993), p. 65. **87** *Freeman's Journal*, 1 June 1818.   **88** *Lady Morgan's memoirs*, i, p. 194.   **89** Charles Egan, *The royal harp director* (London, 1827). A few years earlier, the harpist N.C. Bochsa, Charles Egan's teacher, had invented the 'harp brace', a device to fix the harp at a constant angle of 20 degrees. The apparatus was screwed onto the bass of the harp between the pedals. Described in his *Nouvelle méthode de harpe* (Paris, c.1814), Bochsa claimed the device allowed young women to study the harp without the fear that the constant pressure on the right shoulder might twist their body (see chapter 6, pp 169–70).   **90** Charles Egan, *The royal harp director* p. 8.

active innovation. Whereas the dital-harp was short-lived, Egan's Portable Irish Harp fulfilled a greater cultural need.[91] The ultimate triumph of the instrument's longevity lay in its perceived symbolism linked to national identity, and for many, the vision of Irish airs played on a small Egan harp was an intangible link to the romanticized notions of 'Dear harp of my country'.

91 Only a distant relative of Light's dital-harp exists today: the harp-guitar. Its shape hints of Light's dital-harp, but the harp-guitar has reverted back to metal guitar strings, a flat guitar back and no ditals. See Gregg Miner's informative work on the harp-guitar at harpguitars.net.

5 / Royal appointments

Beyond the lighthouse and craggy island cliffs, the blue-grey sea stretched out as far as the eye could see, and on the hazy horizon, minute specks appeared and gradually morphed into the discernible shapes of sailing vessels. As they approached with white sails billowing, the ships glided past Ireland's Eye towards Howth harbour, where a small group of people had gathered on the pier one momentous Sunday afternoon, 12 August 1821. Rumours had circulated at morning church services of an important imminent arrival, prompting the congregation to hurry down to the pier. Apparently a royal carriage had been spotted in the village the night before, despatched by King George IV's private secretary, Sir Benjamin Bloomfield, who was still on the lookout nearby.[1] All signs seemed to indicate that the king would arrive that afternoon at Howth, rather than the appointed destination further south.

This was a surprising turn of events, for the king's yacht, the *Royal George*, was officially due to land in Dunleary and almost all of Dublin had made their way south that morning on foot, horseback or via one of the many carriages that formed a lengthy procession stretching several miles along the road. Thousands of spectators already lined the nearby shores and surrounding hills in a festive scene with many waving green banners and ribbons. On a crowded pier, the lord mayor, civic personages and noble ladies in their finery stood alongside people from all walks of life as they anxiously awaited the landing in Ireland of George IV (figure 5.1).[2] However, strong winds at Holyhead, his port of embarkation, had influenced the king's spontaneous decision to abandon the royal yacht altogether and travel instead on the *Lightning*, the new Post Office steam packet bound for Howth. Along with its twin the *Meteor*, the steam-powered vessel recently had been adopted to provide a faster postal service between Holyhead and Howth. The king, eager to be underway, had already been forced to delay his journey for a few days. Shocking news had reached him of the sudden illness and subsequent death of his estranged wife, Queen Caroline, and out of respect, the trip had been temporarily postponed. Now, in his bereavement, it seemed a fitting alternative to forego the public festivities at Dunleary for a more private

1 *Dublin Evening Post*, 14 Aug. 1821. 2 Ibid.

5.1 King George IV by Charles Turner, after Sir Thomas Lawrence, 1824. © National Portrait Gallery, London.

landing at Howth. Eager to travel incognito on the speedy *Lightning*, the king was actually in high spirits that day, for it was his fifty-ninth birthday. Once underway, he downed huge quantities of goose pie and whiskey punch with fellow travellers as they sang joyous songs![3]

3 Christopher Hibbert, *George IV, the rebel who would be king* (New York, 2007), p. 621.

At around half past four in the afternoon, a man at Howth with field glasses spied a wisp of smoke coming from the chimney of an approaching vessel. The angular, black *Lightning* came into view, slowly advanced and finally docked near the pier head. As the assembled crowd awaited news, suddenly a royal coach-and-four briskly advanced towards the pier. In due course, a figure emerged on the deck of the *Lightning*; distinctly dressed in blue trousers, a long blue coat, a black cravat and a travelling cap with a gold band, and the king was immediately recognized. A man on the pier shouted, 'The king! God save the king!', and the crowd erupted in ecstatic cheers, with ladies waving their handkerchiefs and gentlemen lifting their hats. It had been four hundred years since a reigning British monarch had made a state visit.

It was a grand arrival, despite the common Post Office steam packet, but the unusual and somewhat unorthodox mode of transport suited the temperament of this king. Hoping to enter the country unnoticed, the monarch was nonetheless moved by the cheers of the people gathered on Howth's pier, and he removed his cap, waving it with a flourish over his head several times. He made his way through the crowd, shaking hands with acquaintants Lord Kingston and Mr Bowes Daly, as well as strangers.[4] The royal carriage departed for Phoenix Park, followed by several gentlemen on horseback and dozens more on foot. When they reached the entrance to the demesne of the Viceregal Lodge,[5] servants attempted to close the gates against the following crowd. However, the king invited the cheering throng to follow him right up to the house, where he alighted from his carriage and gave a short speech professing that his heart had always been Irish and he had long wished to visit them, and it was one of the happiest days of his life.[6] To ensure a loyal public reception for the king, the Dublin press had published a series of favourable articles to promote the forthcoming royal visit. It is also apparent, however, that a certain fervour naturally spread throughout the country, and for several individuals, including members of the Egan family, the opportune state visit would affect their future.

It was significant that George IV had chosen Ireland for his first official state visit as king, and he seemed to be enormously popular in the country. Many remembered George's open opposition to the military force used against the Irish in 1797.[7] As a prince, George had long wished to visit the country and at one time he even entertained the improbable notion of residing in Ireland as

---

4 *Dublin Evening Post*, 14 Aug. 1821. 5 The Viceregal Lodge is now Áras an Uachtaráin (Irish for 'the President's House') and is the official residence of the president of Ireland. 6 See S. Hubert Burke, *Ireland sixty years ago: being an account of a visit to Ireland by H.M. George IV in the year 1821* (London, 1885). 7 For additional background information on George IV's visit and his relationship with Lady Conyngham, see Tom Ambrose, *The king and the vice queen: George IV's last*

the lord lieutenant. Several of the Irish members of parliament were part of the king's Carlton House set in London.[8] His private secretary, Sir Benjamin Bloomfield, was Irish, and the British foreign secretary, Lord Castlereagh, marquess of Londonderry, was Dublin-born. And the person closest to the king, his mistress Lady Elizabeth Conyngham, had a country estate in Ireland and would certainly have relished the idea of a state visit. She was married to an Irish peer, the 1st Marquess Conyngham, and their Irish residence was the majestic Slane Castle in Co. Meath. Overlooking the river Boyne, Slane would prove to be an idyllic secluded getaway for the king and his mistress during the royal stay, and her obliging husband quietly endorsed the arrangement.

The king's trip to Ireland was seen as an extension of the celebrations surrounding his recent coronation ceremony which had taken place in Westminster Abbey just three weeks before. In Dublin, an atmosphere of pomp and circumstance pervaded all aspects of city life, from decorated buildings and commemorative souvenir medals to endless rounds of planned coronation balls, banquets and concerts. Besides the uplifting euphoria of three weeks of celebrations during the king's stay in Ireland, the visit also generated a whole host of economic and social advantages, although some were more lasting than others. People in all walks of life anticipated direct or indirect benefits befitting their status. For the aristocracy, there would be social honours bestowed, while Dublin's middle-class merchants expected handy profits from the influx of visitors. Even the Catholic nobility and bishops came to town, hoping the king would grant Catholic emancipation.[9] However, he was not interested in issuing substantive political proclamations, but instead preferred to present a grand show of kingly benevolence. Noncontroversial gestures of goodwill were carried out by the king's private secretary, such as the distribution of money, clothing, and small farm animals to the poor. For many more, the mere presence of royalty, nobility and thousands of spectators pouring into the city caused an economic boon. Houses were let and merchants stocked up on high-end provisions for the visiting aristocracy. In the weeks leading up to the state visit, labourers were employed to prepare the roads and construction workers and craftsmen were engaged in the burgeoning building projects in town and country. The spacious Round Room was added to Dublin's Mansion House to accommodate guests for a grand banquet. Likewise, lords of country houses added on Gothic-style banquet rooms with exquisite fan-vaulted ceilings in

scandalous affair (Stroud, 2005). **8** Carlton House was George's official residence as prince regent. **9** William Gregory, *Mr Gregory's letter-box, 1813–1830*, ed. Lady Gregory (London, 1898), p. 151. Lord Talbot made the observation in a letter to Mr Gregory, and although hopes were raised,

anticipation of staging royal dinners. Sumptuous new royal bedchambers were also made ready in hopes of personally hosting the sovereign,[10] and at the Viceregal Lodge, a new bed was ordered. In Dublin Castle, a new throne and wall hangings were brought in to refurbish the Presence Chamber,[11] where the court levees, or receptions, would take place, with members of the nobility and gentry being formally presented to the king.

A veritable whirlwind of social activities was announced, from dinners and garden parties to a series of balls held at the Rotunda under the patronage of the lord lieutenant. A highlight of the state visit was the grand installation ceremony of the knights of the Order of St Patrick, where the king would bestow the high order of chivalry to nine select peers, followed by a formal dinner in Dublin Castle. It was essential to be dressed fashionably in the approved manner for these important occasions, and an announcement in the press conveyed the king's wish that all should approach him dressed in 'Irish manufacture'.[12] The request for Irish-made apparel proved a tremendous stimulus to local cloth manufacturers, and adverts for Irish materials dotted the newspapers. In the *Dublin Evening Post*, George Willis and Co., merchant tailors, announced an ample supply of superior cloth locally manufactured in Kilkenny for court dresses on the occasion of the king's visit.[13] The firm of Henry and John Smith also invited the nobility and gentry to inspect their Irish linen and damask cloth.[14] A penchant for Irish jewellery led to a similar boon for craftsmen and jewellers, who profited by creating special commemorative broaches. Jacob West and Co., goldsmiths and jewellers, advertised 'Coronation Broaches' along with their stock of diamond necklaces, bracelets and head ornaments to be had 'on the most liberal terms',[15] and the jeweller Mullen designed a desirable 'Royal Welcome Brooch', a fastening ornament that was emblematic of the king's visit.[16] John Egan, meanwhile, was also busily engaged in overseeing the finishing touches on harps to be played for the monarch at several state functions, and the astute maker also had a plan to present a truly exceptional gift to the king.

After arriving at Phoenix Park, George IV spent his first few days in seclusion at the Viceregal Lodge (figure 5.2) as a mark of respect for the late queen. The king's public entry into Dublin was planned for later in the week, at which time the official events would commence. Meanwhile, the king was

---

Catholic emancipation was not granted until 1829.   10 At Castle Coole a state bedroom was completed in anticipation of a royal visit but George IV did not stay there. Two other examples of banquet and ballrooms built in the Gothic style in 1821 to impress the king are Slane Castle and Annesbrook.   11 Gregory, *Mr Gregory's Letter-box*, pp 144–6.   12 Burke, *Ireland sixty years ago*, p. 29. 13 *Dublin Evening Post*, 11 Aug. 1821.   14 *Freeman's Journal*, 23 Aug. 1821.   15 *Dublin Evening Post*, 11 Aug. 1821.   16 *Freeman's Journal*, 23 Aug. 1821.

5.2 Nineteenth-century view of the Viceregal Lodge, Phoenix Park, where Charles Egan played an Egan Irish harp for George IV. Alamy.

reunited with Lady Conyngham and their inner circle of friends, and a few private dinners and engagements took place at the lodge. On the king's second night in Ireland, the stately residence was filled with the lively sounds of Irish music played on harp and pianoforte. The event was reported in the press:

> Yesterday evening his majesty was graciously pleased to have at the palace, Phoenix Park, Mr Willis, of the Harmonic Saloon, and Mr Egan, pupil of Bochsa, to perform before his majesty on the pianoforte and harp, several pieces of exquisite music. Our gracious sovereign was pleased to command that none but Irish airs should be performed.[17]

Isaac Willis, well known in Dublin music circles, was a concert promoter who had organized a special series for the royal visit. He was also the proprietor of a major music business in Westmoreland Street, the Harmonic Saloon and Musical Circulating Library, which stocked over a thousand different titles of sheet music and also imported musical instruments from London, primarily pianofortes.[18] Performing with Willis was Charles Egan, John Egan's harpist son, who was currently studying in London with the most celebrated harpist in

---

17 *Yorkshire Gazette*, 25 Aug. 1821; news item within article is dated 14 Aug.   **18** *Saunders's Newsletter*, 8 Apr. 1820. Willis imported pianofortes by Broadwood, Clementi, Goulding and others, and harps by Erard, Dizi and Dodd, and he also sold Egan harps.

5.3 N.C. Bochsa, harpist to the royal family. Illustration in Bochsa's *Nouvelle méthode de harpe*, 1814.

England, N.C. Bochsa (1789–1856) (figure 5.3). A famous French virtuoso, N.C. Bochsa had served both Napoleon and Louis XVIII from 1813–16 and was presently the favourite harpist of George IV. Charles and his harp teacher had travelled together from London and were staying at Egan's premises on Dawson Street.[19] As part of the visiting royal entourage, Bochsa was making his Dublin debut and was billed as a headliner for the grand coronation concerts organized by Mr Willis. Four concert performances at the Theatre Royal were planned, and Charles Egan was also listed on the programme as an accompanist to the singers.[20] It seems Charles Egan's flourishing career in music was a fortuitous by-product of the environment in which he was raised. With a famous master harp builder for a father, Charles was afforded exceptional opportunities to develop his skills on the instrument. He seemed to reap the social benefits of John Egan's well-heeled connections, for a familiarity with his father's aristocratic patrons inevitably opened doors for the son.

19 Ibid., 7 Aug. 1821.   20 Ibid., 17 Aug. 1821.

5.4 Charles Egan, *Ancient Irish melodies: as performed by express command before His Most Gracious Majesty George the Fourth during his memorable visit to Ireland, c.1822.* Courtesy of Beinecke Rare Book & Manuscript Library, Yale University.

The young Charles Egan's charmed journey had now led to this moment of playing before the king at the Viceregal Lodge. Instead of Bochsa, it was his Irish pupil Charles who performed in this intimate setting, honouring the monarch's request for only Irish airs to be played that evening. Fresh from his sea voyage, George IV was filled with gratitude to finally be in Ireland and appreciated the Irish music-making at this happy time. As the twilight faded, the chandelier candles would have cast a soft glow on the rich green satin damask walls of the state drawing room as Egan and Willis played their vibrant and soulful tunes, one after another. The flickering light would have illuminated the ceiling's gold ornate plaster-relief, matched by the sheen of gilt ornament on the harp played by Charles. The informal gathering was an opportune occasion to demonstrate the sound and appearance of the Portable Irish Harp.[21] Charles showcased his father's new model that evening, as evinced in the title of a book of harp arrangements he published the following year: *Ancient Irish melodies*: as performed by express command before his most gracious majesty George the fourth during his memorable visit to Ireland* (figure 5.4). The asterisk is explained near the bottom of the title page: **They are particularly adopted for the newly invented Royal*

---

21 It can be assumed with confidence that an Egan empire-style pedal harp also stood in the elegant Viceregal drawing room, for J. Egan had regularly received commissions from Phoenix Park.

Portable Irish Harp.[22] The Irish airs arranged for harp are: 'Erin go Bragh', 'The sprig of Shillelah', 'Groves of Blarney', 'Aileen Aroon', 'The rose tree', 'Gramachree', 'My lodging', 'The legacy', 'Coulin', 'Pay the reckoning', 'Lost is my quiet', and 'The moreen'. From this extraordinary souvenir of the evening, it is possible to imagine a sound picture of Charles Egan playing on his Egan harp before George IV at the Viceregal Lodge. With the performance, the seeds were sown for further honours to come.

On Friday, 17 August, the king officially entered Dublin under the specially constructed city gates at Sackville (O'Connell) Street. It was a fine day, thousands turned out to welcome the monarch, and many waved banners and streamers in blue, the official 'welcoming colour'. Likewise, George IV, dressed in full military uniform, wore the ceremonial blue ribbon and badge of the Order of St Patrick. The multitudes of spectators halted the royal procession of carriages, and the king stood in his barouche bowing to the masses and pointing to the shamrocks decorating his hat, then touching his heart. In celebration of the visit, the buildings in the city and the surrounding suburbs were festooned with flags, bouquets of flowers, blue and white ribbons and loyal catch-phrases of welcome. Mr Willis' music shop displayed three blue flags with popular slogans in gold: 'Erin rejoice', 'A hundred thousand welcomes' and 'Erin's sons, behold your king'.[23] At nightfall on Friday and Saturday, an enchanting scene was created with special illuminations of public buildings, shops and houses. Coloured lights filled windows, and specially made transparencies, or lit-up images, were projected onto buildings by magic lanterns.[24] On these two nights carriages were generally prohibited so that citizens could freely stroll the streets to admire the incredible light show. Many of the illuminations featured portraits of George IV in his coronation robes and scenes of the king arriving in Ireland. Other common themes were crowns and Hibernia holding a harp. John Egan's Dawson Street house was described in the press as having particularly splendid harp-themed transparencies on display. One reviewer wrote: 'No private house was decorated with more brilliancy, taste, effect, and as truly classical than this.'[25] In the left area, a crown shed its rays over the emblems of the arts, sciences and commerce, and underneath was an 'exquisitely executed harp'. On the right, Britannia was pictured with a shield, lion and cornucopia, along with the union symbols of shamrocks, roses and thistles. And

22 Charles Egan, *Ancient Irish melodies* (London, 1822). This is the only occasion mentioned in the press of Charles Egan playing Irish music for the king during his visit to Ireland.   23 *Morning Post*, 24 Aug. 1821.   24 The lantern slide, a small sheet of glass with a painted picture, was magnified by a mirror at the back of an oil lamp and projected onto the building or window. 25 Anonymous, *The royal visit, containing a full and circumstantial account of every thing connected with the king's visit to Ireland* (Dublin, 1821), p. 58. Also, *Morning Post*, 24 Aug. 1821.

in the centre, the sovereign in his royal robes was seated on a throne, as Hibernia was 'presenting a portable Irish Harp, beautifully illuminated' to the king, while a bard 'dressed in ancient costume' observed. Above the main transparency, yet another harp was depicted, in the size and shape of the famed Brian Boru harp in Trinity College, and on either side of it were the initials *G. IV. R.* and 'over all a splendid imperial crown'.[26]

Egan's illuminated picture of the king receiving a Portable Irish Harp might be seen as art imitating life in that Charles Egan, a sort of modern-day bard, had introduced and played the Portable Irish harp to his majesty just days before. But it would be truer to say the picture was ultimately a case of life imitating art, for the scene cleverly foretold Egan's imminent plan. Within days, a 'beautifully illuminated' Portable Irish Harp *was* presented to the king. On 22 August, a report in the *Freeman's Journal* conveyed the news that Mr Egan had made a very special harp for his majesty. The 'superb Portable Irish Harp' capable of making key changes and displaying 'exquisite workmanship' was fashioned in a strikingly unusual form. According to the correspondent,

> The instrument, is quite characteristic of the country – the curved pillar represents the figure of Hibernia, with a wreath of shamrocks round her head – the neck of the harp that contains the machinery, forms a wing that springs from her shoulders, terminating in a beautiful curve, surmounted by the British crown. The colour of the harp an emerald green, ornamented with gold shamrocks. The pins in the sounding board inlaid with Irish diamonds. [...] Richly engraved in the brass machinery is the mighty monarch's name – the inventor has manufactured it for, and the memorable and happy era for Ireland, 1821 – and in this specimen of native ingenuity and talent, after ages may see the great perfection the arts had arrived to in Ireland, in the reign of the beloved, George the Fourth.[27]

The circumstances of the actual presentation of the harp to the king are unknown, but the direct after-effect of the resplendent gift to his majesty is clear. Seven days later, a letter to Egan arrived from the king's secretary, Bloomfield, bearing an important communication from his majesty:

> Sir Benjamin Bloomfield presents his compliments to Mr Egan, and is commanded to acquaint him, that the king approves of the harps, and is much gratified by his dutiful attention. Sir Benjamin has further to communicate, that orders have been given to appoint Mr Egan, harp maker to his majesty. – Stephen's-Green, 29 Aug. 1821.[28]

26 Ibid., pp 58–9.   27 *Freeman's Journal*, 22 Aug. 1821.   28 *Dublin Evening Post*, 1 Sept. 1821.

5.5 Announcement of John Egan's appointment as 'harp maker to his majesty' in the *Dublin Evening Post*, 1 Sept. 1821.

Announced in the press (figure 5.5), the royal endorsement of John Egan harps was highly significant on both sides of the Irish Sea. With a royal warrant, the harp firm was afforded the highest reputation attainable at the time and was assured of extraordinary notoriety for years to come. Royal appointments were awarded to only a few select tradesmen who were already regularly supplying high-quality goods and services to the royal household, and evidence suggests that this was the case for Egan. In the previous year, the harp maker had begun a trade relationship with the crown, according to a mention in the press stating orders for Egan harps had arrived 'from the royal palaces of Carlton House and Hampton Court'.[29] The introduction of Egan harps to the king's palaces was most likely engineered by Bochsa, harpist to the royal family. By 1821, Charles Egan was residing with Bochsa at his residence, 2 Bryanstone Street in London, and Egan harps were advertised as sold from this address.[30] Thus, the king was already acquainted with Egan harps, but the presentation of the special golden winged-maiden harp was the masterstroke that secured the coveted appointment.

29 *Morning Post*, 25 Sept. 1820, reprinted from the *Freeman's Journal*. Details of the harps supplied to Carlton House and Hampton Court palace are not known. The Royal Archives at Windsor Castle confirmed in a 29 October 2014 communication that there are no Egan harps remaining in the Royal Collection.   30 *Morning Post*, 5 June 1821.

HARP MAKER TO HIS MOST GRACIOUS MAJESTY

Egan also broadcasted the news of his award in the *Freeman's Journal* on 29 August:

> The appointment of Mr Egan, of this city, to be harp maker to his majesty, has given universal satisfaction, and is a further proof of his majesty's gracious disposition to reward merit – the perseverance and ability this distinguished artist has displayed these number of years in improving the harp, is highly creditable to himself – and the History of Dublin and other works has made honourable mention of his successful exertions.[31]

As custom permitted, Egan's newspaper adverts from this time on included the phrase 'by appointment' and also the eye-catching royal coat of arms. From 1821, the brass plates on Egan harps were engraved with *Harp Maker by Special Appointment To His Most Gracious Majesty George IV*.[32] By 1823, the dedication was extended to include *& the Royal Family*, and from 1825, inscriptions were lengthened to become *Harp Maker by Authority of the ROYAL WARRANT To His Most Gracious Majesty George IV & the Royal Family* (figures 5.6 and 5.7).[33] The Portable Irish Harp model was duly renamed the *Royal* Portable Irish Harp, and Egan adverts now touted, 'patronized by the king' and mentioned that Egan harps had 'attracted the notice and obtained the approbation of majesty itself'.[34]

A time honoured tradition dating back to medieval times, royal warrants were awarded by members of the royal family to a wide range of manufacturers and tradesmen. George IV issued warrants to wine merchants, comb manufacturers, button makers, pottery firms and many others. However, for musical instrument makers, there seem to have been relatively few royal appointments bestowed by the king. Broadwood pianos, warrant holders since the early 1700s, advertised as 'Pianoforte Manufacturers to King George IV', and the delivery in 1821 of a Broadwood pianoforte to the Brighton Pavilion is

---

31 *Freeman's Journal*, 29 Aug. 1821. The mention of the 'History of Dublin' refers to the 1818 publication by Warburton, Whitelaw and Walsh which praises John Egan's harp innovations. 32 A few Royal Portable Irish Harps have the inscription painted on the soundboard rather than engraved on a brass plate.   33 Inscriptions align with dates in my catalogue of John Egan harps (appendix 3). A rare example in the NMI is a pedal harp, no. 1918, with an engraved inscription on the brass plate, *Harp Maker by Special Appointment*, as well as a small brass banner attached to the opposite brass plate stamped *by Authority of the Royal Warrant*, presumably added later when the official warrant was received. The warrant has not survived and predates warrant records. Pippa Dutton, assistant secretary of the Royal Warrant Holders Association, confirmed by email on 2 May 2008 that records do not go back as far as George IV.   34 *Freeman's Journal*, 17 Jan. 1822.

5.6 (*left*) Royal warrant and crest engraved on the brass plate of an Egan Royal Portable Irish Harp. Photo by Nancy Hurrell, courtesy of the Irish Collection, John J. Burns Library, Boston College.   5.7 (*right*) Royal warrant and crest painted on an Egan Royal Portable Irish Harp in the Museum of Fine Arts, Boston (formerly in a private collection). Photo by Nancy Hurrell.

documented.[35] Sébastien Erard had been granted patronage from the royal family earlier in the century, and apparently he was harp maker to Caroline, George's estranged wife. According to the Erard stock books, Princess Caroline commissioned a pedal harp from the firm in 1800.[36] By 1817, Erard harps were likewise endorsed by Princess Charlotte, the daughter of Caroline and George IV.[37] Several Erard Grecian pedal harps display the engraved inscription *Maker by Special Appointment to His Majesty and the Royal Family*, which suggests a royal warrant, although there is a noticeable lack of a dedication to 'George IV' on harps from this maker.[38] In light of the seemingly limited number of royal warrants awarded to musical instrument makers and the selectivity of the process, Egan's appointment is significant. The accolade bestowed upon Egan was well-deserved considering the quarter of a century he had devoted to the design and production of innovative harp models. The coincidental visit of George IV to Ireland and the king's attachment to the Irish people may also have played a part in the auspicious appointment.

35 'John Broadwood & Sons', broadwood.co.uk/history.html.   36 Elizabeth Wells and Chris Nobbs, *European stringed instruments* (London, 2007), p. 44. A famous portrait in the Royal Collection depicts Princess Caroline tuning her Erard harp. *Caroline, princess of Wales, and Princess Charlotte* was painted by Thomas Lawrence in 1801. See royalcollection.org.uk.   37 An 1816 Erard harp in the collection of Rosemary Hallo is inscribed *Maker to HRH the Princess Charlotte of Wales*, in Hallo, 'Erard, Bochsa and their impact on harp music-making in Australia (1830–66): an early history from documents' (PhD, University of Adelaide, 2014), p. 24. Also, an Erard advertisement carried the endorsement, 'Sebastian Erard, Harpmaker to her Royal Highness the Princess Charlotte of Coburg' in the *Dublin Evening Post*, 11 Nov. 1817. Princess Charlotte had married Prince Leopold of Saxe-Coburg the year before, and unfortunately she lost her life in childbirth around the time this advert appeared.   38 In Adelson et al., *The history of the Erard piano and harp*, i, p. 10,

THE WINGED-MAIDEN HARPS

Portable Irish Harps, RAM Museum, London and Museo dell'Arpa (Salvi Museum), Italy
Two rare Egan Portable Irish Harps, each in a winged-maiden form, still survive in museum collections.[39] The one in the Royal Academy of Music Museum, London (plates 18–20), is believed to be a prototype for the harp presented to the king, presumably the one in the collection at the Victor Salvi Museum (Museo dell'Arpa) in Piasco, Italy (plates 21, 22).[40] Each of these two harps is extraordinary as an art object and also as an historical artefact of Irish culture. An impressive display of craftsmanship, the innovative harp design is loaded with Irish symbolism. The striking figure on the pillar is Hibernia, the female personification of Ireland. She wears a wreath of shamrocks, understood as a native Irish crown, and the instrument is painted in the green shade of the Emerald Isle and adorned with gold shamrocks. This clever, playable symbol of Ireland was the ultimate souvenir of the king's visit.

The two surviving harps are almost identical in form, but each instrument bears its own unique inscription. The harp design has a characteristic Irish bowed pillar, and Hibernia's wings form the neck. Similar to other portable harps, the rounded back of the soundbox is made like a smaller version of a pedal harp, and it has four pairs of elongated sound holes. But beyond this, the harp shape is really quite new, for the back of the harp is actually taller than the front. Usually the highest point of a harp is the top front of the pillar. However on this model an elongated knee-block section seems to defy standard harp construction. Its elegantly curved extension rises dramatically towards the pillar, culminating in a scroll.

The extraordinary shape serves a symbolic purpose, for a small golden crown is attached to the top of the scroll on the Salvi harp (no crown survives on the RAM harp). In this clever design, Egan managed to place the British crown 'above' Hibernia, signifying British sovereignty over Ireland, thus replicating the

a royal privilege awarded by George IV to the Erard firm in 1829 is mentioned, but it is unclear whether it applied to the harp or the piano. One example of an English-made Erard harp with 'by special appointment to his majesty' in the inscription is in the collection at the Fitzwilliam Museum in Cambridge, England. The harp, inscribed *Patent N.3908*, dates to 1826, according to the London Erard stock books.   **39** The RAM Museum harp was restored by Michael Parfett and Yuqi Chock, London, in 2015 and is exhibited in the museum.   **40** The Salvi Museum prefers to keep the provenance of their Egan harp private. The RAM harp was bequeathed to the academy in 1899 by Mrs E.R. Hastings-Parker, with the accompanying note: 'Together with one more the only exactly similar ... in existence also by Egan made to present to George IV on his visit to Ireland ... Pegs studded with Irish diamonds, tone very sweet, and it will be observed that the compass is that of the old single-action French harp. Played by resting in a small rest ...

iconic symbols seen on flags and coinage of the period whereby a winged-maiden harp appears under a British crown with the name 'Hibernia' stamped next to it. How curious that such a harp, fashioned as Hibernia, once understood as an emblem for Irish independence, should be presented to the king of England. However, the winged-maiden certainly had multiple meanings, and at the time of George IV's seemingly unprecedented popularity in Ireland, the British imagery of crowns, roses and thistles happily merged with Hibernia, shamrocks and harps.

The winged-maiden harp design also exhibits characteristics of the fashionable neoclassical style. In the sculptural tradition of classical antiquity, Hibernia is sublime and expressionless and wears a Grecian gown. The hem is artistically tied in a knot, and at each shoulder, the sash morphs into oak leaves spiralling around a rosette. Hibernia's hair is styled in a chignon bun, with locks artfully draped down her neck. The decorative motives on the soundbox and pillar combine neoclassical anthemion and acanthus with native shamrocks, all in gold. The emerald-green background is a brilliant, lustrous colour due to the special japanning technique used, wherein gold leaf was applied as a base under the green lacquer.[41] The gilded figure and wings create a rich, 'illuminated' effect. Parts of the wings are cast in brass, and a handy panel of the wing can be removed to access the rods underneath. Both harps are equipped with Egan's dital mechanism, with *fourchette* discs on the neck operated by ivory ditals on the inner pillar for changing pitches and keys. Inside the soundbox of the RAM harp is a retractable rod, and the harp survives with a small stand decorated in the same style and colours of the harp, with vines of shamrocks on the top surface and acanthus leaves on the base. The RAM harp is a little taller (103.9cm) than the Salvi harp (102.5cm), and the RAM harp has twenty-nine strings, one more than the Salvi harp. The string pegs are studded with Irish diamonds.[42]

The most striking contrast between the two instruments appears in their differing inscriptions. The Salvi harp has a gold heraldic shield attached to the upper surface of the neck, nestled between the two wings. The inscription is *This improved Irish harp was invented & made by John Egan, Dublin, & his two sons John & Charles Egan, 1820.* The RAM harp is without a shield, and instead, has a painted gold-leaf inscription on the lower soundboard. On the left (facing) is *J EGAN/*

and ribbons round the neck to keep it in place, 1899.'   41 The layer of gold leaf as a base for japanning to produce a brilliant effect was discovered during the restoration of the RAM Egan harp by Michael Parfett and Yuqi Chock in 2015. The process is described in William N. Brown, *Handbook on japanning* (London, 1913).   42 On the RAM harp, the Irish diamonds in the string pegs were examined in 2003 by Graham Wells of Sothebys and were found to be made of paste, which would make sense on a prototype instrument.

INVENTOR/ 30 DAWSON ST./ DUBLIN, and on the right is *MAKER/ by Special Appointment/ TO HIS MOST GRACIOUS/ MAJESTY/ GEORGE IV*. His signature appears again, above the soundboard on the inner knee block as, *JOHN EGAN/ INVENTOR/DUBLIN*. The disparate inscriptions on the two harps raise some interesting questions. The theory is that the academy's harp was the prototype for a second harp made for the king. The sequence of events suggests that Egan's appointment as harp maker to the king resulted from having gained his majesty's favour with the gift of the harp. The question then arises, why would the prototype be inscribed with 'maker by special appointment' if it was made prior to the king's visit and before the appointment was actually granted? Perhaps the harp is not actually the prototype, but was made at a later date? Another, more plausible, explanation is that the inscription was added later, after the king's visit. It's even conceivable that the harp might have been used as a marketing device for Egan's shop window on Dawson Street following George IV's visit. It would have been quite an attraction to display a *copy* of the famous gold harp played in the royal palace, and the inscription would advertise Egan's prestigious new appointment. However, there is still another puzzling issue. The Salvi harp lacks any royal dedication to George IV. The announcement in the newspaper in 1821 described the king's harp as, 'richly engraved in the brass machinery is the Mighty Monarch's name'. Neither the RAM harp nor the Salvi harp have the monarch's name 'engraved in the brass machinery'.

The succession of ownership for each winged-maiden harp has yet to be fully documented. Nonetheless, proof of a winged-maiden harp played at court exists in a painting by Sir Thomas Lawrence (1769–1830), George IV's royal portrait painter. In 1824, Lawrence completed a set of two paintings of the daughters of the Marchioness Conyngham. Lady Maria Conyngham appears in her portrait with her favourite dog, and Lady Elizabeth Conyngham is pictured tuning the iconic winged-maiden harp (plate 23).[43] The painting shows the common practice of attaching a ribbon with a decorative bow to the portable harp to act as a strap, and it also shows the harp resting on a padded stand. The portrait is not only a tribute to the recognized fine appearance of the instrument but also provides important historical documentation of the harp's presence in the royal household.

---

43 The painting is currently in the Calouste Gulbenkian Museum, Portugal. Unfortunately, in Roslyn Rensch's *Three centuries of harpmaking* (2002), the sitter in the painting was misidentified as her mother, George IV's mistress, also named Lady Elizabeth Conyngham. And, similarly, in Adelson et al. (eds), *The history of the Erard piano and harp*, ii, p. 762, the painting appears with the sitter cited as a 'mistress of George IV and client of the Erard firm', in spite of the fact the portrait features the younger Lady Elizabeth playing an Egan harp.

HARP MUSIC FOR THE ROYAL VISIT

A remarkable range of Egan models, from gut-strung pedal and portable Irish harps to wire-strung Irish revival harps were played in performances during the monarch's visit. The most highly publicized musical events were undoubtedly the four grand coronation concerts held at the new Theatre Royal. In addition to Bochsa and Charles Egan, in hopes of attracting large audiences, the promoter, Mr Willis, engaged local favourites Miss Cheese and Mrs Vincent, and also imported Covent Garden legend Miss Stephens, as well as Monsieur Begrez, a tenor from London's King's Theatre.[44] Other vocalists, Mr Duruset and Mr Rolle, were leading performers from the London Philharmonic Concerts, and guest instrumentalists included professional players of violin, flute, clarinet and pianoforte. The eclectic concert programme opened with Haydn's *Grand symfonia*, followed by a succession of Italian opera selections by Mozart and Rossini, and inserted in between were several lighter 'glees', such as 'Young lovers'. It was in 'Hark Apollo strikes the lyre' that Charles Egan made his brief appearance, accompanying singers on harp, but the harp celebrity of the evening was clearly his teacher, Bochsa. It's noteworthy that in this mainly vocal programme, Bochsa was featured in two prominent segments playing harp solos. Bochsa's 'Grand military concerto' (with full accompaniments) closed the first half of the show, and in the second half, the harpist had the honour of performing the last piece on the programme before the finale. The pride of place in the concert order reflected the high regard for both the artist and the instrument, and his dazzling harp skills apparently did not disappoint. Bochsa's composition 'Irish air, with variations' was conspicuously one of only two Irish pieces on the programme, the other being 'Song of Ireland – the prince of our love, George our father and king', a vocal piece in the genre of Moore's *Irish melodies*. Sung by Miss Stephens, the contemporary lyrics honoured the king and were set to an old Irish melody. In similar fashion, Bochsa's harp solo was based on an Irish melody, but beyond the initial theme, the variations were presented through a European 'classical' filter. The harpist's trademark compositional method was to employ virtuosic techniques to create a showpiece in the style of Continental art music in which each progressive variation was ever more impressive than the last, with increasingly rapid arpeggios combined with glistening harmonics. Presenting a native Irish tune in this elegant manner on a pedal harp was pleasing to Anglo-Irish ears, and the reviewer in *Saunders's Newsletter* stated that the harpist had 'enraptured and astonished every individual present' with his compositions, confirming his legendary reputation as 'the first

---

44 *Saunders's Newsletter*, 17 Aug. 1821.

performer in the world' on the harp.[45] One correspondent years later described Bochsa's extraordinary command of the instrument:

> The harp in his hands is full of splendid effects; it is capable of infinite variety in power and quality of tone, full of delicacy and of lyric fire [...] His hands wander all over the strings and produce sounding arpeggios, rapid sparkling passage above, and harmonics as pure and silvery as we may imagine to come from the golden wired harps of the cherubins.[46]

A token Irish melody played on an exquisite harp was assured of success in Dublin, and it mattered not that it was played in a decidedly Continental style and performed by a Frenchman. At least the harp on which Bochsa created his magic for the coronation concerts was Irish-made, for he performed on a double-action pedal harp by Egan. Based on surviving instruments from the period, it would have had an imposing presence on stage, with a gold column and a crowned capital with dancing Grecian figures holding lyres. On the body there would have been further ornate Grecian figures painted in gold on perhaps a blue lacquer ground, and the harp would have had a standard height of 170cm and forty-three strings. It is a tribute to the harp's quality of construction and strength of tone that it successfully projected in the substantial 2,000 seat Theatre Royal concert hall in Hawkins Street. Bochsa seems to have been so pleased with the instrument loaned to him that afterwards he placed an order for an Egan pedal harp, to be delivered to his house in London.[47] The virtuoso's letter to Egan, reprinted as an ad in the *Freeman's Journal*, stated, 'Of your double action pedal harps I have given a convincing proof of their merits, by playing on one of your make on Friday, at the coronation concerts, Theatre Royal.'

Audiences were offered another opportunity to hear Bochsa's harp-playing in a 'grand installation oratorio' held in St Patrick's cathedral on 30 August 1821. In the cathedral just two days before, George IV had presided over the installation ceremony of the Order of St Patrick. This aspect of the royal visit had caused a frenzied 'scramble for honours', for there was great competition for the limited number of places. The Irish honour had been instituted in 1783 by George III as 'the Most Illustrious Order of St Patrick', the Irish equivalent of the Order of the Rose in England and the Order of the Thistle in Scotland. To be made a knight was evidence of high social standing, and with it came the privilege of wearing a large ceremonial medal with the eight-pointed star of St Patrick surrounding a shamrock on a red saltire.[48] The ceremony exhibited the

---

45 *Saunders's Newsletter*, 20 Aug. 1821.   46 *American Review; a Whig journal devoted to politics, literature, art and science*, 6 (1847), 549.   47 *Freeman's Journal*, 31 Oct. 1821. In the letter, Bochsa also orders a Royal Portable Irish Harp and a triple-action pedal harp.   48 A saltire is a diagonal cross.

pageantry of romantic chivalry in olden days, with the knights donning helmets and carrying swords and spears, while the wives of the honourees also contributed to the magnificent display:

> Such an assemblage has been but seldom witnessed in Dublin; – the number of towering plumes of ostrich feathers, contrasted with the dark locks from which they seem to spring; the richness of the tiaras … the brilliancy of the diamonds … presented a constellation of beauty and brilliance. The prevailing colours of the ladies' dresses and feathers were light blue and white, corresponding with those of the knights.[49]

Installation events included the dinner at Dublin Castle, a ball at the Rotunda, and a concert in the cathedral. The installation oratorio afforded a chance to experience the 'splendid state of the cathedral' as seen for the recent installation, with branches hung from the Gothic ceiling and blue cloths draped on the floors. Bochsa presented a harp solo on the programme of sacred vocal works by Beethoven, Haydn, Mozart, and Handel, including the 'Hallelujah chorus'.[50]

A much anticipated highlight of the king's state visit was the Grand Corporation Banquet held on the 23 August at the Mansion House on Dawson Street. The new Round Room had been built in just six weeks for the purpose of entertaining George IV. An architectural marvel, it was constructed without pillars, and it had an impressive diameter of 90ft.[51] The banquet space was designed to represent a Moorish palace open to the sky. John Wilson Croker gave a glowing description of the scene: 'It was lighted by a vast circle of light, hung by invisible wires, which had a wonderfully curious and fine effect.'[52] The gallery was filled with music, and the ladies wore Spanish dresses in bright blue silk. Upon the king's arrival, the lord mayor toasted him and the orchestra played 'God save the king'. Later in the evening the national anthem was thrillingly sung by Miss Stephens and the other London vocalists. The tables were covered in a 'profusion of all the delicacies of the season' and 'Champagne corks stormed the ceiling' on this historic night.[53]

The function, sponsored by the city of Dublin, also highlighted Ireland's own native musicians. A group of four Irish harpers presented a programme of traditional Irish melodies for the king, 'introduced with appropriate regard to our national character, performed with feeling and taste until a late hour in the night'.[54] One harper who performed, Valentine Rainey, was said to have been

49 Anonymous, *The royal visit* (Dublin, 1821), p. 108.   **50** *Freeman's Journal*, 30 Aug. 1821.   **51** Revd G.N. Wright, *An historical guide to ancient and modern Dublin* (London, 1821), p. 208.   **52** John Wilson Croker, *The Croker papers*, ed. Louis J. Jennings (New York, 1884), p. 189.   **53** *Freeman's Journal*, 24 Aug. 1821.   **54** Ibid.

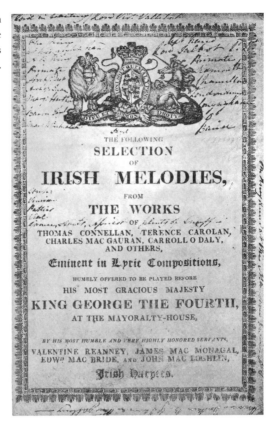

5.8 Printed programme of Irish harpers performing before George IV, in R.B. Armstrong's *Musical instruments*, i, 1904.

dressed as an ancient bard.[55] A robed and caped bardic figure plucking a plainly built wire-strung harp may have appeared as a curious relic to the king and his English entourage, but to the Dublin civic personages, the Irish harpers symbolized a cherished aspect of national identity. A rare programme of the evening, reprinted in the first volume of R.B. Armstrong's *Musical instruments* (figure 5.8), documents the harpers and the music performed, which included Irish melodies by Thomas Connellan, Terence Carolan, Charles MacGauran and Carroll O'Daly as played by Rainey, James MacMonagal, Edward McBride and John MacLoghlin.[56] Of the thirty-four melodies played, ancient harp tunes like 'The green Woods of Tru'ach' were performed as well as several planxtys and 'Carolan's Concerto', many of the same tunes Bunting had collected from the old harpers twenty years before.

---

55 *Belfast News-Letter*, 26 Sept. 1837, as cited in McClelland. Rainey is also known as Rennie or Reanney. 56 Armstrong, *Musical instruments*, i, p. 52. At least two of the harpers, Rainey and McBride, are known to have been students at the Belfast Harp Society school in 1811, and McBride was the current teacher for the school in 1821, with Rainey succeeding him two years later.

Harps played at the grand corporation banquet

The harps played at the banquet that evening were of modern construction, formed in somewhat of an ancient shape with high head and bowed pillar. Valentine Rainey was known to play a harp made by James McBride, a wheelwright and amateur harper who was Edward's father.[57] MacLoghlin's harp was a wire-strung Egan Improved Irish Harp made for the Belfast Harp Society,[58] so it would probably have been 153cm in height, with thirty-seven strings and decorated with green painted shamrocks on a natural background. New research makes a plausible connection between the wire-strung Egan harp held in the National Museum of Ireland (see pp 88–9) and one of the performers at the corporation banquet held for the king in 1821. On the harp's soundboard, below the figure eight pattern of shamrock vines and the Gaelic phrases 'Love Music' and 'Sweet music of Ireland' are two badges providing clues to the provenance of the instrument. On the left (facing) is the badge of the red hand of Ireland, and on the right (facing) is the Order of St Patrick. In *Ireland sixty years ago*, Hubert Burke states that two of the harpers at the banquet were sent by the lord of Shane's Castle, and they were dressed in the ancient costume of the O'Neills.[59] The patron of the two harpers was Charles O'Neill, 1st Earl O'Neill (1779–1841), and the red hand symbol was the family's coat of arms. The harp's other painted emblem, the Order of St Patrick with crowned shamrock leaves on a red saltire, also points to Charles O'Neill, who was installed as a knight of the order in 1809, and was the only O'Neill to attain the honour. It is reasonable to assume that the harp belonged to one of the O'Neill harpers sent to Dublin to perform at the banquet, and it's not impossible that it may have been specially commissioned by Charles O'Neill for the historic performance before the king. Charles O'Neill was well-known for his patronage of harpers, and Arthur O'Neill, the first teacher of the Belfast society's school, had played at Shane's Castle in the early 1800s.

A curious anecdote from Bochsa, who was not immune to elaborating a story, relates that he also performed at the lord mayor's banquet that same evening. Writing in *Bochsa's history of the harp*, the harpist recalled his experience of playing the Brian Boru harp.[60] Bochsa claimed he accompanied Miss Stephens in Moore's ballads 'The last rose of summer' and 'The harp that once through Tara's halls' and laments that by the end of these pieces his fingers were

---

57 See John Bell's notes of 1849 in Henry George Farmer, 'Some notes on the Irish harp', *Music and Letters*, 24:2 (Apr. 1943), 104. Presumably Edward McBride's harp was also made by his father James. **58** MacLoghlin played the harp in the 1829 O'Connell Procession after the passing of the Emancipation Act. It was later purchased by Dr Petrie (O'Curry, *On the manners and customs of the ancient Irish*, iii, p. 296). **59** Burke, *Ireland sixty years ago*, p. 20. **60** N.C. Bochsa, *Bochsa's history of the harp*, ed. Patricia John (Houston, 1990), p. 7.

'nearly cut to pieces by the thick brass wires'. Although other contemporary reports of the corporation banquet make no mention of Bochsa, perhaps the harpist was present at the event and played a wire-strung harp for an impromptu duet with Miss Stephens.

On the next morning, 24 August, George IV's busy public schedule continued with a visit to the Royal Dublin Society. After touring the museum, the monarch surveyed the impressive scene on the lawn of about forty tents. Near a special marquee for the king fitted with a scarlet canopy, entertainment was provided by three harpers dressed in the 'antique garb of minstrels'.[61] Possibly the same harpers who played the night before, little else is known of them, but their presence once again reflects the use of the harp as a signifier of national identity. The king scarcely heard their music it seems, for he appeared on the lawns only briefly before boarding his carriage for Slane Castle. Anxious to meet up once again with Lady Conyngham, it was reported that the king crossed the country at the great speed 'of ten Irish miles an hour' and 'none of his suite were able to keep up with him'.[62]

The next few days spent at Slane were happily filled with excursions in the surrounding countryside including a tour of the historic site of the Battle of the Boyne. Dinners at Slane with the local gentry seemed to suit the king, who once again offered to switch places with Lord Talbot and remain in Ireland as the lord lieutenant. The sovereign seemed to charm those he met with his approachability, as recounted by Chief Justice Bushe, who attended a dinner at Slane:

> The king put everyone at ease […] He is a perfect master of society […] with all the advantages of great quickness with natural humour, a wonderful memory, the opportunities he has had of hearing, witnessing and collecting all the good anecdotes of every kind, and a talent for mimicry quite surprising […] He is a perfect story-teller.[63]

The state visit seemed to strengthen the king's public popularity, although the cheering crowds may also have been due to the sheer novelty of a never-before-seen royal spectacle in Ireland. At the time, George IV was far less popular in his own country where over the years his regal position had been greatly tarnished by unflattering reports of personal compulsions of over-spending, excessive drinking and eating, and a succession of royal mistresses, many already married. At the same time, in stark contrast, the unorthodox King George IV was a connoisseur and a great patron of the arts who left a

61 Anonymous, *The royal visit* (Dublin, 1821), p. 96. 62 Ibid., p. 97. 63 Gregory, *Mr Gregory's Letter-box*, p. 155.

substantial cultural legacy in Britain. The period of the Regency, named for his temporary reign as prince regent (1811–20) during his father's illness, was known for exceptional art, fashion and architecture. Prince George's favourite architect, John Nash, was responsible for altering the face of London in a massive redevelopment scheme in which small dwellings were removed for a new broad way, Regent's Street, an avenue leading directly from George's residence, Carlton House, to the elegant new Regent's Park.[64] George IV's passion for architecture, and Nash's skills, also led to the transformation of Windsor Castle and Buckingham Palace, and the magnificent Royal Pavilion at Brighton. With an eye for style and a capacity for unrestrained lavish spending, George IV collected stunning pieces of furniture, ceramics, silver and paintings. He acquired works by British painters Stubbs and Gainsborough and the Dutch masters Rembrandt and Rubens, and commissioned numerous portraits by Sir Thomas Lawrence, all now preserved in the Royal Collection.[65] Unlike his father George III, or his brother and successor William IV, King George IV was notably a taste-leading monarch, and his patronage of certain luxury British and Irish goods greatly influenced the national appetite for these products, benefitting scores of artists, designers, craftsmen and manufacturers.

The king's visit to Ireland ended in early September with the monarch making his departure on the royal yacht from Dunleary Harbour, and the town was renamed Kingstown in his honour. The excitement of the previous three weeks now entered a phase of memory and legend. There was a mixed review for concert promoter I. Willis, noting that for the last coronation concert, 'The house was fashionably, although not numerously attended.'[66] Bochsa was again singled out for his performance of 'Extempore fantasia', in which he had introduced 'beautiful Irish airs', and which the article said was 'the object of universal admiration'. However, it seems proceeds were generally disappointing and the London performers were not fully compensated with the agreed fees:

> We regret that these concerts that were so creditably got up, took place generally under circumstances that were so unpropitious as to afford, we fear but little compensation to the individuals concerned, for the very heavy expense they must have incurred in their arrangements and preparations.[67]

However, Willis' music business had fared somewhat better, and it may have had something to do with the pleasurable evening of Irish airs played on the

---

64 J.B. Priestley, *The prince of pleasure and his regency, 1811–20* (London, 1969), p. 290.   65 See royalcollection.org.uk.   66 *Freeman's Journal*, 4 Sept. 1821.   67 Ibid.

pianoforte and harp at the Viceregal Lodge. Willis and Charles Egan had apparently managed to ingratiate themselves with the king, for Willis was subsequently favoured with a coveted royal warrant, his Harmonic Saloon becoming the *Royal* Harmonic Saloon. And Charles Egan in the following year became professor of harp to the king's sister, Princess Augusta. An article in the *Morning Post* announced that Egan was enjoying his distinguished new office, and in tribute to his majesty, the harpist had just written a new stanza of 'God save the king'.[68] The Irish harp maker's son had been elevated to a position of significant social standing, and the notoriety also enhanced his reputation as a performing harpist. The providential royal visit to Ireland had shaped the destinies of John Egan and his son Charles, ensuring bright futures for both. In Charles' book *The royal harp director* (1827), the dedication to the king nostalgically paid homage to that fateful evening:

> It should ever gratefully live in the memory of the professors and amateurs of the harp, that, on your majesty's memorable visit to the sister kingdom its native melody was heard and appreciated in the royal palace; and that under your majesty's auspicious encouragement this national instrument has arrived at the highest state of perfection.[69]

---

68 *Morning Post*, 4 Sept. 1822.   69 Charles Egan, *The royal harp director*.

6 / One story draws another

Charles Egan was well suited to his new position, for Princess Augusta (figure 6.1) had a particular fondness for Irish airs, and as her new harp professor, Charles obliged by providing countless harp solos based on Irish melodies. An early handwritten manuscript of Irish pieces arranged by Charles Egan still survives in Princess Augusta's music collection held at the Beinecke Library at Yale University (figure 6.2).[1] In Egan's signature hand in black ink, the title page reads, 'A selection of preludes and airs arranged for the Royal Portable Irish Harp invented by J. Egan harp maker'. Dedicated to Princess Augusta and her brother the king, the title page continues with, 'This selection are a number of celebrated Irish Airs composed many ages back on the ancient Irish harp' and 'They are adopted to the Royal Portable Irish Harp'. The collection appears to be an earlier version of Egan's published volume in 1822, *Ancient Irish melodies*, for the majority of the same tunes appear in both.[2] The autograph mainly differs from the published *Ancient Irish melodies* in that it includes 'preludes', a common teaching device used in the eighteenth and nineteenth centuries. The preludes, composed of chords, scale-wise passages and arpeggios, are individually paired with an accompanying piece, both in the same key, and a variety of key signatures is represented in the manuscript.[3]

Tucked away in Princess Augusta's music folio next to 'A selection of preludes and airs' is a rare handwritten five-page letter from Charles Egan. As an introduction to the music manuscript, it contains a commentary on Ireland's harp tradition and ancient melodies, as well as notes on his father's inventions. In Charles' thin, lacy script, the first page opens with a florid dedication in 'humble gratitude', acknowledging the princess as the 'St Cecilia of the day' for her generous patronage of the fine arts.[4] Alluding to himself as a child 'from

---

1 Charles Egan's handwritten manuscript, 'A selection of preludes and airs', and his autographed letter to Princess Augusta are preserved in the Hanover Royal Music Archive (OSB MSS 146, Box 33, Folder 169), James Marshall and Marie-Louise Osborn Collection, Beinecke Rare Book & Manuscript Library, Yale University.   2 Two tunes in the manuscript, 'Peggy Ban' and 'Kitty Tyrrel', are replaced in the published edition by the airs 'Pay the reckoning', 'Lost is my quiet' and 'The Moreen'.   3 One function of presenting pieces in the collection in a variety of keys was to demonstrate the chromatic capabilities of John Egan's Portable Irish Harp with dital mechanism.   4 C. Egan, 'A selection of preludes and airs'.

6.1 Princess Augusta Sophia by Samuel William Reynolds and Samuel Cousins, after Sir William Beechey, 1824. © National Portrait Gallery, London.

6.2 Charles Egan's handwritten manuscript, *A selection of preludes and airs arranged for the Royal Portable Irish Harp*, in Princess Augusta's music collection. Beinecke Rare Book & Manuscript Library, Yale University.

the Land of Song', he expresses the hope that 'those strains of other days may long delight your royal highness' harmonious ears'. The second page of the letter discusses the 'Improvement of the ancient Irish harp' as related to his father's inventions, and several new harp accessories are introduced: the 'leaf turner' for turning pages, the 'hand director' for facilitating a graceful position, and the 'harp rest' for supporting the weight of the instrument. Then a brief historical overview covers subjects such as the celebrated harpers, the famous Brian Boru harp and the ancient Irish airs themselves. Charles recounts the romantic legend of 'Aileen Aroone', a tune in the collection:

[A] Simple but beautiful air Aileen Aroone was composed by Carrol O'Daly an Irish chieftain who was in love with Ellen Kavanagh the daughter of another Irish chieftain – but was refused her by her parents in consequence of some feuds existing between the families – her parents gave her in marriage to another chieftain and on the day of the marriage O'Daly her former lover came to the wedding disguised as a harper and began to play this air – Aileen Aroone which he composed at the time – this attracted the fair Ellen's notice she knew her lover in his disguise and eloped with him that evening – [5]

Irish airs such as this one, explains Egan, typically portray tales of love and chivalrous deeds. The choice of 'Aileen Aroone' in the letter is significant for its overtones of the princess' own story, a real-life saga filled with secret romance and family opposition to her proposed marriage to an Irishman, bringing poignancy to the appointment of Charles Egan as her new harp professor.

Princess Augusta Sophia (1768–1840) grew up with her older sister Princess Charlotte, and her younger sister Princess Elizabeth.[6] The three princesses were the elder daughters of King George III and Queen Charlotte,[7] and they had a sequestered childhood. As adults, the princesses continued to be somewhat isolated from society, regularly accompanied by their parents to concerts and court functions, and their private lives were devoted to the 'feminine' pursuits of music and art. The king and queen, reluctant to part with their daughters, resisted several marriage offers from royal princes in foreign courts. The Royal Marriages Act (1772) dictated that each member of the royal family must have the consent of the reigning monarch to proceed with a lawful union, thus ensuring a 'suitable' partner.[8] Eventually, in 1797, Charlotte was allowed to marry Prince Frederick of Württemberg, and some twenty years later, in 1818, Elizabeth wed Prince Frederick of Hesse-Homburg. But a different fate was in store for Princess Augusta, who, like the chieftain's daughter Ellen in 'Aileen Aroone', was trapped by her royal position and forbidden to marry her chosen partner. Her misfortune was to have fallen in love with an Irishman, General Brent Spencer, who was not her match in birth or station.

General Spencer had served for a time as an equerry between the duke of York and King George III, and on his visits to Windsor Castle, by chance had met and formed a relationship with the princess. The gallant General Spencer, at age 39, had already distinguished himself as commander of the 40th

---

5 Ibid.   6 For further reading see Flora Fraser, *Princesses: the six daughters of George III* (London, 2004).   7 George III and Queen Charlotte had fifteen children.   8 Fraser, *Princesses*, pp 262–3.

Somersetshire Regiment in the West Indies.[9] Frequently in danger, he was recognized in 1807 for his bravery in military activities in Denmark, and in Portugal, his courageous acts in the Peninsular War earned him the Order of the Bath.[10] For years during his tours of duty, the couple carried on an uncertain, long-distance courtship, with the princess anxiously awaiting news of his safe return. Having formed a mutual attachment, the next step was to have the proposed union sanctioned by the reigning monarch, her brother, the prince regent. In 1812, Princess Augusta wrote to Prince George for permission to marry. She was keenly aware of the queen's opposition to the match, but at age 43 she fervently hoped that a private marriage might take place. In the letter, the princess conceded that Sir Brent was not an equal by birth, however twelve years had passed since they first met, and she had been faithfully attached to her secret love for nine of those years.[11] Unlike the fairy tale ending in 'Aileen Aroone', the princess' story had a different conclusion. A written answer from the prince regent has not come to light, and there seems to be no documentation of a marriage having taken place. The only remnant of the romantic relationship was a locket bearing Augusta's picture that was worn around the General's neck which was taken from him upon his death in 1828.[12]

With her dreams of marriage unfulfilled, the princess filled the hours, days and years with her beloved music, including at Frogmore House, which around 1819 became her cherished personal residence. An estate on the grounds of Windsor Castle, Frogmore had been Queen Charlotte's retreat, and after her death the house passed to Augusta, being the eldest unmarried daughter. The Frogmore gardens, filled with rare species of plants and trees, enticed the princess to pursue gardening as a pastime, but music prevailed as her principle avocation, and she sang and played the harp and pianoforte daily. The princess was joined at Frogmore by her companion, Lady Mary Taylor, and on most evenings, two hours were devoted to playing harp and pianoforte duets.[13] By the time Charles Egan was appointed professor of harp to the princess, she had reached the age of 54. A decade had passed since her thwarted attempt of marriage to Sir Brent Spencer, and yet a curious twist of fate had once again brought an Irishman within her realm, with sounds of Irish harp airs wafting through the rooms of Frogmore House.

Music had always been a source of pleasure and solace for the princess. As a child she was delighted to be given her own harpsichord for her rooms at Windsor, and for a time she received keyboard lessons from the music master, Charles Horn.[14] In her youth, Augusta attempted a few simple original keyboard

---

9 Ibid., pp 184–5.   10 Ibid., p. 223.   11 Ibid., p. 263.   12 Ibid., p. 265.   13 Ibid., p. 341.   14 Ibid., p. 100. Keyboard manuscripts in the hand of Charles Frederick Horn survive in Princess

solos, and her early interest in composing seems to have continued throughout her life. As she matured, Princess Augusta, an avid admirer of Thomas Moore's *Melodies*, took to arranging her own versions of his popular songs for the pianoforte. In 1815 a friend of Moore's, Mary Godfrey, informed the poet that Princess Augusta had composed her own variations to his air 'Love's young dream'.[15] Years later, in 1824, an occasion presented itself wherein Moore was able to hear the princess' compositions first-hand at a gathering hosted by Lady Donegal, where Princess Augusta sang and played a couple of Moore's songs in which she had composed 'new airs'. In his journal, Moore recalls her version of 'The wreath you wove' as 'rather pretty'.[16] At the gathering, the princess also played an original march she had composed for her brother, the duke of York, and as the music-making continued, Moore boldly sang his anti-British rebel song, 'Oh where's the slave'. He was unexpectedly joined in the chorus by the princess, who was presumably oblivious to the inherent political message. Another chronicler from the period, the English novelist Fanny Burney, also noted Princess Augusta's adeptness at composition, recounting three different occasions at Buckingham House in which the princess 'played for me and sang to me airs of her own composition ... very pretty, and prettily executed – with touching words of innocent ardour of sentiment'.[17] Composing and arranging was undoubtedly one of the princess' regular pursuits, affording her an outlet for personal expression, and a manuscript of arranged songs and dances in the princess' hand still survives in her music archive.[18]

At the start of harp lessons with Charles Egan, the royal pupil was already a seasoned amateur composer, with over thirty years' of casual experience writing music for voice and pianoforte, and duets for harp and pianoforte. In the mutually beneficial teacher-student relationship, Charles found in the princess a committed student with significant experience in composing, while Charles himself was still a young man in the early stages of launching a career as a composer-arranger. For whatever reason, his first decade as professor to Princess Augusta was an incredibly fruitful period, yielding nearly fifty 'C. Egan' published works scored for voice, harp and pianoforte as listed in an 1829 'Catalogue of music, composed and arranged by Charles Egan'.[19] With their shared interest in arranging, the princess and her professor likely exchanged

Augusta's music collection in the Hanover Royal Music Archive. See hdl.handle.net/10079/fa/ beinecke.hanover.   **15** Lord John Russell (ed.), *Journal and correspondence of Thomas Moore* (London, 1853–6), viii, p. 203.   **16** Ibid., iv, p. 193.   **17** Joyce Hemlow (ed.), *The journals and letters of Fanny Burney (Madame d'Arblay)* (Oxford, 1984), xi, p. 111, n. 1.   **18** Hanover Royal Music Archive, James Marshall and Marie-Louise Osborn Collection, Beinecke Rare Book & Manuscript Library, Yale University.   **19** A list of the published works of Charles Egan appears as the index of his 1829 book, *The harp primer* as 'Catalogue of music, composed and arranged by Charles Egan, professor

points of view on harmony and style in their lessons together. In discussions, royal protocol would have been strictly observed by Charles, but at the same time, the underlying gender roles of the day would have afforded him some sense of male authority. As her instructor, Charles undoubtedly brought to the lessons his expertise in the established harp-playing techniques of the day, acquired from Bochsa, and the princess also valued his Irish heritage and the national airs learned in the lessons.

Charles also brought with him a unique first-hand knowledge of the various mechanisms on Egan's 'new, improved' harp models, which proved to be useful to Princess Augusta in that she played several of Egan's harp models. In fact, she was an extraordinarily supportive patron to John Egan, who in 1822 became 'Harp Maker to her Royal Highness the Princess Augusta' in addition to 'Harp Maker to the King', according to a notice in the *Freeman's Journal*. The article also announced a new harp made for the princess 'in addition to the harps her royal highness already has of his make'.[20] Details of the individual harps the princess owned are not recorded, nonetheless the title pages of her music books clearly indicate the harp models she played. The pedal harp solos suggest she owned the primary form of harp in use, the empire-style pedal harp, and it is also reasonable to assume that while the princess would have played a single-action harp earlier in the century, she later acquired a double-action harp to accommodate the chromaticism in the Bochsa solos present in her collection. Several of the princess' music books are specifically arranged for the Royal Portable Irish Harp, indicating ownership, and she may well have plucked the strings of the golden winged-maiden portable harp brought back from Ireland by the king in 1821. Subsequently a Royal Portable Irish Harp would have been commissioned and made to her specifications. There is recorded confirmation of an order placed for another Egan harp model in 1822, made in a new groundbreaking design – a *triple-action* pedal harp.[21]

THE TRIPLE-ACTION PEDAL HARP

The paths of John Egan and his son Charles were necessarily intertwined, with the success of one benefitting the other. Working in tandem, the inventor relied on his harpist son, well placed in London for showcasing new models, and for Charles, performances on his father's innovative harps brought greater notoriety. The invention of the triple-action pedal harp may have even played a part in

of the harp to her Royal Highness the Princess Augusta, & first harpist to her Royal Highness the Duchess of Clarence'.   **20** *Freeman's Journal*, 16 June 1823.   **21** *Saunders's Newsletter*, 6 Aug. 1822.

Charles' royal appointment. An article in *Saunders's Newsletter* in August of 1822 announced that 'Mr Charles Egan, son of the inventor, had the honour of performing on the triple-action harp at the palace, and received the royal approbation.'[22] The piece continued with news that the young artist 'has been appointed Professor of the Harp to her Royal Highness the Princess Augusta', seemingly linking the two events. Charles Egan had already gained the king's favour in Ireland in 1821 when he debuted his father's Portable Irish Harp at the Viceregal Lodge. Once again the harpist demonstrated the latest Egan model to members of the royal family, which was noticed by the palace's most proficient harpist, Princess Augusta. Captivated by the ingenious invention, she immediately commissioned one to be made for her, and, obviously, specialized instruction on the instrument would have been advantageous. The princess would have needed assistance on how to operate the harp's baffling triple-action pedals, and additional expert guidance on how to effectively work the ditals on a portable harp would also not go amiss. Thus, the harp maker's son was duly appointed as professor of harp to Princess Augusta.

The triple-action pedal harp had long been considered the ultimate achievement in the overall development of the pedal harp, for the instrument could play in every major and minor key. Capable of producing extreme sharps and flats, the model had additional slots for the F, C and G pedals, corresponding to additional *fourchette* mechanisms on the neck. In a personal letter from Charles Egan to Princess Augusta, he explained that 'the necessity of the invention of the triple-action harp has been alluded to many years since by Bochsa & others in their writing on the theory of the harp'.[23] In Bochsa's 1819 book *A new and improved method of instruction for the harp*, he wrote that on the double-action harp, borrowed notes could be substituted for some of the double sharps and double flats in the scale, but eventually a 'third action of the pedals' was necessary, although unfortunately a third action of the pedals 'would render the mechanism too complicated'.[24] Within two years of Bochsa's published statement, John Egan achieved the unimaginable by successfully producing a harp with the complicated triple-action mechanism. In spite of the complexity – or perhaps because of it – it seems the inventor Egan was drawn to the challenge, and Bochsa was able to personally examine the technological marvel that same year while staying at Egan's on Dawson Street during the royal visit. Subsequently, in a letter to Egan from London, Bochsa not only placed an order for a triple-action harp but also publicly lauded the invention as 'the highest degree of perfection the harp can arrive at',[25] and the congratulatory catchphrase

22 Ibid.   23 Charles Egan in a letter to Princess Augusta, Hanover Royal Music Archive (OSB MSS 146, Box 33, Folder 169).   24 Bochsa, *A new and improved method of instruction for the harp*, p. 44. 25 *Freeman's Journal*, 31 Oct. 1821.

> Dublin, Sept. 8, 1821.
>
> Dear Sir—I have great pleasure in informing you the Royal Portable Irish Harp, invented by you, has my decided approbation. Its peculiar sweetness of Tone, so admirably adapted for accompanying the voice—the great facility of changing the Keys, and its portability, make it a desirable Instrument to proficients on the Pedal Harp.
>
> Of your Double Action Pedal Harps I have given a convincing proof of their merits, by playing on one of your make on Friday, at the Coronation Concert, Theatre Royal; and, as a further proof, I request you will make for me a Double Action Pedal Harp, a Royal Portable Irish Harp, and also one of your newly-invented Triple Action Pedal Harps, which invention I do consider the highest degree of perfection the Harp can arrive at. When finished please to forward them to me, at No. 2, Bryanstone-street, Portman-square, London. Wishing you all the success your abilities deserve, I am, dear Sir, your's, most truly,
>
> N. C. BOCHSA.
>
> To Mr. Egan, Harp Maker to his Majesty.

6.3 Congratulatory letter from N.C. Bochsa in *Freeman's Journal*, 31 October 1821.

was duly reproduced in adverts as a marketing tool to promote the instrument (figure 6.3). By January of 1822, Egan's triple-action harp was in limited production, and an ad for the new invention appeared in *Saunders's Newsletter*, describing it as 'invented and only manufactured by him [Egan]'.[26] Presumably by the summer a triple-action harp had been delivered to Bochsa at his address on Bryanstone Street, Portman Square, where Charles Egan was currently residing, and the harp maker's son may well have performed on Bochsa's prototype of the triple-action harp for the model's debut at the palace (figure 6.4).[27]

Princess Augusta's triple-action harp, which took a year to produce, was described in the press as 'a beautiful specimen of Irish ingenuity and workmanship'.[28] After it was delivered to Frogmore House, Egan received a message:

> Lady Mary Taylor informs Mr Egan that his triple-action harp, manufactured for her Royal Highness the Princess Augusta, is safely arrived at Frogmore, and Lady Mary is happy to assure him her royal highness approves of it most highly.[29]

News of the special harp made for Princess Augusta reached as far as France, and was deemed newsworthy enough to be mentioned in *Galignani's Messenger*, a daily English newspaper in Paris. In the press release, the harp was described as,

26 *Saunders's Newsletter*, 16 Jan. 1822.   27 Ibid., 10 Aug. 1822.   28 *Freeman's Journal*, 16 June 1823.
29 Ibid., 13 Nov. 1824.

6.4 Triple-action
harp announcement
in *Saunders's Newsletter*,
6 August 1822.

NEW IMPROVEMENT OF THE HARP.—We are happy to understand the Treple Action Harp, that great desideratem to proficients on the Pedal Harp. (the only instrument of the kind in the world, invented and manufactured by Mr. EGAN, of this city, Harpmaker to his Majesty,) has been honoured with the Royal notice and approbation. It is highly gratifying that the Royal patronage has been extended to our ingenious countryman, who has devoted the principal part of his life in improving the Harp. The mechanism of his Single and Double Action Pedal Harps is universally admired for its simplicity and excellent workmanship, as well as superior tone. His invention of the Triple Action Pedal Harp, and Royal Portable Irish Harp, strung with gut, entitles this Artist to great praise from the musical world, and from his country in particular, he having removed from our national instrument the original imperfection it had laboured under for so many centuries, being heretofore incapable of making accidental flats and sharps; and by his conferring on it imperishable features of perfection, has been the means of having it heard again in the Palaces of Kings, and honoured by the hands of even Royalty itself. We are also happy to hear that Mr. CHARLES EGAN, Son of the Inventor, had the honour of performing on the Triple Action Harp at the Palace, and received the Royal approbation. This young Artist, pupil to the celebrated Bochas, in his professional career, has received that portion of the patronage which that illustrious and munificent Family so liberally bestows on native genius—he has been appointed Professor of the Harp to her Royal Highness the Princess Augusta.

'painted a dark ground, richly ornamented with gold vignettes, gold borders, and emblematic figures playing on lyres'.[30] The gilt column was surmounted by a crown, and the brass plate was engraved with 'Royal arms and the name of the illustrious personage' for whom it was made. Princess Augusta had also ordered Egan's recommended harp rest, a device that was becoming increasingly popular, and it was installed on the harp.

Egan's harp rest, an apparatus similar to Bochsa's harp brace, became a popular accessory for harp students. It was even adopted for use in 1822 at a Dublin harp academy run by Miss Rudkin, who asserted with confidence that children aged 10 or 11 could learn to play the harp without 'the slightest injury to figure or shape' due to the use of Mr Egan's harp support.[31] So popular was the accessory that in the same year it attracted the attention of Pierre Erard, manager of the Erard harp firm in London. In a letter to his Uncle Sébastien, Pierre outlined his plan to directly copy Egan's device and obtain a patent for

30 *Galignani's Messenger*, 24 Apr. 1824.   31 *Saunders's Newsletter*, 19 Oct. 1822. Miss Rudkin's academy also provided harps in various sizes adapted to the ages/sizes of her pupils.

it from the attorney general, writing, 'This machine for which I am sending the sketch is made by an Irishman in Dublin,' and 'He has no patent.'[32]

In the city of London, with a community of several resident harp makers engaged in fierce competition, new ideas were constantly imitated and there was a real necessity to protect inventions with legal patents. It was different for Egan, separated by a great distance from the London harp workshops, and yet the maker was still cognizant of the innovations of the age. Like other harp makers, Egan understood the attraction of ladies to newfangled harp accessories, and the triple-action harp epitomized the current fascination for mechanical 'improvements' to instruments. In the 1824 *Pigot & Co.'s* directory, a complete range of harp models was advertised in the maker's listing: 'manufacturer of single, double and treble action pedal harps, and Royal Portable Irish Harps by special appointment to his Majesty the King and the Royal Family, 30 Dawson street'.[33] In spite of achieving the ultimate in harp design, it seems possible that Egan eventually encountered various structural difficulties with his triple-action harp, for production of the model was short-lived. In the very next year and beyond, Egan's Royal triple-action pedal harp ceased to be mentioned in directory listings and disappeared altogether from adverts. Although a technically advanced instrument, its practical usefulness for most amateur harp players is highly questionable. The capabilities of extreme sharps and flats, seldom used by harpists, would hardly warrant the extra effort of a player adjusting to the additional pedal slots. Extremely challenging to produce, the model's extra mechanisms may have put too much strain on the harp frame, and it was obviously a nightmare to regulate pitches in all the various pedal settings. Production ceased after only three short years, and none of the triple-action harps seem to have survived.

However, the idea of a triple-action harp did not totally die away. The French conductor-composer Hector Berlioz (1803–69) was still longing for a fully chromatic harp in his 1844 landmark orchestration manual *A treatise on modern instrumentation and orchestration*.[34] This indicates that the composer was unaware of Egan's model, which had been developed twenty years earlier. Apparently the perceived need for extreme chromatics on the harp was conveyed to Berlioz by the harp virtuoso, Elias Parish Alvars (1808–49). A former student of Bochsa, the harpist's dazzling technique made use of enharmonics and

---

32 Adelson et al. (eds), *The history of the Erard piano and harp*, ii, p. 788. While it seems Pierre Erard had no qualms about copying Egan's newly invented device, at the same time he considered taking legal action against Egan for copying Erard's *fourchette* mechanism, although it was universally copied by all the London makers.   33 *Pigot & Co.'s City of Dublin and Hibernian Provincial Directory* (Dublin, 1824).   34 Hector Berlioz, *A treatise on modern instrumentation and orchestration*, trans. Mary Cowden Clark (London, 1844), p. 66.

glissandos, a feature idiomatic to the harp through the clever use of multiple combinations of various pedal settings. For instance, setting the pedals for D-sharp and E-flat creates a series of strings which double the same note sound, and the doubling of tones in rapid succession on the resonant harp is a unique feature of the instrument's capabilities. By engineering sound clusters of hauntingly beautiful chords through pedal settings, the player then merely brushes the strings from top to bottom to create the quintessential harp effect, the *glissando*. Parish Alvars named these double notes on the harp *'synonimes'*, and through complicated pedalling, he flawlessly executed a seemingly impossible succession of passages with rapidly changing layers of harmonies. In his quest to further expand the tonal range of *synonimes*, Alvars proposed the construction of a triple-action harp to include the missing *synonimes* for pitches D-natural, G-natural and A-natural.[35] This was the precise solution enacted by Egan who had added pedal slots and mechanisms to the F, C, and G pedals, thereby doubling the pitch sounds for D (C-double sharp), G (F-double sharp) and A (G-double sharp).[36] Charles Egan wrote that the 'triple movement harp' was capable of playing in 33 keys – 18 major and 15 minor – and that the key of A-sharp major was possible.[37]

MUSIC FOR NEWLY INVENTED EGAN HARP MODELS

In the nineteenth century, when a new instrument model was introduced, it was common practice to issue a practical instruction manual with appropriately arranged pieces idiomatic to the model. In the Egan enterprise, Charles Egan provided this essential service. The Egan firm, excelling in the marketing practices of the time, garnered the public's anticipation for the forthcoming book on the new portable harp by announcing 'the expected work on the powers and practice of the Royal Portable Irish Harp' had been purchased by a music company and 'will shortly be laid before the public'.[38] The first tutor, *A new series of instructions arranged expressly for the Royal Portable Irish Harp*, was actually published by John Egan (figure 6.5). In the ever expanding father-son collaboration, the attribution on the title page reads, 'Dublin. Published for the author by John Egan Harp Maker to His Majesty & the Royal Family.' Charles Egan's arrangements fit the small range of the instrument, and his books fulfilled a desire of harpists to play Irish airs on their small Irish harps. C. Egan continued

---

35 Ibid., p. 66. The modern term is *enharmonic synonymes*.   36 Parish Alvars studied harp with N.C. Bochsa in the 1820s and possibly would have known Charles Egan. It is questionable whether Alvars knew of J. Egan's triple-action harp, for at the time of its invention, in 1822, Alvars was only 14 years of age.   37 Charles Egan, *The royal harp director*, p. 15.   38 *Dublin Correspondent*, 8 Nov. 1823.

6.5 Charles Egan, *A new series of instructions arranged expressly for the Royal Portable Irish Harp*, 1822. Beinecke Rare Book & Manuscript Library, Yale University.

to publish several more collections of Irish pieces for the portable harp, including *A selection of ancient Irish melodies* (*c.*1822), *Ancient Irish melodies* (1822), and *A selection of favourite airs, with variations arranged for J. Egan's newly invented Royal Portable Irish Harp* (n.d.).[39]

For the debut of the triple-action pedal harp, once again Charles Egan brought out a printed book to explain the capabilities of the new instrument. The tutor was titled *The royal harp director, being a new and improved treatise on the single, double & triple movement harps* (1827) and was written as an introductory manual primarily for the novice player (figure 6.6). In the book, essential basics are given on learning how to play the three different types of pedal harps, with instructions on tuning and how to set the pedals for each harp model, and on a page devoted to the triple-action harp, a list of additional key signatures possible to access through various pedal settings is given. Other topics covered in *The royal harp director* are the basic techniques of fingering, scales, arpeggios,

---

39 *Freeman's Journal*, 27 Nov. 1824. In Ireland, the *Ancient Irish melodies* were promoted and sold by Charles' colleague I. Willis at the Royal Harmonic Saloon.

6.6 Charles Egan, *The royal harp director*, 1827. Courtesy of the Library of Congress.

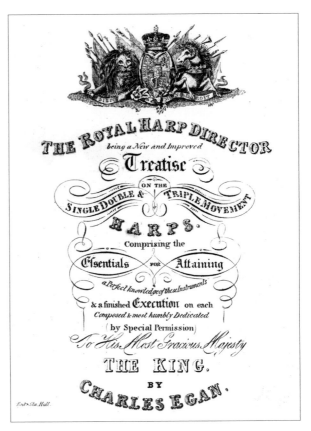

harmonics and the shake (trill), and the latter part of the book is devoted to sheet music of preludes and airs presented in a variety of keys and musical styles. An eclectic combination of pieces, from 'God save the king' to simple arrangements of Mozart and Handel, the collection also includes the national airs of different European countries. In addition, *The royal harp director* has an arrangement of 'Waltz from *der Freischutz*', the most popular opera theme of the day, and a charming original piece by C. Egan, 'Love they say is like a flower'.[40] Finally, a prelude titled 'Modulating through various keys to facilitate the use of the pedals' furnishes the student with a practical exercise for learning the standard pedal sequences from E-flat major to C major.

Charles Egan, in line with other contemporary harp professors, now had the requisite two method books to his name: *A new series of instructions arranged expressly for the Royal Portable Irish Harp* and *The royal harp director*. In 1829, he brought out a third tutor, *The harp primer, being a familiar introduction to the study of the harp*, this time

40 'Waltz from *der Freischutz*', 'Love they say is like a flower' and other C. Egan arrangements can be heard on Nancy Hurrell, *The Egan Irish harp* (CD, 2011).

written for the complete beginner.[41] One of the impressive features of the book
is a detailed engraving of a pedal harp with the red and black strings in colour.
The introduction states that the book is a simple 'initiatory work' combining
the rudiments of music with the principles of the instrument, and the chapters
cover topics such as the musical staff, notes, time and keys, plus basic guidance
on harp-tuning and pedal settings for single-action and double-action harps
(with the triple-action harp conspicuously absent). Charles marketed the work
as 'simple and scientific', and a favourable notice in the *Morning Post* gave the
endorsement, 'It is an excellent little work, well written, and admirably calculated
to assist beginners in acquiring a knowledge of that delightful and favourite
instrument. – John Bull.'[42] Unfortunately, Bull's positive opinion was not
universally shared, for a reviewer in the *Spectator* called the book 'the most
impudent piece of quackery that ever fell under his notice', adding that it
'pretends to be an introduction to the study of the harp, but it is no such
thing'.[43] The reviewer complained that the bulk of the book covered the 'ABC
of music' rather than actual harp instruction. Incensed by this affront to his
reputation, Charles countered with the argument that the rudiments of music
were a necessary preliminary step in the study of *any* instrument.[44] How could
a child read a book without first learning the alphabet? he asked. According to
Charles, his tutor was specifically promoted to *beginners* and therefore, 'Where is
the atrocious imposture?' He demanded the editor make amends for the
reviewer's 'dastardly attack on his work and reputation' by printing a reparation
of the wrongful complaint in the next issue of the *Spectator*, but in case a
retraction would not be forthcoming, Charles includes a postscript asking the
editor to at least print his letter.[45]

Further glimpses of the self-assurance of the Egan favourite son are seen in
his glowing, self-promoting advert for the *Harp primer*: 'Mr Egan is already
favourably known to the musical world by compositions of very decided ability
– the present work cannot fail to enhance the reputation he enjoys as a clever
and intelligent instructor.'[46] After moving to London and taking up his position
as royal harp professor, Charles Egan seems to have enchanted the genteel
acquaintances he met as he moved in London social circles, dedicating harp
works to several illustrious patrons. One notable example is his *Harp primer*,
which was dedicated to the duchess of Bedford, Lady Georgiana Gordon (1781–
1853), 'with admiration for the refined taste and musical acquirements of her
grace [...] warmest gratitude for the distinguished patronage'. A similar

---

41 Armstrong suggests that the *Harp primer* was originally published in 1822 and was reissued in
1829. 42 *Morning Post*, 29 Aug. 1829. 43 Ibid., 21 Nov. 1829. 44 Ibid. 45 Ibid. 46 *London
Courier and Evening Gazette*, 31 Oct. 1829. Presumably Charles Egan composed the advert.

inscription on a harp solo is inscribed to the duchess' daughter, Lady Sophia Georgiana Lennox (1808–1902), appearing on the title page of his 'Fantasia on a national Sicilian melody and grand march'. Other dedicatees of Egan's harp pieces include the duchess of Clarence (1792–1849), the marchioness Conyngham (1769–1861) and Lady Bloomfield (1822–1905), as well as a string of untitled ladies: Miss C. Walpole, Miss Jane Rhodes, Miss E. Farquharson, Miss J. Stevenson and others, suggesting that in some cases, perhaps the person honoured was a harp student who engaged Charles as teacher.

Charles' gesture of paying tributes with engraved dedications to his benefactors on printed books of music is reminiscent of Turlough Carolan a century earlier, who consistently named his tunes for the noble patrons who supported him. Like Carolan, Charles Egan was becoming increasingly popular as a performer and composer, or more accurately, an arranger. An indication of his notoriety and attractive personal features is revealed by the fact that paper copies of his likeness were commercially printed and sold to the public in 1826.[47] A common practice at the time, painted portraits of famous persons were translated into black-and-white engravings on paper for sale, and a painting of Egan by the artist Gubbini provided the template for a commercial print of the harpist.[48]

By 1829, in addition to his harp tutors and collections of Irish airs, the harpist-composer had a variety of other musical offerings in circulation. A catalogue of music printed in the *Harp primer* lists Egan's compositions, arranged in categories: 'elementary works', 'solos', 'duets', 'vocal works', 'new songs' and 'sacred music'. Harp solos include fantasias, impromptus, marches and opera airs, plus Irish and Scottish melodies, and the duets consist of opera themes arranged for harp and pianoforte. In the 'vocal works' category is Egan's notable book *A selection of national lyrics* based on poetry of Edward Dowling esq., and under the heading 'sacred music' is Egan's *Selection of original sacred airs* for harp or pianoforte, dedicated to James Duncan esq., organist of His Majesty's Castle Chapel Royal, Dublin. Charles Egan followed the growing trend in music publishing of the early 1800s whereby composers moved away from serious, technically challenging solos in favour of simpler pieces based on recognizable melodies. The shift was partly due to the rise of the middle classes, who began to purchase the symbols of gentility, such as a pianoforte or a small harp. Music publishers, catering to a widening audience, encouraged musicians to base their piano sonatas on more familiar Scottish tunes rather than classical themes.[49]

---

47 *Freeman's Journal*, 20 May 1826. **48** Ibid. The commercial portraits were reproduced on India paper and sold by J. Wiseheart for 2 shillings. The location of the original painting is not known. **49** Arthur Loesser, *Men, women and pianos: a social history* (New York, 1954; repr. 1990), p. 252.

Likewise harpist-composers provided endless variations based on Irish and Scottish airs in solos with titles including the words fantasia or impromptu. Examples of this genre in Princess Augusta's harp collection include Egan's 'Kinloch of Kinloch' and 'O' Kenmure's on and awa', both with variations, and the 'Impromptu for the harp' is similarly based on familiar Scottish and Irish melodies. In addition to music based on native airs, Egan also turned to recognizable opera themes for his arrangements. A work for harp and pianoforte titled 'A selection of airs from the celebrated opera of Zelmira, composed by Sig. Rossini' was dedicated to Lady Mary Taylor, the princess' duet partner. To complete the well-rounded range of harp books in the princess' music collection, a copy of Egan's instructional work for practicing pedal changes is also present, his *Brillantes courtes et faciles: preludes for the harp in various major & minor keys*.[50]

As an aspiring harpist-composer, Charles Egan followed in the footsteps, or rather the shadow, of his brilliant teacher, N.C. Bochsa. Early in Egan's career, a telling review of new harp compositions in the *Quarterly Musical Magazine* in 1823 contrasted the skills of the two composers. Next to the glowing critique of Bochsa's solos was a less than enthusiastic comment on Egan's composition 'The Bavarian or Tyrolese air', in which the reviewer felt the 'young Irishman' was still finding his way in composition.[51] It was suggested Egan might have more success if he 'trusted more to his imagination, and adhered less to the hacknied [*sic*] forms of triplet, arpeggio, and octave', but if rapidly executed, the piece would affect the 'brilliant character of the instrument'.[52] In contrast, there was complete admiration for a new march and fantasia by Bochsa, whose works showed 'great ability and taste' and 'ease, brilliancy and utility'. Bochsa, trained in the Paris Conservatoire in the early 1800s, was a naturally gifted composer and author of a staggering number of works, from ballets, operas and symphonies to countless solos and method books for harp. Egan continually learned from Bochsa, and in time the student's arranging skills developed and improved, as evidenced in his 1830 composition 'The Muliteer', described as incorporating a series of interesting modulations to various keys.[53] A novel approach in Egan's 'Military divertimento' placed the melody in the left hand in tenths while the right hand accompanied the bass, and Egan remarked that 'This ambidexterity has frequently elicited admiration in the performances of the author.'[54]

Perhaps the best judge of merit is the test of time, which preserves some solos in the canon of harp music while discarding others. Bochsa's compositions and method books are still reprinted today and are in use in serious harp

50 Hanover Royal Music Archive, Yale University.   51 'Grand Russian march for the harp' in *Quarterly Musical Magazine and Review* (Oct. 1823), 543.   52 Ibid.   53 *Dublin Morning Register*, 5 Jan. 1830. 54 Ibid.

pedagogy around the world, whereas Charles Egan's works are found mainly in the archives of a few national libraries.[55] However, Egan's books of Irish tunes were significant in their day as the first music written specifically for the Portable Irish Harp, furnishing a template for Irish harp music. Arranged for the small harp, the pieces were more idiomatic to the instrument than Bunting's Irish collections written for the pianoforte, and the main appeal of Egan's music was easy accessibility for amateurs who did not aspire to the technical brilliance of Bochsa solos. An anecdote of an amateur public performance gives a glimpse into the functionality of Egan's music. The performer, Miss Jarmon, sang and accompanied herself on the harp with 'pathos and sweetness' as she performed Egan's 'Ah! wilt thou leave Mary?' The reviewer called the piece 'poetically simple' and 'well adapted to the sweetness of the melody'.[56] In other words, it was an adequate composition for an amateur performer, but the degree to which the correspondent was actually listening to the music is compromised by his comment that 'Miss J.'s fine figure renders her a most interesting object presiding at the Harp – she was loudly and deservedly encored.'[57]

Charles Egan often performed his own musical compositions on recitals, and in 1829 he toured with a series of concerts in Bath, Bristol and Clifton.[58] In London he made news in 1828 as the featured artist on a charity concert benefitting the Society of Friends of Foreigners in Distress. Attended by the duke and duchess of Clarence, in the performance the harpist accompanied singers and played an original solo:

> In the course of the evening, Mr Egan at the command of his royal highness, executed in a masterly style his Fantasia, dedicated to her Royal Highness the Duchess of Clarence. The performance of this composition drew down the plaudits of his royal highness and the rest of the distinguished company. The beautiful melody 'And doth not a meeting like this make amends' was introduced with peculiar pathos and the happiest effect.[59]

His playing was greatly admired by the duchess of Clarence, sister-in-law to Princess Augusta. In 1828, she granted Charles a royal warrant.[60] The duchess,

---

55 Copies of *The royal harp director* are held in the Library of Congress (Washington, DC) and the British Library (London). A copy of *A selection of ancient Irish melodies* is available in the Irish Traditional Music Archive. Various C. Egan harp solos are catalogued in the National Library of Ireland. *A new series of instructions for the Royal Portable Irish Harp* and numerous harp solos are preserved in the Hanover Royal Music Archive, Yale University. The *Harp primer* is accessible online on Google Books.   56 *Saunders's Newsletter*, 17 May 1826.   57 Ibid.   58 *Dublin Evening Packet and Correspondent*, 17 Jan. 1829.   59 *Saunders's Newsletter*, 20 May 1828.   60 *Morning Post*, 11 Feb. 1828.

Adelaide of Saxe-Meiningen (1792–1849), became queen two years later when her husband ascended the throne as William IV. At that time Charles' title was elevated accordingly to 'harpist to the queen', and in the same year he was elected an honorary member to the prestigious Royal Academy of Music.[61] During this period Charles resided at a well-appointed address at 2 Wilton Street, Grosvenor Place, a convenient ten-minute walk to Buckingham Palace. From his upscale Georgian terraced house on a respectable leafy avenue, Charles offered harp instruction and also operated a little shop where he sold Royal Portable Irish Harps along with his *Royal harp director* and other published music collections.[62] From time to time Charles returned home to Dublin for short periods and advertised harp instruction for students while visiting family, but his adult life was mainly lived in London. Eventually Charles Egan, residing in fashionable Belgrave Square, married into a privileged class of society, becoming brother-in-law to Lord Langford of Summerhill House, Co. Meath.[63]

THE DUBLIN FAMILY FIRM

While Charles led a charmed life performing in royal palaces and publishing collections of Irish airs for harp, his brother John Jnr, back in Ireland, was involved in the hands-on work of constructing harps. John Jnr became foreman of the Egan manufactory, and in the 1820s, business was booming. The family firm produced an astonishing array of harps in this decade. Pedal harp models included single-, double- and triple-action harps, and instruments were equipped with shutter panels on the back for altering the volume of resonance.[64] Three types of Royal Portable Irish Harps were also manufactured, equipped with ring stops, single-action ditals or double-action ditals, and additionally, the wire-strung Improved Irish Harp model for students at the Belfast Harp Society school was in production. Within the range of models, one could select the amount of decoration desired, which affected the harp's price. Royal Portable Irish Harps ranged from 8 to 24 guineas, according to mechanisms and decoration. The cost of a single-action pedal harp, varnished and gilded, was

---

61 Egan's teacher, Bochsa, provided key assistance in the founding of the Royal Academy of Music in 1822 and was appointed its first harp professor. He was subsequently dismissed in 1826, owing to attacks on his character relating to some unfortunate unresolved business in France. 62 *Morning Post*, 15 Feb. 1827.   63 *Dublin Morning Register*, 28 Oct. 1830. Details of Charles Egan's marriage and wife are not known. A reference to Charles introducing his 'amiable lady' to the vocalist Madame Catalani appeared in the *Bath Chronicle and Weekly Gazette*, 20 Nov. 1828. 64 Shutter panels were an invention of Johann Baptist Krumpholtz (*c*.1745–90) whereby an eighth pedal or 'swell' pedal operated small hinged doors in the rectangular soundholes on the back of the harp. See Rensch, *Harps & harpists* (Bloomington, 1989), p. 173.   65 *Freeman's Journal*, 6 July

40 guineas, rising to 45 guineas if ornamented and lacquered in a colour. Similarly, a double-action pedal harp, varnished and gilt, sold for 60 guineas, with the top-of-the-line instrument, a lacquered and ornamented harp, selling for 65 guineas.[65] Offering harps at low prices was a primary element of John Egan's sales strategy, with his oft-repeated slogans in adverts 'For nearly *one-half* less than harps of the same quality [that] are imported.' The claim is corroborated by comparing a contemporary *Morning Post* advert of a London-made Erard double-action pedal harp priced at 120 guineas.[66]

The fact that Erard harps were regularly imported to dealers in Dublin apparently did not pose a threat to Egan, for he had cornered the market as Ireland's native harp maker. In 1816 Pierre Erard contemplated opening a shop in Dublin to sell directly to the public rather than continuing to offer Erard harps through dealers.[67] Apparently Erard harps on commission to a particular Dublin dealer were not selling well, prompting Pierre to travel to Ireland to investigate, and upon arrival, he discovered that the dealer had actually gone bankrupt. Consequently Erard retrieved the harps and rented an apartment at 2 Lower Sackville Street for his own warehouse. Despite great expectations, Pierre returned to London empty-handed. Although there had been some interest expressed in his harps, no actual cash sales occurred. His trip to Ireland, however, proved useful in ascertaining the challenges of importing harps across the Irish Sea. Pierre wrote of the double threat to selling harps in Dublin: firstly, the dangers of shipping harps, and secondly, the formidable presence of a local harp maker:

> In Dublin there is a maker named Egan [...] [H]e is selling and has sold many of his single-actions because there are a thousand problems related to importing harps from England: the crossing of the sea, the worry of being obliged to keep an instrument that one does not like, the difficulty of repairing it, the desire to give preference to those who are established in one's country, etc. [...] This national spirit has won friends for Egan [...][68]

1822. Nex compares piano and harp prices: a Broadwood grand piano (six octaves), £94 in 1818; a Broadwood square piano, £32 in 1818; and an Erard double-action pedal harp, £126 in 1817. Nex, 'The business of musical instrument making in early industrial London'.   **66** *Morning Post*, 19 May 1817.   **67** Adelson et al., *The history of the Erard piano and harp*, ii, p. 634.   **68** Ibid., p. 637. In the letter, Pierre Erard scathingly calls Egan's harps 'worse than everything one makes in London'. An early example of an Egan harp on view at Avondale House (see pp 41–2) certainly lacks the professional finished look of his later harps, however the subjective comment might reflect P. Erard's disdain for an Irish competitor. He also mentions the simplification of rods in Egan's mechanism as a disadvantage. These statements can be viewed in the context of the general tone of all of P. Erard's letters, which is tinged with professional arrogance and shows a complete

Pierre Erard never managed to get past the impenetrable barrier of loyalty exercised by the Irish and Anglo-Irish for their native harp maker. The Erard shop on Lower Sackville Street briefly sold single and double-action harps but was in operation for less than a year. In the end, Pierre Erard was defeated by the strength of patronage for Egan, and also the Irish maker's competitive pricing. However, several music and instrument sellers continued to import Erard harps from London.

Experiencing a booming trade, the Egan shop offered a complete range of matching accessories, such as music stands painted and gilded to match one's harp, and in addition to Egan models, a variety of second-hand harps by other makers. Old harps could be exchanged for new ones, and the Egan enterprise continually shaped its sales with offers seemingly too good to refuse. With the purchase of a harp came the added perks of the harp being 'kept in strings free of expense, for one year – and tuned free for a year, if in Dublin, or four miles from it'.[69] It might seem extravagant to provide a tuning service for a harp, but ladies of the nobility and gentry expected such things to be done for them. In addition to tuning, the full-service Egan operation promised to oversee repairs, varnishing and gilding 'on the most moderate terms'.[70] Of special importance, the harp business boasted its own covered caravan, which was specially constructed to transport harps and pianofortes in town and country. An ad in the *Dublin Evening Post* headed 'Great advantages to ladies hiring harps' touted harp rental as an attractive alternative for aspiring harpists in middle-class families who considered a harp purchase prohibitive.[71] Harps could be hired by the night, week, month or year, and free strings and tuning were applied to the arrangement. If the harp was bought within six months, the rental was applied towards purchase, making this an affordable option for many customers, and the arrangement could be extended for a number of years, barring any accidents.[72]

John Egan acquired a private residence in Coldblow Lane (Belmont Avenue) in Donnybrook,[73] and towards the end of the decade a momentous change took place in the business with the firm officially becoming John Egan & Son in 1828. The father-son harp company continued to attract patronage from Dublin Castle, including appointments from both the marquis of Anglesey and the duchess of Northumberland. The 1st marquis of Anglesey, Henry William Paget, served as lord lieutenant of Ireland (1828–9) and was succeeded by Hugh Percy, 3rd duke of Northumberland (1829–30), and as was the custom, Egan

contempt for his competitors. For example, he called Dizi's harp a 'worthless machine' and Delveaux's harps 'monstrosities'.   **69** *Dublin Evening Post*, 4 Apr. 1822.   **70** Ibid.   **71** Ibid. **72** Ibid.   **73** Coldblow Lane and Dawson Street are both given in the listing for John Egan's will.

harps were provided to their wives, Lady Charlotte Wellesley and Lady Charlotte Percy. The appointments capped an impressive span of twenty years of patronage from the wives of the lord lieutenants at Dublin Castle, commencing in 1809 with the initial pedal harp made for Egan's first patron, the duchess of Richmond.

'HARPS OF SUPERIOR FINISH'

The surviving pedal harps produced by John Egan and the later phase of the firm, John Egan & Son, can be classified into two distinct stylistic periods, distinguished by the capital designs: Grecian figures playing lyres (*c.*1817–25) and stylized winged caryatids (*c.*1825–35).

CAPITAL STYLE 1: GRECIAN FIGURES PLAYING LYRES, *c.*1817–25

The capital motif consists of three dancing Grecian figures playing lyres. The upper band has either oak leaves and acorns, or a winged cherub holding a lyre while riding on a pair of lions, or alternately, groups of winged putti. The base front is adorned with either a single winged cherub on lions, or putti, with all motifs uniformly moulded in composite material and gilded. The neoclassical motifs used to decorate the column, base, soundboard and back are all derived from the arts and architecture of ancient Greece, particularly the capital adorned with figures (figure 6.7).

Single-action pedal harp, Irish Linen Centre & Lisburn Museum, Lisburn
This harp has striking gilt soundboard motifs with two large Grecian figures holding lyres on a blue lacquered ground (plates 24–6). On the knee block is an animated trio of small lifelike angels: a winged boy angel sits on a grassy knoll playing a trumpet, his hair blown back as if by a strong wind; a second angel with outstretched arms is running; and a third boy angel with a lyre sits on a rock and appears to be waving his hand in a greeting.[74]

Single-action pedal harp, Newbridge House, Donabate, Co. Dublin
An extraordinary arabesque of angels, cupids and mythological figures is painted in gold on a blue background (plates 27–9).[75] At the bottom of the soundboard

---

74 A fascinating description of the harp's restoration is given by the restorer, Michael Parfett, 'The death and life of an Egan harp', *Conservation News* (Nov. 2003/ July 2004/ July 2005). For information on the last owner of the harp, Miss Maud Hunter (1860–1952), and restoration of the instrument, see Ian Vincent, 'New life for an Egan harp', *Lisburn Historical Society Journal*, 10 (2005–6), 1–5. In Vincent's article, there is some confusion as to the difference between Egan's revival Irish harp models made for the Belfast society's school as opposed to the earlier *cláirseachs* played at the 1792 Belfast Harp Festival produced by other makers. 75 This rare harp was

6.7 Greek ornament on Athenian columns as source motifs for neoclassical harp decoration, from Speltz's *The style of ornament*, 1904.

are two winged devils saluting each other with sheaves of wheat, perhaps a scene from the underworld. Symbolically and physically above them are heavenly angels with benevolent outstretched arms. Next are a male and a female figure with flying cupids whispering in their ears. Decoration combining myth with the stages of life continues with the Greek goddess Artemis, protector of childbirth, complete with a quiver of arrows strapped to her back, and she holds an infant. Grecian ladies holding garlands fill the upper section of the soundboard, and at the top of the base are two figures holding wheat and bowls to represent Demeter, the Greek goddess of agriculture and fertility. On the back are fanciful peacocks, doves and pheasants, as well as a merman with a platter of fruit on his head.

Double-action pedal harp no. 1918, National Museum of Ireland, Dublin
On a black background, two large Grecian figures are depicted on the lower soundboard; one plays a lyre and the other shakes a tambourine. The shutter panels on the back are decorated with mythological characters, including a

purchased by Alec Cobbe for his family home, Newbridge House, which was later acquired by Fingal County Council.   76 Dr Panagiotis Poulopoulos describes the function of the ratchet and pawl mechanism as, 'to activate springs inside the neck of the harp, which control the tension needed for the draught and return of the pedal' (email communication 4 July 2018). Seven Egan harps with ratchet and pawl mechanisms have come to light. The Erard early ram's head single-action harps are sometimes equipped with ratchet and pawl mechanisms, for example Erard

6.8 Ratchet and pawl mechanism on Egan single-action pedal harp no. 1918. Photo by Nancy Hurrell, courtesy of the National Museum of Ireland collection.

Greek satyr mask and trophies of instruments. The harp has an unusual ratchet and pawl mechanism on the back brass plate that adjusts the springs in the action, thereby controlling the tension needed to pull each pedal into the pedal-slot positions (figure 6.8).[76]

CAPITAL STYLE 2: STYLIZED WINGED CARYATIDS, c.1825–35

Three stylized winged caryatids with plumed headdresses are linked by wreaths, and within each wreath is a tiny inscription: *J EGAN/ DUBLIN*. Each figure morphs into decorative acanthus, and the spaces between the figures are filled with anthemion and rosettes. In the upper band are winged griffins with lyres. A satyr head and winged griffins adorn the front of the base, with all decorations moulded and gilded.

Double-action pedal harp no. 2040, Hatchlands Park, England
On the soundboard are imaginative arabesques in a Pompeiian style, with acrobatic figures, birds, winged cherubs and dragons, all in gold with red accents and detailed pen work. The figurative motifs in the arabesque, in mirror image, are vertically linked by pearls, scrolls and acanthus (figures 6.9 and 6.10).[77]

Double-action pedal harp no. 2066, National Museum of Ireland, Dublin
An example from Egan's later design period, a naturally varnished soundboard is overlaid with a rich pattern of acanthus leaves in gold. Gradated spiralling leafy vines each culminate with a rosette, and leafy bouquets adorn the back (figure 6.11).

no. 207 in the Museo dell'Arpa Victor Salvi, and no. 333 in London's RCM, and it is quite possible that Egan imitated Erard's use of the mechanism. The more usual practice is to place springs in the pedal box, as seen on the Grecian Erard harps and Egan's later harps.   **77** The harp is owned by Alec Cobbe, Hatchlands Park.

6.9 (*left*) Egan double-action pedal harp no. 2040 at Hatchlands Park. Photos by Nancy Hurrell, courtesy of Alec Cobbe.

6.10 (*right*) Painted arabesques on the soundboard of Egan harp no. 2040.

6.11 Egan double-action pedal harp no. 2066. Photo by Nancy Hurrell, courtesy of the National Museum of Ireland collection.

6.12 Egan single-action pedal harp no. 2078, with painted arabesques on the soundboard. Photos by Nancy Hurrell, courtesy of the Fenton House collection and the National Trust.

6.13 (*top left*) Grecian capital with winged caryatids on Egan harp no. 2078.   **6.14** (*top right*) Shutter panels on the back of harp no. 2078 at Fenton House.

6.15 (*bottom right*) John Egan & Son double-action pedal harp no. 2082. Photo by Nancy Hurrell, courtesy of Clive Morley Harps.

Single-action pedal harp no. 2078, Fenton House, London
On the harp's blue lacquered ground are exquisite neoclassical arabesques with fanciful combinations of swags, flowers, egrets, bunches of grapes with dangling pearls on strings and shells, all combined with symmetrical patterns of scrolling acanthus leaves (figures 6.12, 6.13 and 6.14).

Double-action pedal harp no. 2082, Clive Morley Harps, Lechlade, England
This extremely unusual harp produced by John Egan & Son in green has the
same shamrock decoration as the Royal Portable Irish Harps. Original strands
of shamrocks within lined borders adorn the back and neck, and presumably
would have decorated the soundboard, although it has been replaced (figure 6.15).

THE END OF AN ERA

At the pinnacle of success, the Egan family was suddenly struck by tragedy. In
1826, John Egan lost his wife; the cause of her death is unknown. An
announcement in the *Dublin Morning Register* simply described her as 'Mrs Egan,
wife of Mr Egan, Harp-maker, of Dawson-street.'[78] Two years later John Egan,
still recovering from the loss, became terminally ill and passed away.[79] Learning
the tragic news, Charles returned to Dublin in April of 1829, as reported in the
Freeman's Journal:

> Mr Charles Egan has arrived at Macken's Hotel, Dawson-street, from
> London. We regret that our talented countryman's visit is not a
> professional one; that it arises from a cause which we, in common with
> our fellow citizens, sincerely deplore, the recent sudden demise of his
> estimable father.[80]

John Egan's illness had precipitated the need to plan for the future,
prompting the partnership of John Egan & Son the year before the elder maker's
death. Now, as the surviving partner, it was up to John Jnr to assume the burden
of responsibility for the firm. Apparently, he adopted a plan of 'business as
usual' and there was no curtailing of the several harp models produced. A survey
of the dozen or so surviving harps inscribed *John Egan & Son* (figure 6.16)
confirms the continued manufacture of single- and double-action pedal harps,
Royal Portable Irish Harps and wire-strung Irish harps. In fact, the extensive
range of harps produced in this period may well have led to the firm
overextending itself, especially at a time when the demand for harps was
beginning to wane.

It seems that towards the end of his life, John Egan may have encountered a
cash-flow problem. Issuing extended credit to customers was a common practice

78 *Dublin Morning Register*, 26 Sept. 1826.   **79** *Appendix to the thirtieth report of the deputy keeper of the*
public records and keeper of the state papers in Ireland (Dublin, 1899), p. 323. The National Archives of
Ireland confirm that the will was destroyed in a fire in 1922 during the civil war. The official index
of wills at the archive lists the document under the surname Egan, as 'John, Dawson-street, and
Coldblow-lane, Donnybrook, co. Dublin' with the date 1829.   **80** *Freeman's Journal*, 9 Apr. 1829.

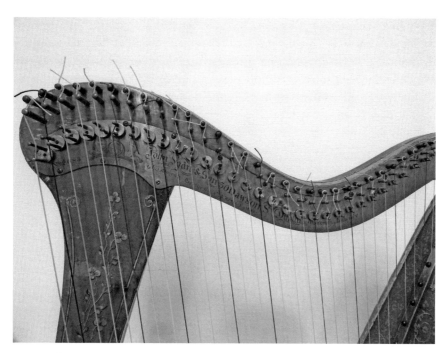

6.16 Royal Portable Irish Harp no. 2085 by John Egan & Son. Photo courtesy of Hamamatsu Museum of Musical Instruments, Japan.

for instrument makers, and there may well have been numerous unpaid bills for harps that had been delivered. Collecting payment would have been a sensitive issue for a merchant like John Egan, who prided himself on good relations with the upper classes. A common predicament for instrument makers, both the Erard and Broadwood records confirm the difficulties experienced by makers in extracting funds from customers, and several English musical instrument firms struggled and eventually went bankrupt.[81] There may have been other issues at play in the case of the Egan business, but for whatever reasons, after inheriting the firm John Jnr found himself in grave financial difficulty, and in 1830, nearly a year after his father's death, John Jnr was declared an insolvent debtor.[82] The rocky road to regaining financial stability continued for several years, and in 1836 he hoped for a fresh start, as announced in *Saunders' Newsletter*:

> Pedal harp manufacturer. John Egan, (Son of the late John Egan, of Dawson-street) begs to acquaint the nobility, gentry, and the public in

81 Nex, 'The business of musical instrument making in early industrial London', p. 274.
82 *Dublin Morning Register*, 2 Feb. 1830.

general, that having surmounted the difficulties he has been lately reduced to by means of his liabilities to his father's debts, as his partner in the above business, has recommenced the manufacturing of harps on his own account, and most gratefully returns his sincere thanks for the liberal support he and his Father received from the nobility of the United Kingdom for upwards of 40 years.[83]

In an attempt to rejuvenate the business, John Jnr offered even more generous terms of service than his late father had. With a harp purchase, an extended *three*-year warranty for servicing was included, and with a harp rental, Egan & Son provided free tuning. He slashed harp prices, announcing that 'To meet the pressure of the times, he has made a most considerable reduction in the prices of his new harps,' and likewise harp strings were sold 'considerably under the usual price, by the set or single string'.[84] Another marketing angle was to stress his advantage of being a performer on the harp, as well as working in the factory. As a player, John Jnr expected a harp to be perfectly in tune in all the different key signatures, and thus, the Egan harps regulated by him were guaranteed to have uniformly accurate semitones.[85] In trying to rebuild the Egan brand, John Jnr sought to emphasize the firm's royal patronage and its long-standing reputation, which he exaggerated in an advert as 'established upwards of 50 years', unscrupulously inflating the actual time frame of the enterprise by two decades.[86]

Changes were also taking place in John Jnr's personal life. With both parents gone, no one stood in the way of him marrying the bride of his choice, and in September of 1830, John Jnr married Catherine Dovey at St James church, Liverpool.[87] The eldest daughter of the late W. Joseph Dovey esq., a ship's anchor smith and ironmonger in Liverpool's dock area, Catherine would likely have been impressed by Egan's standing as a merchant to the Anglo-Irish aristocracy and the royal family. An announcement of the marriage named the groom's position of 'harp manufacturer to his majesty' in sharp contrast to that of the bride's father, an 'anchor smith of this town'.[88] The marriage appeared to be quite an advantageous match for a blacksmith's daughter, but in reality the

---

83 *Saunders's Newsletter*, 25 Apr. 1836.   84 *Dublin Morning Register*, 27 Sept. 1831. The advert lists Egan's address as 23 Dawson Street instead of 30 Dawson Street and he may have moved as a further cost-cutting measure.   85 Ibid., 21 Feb. 1832. Harp regulation, performed by trained technicians, is the process of adjusting the positions of the *fourchette* discs so that the semitone pitches in all the pedal settings are accurate. Over time the precise position of where the 'fork' stops the string needs adjustment as the natural bowing of the soundboard from string tension alters the string's length.   86 Ibid.   87 *Dublin Evening Packet and Correspondent*, 30 Sept. 1830. The couple was married by the Revd Mr Smyth in the Anglican church.   88 *Gore's Liverpool General Advertiser*, 23 Sept. 1830.

groom's famous father had also started out as a humble smith. Following the wedding, John Jnr and his bride settled in Dublin, and the union also became a business partnership.

In John Jnr's ongoing efforts to revive his ailing harp business, a reorganization took place. In 1832 a press announcement with the heading 'Old established harp manufactory' said a rejuvenated company was headed by the proprietor, 'E. Dovey',[89] and John Egan, no longer the legal owner, was instead the foreman of the business.[90] Hard times had forced John Jnr to abandon Dawson Street, and the company's new address was just around the corner at 52 Grafton Street, St Stephen's Green. It appears the insolvent debtor Egan had liquidated his assets to pay off his creditors, and he was then able to restructure a new harp company in his wife's family name. In an effort to rein in spending, and presumably also to reduce the number of workers, the business sold only one type of harp: the double-action pedal harp. John Jnr courted public sympathy with ads referring to his personal sacrifice ('John Egan, having worked at all the branches of harp-making during his father's long illness') and with self-promoting statements such as, 'being considered a good performer on the harp'.[91] If that weren't enough to attract customers, he also offered a novel perk with each harp purchase: customers received a free course of 'Bochsa's instructions' taught by John Egan. Additionally, John Jnr promised to teach ladies to tune their own harps in only a few lessons!

SIBLING RIVALRY

The Egan family history appears to be the age-old tale of two brothers, one remaining at home and the other seeking his fortune abroad. John and Charles were alike in that they both became harpists and teachers, but their fortunes were very different. As young men, John stayed in Ireland to work in the family firm while Charles went to London and assumed a high-profile position in the royal household. By the 1830s, their paths had grown even further apart, as had their standings in society. Charles Egan had become harpist to the queen, was a member of the Royal Academy of Music, and through marriage had become the brother-in-law to the aristocrat Lord Langford. John Egan Jnr, on the other hand, had become an insolvent debtor, a foreman in a struggling harp business, and had married a smith's daughter from Liverpool. The unequal positions in society likely created personal resentment. In this family dynamic there was also

89 John Egan Jnr's wife was Catherine Dovey. E. Dovey may have been her business name or it may have been another member of her family.   90 *Saunders's Newsletter*, 12 Oct. 1832.   91 Ibid., 6 Dec. 1832.

another strong player, who, as a woman, has been totally overlooked in the history of what was perhaps Ireland's most prestigious harp-making business. John and Charles had a sister, Miss Egan, whose Christian name is not known.

As a young woman in early nineteenth-century Ireland, Miss Egan would not have been groomed for a career, but rather to play the harp and to marry. Like her brothers, Miss Egan also became a performing harpist and a teacher, and the sons and daughter of Ireland's celebrated harp maker were often in the public eye, at times performing together on concerts. For example, in 1825, John Jnr and his sister joined forces in ensemble playing for a benefit concert organised by a colleague, Miss Ashe, in a performance of 'A grand bardic overture for six harps' by Bochsa.[92] The Egans were among the Dublin performers billed as 'six principal teachers of the harp'. In spite of the close proximity of John Jnr, it was to her illustrious brother Charles that Miss Egan formed an attachment, and she visited Charles in London for harp tuition for a brief period in 1831.[93] Later, Charles Egan paid tribute to his sister by dedicating a work to her. Egan's *Brillantes courtes et faciles: preludes for the harp* was inscribed, 'Composed & respectfully dedicated to Mrs Jackson', his sister's married name. Over the years in the Egan harp factory, a romantic affair between the owner's daughter and one of the workers, William Jackson, had taken place, resulting in their marriage, and by 1830, the couple lived at 38 Grafton Street.[94] Mrs Jackson, with several years' experience teaching privately, established a harp academy at their residence, where she taught both harp and pianoforte.[95] Well-known to the public as John Egan's daughter, she chose as her professional title 'Professor of the harp – daughter of the late celebrated harp manufacturer, Egan of Dawson-street'.[96] After two years of managing the harp school, she considered expanding her business pursuits. A confident young woman, possessing the self-reliant traits of her late father, Mrs Jackson made the momentous decision to follow in her father's footsteps and to manufacture and sell harps. Jennifer Nex observes the gendered nature of historical writings, in that the significant roles of women in musical instrument-making has yet to be fully acknowledged, for they are often invisible in historical archives.[97] Women were involved in family businesses as widows, sisters and daughters, and in many cases, including the Egans of Dawson Street, were ultimately responsible for the continuance of the family firm.

Mrs Jackson's foray into starting a harp-production workshop had great prospects, for her husband William already had the crucial hands-on training

92 *Freeman's Journal*, 1 June 1825. Charles Egan was living in London at this time and did not take part.   93 *Dublin Morning Register*, 14 Dec. 1831.   94 See Dublin Music Trade, dublinmusictrade.ie.   95 *Dublin Morning Register*, 20 Oct. 1830.   96 *Saunders's Newsletter*, 10 Dec. 1832.   97 Nex, 'Gut string makers in nineteenth-century London', 132–3.

and experience in harp-making. She began by offering a few double-action harps 'of superior brilliancy of tone' for sale, at half the price of London imports, implying that they were of Egan manufacture. Her start-up coincided with her brother's liquidation of property, and it seems likely that she acquired her initial stock of harps from him. In a curious turn of events, Mrs Jackson and John Jnr now both had harp businesses only steps away from each other on Grafton Street, and a brother-sister rivalry, perhaps simmering for years, finally came to a head. John Jnr, claiming superiority, began to refer to his company in ads as 'The *only original* harp manufactory in Ireland', spurring a fight with his sister for dominance in Dublin's harp trade.[98]

Three years on, in 1835, Jackson's Harp Manufactory was thriving and it relocated to 7 Molesworth Street, where the company offered a variety of new double-action harps in addition to used Egan harps (for example, a Portable Irish Harp was on offer, complete with stand, cover and travelling case).[99] The new harps were inscribed with the 'Jackson' name, but in reality they were essentially Egan-type instruments, for Mrs Jackson's workshop was staffed by craftsmen from the old Egan factory.[100] In the press, she described her employees as 'artists of the greatest experience, who served under her father, the late Mr Egan, for many years'.[101] It is significant that Mrs Jackson, instead of her brother, had retained the craftsmen from the family firm, in spite of the fact (or because of it) that John Jnr had been their foreman at Egan & Son. Now led by William Jackson, the experienced workers at Jacksons constructed, gilded and varnished new harps and also repaired harps of other manufacturers. Jackson harps steadily attracted attention, and two new harps from the Jackson workshop were displayed at the Royal Dublin Society's Exhibition of Irish Manufacturers, with Mrs Jackson awarded a prestigious silver medal by the committee.[102] A further endorsement for Jackson harps came from the Viceregal Lodge the same year, in 1835, and Mr Jackson was appointed harp maker to the lord lieutenant's wife, the countess of Mulgrave who was 'very much pleased with the tone and sweetness of the harp'.[103]

Not to be outdone by his sister, John Egan Jnr also courted and received patronage from the Countess Mulgrave for a harp presented to her by the Egan, Read & Taylor company. Egan had recently begun to manufacture harps again by joining forces with Nicholas Read and John Taylor, and they sold single- and double-action pedal harps and also portable harps. After a short time, Taylor

---

98 *Saunders's Newsletter*, 6 Dec. 1832.   99 Ibid., 14 Nov. 1835.   100 A surviving Jackson harp in a private collection is inscribed: *Jackson Late of Egan's/ No. 7 Molesworth St. Dublin/ No. 110/ Harpmaker to Her Excellency.*   101 *Saunders's Newsletter*, 26 Dec. 1836.   102 Ibid., 20 June 1835.   103 Ibid., 20 June 1835. The countess, Maria Liddell, was the wife of Constantine Henry Phipps, 1st marquis of Normandy, who served as lord lieutenant of Ireland, 1835–9.

left the firm, and the 1836 *Watson's or the Gentleman's and Citizen's Almanac*, lists the business on 21 Aungier Street as, 'Egan, Read, and Co., portable and pedal harp manufacturer to his Majesty'.[104] The business merger of Egan, Read & Taylor, far from being successful, actually led to further financial misfortune for John Jnr, and in February of that year, he once again found himself declared an insolvent debtor. It appears that he had fronted the enterprise, for the debtor listing was 'John Egan, late of Aungier-street, Dublin, lately trading with Nicholas Reed [*sic*] and John Taylor, as harpmakers'.[105]

Egan, Read & Taylor Royal Portable Irish Harp, 1835, National Museum of Ireland, Dublin
A rare example of the firm's production survives in the National Museum (figure 6.17). Similar to the later Egan portable harps, it is 90cm high and has thirty-three strings.[106] An inscription painted in gold on the neck reads *EGAN, READ & TAYLOR. MAKERS TO HIS MAJESTY. 21 AUNGIER. ST. DUBLIN*. The harp has a naturally varnished ground with painted gold shamrocks within lined borders on the soundboard, column and back. Gilt foliate scrolls decorate both sides of its head. The most striking difference between this harp and the portables produced by John Jnr's father at the end of his career is the mechanism. Instead of ivory ditals and *fourchette* discs, the makers reverted back to the earlier ring stops, on this harp appearing in groups of three in each octave.

The success of Mrs Jackson must have irritated her brother, and their growing rivalry continued to unfold in the press for several years. She made it clear to customers: 'Mrs Jackson begs to state that she is no way connected whatsoever with any other harp manufactory in the city.'[107] John Egan Jnr retaliated by publishing an extraordinary list of 'references', a thinly veiled term for a tally of persons who took his side against his sister in the growing feud:

> Reference can be had to the first nobility in the kingdom as to ability and promptitude; also, to professors the Misses Ashe's, Ely-place; Miss Cheese, at Messrs. Robinson and Bussell's, Mr Connell, Mr Lewis, and to Messrs. Moses and Pigot, Westmoreland-street; Mr McCullagh, Suffolk-street and Grafton-street; and Mr Ellard, Sackville-street, Manufacturers, with whose houses Egan has connection, and none other in Ireland.[108]

---

104 In 2013, an Egan, Read & Company double-action pedal harp was for sale at Railway House Antiques in Cape Town, South Africa.   105 *Saunders's Newsletter*, 29 Feb. 1836.   106 Inside the soundbox, written in ink, is the inscription: *Catherine Murtagh From 11 Morton, 23rd. July, 1835.* 107 *Saunders's Newsletter*, 4 Jan. 1836.   108 Ibid., 25 Apr. 1836. This mention of the music business Robinson & Bussell raises the interesting possibility that perhaps, in 1840, John Egan Jnr found work at the company producing portable harps. See chapter 8, pp 227–8.

6.17 Portable harp by Egan, Read & Taylor. Photo by Nancy Hurrell, courtesy of the National Museum of Ireland collection.

In spite of the support of friends and colleagues, John's dream of reviving the Egan enterprise was beginning to fade. An ad informed the public that messages could be left for him at either 19 Stephen's Green North, an instrument wareroom of Mr N. Walsh, or 21 Aungier Street, the shop of his former partner, Nicholas Read.[109] In the next year John rebounded temporarily following a visit to London where he spent some time with N.C. Bochsa. The London harpist-composer impressed upon Egan the absolute necessity of a correctly regulated harp for playing his 'new effects', and with his confidence bolstered, Egan announced plans to once again manufacture harps 'on the newest principles'.[110]

109 Ibid. 110 Ibid., 9 Jan. 1837.

In his book *Bochsa's explanations of his new harp effects and passages* (1832), the harpist-composer had introduced dazzling techniques such as 'enharmonic arpeggios', 'undulated sounds' (pedal slides) and the 'double glissando', all of which required extremely accurate semitones in every key signature.[111] Harp music in the nineteenth century gradually moved towards a stylistic transformation, abandoning the former traits of Alberti bass accompanying a treble melody. With the double-action harp and the special effects introduced by Bochsa, compositions relied less on melody and more on modulations of tone colour manifested by glissandi and resonating arpeggios. As observed by Zingel, the new style of harp compositions exploited the special nature of the harp, and the repertoire of the harp and piano, formerly interchangeable, began to follow different paths stylistically.[112] John Egan Jnr was able to capitalize on the popularity of Bochsa's new techniques: now trading from 12 Duke Street, Egan promoted his harp-regulation, tuning and stringing services. John's feud with his sister was still ongoing, and he issued a combative statement: 'Mr Egan begs to say he has no connection whatever with the proprietor of the shop, 7, Molesworth-street, though falsely represented during his stay in London.'[113]

A final address for John Egan Jnr in the 1838 *Pettigrew and Oulton* reveals yet another move, to 57 Bride Street, and his professional title is 'John Egan, harp manufactr'.[114] It is unclear whether 'manufacturer' is meant in the present or past tense, however no harp engraved with this address has come to light. Lasting success seems to have evaded John Jnr due to the initial hurdle of inheriting his father's debts, and unfortunately his problems seemed to continue throughout the subsequent decade. The collaborations with E. Dovey and later Read & Taylor seem to have lasted only briefly before falling apart. In coping with his setbacks, John continued to rely on his late father's accolades to boost his own self-image, as evinced in his professional title of 'John Egan (son and successor of the late John Egan, of Dawson-street) harp-maker, by appointment, to the royal family'.[115] Granted, John Jnr had worked with his father for several years and rightfully shared his late father's distinction, however the son never attained the level of celebrity of the father, nor of his brother Charles, and due to a myriad of circumstances, he was unable to fulfil the expectations for him to successfully carry the family business into the future.

---

111 N.C. Bochsa, *Bochsa's explanations of his new harp effects and passages* (London, 1832).   112 Hans Joachim Zingel, *Harp music in the nineteenth century*, trans. and ed. Mark Palkovic (Bloomington, 1992), p. 26.   113 *Saunders's Newsletter*, 9 Jan. 1837.   114 *Pettigrew and Oulton, Dublin Almanac and General Register of Ireland* (Dublin, 1838), p. 541.   115 *Saunders's Newsletter*, 30 Jan. 1837.

WILLIAM JACKSON JNR, 32 DAWSON STREET

In the custom of primogeniture, the eldest son inherits the family business, and it is assumed the enterprise will continue to thrive through the male line. The Egan sons did play an important part in promoting the Egan harp enterprise, but in reality it was the daughter who kept the family's harp-making tradition alive. A self-assured businesswoman in a predominantly male field, Mrs Jackson surpassed her brother in the end. This formidable competitor, with the help of her husband and the former Egan factory workers, managed to put John Jnr's harp shop out of business. And through Mrs Jackson, the family trade was passed on to the next generation, for her son William also became a harp maker. William Jnr, like his mother, was raised in the atmosphere of wood, strings and paint, and at an early age he took on jobs for the firm. By 1836 William Jnr was stringing and tuning harps and was mentioned in Mrs Jackson's advert: 'Harps strung and tuned in town and country, with the greatest accuracy, by her son'.[116] By the early 1840s, William Jnr became a partner in the business, and in the 1841 *Pettigrew and Oulton* directory he is listed as 'William Jackson, jun. harp manufacturer', working from the address 3 Molesworth Street.[117] In 1843 William Jnr became a partner in the company, according to the *Post Office Annual Directory and Calendar*, which advertises 'Jackson and Son, harp makers'.[118] After collaborating with his son for four years, William Snr retired in 1844 to the family's residence, Annefield, at Booterstown Avenue, and shortly after, passed away. With his father's death, William Jnr inherited the Jackson harp business.[119] For seven years, Mrs Jackson's manufactory had operated on Molesworth Street, but when her son inherited the harp business, an historic move was made to new premises.[120] An advertisement in the press has the heading 'Egan's old established pedal harp manufactory, 32 Dawson street, Dublin', followed by 'William Jackson *grandson and successor to the late J. Egan*' (figure 6.18).[121] The grandson of John Egan was now crafting and selling harps in the old family factory on Dawson Street.

William Jackson sold both single- and double-action harps of his own manufacture and also harps by London makers including Erard. Promoting harps by Erard, his grandfather's greatest rival, would have been unthinkable in

116 Ibid., 26 Dec. 1836.   117 *Pettigrew and Oulton, Dublin Almanac and General Register of Ireland* (Dublin, 1841), p. 692.   118 *The Post Office Annual Directory and Calendar* (Dublin, 1843), p. 277.   119 Dublin Music Trade, dublinmusictrade.ie.   120 Ibid. The directories list the Jackson business at two locations on Molesworth Street: 7 Molesworth Street (1836–9) and 3 Molesworth Street (1840–3). It might be the same premises if the street numbers changed.   121 *Dublin Weekly Register*, 31 May 1845. Number 32 on Dawson Street, designated as the old Egan manufactory, indicates that the street numbers had changed since John Egan's former tenure was at 30 Dawson Street.

EGAN'S
OLD ESTABLISHED PEDAL HARP MANU-
FACTORY.
32, DAWSON STREET, DUBLIN.
—
WILLIAM JACKSON
Grandson and Successor to the late J. Egan,
BEGS to inform the Nobility and Gentry that he
is constantly supplied with an assortment of DOUBLE
and SINGLE ACTION HARPS, of his own and Lon-
don Manufacture, which he will dispose of on MODERATE
TERMS.
Harps carefully repaired. Painted, Varnished, Gilt,
Strung, and Tuned in Town and Country.
A constant supply of London Silver, Gut, and Bochsa's
Metallic Harp Strings.
Portable and Irish Harps made to order.

6.18 William Jackson announcement of the return to the Egan Dawson Street manufactory, in *Dublin Weekly Register*, 31 May 1845.

Egan's day. However, a quarter of a century later, William explored a range of opportunities to ensure the continued success of his music business. In addition to producing Jackson harps, he became somewhat of a shrewd dealer of imported harps, taking annual business trips to London, where he met with the Erard company and the other harp makers to arrange competitive pricing for harps shipped to Dublin. Low-priced harps had always been a cornerstone of the Egan sales strategy, and William promised customers his imported harps were sold 'at lower prices than any other house in Dublin'.[122] He primarily retailed pedal harps, but other models could be requested such as 'Portable and Irish Harps made to order'.[123] Another marketing technique was to offer something for free to attract customers. With the purchase of a set of strings, harps would be strung and tuned 'free of expense', and the usual services of repairing, painting and gilding were offered for harps, and also guitars.[124]

Harp lessons with a Miss Jackson could also be arranged at the shop on Dawson Street. A professor of the harp and pupil of Bochsa, presumably Miss Jackson was William's sister.[125] Their mother, Mrs Jackson, returned to her former profession as a harp teacher, now that William had taken charge of the Jackson business. In 1846 Mrs Jackson moved to Belfast and began a teaching practice in her new home on 14 Donegall Street, as reported in the *Belfast Commercial Chronicle*:

> We understand the lady who is now a resident of this town, is daughter of the late Mr Egan, the well-known harp manufacturer, and is perfectly qualified to give instructions on this delightful instrument.[126]

122 Ibid., 5 Sept. 1846.   123 Ibid., 7 Dec. 1844.   124 Ibid., 5 Sept. 1846.   125 Ibid., 31 Jan. 1846.
126 *Belfast Commercial Chronicle*, 25 Nov. 1846.

Mrs Jackson left Dublin knowing that in her lifetime she was responsible for extending the Egan harp-making legacy, enabling three generations of the family to produce harps in the Dawson Street factory.

NEPHEW AND SUCCESSOR TO THE LATE JOHN EGAN

It was a fairly common practice in the nineteenth century for a family trade to be passed on to succeeding generations. John Egan set a high standard for quality Irish-made harps, and building upon his reputation, his son, daughter and grandson enabled a family legacy of fifty years of harp-making in Ireland. Attracted by the Egan family success in the commercial marketplace, Francis Hewson, John Egan's nephew, also became a harp maker. In 1844, the dominance of the Egan harp trade was evident from the awards presented at the Royal Dublin Society's annual exhibition, where Egan's grandson and nephew took top honours with the medals for double-action harps awarded to W. Jackson of Dawson Street and to F. Hewson of King Street.[127] Francis Hewson's workshop on South King Street was active from the 1840s to the 1860s, and his final address listed in the 1868 *Thom's Irish Almanac* was 3 York Street. Although Hewson produced both pedal harps and Irish harps, only two of the latter survive in the National Museum of Ireland (figure 6.19). His familial connection to Egan is highlighted in the painted inscriptions on the two harps: FRANCIS HEWSON./ *MAKER/ Nephew & Successor/ To the late JOHN EGAN/ HARP-MAKER/ To the ROYAL FAMILY/ 37, SOUTH-KING St./ Dublin/ 1849.*

The instruments are formed in the same shape and size as John Egan's Improved Irish Harp model made for the Belfast Harp Society school. Like Egan's wire-strung harps, on the central strip of the soundboard staples appear by the string holes to protect the wood from the wire strings. The soundboard decoration was also inspired by the earlier Egan harps, with vines of shamrocks artistically arranged, and gold spirals that culminate in rosette flowers. Near the bottom, in the same position as seen on Egan harps, an official crest in gold accompanies the maker's inscription. It appears to be a royal crest, but a closer look reveals a coat of arms composed of Irish symbols. Whereas the royal crest has a lion and unicorn guarding the British shield, Hewson's version presents two seated wolfhounds guarding a shield adorned with the Brian Boru harp. An antique Irish crown replaces the English royal crown above the Irish harp. Below the shield an inscribed banner again replicates the British crest but alters the message. The official British banner bears the inscription *Dieu et mon droit*,

---

127 *Statesman and Dublin Christian Record*, 18 June 1844.

6.19 Irish harp by Francis Hewson, John Egan's nephew. Photo by Nancy Hurrell, courtesy of the National Museum of Ireland collection.

meaning 'God and my right', to denote the sovereign's divine right to rule. In contrast, Hewson's banner has the Irish proverb 'Gentle when stroked, fierce when provoked', and the two wolfhounds display fierce expressions. In spite of this pro-independence messaging, Hewson had no hesitation in also capitalizing on his uncle's appointment to the British royal family, which is referred to in the inscription on the harp. Manufacturing wire-strung models well into the 1860s,

Hewson supplied instruments to blind harpers, enabling the survival of their unique musical tradition. One of Hewson's harps, pictured in the *Journal of the County Louth Archaeological Society*, was owned by the blind harper Hugh O'Hagan, who was once again given the ubiquitous designation of the 'last minstrel' of Co. Louth.[128]

In addition to the Egan family businesses, the craftsmen from the Egan factory continued to make similar harps for other instrument companies. One former worker from the Egan factory even produced his own harps, as described in an 1872 issue of *English Mechanic and World of Science*:

> Egan himself is now no more, but I found one of his workmen on York-street Dublin. His daughters were seamstresses, and this workman resided with them. He offered to supply a superior harp for £10. An equally effective but not so handsome an instrument may be constructed for a considerable less sum.[129]

128 Anonymous, 'The harp of the last minstrel of County Louth', *Journal of the County Louth Archaeological Society*, 1:4 (Oct. 1907), p. 104. 129 *English Mechanic and World of Science*, 384 (2 Aug. 1872, London), 510.

7 / Players and prototypes

The timing of the Egan harp enterprise, operating in the early 1800s, was fortuitous in that it coincided with several key cultural developments – the crucial status of the harp as a signifier of national identity in post-union Ireland, the new social mobility of Dublin's merchant class, and Anglo-Irish society's unprecedented infatuation with the pedal harp. An ornate, elegantly shaped harp was highly desirable for music-making in aristocratic social settings, and the Egan workshop flourished in a golden age of harp-playing. As a coveted luxury item, a gilded statuesque pedal harp was a mainstay in the aristocratic music room, and a smaller shamrock adorned Portable Irish Harp projected a genteel patriotism. The indisputable visual impact of the instrument was exploited by artists who regularly incorporated harps in late eighteenth- and early nineteenth-century portraiture. Several well-known English artists such as Thomas Gainsborough (1728–88), Joshua Reynolds (1723–92) and George Romney (1734–1802) created striking portraits of prominent ladies posing with their decorative pedal harps, to accentuate beauty by association of both player and instrument.[1] One of the most widely recognized paintings from this era of harpist portraiture is *Self-portrait with harp* (1791) by Rose Adélaïde Ducreux (1761–1802), which epitomizes the visual splendour of a young harpist dressed in an exquisite Pompadour-striped silk gown,[2] nonchalantly strumming a handsomely carved harp.[3]

Beyond the harp's desirable appearance and role as a high-status instrument, the pedal harp also fulfilled an important sociological function, for owning a harp was perceived as a necessity for a young lady to ascend in society. In upper-class Irish and Anglo-Irish families with daughters, a diligent father felt obliged to purchase a harp to further his daughter's prospects. The ability to play the harp or the pianoforte was considered one of the suitable 'accomplishments' of a cultivated lady, along with drawing, fine embroidery and dancing. Perceived as

1 For example, see Gainsborough's *Portrait of Louisa, Lady Clarges*, Reynolds' *The countess of Eglinton* and Romney's *Lady Louisa Hervy, countess of Liverpool*.   2 The distinctive stripes in the fabrics of gowns worn by Madame de Pompadour were imitated in harp decoration with stripes painted on the sides of the bases of some late eighteenth-century pedal harps.   3 This painting is in the collection of the Metropolitan Museum of Art.

'ornaments' in society, unmarried females were meant to be admired, and the display of a lady's musical talent attracted further attention and esteem. It was felt that skilful harp-playing acted as an entrée into fashionable company, where she could be noticed by an eligible bachelor. In contemporary manuals on conduct published for young ladies, instructions were given on deportment and also the importance of a lady's accomplishments as a stepping stone to achieving a good match and a prized marriage. In one such manual, the wise words of a 'cabinet council of mothers' explain the demand for female accomplishments in the fashionable world:

> 'A young lady,' they say, 'is nobody, and nothing, without accomplishments; they are as necessary to her as a fortune: they are indeed considered as part of her fortune, and sometimes are even found to supply the place of it. Next to beauty, they are the best tickets of admission into society which she can produce; and everybody knows, that on the company she keeps, depends the chance of a young woman's settling advantageously in the world.'[4]

Parents were convinced that several hours of daily harp practice was a wise investment, and the time-consuming pursuits of music and art were also useful for keeping daughters productively occupied at home, safely sheltered away from unseemly temptations.

Visually, an exquisite empire-style pedal harp was the perfect prop in the ongoing drama of courtship unfolding in the music room. A finely decorated instrument drew attention to a young woman's own loveliness, for the harp's classical ornaments, by association, were meant to suggest an ideal of perfection in both instrument and player in this age dominated by a fashionable neoclassicism. The sublime Grecian figure motifs adorning the harp capital and soundboard signalled the harpist's own classical beauty, and the harpist reinforced the idealized image with her choice of apparel. With upswept hair in curls and dressed in a white flowing high-waisted Grecian gown, the harpist fabricated a resemblance to the exquisite Greek and Roman marble statues of goddesses sent home to the great houses of Ireland and England following the grand tours of Italy. The Egan harps adorned with lyre-playing angels hinted of the heavenly sounds created by the 'divine' harpist. The act of harp-playing itself seemed to affect the onlooker, for the graceful movements of a harpist plucking the strings drew attention to her attractive arms and hands, and the delicate tones from an expressive touch on the strings never failed to charm. In *The mirror of the graces*

4 Maria Edgeworth and Richard Lovell Edgeworth, *Practical education* (New York, 1801), ii, p. 120.

(1830), young women are encouraged to assume an 'easy' attitude, with a 'polished turn' of the hand and arm, 'gentle motion of a lovely neck' and a sweet expression of 'intelligent countenance' while performing at the harp.[5] Just as Sydney Owenson's fictional harpists projected visual beauty with ethereal harp sounds, in Jane Austen's novel *Mansfield Park* the powerful allure of the instrument is woven into the story:

> A young woman, pretty, lively, with a harp as elegant as herself; and both placed near a window cut down to the ground, and opening on a little lawn, surrounded by shrubs in the rich foliage of summer, was enough to catch any man's heart.[6]

The novel's harpist, Miss Crawford, used her playing to attract the romantic attentions of Edmund, who was so enamoured with the instrument that he came to hear her play every day. Austen observed that Miss Crawford's harp 'added to her beauty, wit, and good-humour', and in her expressive playing, 'there was something clever to be said at the close of every air'.[7]

For daughters in upper-class families, the requisite harp lessons took place in their homes where they were taught by either a resident governess or a professional harp master. A harp purchase was also deemed a good investment for a lady's future domestic life. John Bennett, in *Letters to a young lady* (1789), instructs his lady readers that playing an instrument will enable them to entertain their friends, increase their own happiness and also 'inspire tranquillity' for the 'ruffled or lonely hours' of a married lady's life at home.[8] Typically a lady's performances of enchanting harp solos were solely for the benefit of a private drawing-room audience of family and friends, and a refined married lady was discouraged from performing outside the home, as it would inappropriately draw attention to herself and upstage her husband. Richard Leppert in *Music and image* (1988) observed that 'A well-bred woman who took music so seriously constituted a threat to social boundaries.'[9] Different customs were observed, however, for women in the middle classes, like Miss Egan, Miss Cheese and their contemporaries who regularly took part in public concerts and offered harp lessons in their Dublin music academies. In classes for the daughters in merchant families, harp teachers passed on coveted harp skills to students who also aspired to gentility by learning the instrument.

5 *The mirror of the graces: or, the English lady's costume … by a lady of distinction* (Edinburgh, 1830), p. 154. 6 Jane Austen, *Mansfield Park* (London, 1814), pp 57–8.   7 Ibid.   8 John Bennett, *Letters to a young lady, on a variety of useful and interesting subjects*, 2 vols (Warrington, England, 1789; repr. Philadelphia, 1793), i, p. 103.   9 Richard D. Leppert, *Music and image* (Cambridge, 1988), p. 40.

7.1 Birr Castle, Co. Offaly. Photo by Nancy Hurrell.

Egan harps were primarily owned by the established families in Ireland's castles and great country houses. By looking at the historical archives for a few individuals from the period who played Egan harps as an amateur pursuit, attitudes towards the instrument and its music are revealed. For example, two known players of Egan harps – Lady Alicia Parsons at Birr Castle and Frances Power Cobbe of Newbridge House – were encouraged to play the harp at a time when the culture greatly valued feminine musical accomplishment.

LADY ALICIA PARSONS OF BIRR CASTLE

Egan harps are currently displayed in several historic house museums in Ireland and England, but many of these antique harps were either purchased in modern times or donated to museums, as opposed to being a surviving family heirloom original to the house. The likelihood of a historical harp having been passed down in a family over two centuries is fairly remote, as instruments are typically sold over time, and the more usual provenance of a historical harp includes a succession of private owners and instrument dealers.[10] A notable exception is

10 For instance, the Egan harps produced for members of the royal family are no longer part of the Royal Collection.

the Egan Portable Irish Harp at Birr Castle (figure 7.1), displayed in the magnificent Gothic music 'saloon'. The beautifully preserved instrument has remained in the family for nearly two hundred years, and it is still played occasionally for special performances.[11] The harp was purchased by Sir Lawrence Parsons (1758–1841), the 2nd earl of Rosse, for his daughter, Lady Alicia Parsons (*c*.1815–85) (figure 7.2).[12] A member of the Irish parliament, Sir Lawrence was known as a patriot statesman with nationalist political sympathies. Thuente counts Parsons as an early influence on Theobald Wolfe Tone, and in the 1780s he was involved in the Volunteer movement with Lord Moira, Charles Vallancey, Henry Grattan and Henry Flood.[13] A prominent opponent of the Act of Union of 1801, following its passage, Sir Lawrence retreated to his country estate, turning his energies towards rebuilding the castle. Among the improvements undertaken in the early 1800s was the addition of the spacious music saloon (plate 30). Prized for its acoustics and architectural beauty, the great room has continued to be a favourite setting for concerts and music-making by succeeding generations.[14] The main feature of the Gothic-style space is a dramatic fan-vaulted ceiling, and the room's majestic pointed-arch windows overlook a picturesque waterfall on the river Camcor. Here in the music saloon, Lady Alicia's sparkling harp tones were accompanied by the rippling sounds of the waterfall as she played her pieces. Sir Lawrence and his wife Alice Lloyd chose to school their children at home, and proficiency in harp-playing was part of Lady Alicia's education. The small Irish harp was appropriately sized for the young Alicia, and the instrument's nationalistic decoration would not have been lost on Sir Lawrence.

On her green Irish harp, Lady Alicia played the fashionable music of the day and seems to have been a proficient harpist, according to her surviving harp books.[15] The collections illustrate the range of musical genres in vogue: Irish melodies, opera themes, and also *quadrilles*, which were accompaniments for the new dance trend. Alicia's books of harp arrangements by N.C. Bochsa include *Les plaisirs de la mémoire*, a compilation of arranged melodies by various composers, with a subtitle suggesting the pieces are 'Calculated for the drawing room as well

11 Lord and Lady Rosse kindly allowed me to perform a concert on the Egan harp at Birr Castle on 22 July 2012. Kathleen Loughnane has performed on the harp several times, the first occasion in 1997, and the instrument is pictured on the cover of her CD, *Affairs of the harp* (Galway, 1997). The harp was restrung by Paddy Cafferky, who used modern gut stringing tuned down to a lower pitch (personal communication, 25 Mar. 2010).   12 Birr Castle, 'Family history of the Parsons family', birrcastle.com/family, accessed 1 July 2012. Alicia's older sister, Lady Jane, is also believed to have played the family harp.   13 Mary Helen Thuente, *The harp restrung: the United Irishmen and the rise of literary nationalism* (Syracuse, 1994), pp 36–40.   14 Lord and Lady Rosse present an impressive concert series annually.   15 Lord and Lady Rosse kindly allowed me to examine the music books of Lady Alicia at Birr Castle in July of 2012. A few of the pieces are hand stamped

7.2 Portrait of Lady Alicia Parsons, courtesy of Oxmantown Settlement Trust, Birr Castle.

as for the boudoir, and intended to be performed from memory'. Another work
arranged by Bochsa, 'Fantasia for the harp', contains favourite themes from the
operas *Don Giovanni, Otello* and *The barber of Seville*. Also included is sheet music
designated for the pianoforte, which Lady Alicia may have adapted to the harp.
Sight-reading piano music at the harp to broaden one's repertoire was a
common practice and was recommended by Bochsa in his method book.[16]
Among Alicia's piano music is the favourite Italian song 'Sul margine d'un Rio',
and in a collection by Constantine Montague, *Fashionable quadrilles and German
country dances*, is the well-liked 'Minuet de la cour'. Alicia's Irish music is in the
format of familiar melodies arranged with harpistic variations, for instance
'Fantasia Irlandoise for the harp' by French harpist Théodore Labarre, as well
as his 'Brilliant fantasia for the harp, introducing the three much admired Irish
melodies "Sly Patrick" – "The Moreen" – & "Nora Creena"'. Thus, the well-
known Irish songs were enveloped in a desirable classical Continental style. Little

'Sold by I. Willis, No. 7 Westmoreland St. Dublin'.   **16** Bochsa, *Nouvelle méthode de harpe*, p. 8.

is known of Lady Alicia's harp-playing, but these important social artefacts of harp and music provide a window into the actual harp sound and the music played in her amateur harp performances.

As a young woman in the 1830s, Lady Alicia divided her time between Birr Castle and the family's London residence at 4 Belgrave Square, and Sir Lawrence was serving as a peer in Westminster's house of lords. One of Lady Alicia's acquaintances in London was Edward Conroy (1809–69), whose father had close ties to the royal family. Sir John Conroy (1786–1854) was the long-time private secretary to the duchess of Kent (1786–1861), having formerly served as an equerry to her husband, the duke of Kent (1767–1820).[17] Conroy was her public-relations officer and confidant, a highly influential position, and he advised the duchess on matters pertaining to her daughter, Princess Victoria, the heir to the throne. Katherine Hudson, in *A royal conflict*, outlines the complex relationship of Princess Victoria and her mother with Sir John Conroy and his family, as they met socially and merged as a single family.[18] Under Sir John's strict recommendations, Princess Victoria led a protected, sheltered childhood in which her friends were principally limited to the Conroys, and the Conroy children were often in Victoria's company at the palace.[19] At the Conroy residence, conveniently located only a short distance from Kensington Palace, the family also hosted parties on special occasions for the duchess and the princess. These were primarily musical gatherings where the Conroy ladies took turns performing pieces on the harp and the pianoforte, and in fact, Edward's mother, Lady Conroy, seems to have been a harpist of note, for N.C. Bochsa dedicated several harp solos to her.[20] At family parties, choruses were sung to the harp, and Edward and his sisters, Jane and Victoire, danced the quadrille with the Princess Victoria.[21]

In the spring of 1837 Edward Conroy described Lady Alicia Parsons in his journal as 'gay and very handsome, sought-after and admired'.[22] Edward, as a childhood friend of the future queen, appeared to have lofty connections, and Malcomson comments that with the expected advancement of the Conroy family to Victoria's court upon her accession to the throne, a marriage to Edward seemed to have 'much to recommend it'.[23] However, the match was resisted by Alicia's family, who expressed concerns as to Edward's character and

---

17 The duchess of Kent, Princess Victoria of Saxe-Coburg had married Edward, duke of Kent, a younger brother to George IV.   18 Katherine Hudson, *A royal conflict* (London, 1994), p. 71.   19 Ibid. The 'Kensington System' was the name given the strict set of rules governing the upbringing of Princess Victoria devised by the duchess of Kent and Sir John Conroy.   20 Ibid.   21 Ibid., p. 72, quote from Queen Victoria's journal, 28 Nov. 1832, the Royal Archives.   22 A.P.W. Malcomson, *The pursuit of the heiress: aristocratic marriage in Ireland, 1740–1840* (Belfast, 2006), p. 158.   23 Ibid.

station, and owing to the opposition, the couple eloped to Gretna Green in Scotland on the 28 May.[24] The surprise elopement, covered for a time in the press, was soon overshadowed by other extraordinary events. Within three weeks, on the 20 June, William IV died, and Princess Victoria ascended to the throne. This altered the fortunes of the Conroy family, but not as anticipated, for the young queen, desiring independence from the overbearing Sir John, dismissed him and his family from court. A pension and a baronetcy was brokered, both of which Edward later inherited. In spite of Queen Victoria's removal of the Conroy family from courtly life in 1837, Hudson cites a notable exception made for Lady Alicia Conroy. Edward's new bride was invited to the palace on the 8 July of that year to meet the queen, who described Alicia in her diary as 'a very pretty young person'.[25]

Lady Alicia fulfilled the expectations for females of her status, which included proficiency on a musical instrument, and it is noteworthy that the instrument purchased for her by Sir Lawrence was Egan's newly invented Portable Irish Harp with dital mechanism. The date 1821 is engraved on a small brass plate attached to the harp, confirming it as an early example of a model in production for less than two years. With the choice of this particular instrument for Lady Alicia, Sir Lawrence demonstrated his patronage for a native Irish harp maker and his innovative design.

Lady Alicia's Portable Irish Harp, 1821, Birr Castle, Co. Offaly
This well-preserved harp is finely decorated with a brilliant green lacquer background overlain with delicately painted gilt motifs of strands of shamrocks on the pillar and neck, and on the back are bouquets of shamrocks, roses and thistles in combination with classical anthemion and acanthus (plate 31). The brass plate is inscribed *Manufactured by John Egan Inventor. / 30 Dawson St. / Dublin*, and on the opposite side is an unusual small brass plate engraved: *J. Egan. Dublin. / 1821* (plate 32). The portable harp is equipped with ivory ditals for sharpening the strings, and inside the soundbox is a stabilizing rod. In excellent

24 Lady Alicia Parsons and Edward Conroy eloped to Gretna Green in May, and a second marriage ceremony was held in July at the Anglican church, Kensington. The marriage certificate, Edward's diary, and letters of Edward and Alicia are held in the Conroy Collection at Balliol College, Oxford University. Lord Rosse and Edward reconciled, and the young Conroy was welcomed into Alicia's family. In 1842 Sir John and his family settled in the Berkshire countryside at Arborfield Hall, and Edward and Alicia lived on the family estate in the nearby Arborfield Grange, where a son, John Conroy, was born to the couple in 1845. Two years later, the couple separated, and although Edward and Alicia never completely reconciled, they continued to live in neighbouring houses on the same large estate amongst rich parklands, meadows and the river Lodden.   25 Hudson, *A royal conflict*, p. 137, quote from Queen Victoria's journal, 8 July 1837, the

structural condition, the harp is still playable and has a superb sound, combining a rich tone with a clear timbre.

FRANCES POWER COBBE OF NEWBRIDGE HOUSE, DONABATE

The Cobbe family's historic account books for Newbridge House (figure 7.3) confirm the purchase of an Egan harp in 1839 by Charles Cobbe (1781–1857) for his daughter, Frances Power Cobbe (1822–1904) (figure 7.4). It had been almost twenty years since the Egan harp was delivered to Lady Alicia at Birr Castle, and yet the custom whereby the head of an aristocratic family provided a harp for his daughter was still in practice. Generations of the Cobbe family had been known for their active interest in music, and Frances Cobbe's grandmother, Anne Power Cobbe (1756–1835), had also descended from a musical lineage.[26] Anne Power Cobbe's mother, Frances Power Trench (*c*.1716–93), was patron to the great harper-composer Turlough Carolan, and the famous song 'Fanny Power' was written for her.[27] Frances Power Cobbe was in fact the namesake of her great-grandmother immortalized in the song, and Frances' own mother, Frances Conway (1776–1847), had been a harpist, pianist and singer, prompting an assumption that young Fanny would follow in her ancestors' footsteps.[28] According to archival records, the Egan harp was purchased for Fanny when she was 17 years old. A 'general accounts' register includes the entry 'To a harp & things … £31', suggesting a Royal Portable Irish Harp model. Another entry reads 'To Mr Egan for harp lessons', and in the following year a sum was paid 'To Mr Egan for harp strings'.[29] Although Frances' harp is no longer held at Newbridge House, the account books supply information on the types of harp services supplied to a country house in 1839–40 by 'Mr Egan', which, given the dates, must refer to John Egan Jnr. The recurrent services of 'tuning piano & harp' in the account entries would have likely been performed by John Jnr, considering his standard catchphrase in adverts was 'harps tuned in town and country'. By 1842, Frances' harp lessons were discontinued, although she was still actively learning new music according to several additional listings of 'music for Fanny'.[30]

At the time of the harp purchase, Frances Cobbe was already familiar with the instrument, having commenced harp studies a few years earlier at Miss Runciman's school for ladies in Brighton.[31] The institution, run by Miss

Royal Archives.   **26** See *The Cobbe family and music in Ireland and Bath* published by the Cobbe Collection Trust, courtesy of Alec Cobbe, pp 6–9.   **27** Ibid. An early printed version of 'Carolan's concerto' in John Lee (ed.), *A favourite collection of the so much admired old Irish tunes* (1778), is titled 'Mrs Poer'.   **28** Ibid.   **29** Charles Cobbe, 'General accounts' pages from 1835–43 in Cobbe Papers, Ce4-3 ii, from Alec Cobbe.   **30** Ibid.   **31** Frances Power Cobbe, *The life of Frances Power Cobbe by herself* (Boston, 1894), i, p. 47.

7.3 Newbridge House, Co. Dublin.
Photo by Nancy Hurrell.

7.4 Frances Power Cobbe, *c.*1900.
The Miriam and Ira D. Wallach
Division of Art, Prints and
Photographs: Print Collection,
New York Public Library.

Runciman and Miss Roberts at 32 Brunswick Terrace, focused on grooming young ladies on the accomplishments of singing, dancing and playing a musical instrument. For Fanny, the strict regime and the choice of subjects taught were a striking departure from her prior home-schooling experience in Ireland. At Newbridge, she had been privately tutored in a wide variety of scholarly subjects, including history, geography, French, poetry, and even harmony and figured bass, taught by a succession of governesses. Young Fanny, who managed to persuade her tutors to forego lessons in the afternoon, spent countless carefree hours outdoors, exploring the park and woods, riding her pony and rowing the family boat on the pond. In 1836 as Fanny was entering her teenage years, Charles Cobbe felt the need to send his daughter to a ladies' school, where her tomboy ways could be transformed into a more acceptable deportment for her eventual entry into society. After the freedom of Newbridge House, Fanny wrote in her memoirs that she found her new surroundings stifling, in spite of the fact that Miss Runciman's was one of the more expensive establishments of the nearly one hundred ladies' schools in Brighton. In her autobiography, *The life of Frances Power Cobbe by herself*, Frances shares her personal experiences at the school and insights into society's limited expectations for women.[32] She writes of the girls at Miss Runciman's, mainly upper-class daughters of country gentlemen and members of parliament, who never dreamed they would achieve anything in life other than becoming an 'ornament of society'.[33] To that end, several hours a day were devoted to lessons in singing and playing the pianoforte, and, Frances wrote, 'Many of us, myself in particular, in addition to these had a harp master, a Frenchman named Labarre, who gave us lessons at a guinea apiece, while we could only play with one hand at a time.'[34] Reflecting the high standards of the school, the gifted French virtuoso Théodore Labarre (1805–70) was engaged briefly as harp master in the 1830s, which was possible owing to his concert schedule in London (figure 7.5).[35] Well-known for his harp compositions, Labarre had studied with the famed masters Cousineau, Naderman and Bochsa, and later in life he assumed the lofty position of professor of harp at the Paris Conservatoire, in 1867.[36]

Lessons with Labarre were an important introduction to the instrument for Fanny, although she later characterized the school's overall focus as 'shallow' and 'pointless'. After two unhappy years at the school, Frances, now age 16, while at home in Ireland for the Christmas holidays, managed to convince her parents

32 Ibid.   33 Ibid., p. 56.   34 Ibid.   35 W.M. Govea, *Nineteenth- and twentieth-century harpists: a bio-critical sourcebook* (Westport, CT, 1995), p. 152.   36 Rensch, *Harps & harpists*, p. 163. Rensch gives additional biographical information on Théodore Labarre including serving as director of the Opéra-Comique orchestra from 1847 to 1849, and was later the conductor of Louis-Napolean's private orchestra. Labarre composed many harp solos and a *Méthode complete pour la harpe*, op. 118,

7.5 Théodore Labarre (1805–70), harp professor to Frances Power Cobbe. Music Division, New York Public Library Digital Collections.

not to send her back. To appease them, Frances made a few attempts to enter Dublin society, attending balls and drawing rooms, but eventually retreated to a quiet life at Newbridge. Her harp studies continued, though, for within a month of her return from Brighton, Charles Cobbe had purchased the harp from Egan, along with lessons. For Frances, playing the harp and pianoforte was not utilized as a social 'accomplishment' in the semi-public drawing rooms of Dublin, but rather for her own pleasure. Her music-making at Newbridge House took place in the spacious red drawing room that had been added at the back of the house by Thomas Cobbe in 1765.[37] With an elaborate rococo plasterwork ceiling, the room is also impressive for its length of 45ft, allowing the space to function as a gallery for displaying the family's formidable collection of old master paintings. A favoured haven for Frances, in the picture gallery she could play her harp pieces while imagining herself in lush Italian landscapes: 'The drawing-room with its noble proportions and its fifty-three pictures by Vandyke, Ruysdael, Guercino, Vanderveld, and other old masters, was the glory of the house. In it the happiest hours of my life were passed.'[38] As the only daughter among four brothers, and her mother an invalid, Frances was free to follow her own pursuits until eventually she became the mistress of Newbridge House and assumed the duties of supervising staff and meals.

with exercises.   37 Desmond Guinness and William Ryan, *Irish houses and castles* (London, 1971), p. 151.   38 Cobbe, *The life of Frances Power Cobbe*, p. 8.

The harp is not mentioned again in Frances' autobiography until the pivotal moment when she left Newbridge House in 1857. After overseeing the household for nearly twenty years, her duties as mistress came to an immediate end when her father died and the house passed on to her older brother and his wife, as was the custom. Frances, who had reached the age of 35, chose to fulfil her long-held dream of embarking on a pilgrimage to Egypt and Jerusalem, touring Switzerland and Italy along the way. Characterizing her leave-taking of Newbridge as the 'worst wrench' of her life, she decided to sell her harp:

> To strip my pretty bedroom of its pictures, and books, and ornaments, many of them my mother's gifts, and my mother's work; to send off my harp to be sold; and make over to my brother my private possessions of ponies and carriage, – (luckily my dear dog was dead), – and take leave of all the dear old servants and village people, formed a whole series of pangs.[39]

After a year spent travelling abroad, Cobbe took a position in Bristol working for Miss Carpenter at the Red Lodge Reformatory, a school for wayward children. Throughout her life, Frances continued to support worthy causes, making a mark as a feminist writer and avid campaigner for women's suffrage.[40] In her writings on gender issues, Cobbe advocates a higher level of education for women, along with greater employment opportunities and equal pay. In an essay titled 'What shall we do with our old maids?' she exposes the constant pressure put on females to marry, describing the 'dinning into their ears from childhood that marriage is their one vocation and concern in life'.[41] Cobbe respects the institution of marriage, but calls for a woman's right to choose independence and worthwhile employment in its place.[42] She draws attention to the inconsistent expectations for women in different classes, in that females of a lower social rank are compelled to work by financial necessity, and yet upper-class ladies who yearn for self-fulfilment are denied a purposeful career outside the home. In Cobbe's articles and books, she was an influential voice on gender issues, the subject garnering greater attention and urgency as the century wore on. Frances Power Cobbe's early experience at Miss Runciman's no doubt coloured her views, and despite her rejection of the concept of harp-playing as a pretentious lady's 'accomplishment', her personal instrument became an intrinsic part of her independent life at Newbridge.

---

39 Ibid., pp 194–5.   40 In 1875 Cobbe founded the Society for the Protection of Animals Liable to Vivisection.   41 Frances Power Cobbe, *Essays on the pursuits of women* (London, 1863), p. 64. 42 Ibid.

WILLIAM VINCENT WALLACE, WATERFORD

Another known player of an Egan harp was the Irish composer William Vincent Wallace (1812–65) of Waterford (figure 7.6), and a harp connected to him survives in the house museum at Bishop's Palace, Waterford Treasures. Wallace, born in a modest house on Colbeck Street, went on to forge an impressive international career as a violinist, pianist and composer, and although his supposed connection to the harp was short-lived, his experience sheds light on a significant strand of Irish harp history, namely harps played in Roman Catholic convent schools. The prevailing nineteenth-century cultural trend of harp lessons being deemed a necessity for upper-class ladies in the big houses was imitated by middle-class women studying harp in Dublin music academies, and the practice was also adopted by Ireland's convent communities, where harp tuition was offered to novices. In the 1830s, William Wallace was a professor of music at the Thurles Ursuline Convent School, giving lessons in harp, piano and violin. Although only 18, the school's youthful music teacher brought with him a wealth of experience, for he had been immersed in a world of band concerts as a child. His father, William Spencer Wallace, was sergeant bandmaster for the Royal 29th Regiment, and young William had played various brass instruments in his father's band, as well as later mastering the violin, piano and organ.[43] Demonstrating a versatile proficiency in instrumental-playing, William was appointed organist at the cathedral in Thurles, which included teaching duties at the adjoining convent school. In addition, he regularly furnished original compositions for the religious services at the cathedral, and it was as a composer that he later gained widespread notoriety.

Students boarding at the Ursuline convent in Thurles obviously did not learn the harp as an accomplishment to attract suitors. Nonetheless, for Isabella Kelly, a 17-year-old novice, the allure of harp-playing did inadvertently spawn a courtship between herself and her harp teacher, mirroring the outside world. Isabella had not yet taken her vows, and in spite of parental objections, the youthful pair married and moved to Dublin, where William found work playing violin in the Theatre Royal Orchestra. From this time on, the couple's brief connection to the harp ended, as the pedal harp was owned by the convent. William focused on violin and piano performances and in 1835 embarked on a lifelong global career of touring. Moving to Australia, he combined concerts with teaching, and he established Australia's first music academy in Sydney. Later, the artist spent time in New Zealand, South America and the US.[44]

43 Maureen FitzGerald, Richard FitzGerald and Robert Phelan, *William Vincent Wallace, composer and musician, 1812–65* (Waterford, 2012).   44 In 1850 William Wallace was remarried in New York to Helene Stoepel, a pianist, and the couple had two sons.

7.6 Composer William Vincent Wallace (1812–65). Music Division,
New York Public Library Digital Collections.

Although generally unknown today, in his time, William Vincent Wallace
achieved worldwide acclaim as a performer and composer of instrumental music
and operas. *Maritana* was considered his greatest success, with the opera making
its premiere at London's Theatre Royal in 1845.[45]

The story of the dashing Irish composer and the harpist novice has become
part of local historical lore, and the actual Egan pedal harp that was presumably
used in the lessons survives as a historical memento of William and Isabella's

---

[45] Dr Una Hunt has resurrected the music of William Vincent Wallace through research and
recordings, including her informative RTÈ Radio Lyric FM programme, 'The Road to Maritana'.
See rte.ie/lyricfm for 5 Oct. 2012.

courtship. Over the centuries, the sisters in the Ursuline convent preserved the instrument,[46] and the splendid gold Egan harp was recently restored.[47] Dating from about 1829, the double-action harp was manufactured by John Egan & Son. The Thurles Convent harp is a reminder of the significant role played by Ireland's Roman Catholic convent schools in the transmission of harping techniques and repertoire, as well as safeguarding instruments, from as early as the 1820s. As the nineteenth century progressed and the pedal harp was overshadowed by the piano as society's instrument of choice, the convents became the repositories of harp methods and instruments.[48] In addition to the Ursuline Convent at Thurles, other communities, such as Loreto Abbey, Rathfarnham House in Dublin, also purchased harps and offered tuition. According to an entry in the Loreto Abbey historical account books, the school purchased a harp in the year 1823–4, which is listed as 'Harp £18.7.9'. However, the maker is not noted.[49] Harp lessons continued to be taught at Loreto Abbey in the late nineteenth and early twentieth century by Mother Attracta Coffey (d. 1920), and her esteemed work enabled a legacy of harping expertise to be passed on to succeeding generations.[50] Similarly, in the 1900s, the Dominican Convent, Sion Hill, was another recognized sanctuary of harp-playing,[51] where celebrity harpists Mary O'Hara and Kathleen Watkins were trained. Known by their numerous appearances playing Irish harps on radio and television, both were once students of the respected teacher Máirín Ní Shéaghdha (Ferriter) at Sion Hill.[52]

---

46 A communication dated 25 Feb. 2016 from Sister Mercedes Lillis, historian at the Ursuline Convent, Thurles, states that the Egan harp was presumably used for teaching after the 1830s, but later the instrument was more of an 'historic precious artefact to be treasured and its history explained to people who saw it'. **47** The harp underwent restoration by Conservation Letterfrack in 2012, although its mechanism was not refurbished and the instrument is no longer playable. **48** For instance, according to National Museum of Ireland records, Egan Royal Portable Irish Harp no. 1886 was purchased from 'Sr Cecily, Dominican Convent' in 1984. Another example is the wire-strung Egan harp at Enniskillen Castle, which was preserved by the Sisters of Mercy, Enniskillen and the Diocesan Museum in St Macartan's College for many years before its donation to the Fermanagh County Museum in 1977. **49** A private communication from archivist Áine McHugh, 7 Nov. 2016. See also Áine McHugh, 'Beyond figures – the first account book' in Loreto Archives International web page, ibvm.org/wpcontent/uploads/ 2014/07/Province_Archivists_Publication_Dec-2012.pdf, accessed 5 Nov. 2016. **50** Sheila Larchet Cuthbert, *The Irish harp book* (Cork, 1975), p. 239. See also Helen Lawlor, *Irish harping 1900–2010* (Dublin, 2012). **51** Further information and a photo of harp students at Sion Hill in 1978 appear in Nora Joan Clark, *The story of the Irish harp: its history and influence* (Lynnwood, WA, 2003), pp 121–3. **52** In a conversation with Kathleen Watkins in 2008, following my lecture at the Royal Irish Academy, she said that her harp teacher at Sion Hill always talked of Egan harps as superior instruments, 'the very best harps'.

7.7 (*left*) Double-action pedal harp by John Egan & Son no. 2083, *c.*1829.   **7.8** (*right*) Brass plate with the royal warrant and crest on Egan & Son harp no. 2083. Photos by Nancy Hurrell courtesy of Waterford Treasures.

John Egan & Son double-action pedal harp no. 2083, c.1829, Waterford Treasures, Waterford
The brass plate bears the inscription: *John Egan & Son 30 Dawson St. Dublin / Makers by Authority of the ROYAL WARRANT to His Most Gracious Majesty / George the IV & the Royal Family* (with royal coat of arms). The Grecian-style capital motif has three stylized winged caryatids wearing plumed headdresses and the figures are linked by small hand-held wreaths. In the upper band are three pairs of mythical winged griffins, and the harp's base is adorned with two trumpeting angels, each holding a sprig of shamrocks for Ireland. The double-action harp has two rows of *fourchette* discs and was originally equipped with shutter panels on the back. The soundboard, composed of sections of horizontally grained wood, is decorated with spiralling acanthus in gold on a natural varnished background (figures 7.7 and 7.8).

THE DUCHESS OF RICHMOND, LORD LIEUTENANT'S WIFE, DUBLIN CASTLE

The provenance of most extant Egan harps is unknown, and similarly obscure are the whereabouts of the Egan harps once played by prominent harpists in history: Frances Cobbe, Sydney Owenson and Princess Augusta. With no surviving record books from the firm, and the scant or non-existent documentation of instrument

7.9 Duchess of Richmond, Lady Charlotte Gordon (1768–1842). Miriam and Ira D. Wallach Division of Art, Prints and Photographs: Print Collection, New York Public Library.

dealers, much information has been lost in terms of players connected to instruments. Still, it is possible to link an historical instrument from a particular time frame to a contemporary harpist who was a known player of an Egan harp. This can be applied to the duchess of Richmond, Lady Charlotte Gordon (1768–1842), who resided in Ireland during her husband's tenure as lord lieutenant (1807–13) (figure 7.9). In 1809, the duchess commissioned an Egan harp to be made for her. Unfortunately the location of the duchess' harp is unknown and it is no longer in the family collection.[53] However, an early Egan

53 According to Rosemary Baird, curator of the Goodwood Collection at Goodwood House, the family seat of the dukes of Richmond, there is no Egan harp in the collection. Private

pedal harp discovered in an antique shop in England is a close match in date to the duchess' harp, and it is the type of instrument she may have played.[54] Upon first impression, the harp appears comparable in decoration to a very pretty, delicately styled French harp from the late eighteenth century. The single-action mechanism suggests pre-1817 manufacture, and it has the type of tuning pins seen on late eighteenth-century harps.[55] The instrument's inscribed address on the brass plate, '25 Dawson St.', is the maker's first recorded business address, providing further confirmation of the harp's early manufacture in about 1809–13.[56]

The harp's most striking feature is its unique Egyptian capital decoration, which pre-dates Egan's capital style of Grecian ladies and subsequent phase of winged caryatids. Produced in an era when the public developed a fascination for the Egyptian culture, the instrument displays themes that were incorporated in furniture as well as harps. Following Napoleon's campaign in Egypt, new archaeological discoveries of ancient Egyptian art and architecture provided inspiration for designers working in the decorative arts. A similarly decorated pedal harp made around 1815 by the London firm Erat and Sons also has a capital with Egyptian figures, and a striped column and pedal box.[57] A slightly different Egyptian mummy design was used by Sébastien Erard on some of his ram's head capitals, produced from 1789 to 1810.[58] The Egan harp with Egyptian capital may have been a 'special' harp design or possibly one in a very early design phase. The fine artistry commends it as a suitable harp to be played by a duchess in gatherings held in Dublin Castle or the Viceregal Lodge, Phoenix Park.

John Egan single-action pedal harp with Egyptian capital, private collection
This harp's unique empire-style capital features stylized Egyptian mummy figures with palm leaves and rosettes in a style imitating an ancient Egyptian

communication, 4 Sept. 2009.   **54** The pedal harp is now in the collection of William and Victoria Bodine in Connecticut.   **55** This pedal harp has 41 strings, whereas all other extant Egan pedal harps have 43 strings. The tuning pins resemble those on eighteenth-century pedal harps: tapered, with a 'brim' for fitting a tuning key. Similarly formed pegs appear on the early Egan pedal harp at Avondale House and also on another Egan harp in a private collection in Belfast. **56** Only one other surviving harp is inscribed with 25 Dawson Street; all other harps have 30 Dawson Street. In *Wilson's Dublin Directory*, the entry for John Egan's business address is listed as '25 Dawson-street' from 1804 through 1820. In 1821 the number changes to '30 Dawson Street'. The listing however was slow to be updated, as proven by the more current newspaper adverts showing Egan's address as '30 Dawson Street' as early as 1817. It is believed the street numbers changed and the maker remained in the same premises, as evidenced by William Jackson Jnr later taking over the same workshop on '32' Dawson street.   **57** The single-action pedal harp, no. 1171, by Erat and Sons, is held by St Cecilia's Hall Museum of Instruments, Edinburgh University. **58** Only a few Erard harps with this design still survive, for example one in storage at the Horniman Museum, London. Erard harp no. 808 has stylized Egyptian mummy figures (although female), acanthus leaves and rams heads instead of rosettes.

7.10 (*above*) Egan single-action harp with Egyptian capital. Photos by Nancy Hurrell, courtesy of William and Victoria Bodine. **7.11** (*top right*) Brass plate engraved with *No. 25 Dawson St. Dublin*. **7.12** (*bottom right*) Pedal box with striped decoration.

pillar (figures 7.10, 7.11 and 7.12). The upper band is filled with neoclassical winged griffins holding lyres, and the top crown has Greek-inspired anthemion in a scalloped border above a decorative ring of beading. The carved fluted column is striped black and gold and culminates in a bulbous section decorated with acanthus leaves. The top of the pedal box is plain, and the sides are carved and gilded in the distinctive Pompadour stripe style of the late eighteenth century. The soundboard of horizontally grained sections of wood, possibly original, has been stained and revarnished, along with the back (a restoration). Engraved on the brass plate is the inscription: *John Egan No.25 Dawson St. Dublin.*

UNUSUAL PROTOTYPE FROM CAMLA VALE

John Egan's body of work demonstrates his ability to produce Grecian pedal harps comparable in quality and decoration to those made in London by competitors Erard, Erat, Barry and others. At the same time, he was capable of extremely imaginative, original harp designs as evinced in an unusual prototype in a private collection in Belfast. The most unorthodox feature of the harp is its thin curved pillar, not of wood but cast in bronze, an unprecedented concept in pedal harp manufacture. Adorned with a spiralling garland of shamrocks in relief, the pillar culminates in a large lion's paw resting on the base, again, unlike any other harp known to exist.[59] Technically, it is impossible for a pedal harp to have a curved pillar, for the standard straight and hollow pillar serves the important function of housing linear metal rods. These rods are crucial to the operation of the pedals, in that they link the pedals to the pitch-raising mechanism on the neck. On this harp, however, the pedal rods are threaded through the soundbox, leaving the pillar free to bend in a most fanciful way.[60] In shape and form, other sections of the harp are also unique, such as the rounded 'head' with flat surfaces, resembling the harp in Avondale House, except that here the head extends downward to create the top section of the pillar. In gilt plaster decoration, an elongated acanthus leaf appears on the front pillar surface, with a corresponding Egyptian palm leaf on the opposite inner face of the pillar. The section then rests on a very unusual quadrangular Grecian-inspired pedestal, which resembles an Ionic capital. The harp's wooden body is lacquered in blue, displaying Regency classical motifs merged with Irish shamrocks. The dramatically curved pillar cast in bronze is a signature John Egan invention, conceptually appropriate from a harp maker who had worked in a blacksmith's forge.

Purchased at auction in 1962 at Camla Vale, Monaghan, the harp was formerly owned by the Rossmore family. It is unclear whether it was original to the family, but if so, the dating corresponds to the time of the 2nd Baron Rossmore, Warner William Westenra (1765–1842), who resided in Rossmore Castle while his brother, Lt. Col. Henry Westenra (b. 1770) made his home in the nearby Camla Vale House. Both were known as gentlemen pipers of proficient musical skill, as was also the case of the 3rd Baron Rossmore, Henry Robert Westenra (1792–1860).[61]

John Egan single-action pedal harp with curved bronze pillar, private collection
The curved bronze pillar adorned with a garland of raised shamrocks culminates in a large lion's paw at the base (plates 33–5). The single-action harp is fitted with a ratchet and pawl mechanism on the brass plate. The harp's

---

59 The pillar somewhat resembles monopodia seen in Regency furniture, but does not have a lion's head at the pillar top. Lion paws typically adorned neoclassical chair and table legs, and an upright piano in the Victoria & Albert Museum by Van der Does, Amsterdam, *c*.1820, has lion monopodia for legs.   60 The Tyrolean pedal harp first used the concept of a curved pillar, and the pedal rods were housed inside the soundbox, but the pillar was made of wood.   61 See James O'Brien Moran, 'Lord Rossmore, a gentleman piper', *Seán Reid Society Journal*, 2 (Mar. 2002). Or

painted soundboard has two large robed figures holding lyres. Framed by arched laurel wreaths, they stand on platforms supported by fanciful lotus bud motifs. The figures, outlined in black, appear in a different style from other Egan harps, and appear to be a later restoration but may reflect the original figurative designs underneath. Similarly, bouquets of gold Irish shamrocks on the back are modern. Composite decoration on the base includes winged mythical creatures on the top surface, palmetto leaves on the corners and egg-and-dart edging on the back.

PETITE 'CHARLEMONT-TYPE' HARP, PHILADELPHIA

In a private collection in Philadelphia, another unusual harp appears to be the work of John Egan. The miniature green harp is formed like a pedal harp but without pedals or ditals. This prototype, although unsigned, is almost certainly by Egan and it bears a close resemblance to another historic instrument known as the Charlemont harp.[62] Named for its owner, Mary, countess of Charlemont (d. 1807),[63] the harp is described in Armstrong as having green and gold decoration and is 'surmounted by a coronet and scarlet cap'. As the Philadelphia harp lacks this feature, it may account for the height discrepancy between the two, with the Charlemont harp measuring 46in, in contrast to the Philadelphia harp's 41in. A photo of the Charlemont harp in *The Harp* by Roslyn Rensch confirms its uncanny resemblance to the instrument in Philadelphia.[64]

Small Charlemont-type harp, private collection, Philadelphia
This harp has a conical soundbox and a straight, fluted pillar with a capital of carved foliate decoration, and it stands on four short legs (figures 7.13, 7.14). With a height of only 41in, the model is slightly taller than a Portable Irish Harp, but in a strikingly different shape. Although no maker's name appears on the harp, Egan's signature decoration of gold shamrocks within lined borders appears on the soundboard, neck and back, indicating that the instrument is almost certainly made by him.[65] The neck has a shallow arc, and the twenty-seven

the harp may have been purchased by Lord Rossmore, the 5th baron, who wrote in his memoir, *Things I can tell* (1912), that Camla Vale was used as a 'storehouse for the various antiques I collect from time to time'. **62** Armstrong, *Musical instruments*, i, p. 105. **63** The countess was Mary Caulfeild who was married to James Caulfeild, 1st earl of Charlemont. **64** Roslyn Rensch, *The harp: its history, technique and repertoire* (New York, 1969), plate 32b. At the time of publication, the harp was in the National Museum of Ireland. Although almost identical to the harp in Philadelphia, there are minor discrepancies as to bridge-pin location, capital decoration and added ring stops. **65** The harp is owned by Fred Oster of Vintage Instruments, Philadelphia, who allowed me to examine it in 2010, along with two other Egan Portable Irish Harps in the collection.

7.13 (*left*) Charlemont-type portable harp. Photos by Nancy Hurrell, courtesy of Fred Oster, Philadelphia.   **7.14** (*right*) Detail of shamrock border and rosettes on pillar of Charlemont-type harp.

strings are equipped with Egan-like ring stops in ones and twos. The capital has a curious V-formation of leaves with the original plasterwork missing.

THE EGAN HARP MODELS

Egan continually pushed the boundaries of conventional harp-making, as seen in the unusual design elements of jutting head shapes on portable harps and a bowed bronze pillar on a pedal harp. Special harps like the winged-maiden model and a well-formed miniature harp with fifteen strings reflect the maker's imaginative concepts. Egan's newly invented mechanisms expanded the chromatic tonalities of harps, from ring stops and ditals to triple-action pedals. In surveying the range of models made by John Egan throughout his thirty-year career, a dozen different types of harps can be identified:

1. Single-action pedal harp
2. Double-action pedal harp
3. Triple-action pedal harp
4. Portable Irish Harp with ring stops
5. Portable Irish Harp with single-action ditals
6. Portable Irish Harp with double-action ditals
7. Winged-maiden dital harp
8. Irish harp with projecting block and wire-strings
9. Improved Irish Harp with wire-strings
10. Tyrolean-style pedal harp with curved bronze pillar
11. Charlemont-type small harp with straight pillar (attributed to Egan)
12. Miniature Irish harp with fifteen strings

Egan supplied quality, locally produced instruments to harpists, and he expanded the range of harps commercially available in Ireland. Egan harps with gut and wire strings were available in a variety of sizes, with different options for mechanisms and decorative finishes to meet the diverse needs and incomes of customers, and as a result, harp-playing thrived in the first half of the nineteenth century. Harps issuing from the Dawson Street workshop were integrated into the diverse fabric of Irish society, played by poor youths in charitable harp schools, the daughters of Dublin shop owners, novices in Catholic convent schools and noble ladies in castle drawing rooms.

8 / The shape of the future

An assessment of John Egan's contribution to Irish harp history might conclude that his range of harp models expanded the culture's access to instruments, and harp-playing significantly increased in the early decades of the nineteenth century. In terms of the influence of an individual harp model on the harping tradition, ultimately the test of time determines the lasting legacy of an instrument or mechanism, as some designs prove to be passing novelties while others survive as enduring concepts. The single most important design concept of John Egan's career was the Portable Irish Harp model, as evidenced in its longevity as the universally adopted form of the Irish harp in the last two centuries. In the immediate decades after John Egan's death, the small Irish harp model was imitated by a succession of subsequent harp makers, and the concept continued to endure into the twentieth century, with an entire lineage of similarly shaped shamrock-covered harps produced by makers worldwide. Versions of the instrument are still made today, maintaining the original structural components of a small conical soundbox and a curved pillar, but with certain aspects altered, for instance size. Today many modern Irish harps are closer in height and proportions to Egan's larger Improved Irish Harp model, but whatever the size, the gut-strung Irish harp or Celtic harp with levers is still prized for its clear sound, portability and ease of playing.[1]

The appeal of a portable harp in an Irish-inspired shape and decoration has proved to be both timeless and universal, and yet it can also be said that the original concept was unmistakably driven by the cultural politics of the time. Launched in a period of heightened nationalism during colonial rule, Egan's harp incorporated independence imagery as the maker cleverly forged the cultural zeitgeist into a modern playable instrument. The Portable Irish Harp entered the marketplace along with other cultural products capitalizing on the public appetite for the Celtic past repackaged in modern commercial forms. Just as Lady Morgan's popular romantic novels were infused with extensive antiquarian footnotes, and Thomas Moore's accessible songs drew on the

---

1 For a discussion of nomenclature, see Anne-Marie O'Farrell, 'The chromatic development of the lever harp: mechanism, resulting technique and repertoire' in Joyce and Lawlor, *Harp studies,*

glorious Gaelic past, Egan's harp design fused an ancient ideal into an up-to-date chromatic instrument.[2] Imported to England and the Continent, the somewhat exotic Irish goods were embraced by enthusiastic consumers, from the nobility and gentry to the royal family. It can be argued that the success of Egan's design, as it continued to be imitated, was in part due to the harp viewed through a lens of novel Irishness. The national branding of the instrument enhanced its long-term success, and eventually a small gut-strung harp adorned with shamrocks came to be regarded as the Irish harp template. This Irish branding also extended to the canon of music played on the instrument, and in the twentieth century the small gut-strung Irish harp was primarily associated with singing and playing Irish music. Lawlor writes of the difficult position of the Irish harp in the mid-twentieth century as it was not yet integrated into mainstream traditional music, and yet the instrument's limited chromaticism (early lever mechanisms) excluded the Irish harp from the performance of Western art music.[3] In contrast, it was John Egan's original intent to introduce a fully chromatic harp capable of playing classical pedal harp repertoire. The maker had prided himself on the invention of an improved Irish harp with ditals and the *fourchette* mechanism characterized as 'equal to the pedal harp', and he presumed this was the way forward for Ireland's harping tradition. Although still with certain chromatic limitations, on a portable harp with ditals, a harpist could adapt selected pedal harp solos of art music and also play traditional Irish airs. The problem of transferring pedal harp repertoire to the portable harp is that one hand constantly leaves the strings to operate the ditals, as Armstrong points out:

> On Egan's harp, to produce a passing accidental, the left hand must drop the strings, and only a practiced performer, who can concentrate his or her attention upon the bass strings, for the time being, can replace the left hand in the proper position without slowing the time.[4]

For playing traditional Irish music, generally less chromatic in nature, the ditals were often not needed and in some cases, even a hindrance. The modal tunings of Irish airs were better suited to individually set ring stops whereby a pitch

p. 210.   2 After 1821, any independence messaging originally implied by Egan's Portable Irish Harp was superseded by royal associations as the model became the Royal Portable Irish Harp. With 'royal' added to the name, Egan's Irish harp was symbolically 'crowned', which was curiously antithetical to the uncrowned harp so revered in the rebel imagery of the 1790s. However, thirty years on and in the aftermath of the popular king's visit, it was an impressive marketing device for Egan harps, one in which 'royal' signified a 'superior' product.   3 Lawlor, *Irish harping, 1900–2010*, pp 54–5.   4 Armstrong, *Musical instruments*, ii, p. 146.

could be sharpened in one octave and remain a natural in another octave. Perhaps for this reason and others, ditals were ultimately abandoned in favour of ring stops. Harps with ring stops were lighter in weight, and the instrument's weight was more evenly distributed. Egan's dital harp was particularly unsteady due to the weighty pillar and mechanism. For subsequent harp makers copying the model, there were obvious advantages in choosing ring stops over ditals, namely the simpler mechanism was less expensive to produce and easier to construct in that the installation of ditals required the special expertise of a skilled technician. John Egan had been personally invested in his invention, but his son John Jnr was forced to make cost-cutting measures when he inherited the family firm. For a couple of years John Jnr continued to advertise both single- and double-action Royal Portable Irish Harps, but in 1832 when the business downsized in the move from Dawson Street to Grafton Street only double-action pedal harps were sold.

Towards the end of his somewhat turbulent professional career, John Jnr did return briefly to the manufacture of portable harps. A surviving Royal Portable Irish Harp dated 1835 from the workshop of Egan, Read & Taylor is displayed in the National Museum of Ireland. The instrument is comparable in form and dimensions to previous Egan portables, but it is fitted with ring stops instead of ditals.[5] The head shape, now lacking an internal mechanism, takes on a slightly new contour of a more horizontally shaped oval, and this became the stylistic design imitated in the next generation of portable harp models produced in Ireland.

IRISH HARP AT ÁRAS AN UACHTARÁIN, PHOENIX PARK

On 29 December 1972, a small green Irish harp with golden vines of shamrocks was presented to President Éamon de Valera by Mrs Julia Fennell, to be permanently displayed at Áras an Uachtaráin, the official residence of the president (figure 8.1).[6] The symbolic gift was a century-old instrument, and it was given pride of place in its own alcove in the Francini, or State Corridor, exhibited alongside the venerable figures of Ireland's past presidents cast in bronze. Here, for nearly half a century, visiting foreign dignitaries, heads of state, presidents and royalty have all filed past the striking green Irish harp upon

5 An interesting example reflecting the preference to abandon ditals in favour of ring stops is an Egan harp in the collection at Castle Leslie in Co. Monaghan. The Portable Irish Harp dating from about 1819 shows evidence of ivory ditals and the mechanism having been removed, and a new brass plate with ring stops having been installed instead. The neck was filled in, but the dital slots still remain on the pillar.   6 The harp presented to de Valera in 1972 by Mrs Fennell was

8.1 Presentation of harp to President Éamon de Valera in 1972. © Irish Photo Archive and Lensmen Photographic Archive.

entering the president's house. Its familiar head shape, mechanism and decoration suggest that it is an instrument from the Egan workshop, but the harp bears a painted inscription on the lower soundboard designating another firm: *ROBINSON & BUSSELL/ Manufacturers/ No. 7./ Westmoreland St./ Dublin.*[7]

Produced in the 1840s for the Robinson & Bussell music company, this important instrument is a rare early imitation of Egan's Portable Irish Harp design. Whereas formerly harps were branded with the name of a single well-known maker, this instrument was produced under the larger umbrella of a general music business, Robinson & Bussell. The maker of this harp may well have learned his craft in the former Egan factory, or if not, he clearly had access to an Egan harp and faithfully copied it. The instrument is identical to the later Egan harps, not only in shape and decoration but also in its construction details, and it is not beyond the realm of possibility that the harp was made by John

given in memory of her late husband, Thomas J. Fennell. Mrs Fennell was accompanied by her daughters Dr Geraldine Fennell and Ms Rosemary Fennell for the presentation. See Irish Photo Archive, at irishphotoarchive.ie. 7 President Michael D. Higgins kindly allowed me to examine the harp at Áras an Uachtaráin on 21 Aug. 2015, as arranged by Pauline Doran, head of protocol.

Egan Jnr, who had begun to offer his services through other companies in the late 1830s.[8] Contract work for craftsmen of instruments was available from different sellers, as suggested by an 1844 advert from the maker William Jackson Jnr: 'Portable and Irish harps made to order'.[9]

Robinson & Bussell Portable Irish Harp, Áras an Uachtaráin, Phoenix Park, Dublin

The similarities to Egan's Portable Irish Harp model are instantly apparent in the Robinson & Bussell instrument (plates 36–8), from the overall appearance down to small details like the brass square on the lower pillar to conceal the screw underneath. The harp's gilded ornaments, painted in the same hand as seen on Egan models, consist of delicate shamrocks within lined borders, neoclassical swirling acanthus on the head, a shield motif on the pillar front, and anthemion on the back. Inside the harp is Egan's invention of a stabilizing rod, and the harp has the familiar ring stops. The green Irish harp at Áras an Uachtaráin is a tribute to John Egan's portable harp design as it continued to be made in the mid-nineteenth century.

The firm of Robinson & Bussell operated at 7 Westmoreland Street from 1843 to 1852 and was one among a long line of partnerships selling music and musical instruments from the address.[10] The company, founded in 1802 as Goulding & Co., was an England-based music business and in a later merger it became Willis & Co. in 1814.[11] After three years, Isaac Willis established his own company, which lasted for over twenty years until it was purchased by F. Robinson, H. Bussell & W. Robinson.[12] A typical Dublin instrument firm, in addition to pianos, violins, violoncellos, flutes and accordions, they also carried single- and double-action pedal harps by Erard, Schwieso and Egan.[13] In the 1840s, the Academy for Musical Instruction was set up inside the store, with singing lessons taught by F. Robinson, and pianoforte lessons offered by his

---

8 In 1836 the contact addresses for John Egan Jnr included the instrument wareroom of Mr N. Walsh and also 21 Aungier Street, the workshop of gilder John Wilkinson, suggesting John Jnr freelanced. Also, John Jnr lists Messrs Robinson and Bussell as one of his references in an advert (see p. 192). The Robinson & Bussell harp displays an inner construction that exactly replicates Egan methods, such as how the pillar is attached to the soundbox in a mortise and tenon joint. Also, the harp's rounded head shape mirrors the Egan, Read & Taylor portable harp in the NMI (produced at 21 Aungier street). The two harps are almost identical in height and have 33 strings, and the gilt shamrocks on the Robinson & Bussell harp mirror the decoration on other Egan portables, indicating a possibility the harp was made by John Jnr with the assistance of gilder John Wilkinson as a commission for the Robinson and Bussell company.   **9** *Dublin Weekly Register,* 7 Dec. 1844.   **10** See dublinmusictrade.ie.   **11** Ibid. In 1821 the I. Willis' music business was called the 'Harmonic Saloon and Musical Circulating Library' and following the king's visit the name changed to 'Royal Harmonic Saloon' to reflect the bestowal of the royal warrant.   **12** *Dublin Evening Packet and Correspondent,* 14 Apr. 1836.   **13** Ibid., 7 Jan. 1837.

8.2 Irish harp by Isaac Willis, *c.*1840 in private collection. Photo by Nancy Hurrell.

partner H. Bussell.[14] By 1843 the company also manufactured military band instruments and advertised as 'Musical Instrument Makers to the Army'.[15] That same year an unexpected tragedy within the factory's working family steered the business in a slightly different direction. A notice in the *Freeman's Journal* titled 'Fatal Accident from Drunkenness' recounted the sudden death of Albion Wyatt, the foreman at Robinson & Bussell.[16] Mr Wyatt's wife testified at the inquest that her husband had gone to the Theatre Royal after meeting socially with some bandsmen, and in his un-sober state he fell down the theatre stairs and later died from his injuries. Within months, adverts for Robinson and

14 Ibid., 28 Oct. 1840.   15 *Dublin Evening Mail*, 26 May 1843.   16 *Freeman's Journal*, 17 Jan. 1843.

Bussell took on a new socially conscious image by championing the temperance societies. With the headings 'To Temperance Societies', ads proclaimed community support, with 'every article requisite for Temperance Bands' supplied on the 'most liberal terms'.[17] At this time, the country's harp, a symbol of cultural pride, came to be aligned with abstinence, as demonstrated by the role of the temperance movement in establishing the Drogheda Harp Society in 1842. For Robinson and Bussell, marketing portable Irish harps alongside instruments made for temperance bands enhanced a principled public image.[18]

The unknown craftsman who made the harp for Robinson & Bussell conceivably also crafted instruments for the earlier configuration of the firm when it was known as I. Willis. Two similarly crafted harps made for I. Willis have come to light, both in private collections. The harps are almost identical in size, shape, and decoration to the Robinson & Bussell harp but lack painted inscriptions (figure 8.2).[19] The evidence of a connection is discovered in the signature markings stamped on the inside base blocks of both harps. The initials 'I W' (Isaac Willis) with serial numbers correspond to the same type of labelling – stamped letters 'R B' (Robinson & Bussell) and serial number – as seen on the president's harp. All three harps are uniformly lacquered in green, with shamrocks and neoclassical motifs, and all are fitted with ring stops in ones and twos, suggesting the same maker(s) in the Westmoreland Street workshop over a span of two decades.[20] The inherited Egan concepts applied to these first generation non-Egan harps were small size, distinctive head and pillar shape and shamrock decoration on a green ground. Also inherited from Egan's portable harp models was the use of lever-type mechanisms and the practice of tuning the gut strings in E-flat major for maximum chromatic possibilities.

Although Irish-made portable harps were sold in the music shops of I. Willis and Robinson & Bussell, both businesses carried greater numbers of imported pedal harps and an even greater inventory of pianofortes, the new instrument in vogue. Musical instrument manufacture was now characterized by a phenomenal rise in the popularity of keyboard instruments, and in the fullness of time the pianoforte eclipsed even the pedal harp as the preferred choice for music-making in the drawing room. I. Willis and his competitors promoted a wide range of pianoforte models from which to choose: grand,

17 Ibid., 2 June 1843.   18 For a discussion on the harp symbol being co-opted by temperance movements in the 1840s, see Emily Cullen, 'Tempering the stereotypes of Irishness abroad: the Irish harp as golden lever of temperance and respectability' in Joyce and Lawlor, *Harp studies*, pp 105–20.   19 The two harps made for I. Willis are around 91cm in height and 49cm depth, with 33 strings, matching the Robinson & Bussell harp.   20 A strikingly similar green harp with gilt shamrocks in the Philharmonie de Paris is constructed in the same shape with identical stringing and ring stops. However, Thierry Maniguet has confirmed that the harp lacks a stamped

cabinet, cottage, harmonic, square and round-cornered.[21] Several London piano makers maintained factories where large numbers of instruments were assembled fairly cheaply, and so the affordable pianoforte was enthusiastically taken up by the middle classes. In addition to the modest price, keyboards required less maintenance than harps (tuning and restringing) and were easier to play. Musical instrument sellers in Dublin expanded their inventories and engaged in highly competitive advertising. Alday and Co. at 10 Dame Street touted their considerable stock of pianofortes and harps as 'upwards of one hundred instruments, a larger assortment than can be seen in a single establishment in London'.[22] Business owners began to refer to their spacious stores as 'warerooms'. The firm of E. McCullagh had one wareroom for selling pianofortes and harps at 22 Suffolk Street and another at 108 Grafton Street for displaying sheet music.[23] On Westmorland Street, Robinson & Bussell at no. 7 had to contend with a nearby competitor, Marcus Moses, who operated from no. 4 on the same street. His pianoforte, harp and music warehouse imported single- and double-action pedal harps in addition to pianofortes from the London makers.[24] The emphasis was obviously on keyboards, with the proprietor claiming to possess a stock of three hundred pianofortes 'of all classes', a truly staggering number even by today's standards.[25]

The inevitable side effect of a marketplace flooded with new pianofortes was a decline in harp production in Ireland. A downturn in portable harp manufacturing that began in the 1850s lasted for a quarter of a century, and other significant events in this period may have also played a part. The Great Famine (1845–52) and the consequent mass exodus of the Irish population to other countries impacted the cultural landscape and influenced societal norms.

GEORGE BUTLER IRISH HARP

Although the extent of harp-making in Ireland in the final decades of the nineteenth century is somewhat unclear, the 1880s saw the beginning of a revival in the production of Irish gut-strung harps. An extant instrument from the time bears evidence that Egan's design continued to be the basic model for the Irish harp. A rare green harp with Irish motifs survives in London's Horniman Museum and is inscribed: *G. Butler / Manufacturer*, denoting George Butler's musical instrument company, a firm known for making brass and woodwind instruments.[26] The harp's inscription, painted in gold within an outline of a

inscription on the inside base block. **21** *Saunders's Newsletter*, 8 Apr. 1820. **22** *Dublin Morning Register*, 4 Jan. 1840. **23** Ibid., 25 Jan. 1834. **24** Ibid., 21 May 1836. **25** *Freeman's Journal*, 4 Apr. 1837. **26** See Nancy Hurrell, 'Historical harps: a harp of Erin rediscovered in the Horniman

shamrock, continues with the addresses, *Monument House, Dublin and Haymarket, London, S.W.*, and the combined addresses establish the harp's date of manufacture as sometime within the period between 1882 and 1926.[27] The elements of shamrock decoration and the harp's distinctively rounded head were no doubt influenced by Egan designs, and in fact the business owned an Egan harp from which to copy. A small Egan harp exhibited at the 1904 World's Fair in St Louis was listed in the catalogue as 'Lent by G. Butler & Sons, Dublin'.[28] Whereas the Egan harp on display in the Irish Industrial Exhibition had 'finger action' or ditals, the Butler portable Irish harp was fitted with ring stops in ones and twos. Inside the soundbox, familiar fittings for a stabilizing rod are present, although the rod is missing. Aspects where the Butler harp differs from previous portable models by Egan and Robinson & Bussell include a slight height increase and a completely different decoration.[29]

G. Butler Portable Irish harp, Horniman Museum, London
A first impression of the harp is that although it resembles previous portable harps in its contour and ring stop mechanism, noticeably absent is the former decoration of gilt shamrocks and swirling acanthus on a green ground (plates 39, 40). Instead, the main body, neck and pillar are simply painted a solid green colour, and the naturally varnished soundboard is filled with exquisitely rendered vignettes, somewhat reminiscent of eighteenth-century harps. Two delicately painted scenes in mirror image on either side of the string strip feature round towers, the figure of Erin or Hibernia and an Irish wolfhound.[30] Above and below these scenes are spirals of prettily painted green shamrocks with pink bows added. In the central area, a realistic image of an ancient round tower is set in a craggy landscape. Eileen Reilly referred to the political messaging of the round tower as 'a suitable image for portraying the antiquity of Ireland's civilization and a period of Irish history which preceded English conquest'.[31]

Another image filling the soundboard's lower area is a finely painted portrait of Hibernia dressed in flowing robes and holding a small harp.[32] Hibernia, seated next to a Milesian crown (or beehive) on a stool, is accompanied by an

Museum', *Folk Harp Journal*, 130 (Winter 2005–6), 45–7.   **27** See 'Butler' in *The new Grove dictionary of musical instruments* (London, 1984). The firm had premises at Haymarket from 1865–1913 and Bachelors Walk from 1882–1926.   **28** *Irish Industrial Exhibition, World's Fair, St Louis 1904: handbook and catalogue of exhibits* (1904). The exhibition featured four Egan portable harps, with two lent by Miller & Beatty of Dublin and another harp was on loan from Lady Florence Bourke (1861–1953).   **29** The Robinson & Bussell harp is 91cm/36in in height whereas the Butler harp is 99cm/39in.   **30** See Jeanne Sheehy, *The rediscovery of Ireland's past: the Celtic revival, 1830–1930* (London, 1980), p. 13.   **31** Eileen Reilly, 'Beyond gilt shamrock' in Lawrence W. McBride (ed.), *Images, icons and the Irish nationalist imagination, 1870–1925* (Dublin, 1999), pp 99–100.   **32** In the painted decoration Erin's hand-held harp appears to be a slender Gothic medieval instrument,

Irish wolfhound wearing a golden coronet collar. The youthful Hibernia is herself about to be crowned with a laurel wreath held by a fluttering angel. A popular theme in independence imagery, the crowning of Hibernia was a metaphor for attaining independence. On the harp's lower soundboard are two curious black shapes of an unknown purpose, but perhaps an inscription was blacked out at some time. The Butler harp with its imagery of shamrocks, harps, round towers, wolfhounds and Hibernia typifies the style of decorative arts in late nineteenth-century Ireland. A Celtic revival swept the country, and the same popular emblems were universally used as motifs in Irish products from jewellery and pottery to furniture and architectural ornaments.

IRISH HARPS BY ENGLISH MAKER HOLDERNESSE

By the late 1800s, harp makers working in London also began to copy John Egan's Irish harp model. As Armstrong observed,

> Egan had imitators, and the writer has seen an early imitation by Serguet, a London maker. Now that there is a seeming revival of the harp, this little instrument is in some demand, and is again being made by Messrs. Holdernesse of Oxford Street, London, by whom a number have been dispatched to America.[33]

The company formed by Charles Holdernesse resembled other musical instrument sellers in that it experienced several reorganizations and address changes during its fifty years in business, from the 1850s to the early 1900s. Primarily a manufacturer of pianofortes, Messrs Holdernesse also sold Erard harps, both single- and double-action models, and at one time the company made portable Irish harps. An extant Holdernesse Irish harp displayed in the Hamamatsu Museum, Japan is unusual in that it is equipped with Egan-inspired ditals on the pillar.

Charles Holdernesse Irish harp, Hamamatsu Museum of Musical Instruments, Japan
This portable harp has a typical Egan contour, dital mechanism and shamrock decoration (figure 8.3). The inscription on the brass plate reads *Charles Holdernesse/ Maker/ 105, New Oxford St./ London*, which confirms that the harp was produced in the 1880s.[34] The naturally varnished body has borders of small

bearing no relation to either the Gaelic harp or Egan's portable model.   33 Armstrong, *Musical instruments*, ii, p. 146. No extant harps by Serguet have come to light.   34 Harp advertisements in *The Era* give the firm's address as 105 New Oxford Street in July, 1887. The harp in the

8.3 Charles Holdernesse Irish dital harp, *c*.1880s. Photo courtesy of the Hamamatsu Museum of Musical Instruments, Japan.

green shamrocks on gilt vines framing the soundboard and back, with similar floral strands on the pillar and neck. The harp contour with extended head mirrors later J. Egan instruments, as does the mechanism with ditals on the inner pillar connected to *fourchette* discs on the neck, and the exact same manner of attaching the pillar to the soundbox with a concealed screw is apparent.[35] Inside the soundbox, there is a fitted metal loop to hold a stabilizing rod, although the rod is missing.

It seems Charles Holdernesse or one of his workers faithfully copied an Egan harp, and evidence suggests that a Portable Irish Harp was at least temporarily in the firm's possession at one time. An Egan dital harp in the National Museum of Ireland, Collins Barracks, has a label on the underside of the neck: *C. Holdernesse & Co,/ Harp & Piano Makers, Repairers & Restorers./ 105, New Oxford Street. LONDON. W.C.* A possible explanation is that during the restoration, measurements and technical drawings were made of the Egan harp with future plans to copy the design for a Holdernesse Irish model.[36]

IRISH HARPS BY ENGLISH MAKER MORLEY

Another London harp maker whose Irish models significantly contributed to the harping tradition was Joseph George Morley (1847–1921) (figure 8.4). In the 1890s, Morley introduced his own version of a small Irish harp in the marketplace in England, and he also distributed his new harp model in Ireland as well. J.G. Morley was born into a family of musical instrument sellers whose history of making and repairing harps dates back to the early 1800s.[37] At one time J.G. Morley apprenticed in the Erard factories in both Paris and London, and later, in the 1890s, he assumed ownership of the London Erard company as well as the Holcombe firm, representing Dodd and Dizi harps.[38] From his shop at 6 Sussex Place, South Kensington Station, Morley showcased the pedal harps

---

Hamamatsu Museum of Musical Instruments was brought to my attention by Jerry Murphy, Boston. **35** The ditals on the Hamamatsu Museum harp are of ebony instead of ivory. The height (89cm) matches the slightly smaller dital harps of John Egan, as opposed to the 91cm harps with a more rounded head design and ring stops produced for Egan Read & Taylor, I. Willis and Robinson & Bussell. **36** The NMI Egan harp with Holdernesse inscription is itself of some notoriety as it was previously owned by the harp historian R.B. Armstrong, who included a picture of the harp in his book, *Musical instruments, ii: English and Irish instruments.* **37** Rensch, *Harps & harpists*, p. 179. The Morley family harp business was started in 1817 by George Morley (1790–1852) at 95 High Street, White Chapel, London and has remained in business in England for two centuries. The harp business Clive Morley Harps is currently located in Lechlade, England. See morleyharps.co.uk. **38** John Marson, *The book of the harp: the techniques, history and lore of a unique musical instrument* (Buxhall, 2005), p. 138.

8.4 Harp maker Joseph George Morley (1847–1921). Photo courtesy of Clive Morley Harps.

of these well-established makers in addition to newly designed harps of his own manufacture.

Not unlike Egan a century before him, Morley constructed several different sized gut-strung harps. His pedal harp with forty-eight strings came to be known as the 'largest pedal harp in the world'.[39] At the other end of the spectrum, the maker also built petite pedal harps in various sizes. An 1894 inventory lists a new 'small portable harp' with pedals as a suitable instrument for beginners. An even smaller 'children's pedal harp' by Morley was available in a choice of colours: natural, blue or black.[40] The idea that small harps were mainly appropriate for

39 Rensch, *Harps & harpists*, p. 179.   40 Morley's small pedal harp model was only 4ft 8in in height.

children as 'stepping stones' to the larger pedal harps may have originated with Morley. A small harp naturally had the appearance of being a child's instrument, and this became a standard marketing strategy that was later copied by other harp makers. Portability was another commercial selling point, and Morley adverts stated that the small harps were perfect for 'quadrille harpists' since the 5ft-tall instrument was 'light and handy and small enough to be taken into a cab'.[41]

J.G. Morley, like the G. Butler Company, owned and exhibited an antique Egan Portable Irish Harp. It was described in Morley's 1894 inventory as,

> Egan, of Dublin, no. 1920, small harp, curved pillar, about 3ft. 6 in., 33 cords, to be held in the lap or on a table, simple movement, no pedals, but 7 ivory buttons, moved by hand, perform the same function as the pedals. Decorations: shamrock decoration on a green ground.[42]

Morley first lent his Egan Irish harp to an exhibition of musical instruments (location unknown) in 1894,[43] and three years later the harp was again exhibited at a another festival, this time in Ireland. The Feis Ceoil (Music Festival) was held in connection with the Gaelic League, an organization formed in 1893 by Douglas Hyde to promote Gaelic language and culture. Various ancillary musical activities such as concerts, competitions and festivals were organized by the League, and J.G. Morley wrote to the Feis Ceoil committee offering the loan of his collection of historical Irish and Welsh harps to be displayed in the festival exhibition.[44] The offer was accepted, and in a curious turn of events, an Egan Portable Irish Harp travelled from England back to its country of origin to be admired as a valued historical instrument among other treasured artefacts of Irish culture.[45]

One cannot discount the possibility that the experience of showing his historical Egan harp at the Feis Ceoil may have prompted J.G. Morley to craft his own Irish harp model, for in the ensuing months he began working on the project, and in the meantime he maintained an amicable relationship with the Gaelic League. Finally, in October, the maker presented the society with his new instrument, the Morley Irish Harp, intended for use in the League's harp classes.

41 See 'Historical documents page' on Clive Morley Harps website at morleyharps.co.uk/historical-documents. 42 J. George Morley, 'Price list of harps by Erard & other good makers at present in stock at the harp factories of J. George Morley'(1894). 43 The location of the exhibition is not known, but pages from the exhibition catalogue are available on the Morley website. 44 *Freeman's Journal*, 25 Mar. 1897. 45 The Egan Irish harp owned by Morley was exhibited again in 1904 at the Music Loan Exhibition held at Fishmongers' Hall, London, according to the catalogue, *An illustrated catalogue of the Music Loan Exhibition* (London, 1909), p. 134. The harp, no. 1920, was later in the Belle Skinner Collection and is now held in the Yale University Collection of Musical Instruments, New Haven, CT.

An announcement in the *Flag of Ireland* informed the public that the harpist Mr Owen Lloyd would conduct classes in Irish harp-playing at the rooms on 24 Upper O'Connell Street, and Mr J.G. Morley of London had generously presented the League with a small Irish harp for the classes.[46] A seasoned entrepreneur, Morley perceived a commercial market for a small harp to once again take hold in Ireland, for at the time apparently there were no native workshops actively producing portable harps. The following year, the English harp maker donated three additional Morley Irish Harps to be awarded as first prizes in each of the three categories of the society's harp competition.[47]

Morley Portable Irish harp, 1908, private collection

This typical example reveals the Egan-inspired contour of the Morley Irish harp (figure 8.5). The high-headed shape reflects Egan's earlier models as opposed to the more rounded head design of the later Robinson & Bussell and Butler harps.[48] The same rounded back soundbox construction was adopted, but a new feature is the presence of four small feet, in pairs on the front and back, to stabilize the harp on the ground.[49] The soundboard decoration of green shamrocks on linear gold vines is an exact match to the trim on the Holdernesse harp, and the duplication can be explained by the practice in both cases of applying 'paper transfers' to decorate the harps. A shamrock motif printed in gold on thin paper was applied face down onto the harp's wet varnish, and the backing was later peeled away leaving an imprint. In addition to shamrocks, Morley's Irish harp has ferocious beasts, in mirror image, near the bottom of the soundboard. Not quite Irish wolfhounds, instead, the animals hark back to neoclassical imagery and resemble horned mythological beasts and are flanked with swirling acanthus. The harp's pillar, neck and back are solid green with linear outlines in gold and clusters of gilt shamrocks with variegated leaves. The maker's signature on the front of the pillar reads: *J. GEO. MORLEY / HARP MAKER * / *from ERARD'S / 6 Sussex Place / SOUTH KENSINGTON, LONDON.*

On Morley harps, with the decoration and inscription uniformly applied as paper transfers, the instruments have a standardized appearance, quite different from the earlier hand-painted Egan models, each with its own character. The method of applying paper transfers – and the later, related procedure of using decals – became the normal procedure for harp decoration in the twentieth century. Another innovation on Morley's Irish Harp was a new mechanism on the neck called 'blades', with one for each string. The blade, a small rectangle of brass, functioned somewhat like a ring stop, in that it was rotated to stop the

---

46 *Flag of Ireland*, 16 Oct. 1897.   47 Ibid., 5 Feb. 1898.   48 The heights of the Butler Irish harp and Morley's Irish harp are the same, about 99cm /39in.   49 The addition of feet perhaps reinforced the notion of a floor-standing instrument suitable for a child.

8.5 Morley Irish harp by J.G.
Morley. Photo courtesy of
Robert Pacey.

string and raise its pitch by a semitone. Although much simpler to produce than
ring stops, a disadvantage was that the blade touched the string in only one place
instead of two, which proved less satisfactory than ring stops for accuracy of
pitch.[50]

Having penetrated Ireland's harp market through an association with the
Gaelic League, Morley likewise introduced his Irish harp to members of the
London branch of the Gaelic League. Morley's wife, an accomplished harpist,
regularly performed Irish airs on the Morley Irish Harp at branch meetings.
Madame Morley, or Cecilia Praetorius, had formerly studied at the Paris
Conservatoire with the celebrated harpist-composer Hasselmans.[51] Her harp-
playing was mentioned in an 1898 review of a League concert held to

50 Blades are notoriously unsatisfactory for being too tight and difficult to turn, or too loose
and slipping out of position, and regulation to obtain the correct semitone pitch is difficult.
51 Rensch, *Harps & harpists*, p. 172.

8.6 J.G. Morley, *A simple method of learning to play the old Irish harp, c.*1898. Courtesy of Clive Morley Harps.

commemorate St Brigid's Day, on which occasion Madame Morley accompanied Gaelic singers in addition to performing harp solos:

> Mr J. O'Finn contributed some delightful selections of Irish music on his flute, and on the national instrument Madame Morley played with much taste and feeling 'An Cuil-fhionn,' 'Sly Patrick,' 'The Moreen,' 'Gradh mo chroidhe,' and 'The Groves of Blarney,' using an elegant specimen of the Irish harp.[52]

The husband-and-wife team further collaborated on the publication of a slim volume of harp arrangements specifically for the Morley Irish harp titled, *A simple method of learning to play the old Irish harp*, and the inside introductory page is headed, 'Instructions for playing Morley's portable harp with exercises and melodies arranged by Madame Cecilia Praetorius' (figure 8.6).[53] The instructions inform the player of the approved Irish harp tuning of E-flat major and the use of brass finger blades to change flat pitches to natural. A series of exercises

---

52 *Flag of Ireland*, 12 Feb. 1898.   53 See J.G. Morley, *A simple method of learning to play the old Irish harp*, archive.org/details/simplemethodofleooprae, accessed May 18, 2017.

mainly consists of chords, arpeggios and scales and is followed by musical pieces, in the standard time-honoured format of harp tutors. However, now the term 'exercise' replaces the former 'etude' or 'prelude' seen in earlier music books. The first pieces in the volume are two Irish airs by Moore, 'The last rose of summer' and 'The minstrel boy'. National airs follow, with 'Russian hymn', the Welsh air 'David of the White Rock', Handel's 'Largo' and the German air 'Die Lorelei'.[54] The selection, although meagre, is not unlike the range of musical genres assembled in the collections of Charles Egan for the Portable Irish Harp a century earlier.

CLARK IRISH HARP IN AMERICA

By the early twentieth century, vast numbers of Irish immigrants had resettled in America's great Irish diaspora, keeping alive their own music and instruments. It was only a matter of time before the romantic ideal of a green Irish harp with shamrocks would cross the Atlantic. In the end, it wasn't an Irishman who brought over an Egan harp, but rather an American from Syracuse, New York who imported an Egan harp and the concept to America. Melville Clark (1883–1953) journeyed to Ireland in 1905, purchased an Egan Portable Irish Harp, later measured and copied it and introduced America's first Irish harp model, the Clark Irish Harp. Born into the music business, like his London counterpart J.G. Morley, Melville Clark was the son of an instrument dealer, George Clark. Much of Melville's childhood was spent in the G.W. Clark showroom filled with various instruments for sale, including harps.[55] A talented musician, Melville performed on the pedal harp from an early age, and as a small boy he stood while playing the large pedal harp, which he later referred to as motivation for producing a smaller harp suitable for younger players. Upon finishing his education, Melville was sent abroad by his father to learn the skills of harp construction. Melville's father, G.W. Clark, was the American supplier for Erard harps, and George Clark used his business connections to arrange for Melville to spend some time in London's Erard factory.[56] While in London, Melville took harp lessons from the renowned harpist-composer John Thomas (1826–1913).[57]

Towards the end of his stay in London, Melville took a side-trip by boat to Ireland, to learn more about the 'famous harps of Ireland'.[58] He met with

---

54 Ibid.   **55** Linda Pembroke Kaiser, *Pulling strings: the legacy of Melville A. Clark* (Syracuse, 2010), p. 29.   **56** During his 1905 visit to the London Erard factory, it is possible he may have encountered a Morley Irish harp.   **57** The celebrated Welsh harpist John Thomas was the harp professor at the Royal Academy of Music, the Royal College of Music and the Guildhall School of Music as well as harpist to Queen Victoria.   **58** Kaiser, *Pulling strings*, p. 41.

Cardinal Logue, who enthusiastically showed the young man his own Irish harp.[59] Clark purchased several Irish harps during his short stay, to take back with him to America. Among the instruments he collected were harps by an emerging Belfast maker, James McFall, and a Portable Irish Harp by Egan, which was said to have belonged to Thomas Moore.[60] No doubt the attribution to Moore was a practice commonly used by dealers to inflate a harp's value, and unsuspecting customers were unaware that Thomas Moore's harp had remained in the Royal Irish Academy since the poet's death. Still, Clark acquired the purportedly famous harp and used it as a template for his new model, as he recounted: 'The Clark Irish Harp is built after the model owned by Thomas Moore, preserving some of its characteristics of size, shape, and construction.'[61]

The idea of manufacturing Irish harps in the US had occurred to Clark while he was still in Ireland, admiring his new purchases. He imagined the potential benefits of introducing an Irish model to America as an alternative to the pedal harp. 'I returned home on the fastest boat possible and began drawing plans and designing my small harp,' he recalled.[62] Clark was attracted to the model's small size, light weight and portability, and on an aesthetic level, he was drawn to the gilt shamrocks, a significant aspect of the instrument's attraction and branding. Like Morley before him, Clark also saw a potential market for the instrument to be sold as a child's harp, as well as appealing to adults. The Egan firm never advertised the portable harp model as a child's instrument; its intentional small size was linked to the Brian Boru harp, however this symbolic referencing would have been lost on both Morley and Clark, working a century later in England and America. Other retail advantages for the Clark Irish Harp were obviously the same as in Egan's day, such as portability and an affordable price. Clark began building prototypes, and by 1909 the first Clark Irish Harps were available for customers, and only two years later, in 1911, the firm was producing thirty-five Irish harps per month. The Clark Irish Harp was skilfully promoted to teachers for teaching students to play the instrument, and the company was overwhelmed with orders. Eventually, to accommodate the demand, the Clark Harp Manufacturing Company entered into a contract with the larger Chicago-based Lyon & Healy Harp Company for assistance with

59 Cardinal Logue was a known proponent of James McFall's revival harp model, and presumably it was a McFall harp in the cardinal's possession at the time of Clark's visit in 1905.   60 A photo in the Linda Pembroke Kaiser Collection displays Melville Clark's harp collection, including three McFall harps and an Egan portable harp. Two of the McFall harps purchased in Ireland by Clark are now in the O'Brien Collection, Chicago.   61 Melville Clark, 'The Irish harp', as quoted in Kaiser, *Pulling strings*, p. 32.   62 Clark, 'How I came to invent the Clark Irish Harp', 1942, p. 2, in Clark Irish Harp folder, Linda Pembroke Kaiser Collection as quoted in Kaiser, *Pulling strings*, p. 32.   63 Kaiser, *Pulling strings*, p. 37.

8.7 Harp maker Melville Clark and his Clark Irish Harp. Courtesy of the Linda P. Kaiser Collection.

production.[63] The collaboration continued over twenty years, lasting until 1935, and later, Lyon & Healy, America's largest and oldest pedal harp manufacturer, brought out their own models of Irish and 'folk' harps, which were sold in immense numbers worldwide.

Clark Irish Harp models

With a high head and curved pillar, the Clark Irish Harp model loosely follows the Egan design in both contour and construction, although with the addition of four small feet (figure 8.7). The Clark 'A' model was larger than the 'B' junior model.[64] The strings are fitted with blades, and the decoration includes shamrock borders on the soundboard, back and pillar, with bouquets on the head – all paper transfers similar to those used by Morley. Additional soundboard motifs are Irish revival Celtic knots, beasts and round disks, closely resembling the style and symbols seen on McFall harps, particularly on one which Clark owned. Instead of a stabilizing rod, the harps are equipped with a four-legged detachable stand, a 'taborette' which raised the Clark Irish Harp off the ground to a height suitable for adults, and when taken off the stand, the harp was appropriately sized for a child. Various Clark harp accessories, similar to those of Egan, included a shoulder strap, a harp cover and a wooden carrying case.

In Ireland, the reemergence of a harp workshop occurred in the 1930s, with harps made by John Quinn. Quinn repaired the instruments at Sion Hill, and music teacher Sister Angela Walshe encouraged Quinn to make Irish harps for the school.[65] Somewhat similar in form to the Morley and Clark Irish harps, Quinn harps were in production from the 1940s to the 1970s. Other companies joined the trend in Irish harp manufacture, and in the 1960s the Japanese company Aoyama, after a visit to Sion Hill, brought out a larger, sturdier Irish harp model, with greater string tension, as described by Janet Harbison.[66] In contour, the Aoyama Kerry model is of the same lineage as the 1840s Robinson & Bussell harp, with a distinctive bowed pillar, rounded head and conical soundbox. As the Irish or Celtic harp gained widespread popularity in the late twentieth century, several small independent harp workshops, particularly in the US, also began building their own versions of portable harps.

---

64 According to Kaiser, the height of the Clark 'A' model was 39in and the smaller 'B' junior model was 25in tall. It's worth noting that the Clark 'A' model is the same height as Morley's Irish harp and the Butler Irish harp, whereas the earlier Robinson & Bussell harp was 36in, closer to the height to the later portable harps by Egan.   65 Nora Joan Clark, *The story of the Irish harp: its history and influence* (Lynnwood, WA, 2003), pp 106–8.   66 Janet Harbison, 'Harpists, harpers or harpees?' in Fintan Vallely et al. (eds), *Crosbhealach an Cheoil, The crossroads conference* (Cork, 1996) as quoted in Lawlor, *Irish harping*, p. 90.

MILDRED DILLING HARPS: THE DITALS RE-EMERGE

Occasionally the provenance of an Egan harp is a story in itself, one in which the instrument was owned by a succession of high-profile harpists. A second Egan Portable Irish Harp that Melville Clark bought to add to his instrument collection, for example, already had a supposed legendary past (figure 8.8). According to the seller, it had once belonged to the rebel patriot Robert Emmet, although there is no record of him ever having played a harp. Besides the unsubstantiated attribution, the dating is also problematical in that the harp had ditals and Egan's dital model wasn't invented until several years after Emmet's death.[67] Still, the so-called 'Emmet harp' kept its title, not unlike its celebrated

8.8 Melville Clark's Egan Portable Irish Harp. Courtesy of the Linda P. Kaiser Collection.

67 Egan's portable model with ditals was invented in 1819 and Robert Emmet was executed in 1803.

8.9 Harpist Mildred Dilling and her John Egan harp. Courtesy of the Mildred Dilling Collection, Brigham Young University, Utah.

ancestor, the Brian Boru harp, which also carries a colourful but misinformed attribution. After Clark's death in 1953, the entire harp collection was purchased by the well-known American harpist Mildred Dilling (1894–1982).[68] Internationally renowned for her concert tours to all parts of globe, Dilling often played various historical harps from her collection, including two Egan harps, as part of her programme (figure 8.9). She was drawn to the sound of the Portable Irish Harp as well as its ingenious concept of ditals to change key, although in performance she found the ivory knobs on the pillar somewhat awkward to reach.[69] Living in New York City, Dilling decided to enlist the help of a local harp maker, James F. Buckwell, to devise a slightly different version of Egan's model, with the hand-operated ditals for the *fourchette* mechanism placed in a more accessible position: on the neck. The result was the new 'Dilling harp' with elongated metal levers, named 'rockers', on the top of the neck, and Buckwell patented the design in 1920.[70] The extended length of the seven rockers

68 Kaiser, *Pulling strings*, p. 135.   **69** See Joyce Rice, 'The Dilling model single-action harp: a short version of the long backstory', *Harp spectrum*, harpspectrum.org/historical/historical.shtml. **70** J.F. Buckwell, 'Harp and harp action', Patent 1,332,885, US Patent Office, 9 Mar. 1920, from

allowed accessibility by either hand, and on the instrument Dilling was able to perform the chromatic jazz tunes of the 1930s. Unfortunately there was only a limited interest in the model, but Dilling held onto the dream of manufacturing the design, and eventually, fifty years later, she revived the project, this time collaborating with harp maker Arsalaan Fay of the Douglas Harp Company in Massachusetts. Fay constructed a larger, sturdier harp with the levers more elegantly attached to the harp's harmonic curve. This version of the Dilling harp went into production, and the model in its present form has been renamed the Douglas Joy Single-Action Harp, in honour of the harpist Jocelyn Joy Chang (1951–2010), who was a great proponent of the instrument and had commissioned several works for the harp.[71] Thus, John Egan's invention of ditals for expanding the tonalities of the small harp survived in yet another generation of instruments. The famous Egan/Emmet/Clark/Dilling harp that inspired the Douglas Joy model is currently on view in the Dilling Collection at Indiana University.[72]

Over the span of a hundred years, John Egan's Portable Irish Harp was imitated by an impressive list of harp makers and instrument companies: I. Willis, Robinson & Bussell, G. Butler, C. Holdernesse, J.G. Morley and Melville Clark. And design aspects of these models, in turn, inspired Irish harps by J.F. Buckwell, Lyon & Healy, Aoyama and Douglas. Just as Moore's *Melodies* endured over the centuries and took on a life of their own beyond Ireland's shores, so too did Egan's Portable Irish Harp live on, as the basic archetype for the modern gut-strung Irish harp. The model was reproduced globally, and in the late 1900s, makers continually explored design modifications such as increased size, innovative levers and different soundbox construction, from stave-back to square-back. The gilt shamrocks were largely abandoned, indeed decoration was generally phased out altogether on modern Irish harps except for special models. However, in the twenty-first century, a new 'special finish' version of the Camac Aziliz lever harp is green with a spray of gilt shamrocks on the harp's head, and borders of shamrocks frame the soundboard and back, bearing a striking resemblance in concept to Egan's pattern of decoration.[73] And remarkably, just as Butler, Holdernesse, Morley and Clark had each possessed antique Egan portable models, the Camac firm likewise owns and displays a green Egan Portable Irish Harp in its Treasures of the Camac Collection based in Ancenis, France.[74] Modern perceptions of the Irish harp still interweave the national symbol with the playable instrument, and shamrocks, the colour green and Irish airs played on the harp continue to reinforce the instrument's perpetual connection to Ireland.

Arsalaan Fay.   71 See website for Douglas Harp Company, douglasharpco.com.   72 See info.music.indiana. edu/news/page/normal/7032.html.   73 See camac-harps.com.   74 Robert Adelman, 'Treasures in the Camac Collection' (brochure).

Epilogue / Museum objects with historical resonance

On a summer's day in 2009, Julie Finch was walking near her Manhattan apartment when she noticed a dumpster on 26th Street and decided to investigate. New York skips are well-known for yielding 'luxury trash' – the castoffs of affluent consumers living in a disposable society – and 'dumpster divers' regularly scavenge them for upscale goods. As Julie peered inside, she scanned the fairly unremarkable jumble of wood scraps and papers. Then an unusually shaped object caught her eye. 'It's a very beautiful shape, which is what drew me to it, and why I carried it home,' she recalled.[1] Although dark and dingy, the triangular shape was clearly a small harp, and it still had a tangle of broken strings attached (figure E.1). Back in her apartment, upon closer inspection of the instrument, Julie saw a glimmer of gold shamrocks underneath the veil of dirt, and she noticed the inscription engraved on the brass plate: *John Egan, Inventor / 30 Dawson St. / Dublin*. An Internet search on the harp maker led to the astounding realization that she had just rescued a 200-year-old Irish harp from a rubbish skip. With the knowledge of the harp's great age came an overwhelming sense of responsibility to preserve it, and she wondered, 'Now what should I do?'[2] This was the question she posed to me later that day, when she contacted me for information on Egan harp history, restoration options and the harp's monetary value.

There was also the intriguing question of why the rare historical Irish harp had unceremoniously ended up in a dumpster. Information from the building superintendent confirmed that the skip's contents were the remnants of a music business, Augustine Guitar Strings, which previously occupied an office but had moved. The harp had belonged to Rose Augustine (1910–2003), the president of the company, who at one time accumulated a small collection of musical instruments.[3] After Augustine's death in 2003, the company relocated to Long Island, and the old harp was simply left behind, for in its deteriorated condition, it was considered to be of no real value to the family estate.[4]

1 Email communication from Julie Finch (30 June 2009). 2 Ibid. 3 Brian O'Connell, 'A fairytale in New York', *Irish Times*, 15 Aug. 2009. The legendary guitarist Andrés Segovia had lived with Rose Augustine and her husband for several years. 4 Colin Moynihan, 'For a rare

E.1 Egan harp discovered in a New York skip in 2009. Photo courtesy of Lorcan Otway, owner.

The incredible story of a centuries-old Irish harp having been found in a New York dumpster soon caught the attention of the news media. Discovering an old discarded harp is an extraordinary occurrence, whether scavenged from a Manhattan skip in 2009 or unearthed from an Irish bog in 1809. In the early nineteenth century, harps found in peat bogs also garnered widespread attention and were considered valuable archaeological relics, with accounts of the exciting discoveries chronicled in respected travel journals and antiquarian lectures. The present-day tale of the 'dumpster harp' lit up Internet sites, was discussed on radio programmes and featured in newspaper articles. The idea that a precious harp with golden decoration would be cast aside in this manner was unimaginable. And the notion of acquiring instant wealth from found treasure was also a captivating aspect of the story, for as the tale of the dumpster Egan circulated, the harp's monetary worth grew with each retelling until it was finally declared 'priceless', on a par with a Stradivarius violin. Serious reporters sought information on the harp's actual rarity and worth, and my historical assessment of the instrument appeared in articles published in the *New York Times* and the *Irish Times* in Dublin.[5] For the simpler questions as to numbers of extant Egan

discarded harp, a chance to sing again', *New York Times*, 9 Aug. 2009.   5 Ibid. and O'Connell, 'A fairy tale in New York'.

harps, my database of known instruments easily supplied the answers.[6] For queries as to the harp's monetary value, the answer was more complex, for the 'value' of an antique instrument tends to be highly subjective. I had seen photos of the dumpster Egan, and with its blue lacquer finish greatly degraded, I estimated that the cost of conservation by an expert would undoubtedly exceed the not inconsiderable purchase price of a new harp.[7]

If an Egan harp over time has remained largely in a good and original condition, it is valuable to a museum or a collector. A damaged historical harp can be cosmetically restored, but the amount and quality of the conservation is critical to determining an estimated worth of the instrument. If the restorative work to the harp's structure and surface decoration is so great that the integrity of the maker's original intent is compromised, the harp becomes less valuable to a museum. However a private collector may prefer the finished look of a restored harp over an instrument in a worn, but more authentic state. In addition to the look of the harp, another consideration is whether or not it is still a functioning musical instrument. If a harp is still playable, or deemed sturdy enough to be restored to playing condition, it is of interest to harpists. And finally, Egan Portable Irish Harps have the added attraction of emblematic Irishness, and it was this aspect that ultimately led to the sale of the dumpster Egan harp. Lorcan Otway, an Irish singer and friend of Julie's, made an offer for the harp, and has since pledged to have it restored to reawaken its voice.[8]

EGAN HARPS IN MUSEUM COLLECTIONS

Egan harps are preserved in over forty museums in sixteen different countries worldwide. Treasured for their Irish symbolism and also as decorative works of art, they are prized for different reasons according to the focus of each individual institution. In Ireland, where historical harps are considered important to the country's heritage, Egan harps are preserved as national artefacts representing the country's leading maker of the early nineteenth-century. The main repository for John Egan harps is the National Museum of Ireland, Collins Barracks, which has nine Egan harps in its collection, including two notable bequests from R.B. Armstrong.[9] In Northern Ireland, local-history

6 At the time the dumpster Egan was found there were 70 Egan harps in my database. By 2018 over 100 Egan harps had come to light.   7 Finch's use of water to clean the harp was unfortunate and added to the deterioration of the painted surface. A professional restorer will clean an antique harp with gentle solvents to protect the surface decoration.   8 The harp was purchased from Finch by Lorcan Otway of New York who plans to restore the instrument.   9 Information on museum records was accessed in 2008 when I assisted Jennifer Goff in cataloguing the Egan

museums also maintain Egan harps in their holdings, including the Fermanagh County Museum at Enniskillen Castle and the Irish Linen Centre, Lisburn. While many Egan harps in museums are displayed in conventional glass cases, other instruments are prominently placed in period rooms as ornate pieces of 'furniture' in historic house museums. A sumptuously adorned harp standing majestically in a drawing room is a wonderful prop for imagining daily music-making in 1800s Ireland, and stately Grecian pedal harps by Egan grace the music rooms of Newbridge House, Avondale House and Waterford's Bishop's Palace, with the neoclassical harps harmonizing in style with the house furnishings.

Decorative Egan harps, with intricate swirling acanthus designs in gold, are also considered to be high-quality art objects, and as such, they are collected by museums specializing in decorative and fine arts. In London's Victoria & Albert Museum, for example, the handsome Egan Portable Irish Harp was added to the collection solely for its artistic value. The priority of the V&A founders in the 1850s was to select only musical instruments of 'outstanding beauty' regardless of any musicological contribution.[10] The V&A Egan harp satisfies these aims with its sculptural form and exquisitely rendered surface paintings of lush acanthus, plump roses, tiny bunches of grapes and feathers.[11] The instrument's ivory ditals, irrelevant to the overall ornamental appearance, have actually been removed, whereas in other historical instrument museums, the Egan Portable Irish Harp with ditals is credited as a harp with an innovative mechanism. Egan portable harps are preserved in several European instrument museums such as Scenkonstmuseet (Sweden), Musical Instruments Museum (Belgium) and Munich Stadtmuseum (Germany), and two distinguished historical harp collections – the Museo dell'Arpa Victor Salvi (Italy) and the Treasures of the Camac Collection (France). Likewise, three major collections in Japan also hold portable harps by Egan: the Musical Instruments Museum (Osaka), MG Museum (Nagoya) and the Hamamatsu Museum.

Museums acquire historical harps by various means, including purchases from antique dealers and private individuals, and donations as parts of bequests. Many of the world's significant musical instrument collections in museums originated with the donation of a nucleus of instruments from a private collector. The practice often arises out of necessity, in that typically a person's assemblage of instruments expands over time, and it becomes necessary to either turn one's house into an independent museum or donate the instruments to a public institution. Collectors have embraced the idea of generously passing on

harps in the National Museum's collection.   10 See V&A website, vam.ac.uk/content/articles/ h/musical-instruments-collection-history.   11 I examined the Egan harp in the V&A storage facility in London in 2012.

E.2 Royal Portable Irish Harp
in Dean Castle, courtesy of
Charles van Raalte Collection,
Dean Castle, Scotland.

their valuables to an established public museum where the instruments can be appreciated by a larger audience.

The concept of assembling a collection of unusual musical instruments originated as a social trend in the late nineteenth and early twentieth centuries. It was customary in England and Ireland for gentlemen of a certain class to display interesting curios acquired on their travels to faraway places for others to admire. In a special 'cabinet of curiosities', musical instruments were on view next to the more exotic souvenirs of stuffed animals, seashells and tribal masks. The musical instruments in collections ranged from highly ornate baroque keyboards to primitive African lyres, and an Egan Irish harp was a particularly sought-after genre of instrument in a comprehensive collection. One notable collector of musical instruments was the Englishman Frederick John Horniman (1835–1906), a Victorian tea trader, who began acquiring objects on his worldly travels in the 1860s. Visiting Egypt, China and Japan, he brought back natural-history artefacts, cultural crafts and musical instruments with a goal of bringing 'the world to Forest Hill', where he lived.[12] The extensive collection eventually exceeded the space in Horniman's house museum, and a new building was

12 See the Horniman Museum website, horniman.ac.uk/about/museum-history.

specially built for the now well-known Horniman Museum. On display in the present-day instrument gallery is an Egan Portable Irish Harp collected by Horniman, along with several thousand sound-making objects representing an array of diverse cultures globally.[13]

In 1884 another Englishman, George Donaldson (1845–1925), who had similarly accumulated a significant array of rare musical instruments, donated his personal collection to the newly opened Royal College of Music.[14] Of the eight splendid early harps in the RCM Museum of Instruments, three were part of the original Donaldson donation in 1894, including an Egan Portable Irish Harp.[15] Another contemporary collector, Charles van Raalte (1857–1908) of Brownsea, Dorset, also purchased an Egan portable harp to add to his personal assortment of instruments, which included rare lutes, viols and keyboards (figure E.2).[16] Van Raalte's daughter Margherita, upon her marriage, later transported many of the instruments to her new home, Dean Castle in Scotland, where today the Charles van Raalte Collection is on exhibit for public viewing. The trend of collecting musical instruments continued well into the early twentieth century, as exemplified by another gentleman collector, Charles Paget Wade (1883–1956), who amassed an eclectic range of musical instruments, along with bicycles, weavers' tools and Japanese armour, all purchased from antique shops.[17] In 1919 Wade acquired a Cotswold manor house in Gloucestershire where he lived and showcased his interesting objects, which include two splendid examples of early Portable Irish Harps on view in a small music room with brass horns, flutes and serpents. Eventually the house, Snowshill Manor, was completely filled with objects, forcing Wade to move out and live modestly in an outbuilding that he named the Priest's House. Devoting his life to the collection, Wade set up a workshop in his small cottage for repairing items, as needed, and in 1951, he donated the manor and its entire contents to the National Trust.

An American counterpart to Wade, Donaldson and Horniman was Mrs John Crosby Brown (1842–1918) who started acquiring musical instruments in 1884 to decorate her music room in New Jersey. Through a friend in Florence,

13 Ibid. The Horniman Museum collection of sound-making objects has grown to 8,000 instruments. Collections within the holdings now include: the Adam Carse Collection, Dolmetsch Collection, Wayne Collection, Boosey and Hawkes Collection and the V&A instruments on loan. 14 Wells and Nobbs, *European stringed instruments*, p. viii. The RCM Musical Instruments Museum also includes donated collections from the Prince of Wales (later King Edward VII) and the Indian instruments donated by Rajah Sourindro Mohun Tagore. 15 See Nancy Hurrell, 'Harps in the Royal College of Music Museum of Instruments', *Bulletin of the Historical Harp Society*, 18:1 (Dec. 2007), 3–9. 16 The Dean Castle musical instruments collection is managed by the East Ayrshire Council in Kilmarnock, Scotland. See futuremuseum.co.uk. 17 See the Snowshill Manor website, nationaltrust.org.uk/snowshill-manor-and-garden.

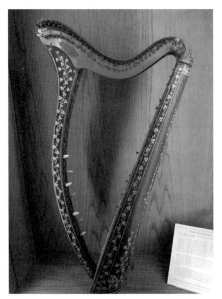

E.3 Portable Irish Harp. Photo by Kathleen
Monahan, courtesy of the John J. Burns
Library, Boston College.

Mrs Brown purchased a few historical instruments, such as a pianoforte, serpent,
harp and mandolin. By 1889, her assemblage had grown to 276 items, and among
the harps is the Egan Portable Irish Harp, inscribed 'no. 1', the maker's first
portable harp with ditals. Arrangements were made for Mrs Brown to donate
her entire collection, known as the Crosby Brown Collection of Musical
Instruments, to the Metropolitan Museum of Art in New York, the first major
instrument collection in an American museum.[18] Egan's Portable Irish Harp
model, which projected Irish identity, was particularly revered by America's Irish
diaspora. A number of Egan portable harps remain in private and public
collections in New England, with examples held in the Boston Museum of Fine
Arts, Harvard University, Boston College and Yale University. Notable
American collectors with Irish ancestors are devoted to preserving pieces of Irish
decorative and fine art in an effort to safeguard their heritage. A well-known
collector of Irish art, Brian P. Burns (b. 1936), is a third-generation Irish-
American and founder of the John J. Burns Library at Boston College, in
honour of his father. Dedicated in 1986, the John J. Burns Library of Rare
Books and Special Collections is world-renowned for preserving early Irish
manuscripts, historical and literary works by Irish authors, and an extensive Irish
music archive. In the library's Irish Room, two Egan Portable Irish Harps are

18 Laurence Libin, *American musical instruments in the Metropolitan Museum of Art* (New York, 1985),
p. 12. The musical instrument collection at the Metropolitan Museum was actually founded a
few years earlier, in 1885, with a smaller donation by Joseph W. Drexel (1830–88). Mrs Brown
continued to add to the Crosby Brown Collection, which numbered 3,000 examples upon her

prominently displayed (plate 41 and figure E.3).[19] In Chicago, the O'Brien Collection is another important assemblage of Irish decorative arts, artwork and historical harps. John and Patricia O'Brien, whose Irish grandparents immigrated to the US a century ago, have made it their mission to collect and conserve rare antiques in an effort to safeguard many of Ireland's cultural artefacts for future generations. Historical harps in the O'Brien Collection include two Irish revival harps by James McFall and two Portable Irish Harps by John Egan.

One of the O'Brien Egan harps was on view in a major exhibition, 'Ireland: Crossroads of Art and Design, 1690–1840', held at the Art Institute of Chicago in 2015 (plates 42, 43).[20] The instrument was among three hundred objects on loan from public and private collections in North America. The O'Brien harp, bright green with gilt leafy scrolls of acanthus and emblematic shamrocks, was the perfect visual symbol signifying Irish artistic design. As such, it became the PR image or logo for the show, and a photo of the harp graced the cover of the exhibition catalogue and appeared on the promotional poster. The green Egan harp was also ubiquitous on websites promoting the important exhibition. Egan's Portable Irish Harp was understood on several levels – as an art object, a national icon, a device for playing Irish music and an ambassador of culture.

Similarly, in 2014, an image of an Egan Portable Irish Harp was chosen for a commemorative Irish postage stamp in the Europa musical instruments series (plate 44). The elegant black harp with gilt shamrocks and scroll is labelled, 'the Irish harp', representing the country's iconic instrument as well as a finely crafted object from early nineteenth century Ireland. In the twenty-first century, the harps of John Egan are gaining notoriety, as the harp maker's place in history is revealed and understood.

EGAN HARPS BROUGHT BACK TO LIFE

Egan harps survive in a range of conditions, from instruments still intact and showing minor signs of wear, to other harps with crackled lacquer, loose joints and missing parts. On several surviving Egan pedal harps, the entire soundboxes have been replaced, and many portable harps have been overpainted in a completely different colour from the original lacquered ground. However, most Egan harps remain in a condition somewhere in between these extremes, with

death in 1918.   **19** One Egan harp was donated by Heidi Nitze via Nancy Hurrell in 2002 and around the same time the other Egan harp, formerly on loan, became a bequest of Dr Frederick and Patricia Selch.   **20** For further reading, see William Laffan, Christopher Monkhouse and Leslie Fitzpatrick (eds), *Ireland: crossroads of art and design, 1690–1840* (Chicago, 2015).

some overpainting and perhaps new feet or side strips added. The ravages of time take a toll on instruments made of wood, and yet it is the material's special quality that gives a harp its unique tone.[21] The stress of string tension over time can have a negative effect on the harp's triangular wooden frame whereby the thin soundboard tends to pull up and the neck twists. Contrary to popular belief, old instruments do not need to be played to stay in good condition.[22] An instrument's material decays from the stress of playing, and wooden instruments seem to have a limited performance life. Instruments that are played more gently seem to fare better, but MFA instrument curator Darcy Kuronen points out that instruments made of wood are subject to the detrimental forces of moisture, dryness, temperature changes, light and even air pollutants, and wood shrinks and swells in response to these fluctuations, with joints loosening over time.[23] Exposed to light and air, painted surfaces often darken and change colour as the paint oxidizes, and varnish can yellow with age or develop a crackled texture.[24] Many harps in Ireland have been structurally weakened by woodworm infestation, and many more unfortunate instruments show signs of damage from being dropped or knocked over, resulting in structural cracks. For these and other reasons, most surviving Egan harps are too fragile to be played. One unfortunate instance of an old Egan harp's fragility was recounted by the actor and author Richard Hayward (1892–1964) in his book, *The story of the Irish harp*. He had recently purchased an Egan Portable Irish Harp, and when he brought the strings up to tension, the harp simply 'collapsed due to woodworm and neglect'.[25] It was later rebuilt with a completely new soundbox, and the actor toured the country playing his restored instrument in a programme devoted to the history of the Irish harp.

Replacing the entire soundbox, or in many cases only the soundboard, is one way to safely bring an historical harp back to life without the fear of further structural damage. Among the few skilled professional conservators working in this field, Howard Bryan in Virginia has restored a number of antique pedal harps in this manner, including at least two Egan Grecian pedal harps (figures E.4 and E.5).[26] Taking precise measurements from the original harp, a new

---

21 For an enlightening overview of musical instruments see Darcy Kuronen, *Musical instruments: MFA highlights* (Boston, 2004).   22 For further reading, see Nancy Hurrell, 'The 100th anniversary of the Boston MFA musical instrument collection', *Bulletin of the Historical Harp Society*, 27:2 (Winter 2018), 11–18.   23 Kuronen, *Musical instruments*, p. 13.   24 Egan portable harps that were originally blue but have darkened over time due to oxidized paint are sometimes mistakenly overpainted black. Another commonly seen restoration is the use of bronze paint applied to the centre and side strips on soundboards and also on the bases and capitols of pedal harps instead of using historically correct, but much more expensive gold leaf.   25 Richard Hayward, *The story of the Irish harp* (Dublin, 1954), p. 23.   26 Howard Bryan has retired, but the company continues to restore antique harps. See the H. Bryan & Company website, oldharpsmadeyoung.com.

E.4 (*left*) Egan single-action pedal harp no. 2081 restored by H. Bryan. Photo by Howard Bryan.
E.5 (*right*) Original soundboard of Egan harp no. 2081. Private collection of Emily Laurance.

soundboard and back are built to the exact same dimensions in an effort to retain the harp's tonal qualities. The soundboard of the harp is considered to be the 'heart and soul' of the instrument, although on Egan harps the soundbox construction also greatly contributes to the tone, according to expert conservator Michael Parfett, working in London.[27] Parfett has had tremendous success rebuilding several Egan pedal harps to playing condition, and he takes great care to conserve as much of the original decoration as possible. A stunning example of his work is a restored and playable Egan Grecian pedal harp in the Irish Linen Centre, Lisburn. The harp's soundboard, neck and pedal box had been significantly weakened by woodworm infestation, and Parfett constructed new parts using traditional methods and materials. Made to the exact specifications as the original, the replacement parts afforded the instrument the

---

27 Email communication from Michael Parfett (1 July 2015). On two pedal harps in which the soundboard was replaced and the soundbox retained, the sound was remarkably the same as that of an Egan harp with an original soundboard.

structural strength needed to withstand the rigors of string tension. It was also a goal of the Lisburn Museum to save the highly decorative painted surfaces of the instrument. In an exceedingly delicate and time-consuming process, Parfett was able to shave off the thin top layer of painted decoration from several sections of the harp, including the soundboard and the rounded neck, and he later carefully reapplied the layers to the newly made harp parts.[28]

Antique Egan harps that are no longer playable are often cosmetically strung at a very low tension, and decoration on Egan harps can be conserved to great effect by a furniture restorer or a highly specialized master gilder like Bart Bjorneberg of Bernacki & Associates in Chicago. Among his projects are the two beautifully restored Egan Portable Irish Harps in the O'Brien Collection. Careful to maintain the original integrity of the period designs, Bjorneberg explains, 'Conservation does not involve artistic choices or material experimentation on the object', and adhering to these principles, he copies existing examples for a historically accurate restoration.[29]

HISTORICAL RESONANCE

In the late nineteenth century, the eminent antiquarian Eugene O'Curry, in his essay 'Of music and musical instruments', described the sound of an Egan harp as 'rich in tone'.[30] Other phrases, like 'sweetness of tone' and 'great brilliancy', were touted by Egan himself in adverts, although these were fairly common catchphrases used in marketing at the time. Using words to convey the particular sound a harp makes is often unsatisfactory, as words tend to be subjective rather than descriptive. Nevertheless, for most of the twentieth century, as antique Egan harps were not generally played, one had to rely on written accounts for impressions of the harp sound. Now, due to the careful restoration of a few instruments to playing condition, Egan harps can once again be heard. Michael Parfett, who has restored historical pedal harps by several different makers, described the tone of Egan pedal harps as not 'brighter' but rather 'rounder and fuller' than the harps of Erard.[31] Parfett attributes the special tonal quality of Egan harps to the thin tapered soundboard and also the soundbox construction, in which Irish oak was used for structural parts and the base blocks.[32] Another

---

28 The fascinating process is detailed in Parfett, 'The death and life of an Egan harp'.   29 See Bart Bjorneberg, 'Renovation, restoration, preservation, conservation', *Conservation and design international* (May/June 2017), conservation-design.com/newsletter1_BA.html. A case in point, on one of the O'Brien portable harps, to replace a small piece of the sculpted decoration, Bjorneberg fashioned a new piece by replicating the decoration on another similar Egan harp. 30 O'Curry, *On the manners and customs of the ancient Irish*, iii, p. 298.   31 Parfett, personal communication, 1 July 2015.   32 Robert Pacey also commented on oak used for the inside

factor contributing to the special Egan pedal harp sound was the use of wooden inserts in the string holes, resulting in a mellow tone.[33] The Portable Irish Harps, although smaller in size, also have thin soundboards with sections of horizontally grained wood and rounded back soundboxes, and the inner structural supports and base block are likewise made of Irish oak, contributing to the distinctive Egan sound.[34]

One way to characterize the particular quality of tone produced by an Egan harp is to contrast it with the more commonly heard modern pedal harp. Obviously modern pedal harps are not all uniform in sound, but have slightly differing 'voices' according to individual makers. However there is a certain commonality in volume, resonance and evenness of tone inherent in modern harps. The distinct differences in the sound projection of modern harps and antique harps are the result of changes in today's construction methods from those of the past. Although the basic structural parts of pedal harps have changed little in the last two centuries, there have been significant modifications, namely increased height, range, dimensions and a strengthening of sections. In the twentieth century, pedal harp manufacturers Lyon & Healy followed two criteria for 'improving' pedal harp design: to increase the volume of sound and to make a sturdier instrument.[35] With a focus on producing an orchestral harp capable of adequately projecting in a large modern ensemble, harps were given extended soundboards, wherein the soundboard flares with greater width near the base to produce louder volume and prolonged resonance. The design alteration was idiomatic to the musical genre of impressionist music in the orchestral repertoire. In atmospheric-themed symphonies, the harp's lush resonant harmonies created tone colour through the layering of long-lasting resonance suspended over the other instruments. In contrast, early nineteenth-century harps with straight soundboards have greater clarity in note articulation, which suited both the style of art music and the more intimate setting of the drawing room. Modern harps today are also built to be indestructible, to counteract the forces of aging, such as a twisted neck or a bowed soundboard from the stress of the strings. Contemporary construction techniques tend to favour thicker wood sections for the neck, and increased lamination of the soundboard in an effort to stabilize any unwelcome movement of parts. However, over-building the instrument has had an adverse effect on the harp tone, which has become duller in timbre. The older pedal harps have a

framework and pedal box on his Egan harp no. 2070 (email communication 16 July 2018). 33 Ibid.   34 A typical feature in Egan-harp construction on all models is the presence of vertical linen strips on the inside backing of the soundboard to provide additional support for the joined sections of wood.   35 A 2009 Historical Harp Society Conference discussion panel on harp construction at the Boston Conservatory with builders Sam Milligan (former harp designer at

noticeably brighter tonal spectrum due to a thinner, more responsive soundboard, which freely vibrates. Parfett describes the soundboards of Egan, Erard and their contemporaries as tapering horizontally from the thickest part in the tenor octave range to the edges, with additional vertical tapering up to the treble and down to the bass end of the soundboard.[36] Although nineteenth-century pedal harps are smaller proportionally in relation to modern harps, they are often surprisingly louder in sound projection due to their thin, flexible soundboards.

My first experience of hearing the sound of an Egan harp came in 2003, when a Royal Portable Irish Harp was acquired by Boston's Museum of Fine Arts.[37] After restringing the harp using thinner, historically correct string gauges, I tuned the harp to a lower pitch (A=415) to lessen the string tension on the soundboard.[38] Parfett refers to the stringing of a historical harp as a 'fine art' that affects the mechanism, playing techniques and sound; an incorrect string tension can 'result in an imperfect tension curve, which can jeopardise the structure of the instrument'.[39] Correctly strung, I was able to hear the harp sound for the first time and was struck by the instrument's thin, clear tone – quite different from modern harps. Then in 2008, I acquired an Egan Portable Irish Harp and came to experience more fully the tonal qualities of an Egan instrument as well as the repertoire of the period (figure E.6).[40] My Egan harp is slightly smaller and with fewer strings than the MFA instrument, and I adapted the museum's stringing chart to the appropriate octaves and gauges, tuning the harp to A=415. When I finally heard the sound of my harp for the first time, I recognized the same distinctive clear tone as produced by the MFA harp, and I was able to reaffirm the descriptions I had so often read in historical sources. The terms 'clear', 'bright' and also 'old' seemed to convey the exceptional timbre produced by both Egan portable harps. While the delicate treble positively 'glistens', the mid-range has a rounded bell-like quality, and the bass has a dry resonance. Present day harp techniques, appropriate for modern taut stringing, are generally not suited to thin, low-tensioned strings on historical harps. The strings feel different in touch, but after adjusting to the slack tension, a whole range of dynamics and nuanced phrasing transports the player into a significantly different soundscape.

Lyon & Healy), Carl Swanson and others.   36 Parfett, 1 July 2015.   37 In 2003 Caroline Gilbert approached me to sell her Egan harp and it was subsequently purchased by the MFA in Boston. 38 I have since played the MFA Egan harp for several gallery talks, and after each demonstration the instrument's soundboard is carefully monitored, and the strings are once again slackened. 39 Parfett, 'The death and life of an Egan harp', part 3, 31.   40 The main structural components of my harp were still intact and only a few parts, such as string pegs and ring stops, had to be replaced before stringing the instrument. Master piano conservator Tim Hamilton, who

E.6 Egan Portable Irish Harp in author's collection. Photo by Matthew Hurrell.

In the performance of early music, one experiences how the musical style of an age perfectly fits the sound quality of the instruments from the period. In my search for music specifically arranged for the Portable Irish Harp, I consulted the rare surviving music collections published by the harp maker's son, Charles Egan, held in the Library of Congress (Washington D.C.) and the British Library (London). The pieces in his *The royal harp director* (1827) range from Irish tunes to opera themes, and are idiomatic to the small harp's crystal-clear attack and short resonance.[41] With a light touch, ornaments such as trills and turns are effortlessly achieved, and the narrow string spacing facilitates rapid scale-wise passages, a stylistic feature in the music. For Irish repertoire, I turned to pieces in Bunting's *The ancient music of Ireland*, arranged for the pianoforte in a period style of chords, arpeggios and Alberti bass. My Egan Irish harp, in terms of its short resonance, slightly resembles an early pianoforte, and the music fits the harp's voice and range, with the more pianistic accidentals in Bunting easily omitted. Additional repertoire sources for the Portable Irish Harp include selected pieces from the pedal harp repertoire of the day, particularly the harp solos by N.C. Bochsa. A typical compositional technique of Bochsa harp solos was the use of a sequence of short melodic motives repeated in different octaves. On a modern harp, repeated motives are somewhat ineffective, due to the smooth homogenous tone throughout the entire range. However on an antique harp, the colour differentiation in the various octaves is heard, from the dark bass to the sparkling treble, bringing to life the musical thoughts within a piece. The experience of playing period music on an Egan harp also creates a connection to the sentiments of another age, as feelings are expressed through stylistic mannerisms in the music, such as Bochsa's wandering scale-wise melodic passages and the sudden shifts from major to minor harmonies for emotive effect. The period pieces played on an Egan harp with its delicate timbre seem to unlock the sounds of another time, and through this unique musical experience, comes a greater understanding of nineteenth-century cultural life.

maintains the museum's historical pianoforte, replicated and replaced two brass ring stops and he also hand carved a complete set of ebony string pegs (original pegs were missing) for holding strings into the soundboard.   41 Harp solos from Charles Egan's books were subsequently recorded on my CD, *The Egan Irish harp* in 2011. The first recording made on Egan harps, the two instruments played on the CD are the MFA Royal Portable Irish Harp and the Portable Irish Harp in my personal collection.

Appendix 1 / Chronology of Egan Harps

1797 John Egan, apprenticed to a blacksmith, constructs his first pedal harp and sells it.

1804 First commercial listing appears in *Wilson's Dublin Directory* as 'Egan (John), Pedal-harp-maker, 25 Dawson-street'.

1805 Sydney Owenson purchases a small gut-strung Irish harp by John Egan.

1809 Egan makes a pedal harp for the duchess of Richmond, wife of Lord Lieutenant Charles Lennox, 4th duke of Richmond.

1809–12 Egan constructs a wire-strung Irish harp to present to the Irish Harp Society of Dublin and he is appointed 'harp maker to the society'. Egan designs a new wire-strung Improved Irish Harp and supplies the harps to pupils at the society's school.

1816 Pierre Erard, Sébastien Erard's nephew, briefly opens an Erard pedal harp showroom at 2 Lower Sackville Street, Dublin, but is unsuccessful and returns to London.

1816–17 Egan receives patronage from the duchess of Dorset, Arabella Diana Cope, wife of Lord Lieutenant Charles Whitworth, 1st earl of Whitworth.

1817 Egan introduces his first double-action pedal harp; the business address in advertisements changes from 25 Dawson Street to 30 Dawson Street.

1818 Patronage is granted to Egan by the Countess Talbot, wife of Lord Lieutenant Charles Chetwynd, 2nd Earl Talbot.

1819–39 John Egan and the later firm, John Egan & Son, supply wire-strung Improved Irish Harp models to the Irish Harp Society of Belfast.

1819 John Egan introduces his newly invented Portable Irish Harp with dital mechanism.

1819 Egan is invited to display harps (pedal and portable) at the Regent's Harmonic Institution, Argyle Rooms, London.

1820 John Egan supplies harps to the royal residences of Carleton House and Windsor Castle in England.

1821 A special winged-maiden Portable Irish Harp is presented to George IV during his visit to Ireland. Sir Benjamin Bloomfield, the king's private secretary, notifies Egan of the award of the royal warrant as 'harp maker to George IV' on 29 August. The Portable Irish Harp becomes the *Royal* Portable Irish Harp.

1821 Egan invents and successfully produces a triple-action pedal harp.

1822 Charles Egan, John Egan's son, is appointed professor of harp to Princess Augusta, George IV's sister.

1823   A Royal Portable Irish Harp is delivered to the poet Thomas Moore.

1824   A triple-action pedal harp is delivered to Princess Augusta at Frogmore House.

1825   Egan advertises a double-action Royal Portable Irish Harp.

1828   The harp firm becomes John Egan & Son. Patronage is bestowed by Lord Lieutenant Henry William Paget, 1st marquis of Anglesey.

1829   John Egan dies, and his son, John Jnr, inherits the Egan harp firm.

1830   John Egan Jnr is declared an insolvent debtor in February. In September, John Jnr marries Catherine Dovey, the daughter of a ship's anchor smith in Liverpool.

1830   Charles Egan is granted a royal warrant as 'harpist to the queen', the wife of William IV, the former Princess Adelaide of Saxe-Meiningen. Charles becomes an honorary member of the Royal Academy of Music, London. Residing in Belgrave Square, he marries the sister of Lord Langford of Co. Meath.

1830   Miss Egan, John Egan's daughter, is married to William Jackson, a former worker in her father's factory. She establishes a harp academy at their residence on 38 Grafton Street.

1831   Patronage for John Egan & Son harps is bestowed by the duchess of Northumberland, wife of Lord Lieutenant Hugh Percy, 3rd duke of Northumberland.

1832   John Jnr abandons the Dawson Street premises and moves into 52 Grafton Street near Mrs Jackson's business at 38 Grafton Street, where she also sells harps, and a professional rivalry ensues.

1835   Jackson's Harp Manufactory, trading from 7 Molesworth Street, begins production of Jackson harps and also sells used Egan harps. John Jnr joins the firm of Egan, Read & Taylor operating from 21 Aungier Street, Dublin.

1836   William Jackson is appointed harp maker to the lord lieutenant's wife, the countess of Mulgrave. Egan, Read & Taylor also receives patronage from the countess.

1836   John Egan Jnr of Egan, Read & Taylor is declared an insolvent debtor.

1838   John Egan Jnr advertises as 'harp manufactr.' at 57 Bride Street in the *Pettigrew and Oulton* directory.

1843   Mrs Jackson's son, William Jackson Jnr, becomes a partner in the business, advertising as 'Jackson and Son, harp makers' in the *Post Office Annual Directory and Calendar.*

1844–68 Francis Hewson, John Egan's nephew, manufactures pedal harps and wire-strung Irish harps from his premises at 37 South King Street. In 1868 a final address is listed as 3 York Street in *Thom's Irish Almanac.*

1844   William Jackson Jnr, grandson of John Egan, inherits the Jackson harp firm and returns the family business to Egan's former pedal harp manufactory at 32 Dawson Street.

Appendix 2 / Glossary of harp terms

back – the rear portion of a harp soundbox, often incorporating soundholes or shutter panels.

base – the lowest part of a harp's body; on a pedal harp, it is a box that houses the pedals.

blades – a mechanism on the neck of gut-strung or nylon-strung Irish harps. A small brass rectangle at the top of each string is rotated by hand to press against the string and raise its pitch by a semitone.

body – the main portion, or soundbox, of a harp.

brass plate – a thin metal plate with engraved inscription indicating the harp maker and address, it sometimes has a serial number, date and a royal warrant. On pedal harps the metal plates (or action plates) also protect the mechanism housed inside the neck.

bridge pins – small metal pins located on the neck, just below the tuning pins; a shallow groove on each pin guides the string to ensure that it lies in the same plane as the other strings. Some pedal harps have adjustable screws to regulate the position of the pins.

capital – an architectural term that refers to the banded sections at the top of a conical harp pillar.

centre string strip – a thin wooden strip affixed to the centre of the soundboard spanning the entire length, pierced with holes into which strings are inserted.

column – see pillar

crochet hooks – a mechanism on late eighteenth-century French pedal harps, in which a metal hook pulls the string against a nut on the harp's neck to raise the pitch by a semitone.

diatonic tuning – a tuning scheme utilizing major and minor scales, with whole tone and semitone pitches.

ditals, ivory stops – seven ivory knobs, one for each note in the scale, project from the inner surface of the pillar on Portable Irish Harps. Invented by John Egan in 1819, the seven hand-operated ivory levers are attached to rods inside the pillar which activate *fourchette* discs on the neck. When a dital is moved down into a slot, the corresponding discs in each octave turn, and strings of that pitch are simultaneously stopped by the disc forks to raise their pitches by a semitone.

double-action harp – invented in 1810 by Sébastien Erard, the double-action pedal harp has two rows of *fourchette* discs to enable three possible pitch sounds for each string: flat, natural and sharp. Each pedal has three slotted positions: flat (open strings), natural (one row of *fourchette* discs activated) and sharp (two rows of *fourchette* discs activated). The double-action pedal harp is tuned in C-flat major. See also **single-action, triple-action.**

empire harp – a style of pedal harp introduced in 1792 by Sébastien Erard, characterized by a conical capital, rounded back and *fourchette* disc mechanism.

feet – the four projecting parts attached to the harp's base, two at the front and two at the back, to stabilize the instrument as it stands and to help balance it when in playing position. The feet are often decoratively carved in the form of lion paws, in the style of neoclassical furniture.

finial – a carved decorative feature at the top end of the pillar on a non-pedal harp.

fourchette **discs** – a mechanism invented by Sébastien Erard, comprised of rotating metal discs with single and double prongs (forks) that stop a string to raise its pitch by a semitone. They may be operated by pedals or ditals.

Grecian capital – a decorative style used for early nineteenth-century pedal harps, distinguished by an upper column adorned with three neoclassical robed female figures or winged-figures, formed in high relief, made of moulded composite material and gilded.

gut strings – made from sheep's gut, the pliable material used for harp strings can be easily pinched or stopped by mechanisms on the neck to obtain semitones and key changes on pedal and portable harps.

head – a shaped area at the top of an Irish harp, where the pillar is joined to the neck.

knee block – the small rounded knee-shaped section where the neck is joined to the soundbox.

neck, harmonic curve – top curved section of the harp that is joined to the pillar and the soundbox.

pedal box – the hollow box-shaped container at the base of a pedal harp that houses the pedals and their springs.

pedal notches, slots – notched openings at the back of the pedal box for positioning the pedals to raise and lower the pitches of strings.

pedal rods – seven thin steel rods, one for each note in the scale, housed inside the hollow pillar, which connect the pedals to the disc mechanism on the neck.

pedals – the foot-operated levers invented in the early 1700s that move into slots to activate a mechanism on the neck for raising and lowering the pitches of the strings.

pillar, column – the vertical support that is joined to the base and the neck.

ring stop, loop stop – a device on Portable Irish Harps by John Egan comprised of a tabbed loop of brass through which a string passes. Operated by hand, as the loop turns, it stops the string in two places, raising the string pitch by a semitone.

scroll top – a carved spiral in a rococo style that often decorates the tops of pillars on late eighteenth-century French pedal harps.

semitone – a musical interval of a half step, or one-half of a whole tone. Harps tend to be tuned diatonically, and various mechanisms can expand the instrument's chromaticism so that a wider range of half steps is accessible.

shutter panels – an invention of Johann Baptist Krumpholtz in the 1780s, the hinged rectangular wooden doors cover the sound holes on the back of a pedal harp. A 'swell pedal' opens and closes the doors to alter the volume of sound or create a tremolo effect.

single-action harp – on early nineteenth-century harps, a single row of *fourchette* discs enables two possible pitches on each string. Tuned in E-flat major, when a pedal is moved into a slot, the corresponding discs turn and stop the string, raising the pitches a semitone, from either flat to natural or natural to sharp. See also **double-action, triple-action.**

soundboard – the flat top surface of the soundbox.

soundbox – the main body of a harp and the instrument's resonating chamber onto which strings are attached.

sound holes – oval or square openings on the back of a harp to emit sound; also used for access in attaching the strings.

stabilizing rod, slide – an invention by John Egan for his Portable Irish Harp, the device consists of a wooden rod culminating with a foot. Housed inside the soundbox and secured by a screw on the back of the harp, when extended to the floor, the rod steadies the harp held in the lap.

stave back – a construction technique of late eighteenth century French harps, in which thin vertical panels are joined edge to edge.

stopped note – an open string is pinched by a mechanism (ring stop, blade, hook, lever or *fourchette* prongs) to shorten the string's sounding length, and the pitch is raised by a semitone.

string peg – a small round peg of ebony, sometimes with an inset of ivory or bone, which plugs into the string hole on the soundboard to keep the string in place.

swell pedal – an eighth pedal operates the opening and closing of shutter panels on a pedal harp to create a crescendo or tremolo effect.

tone, timbre – the tone colour of an instrument's sound, sometimes characterized as 'bright' or 'dull'.

triple-action harp – a harp model invented by John Egan around 1821. Pedals for F, C, and G had an additional third slot and corresponding *fourchette* discs in each octave. The model's chromatic capabilities included thirty-three keys (major and relative minor), including the key of A-sharp major. See also **single-action, double-action.**

tuning key – a device comprised of a wooden handle and a metal shank for turning a tuning pin in order to raise or lower the pitch of the string for tuning.

tuning pins – iron pins inserted horizontally through the neck that turn to alter the string pitch in tuning; the string is threaded in a small hole or slit at one end, and the other end of the pin is tapered to accept a tuning key.

wire strings – strings of brass, bronze, steel or precious metal on Gaelic harps. Wire strings, or strings wound with wire over a silk core, were also used in the bass octaves on pedal and portable harps by John Egan.

Diagram of Action of Harp by John Egan – not to scale.

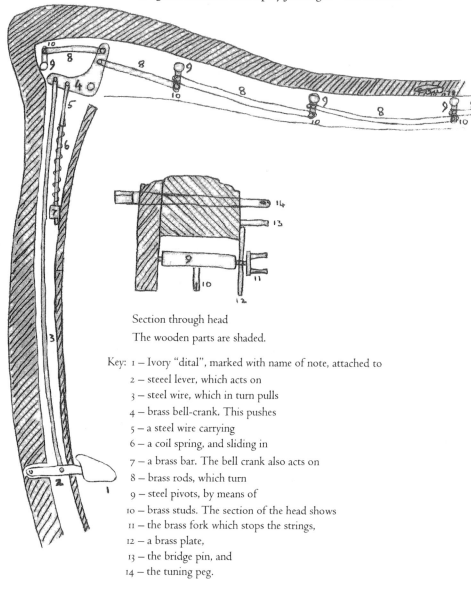

Section through head
The wooden parts are shaded.

Key: 1 – Ivory "dital", marked with name of note, attached to
2 – steeel lever, which acts on
3 – steel wire, which in turn pulls
4 – brass bell-crank. This pushes
5 – a steel wire carrying
6 – a coil spring, and sliding in
7 – a brass bar. The bell crank also acts on
8 – brass rods, which turn
9 – steel pivots, by means of
10 – brass studs. The section of the head shows
11 – the brass fork which stops the strings,
12 – a brass plate,
13 – the bridge pin, and
14 – the tuning peg.

The harp is inscribed – "No. 2098. John Egan & Son, 30 Dawson St., Dublin.
Makers by authority of the Royal Warrant to his most
Gracious Majesty George the ivth. & the Royal Family."

A2.1 'Diagram of action of harp by John Egan' in Chris Warren, 'Some notes on the Egan "Royal Portable" harp', *Folk Harp Journal*, 24 (March 1979), p. 11, reprinted by permission.

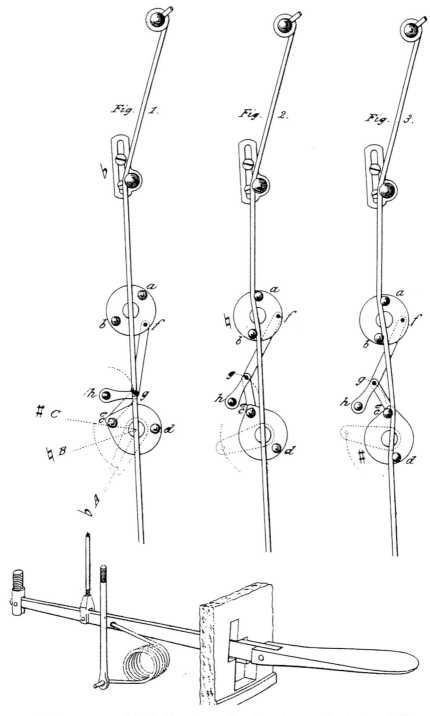

A2.2 The three positions of the double-action *fourchette* discs – flat, natural and sharp – in Pierre Erard's *The harp* (1821).

A2.3 Sections removed from an Egan Portable Irish Harp. Photo by Matthew Hurrell.

Appendix 3 / Catalogue of Egan harps

Serial numbers and production

An analysis of the Egan harp firm's production, such as the numbers of instruments sold, is problematical in that record books are not extant, and only a few harps bear dates. Egan harps made before 1819 do not have serial numbers, and some early harps are without a maker's engraved signature and instead were given a paper label with a handwritten inscription, attached to the inside of the soundbox. Restorers sometimes notice a hand-penned date written on a harp part. A general summary of harp production in the Egan workshop is arrived at by cross-referencing dates on instruments, serial numbers, newspaper adverts, engraved inscriptions and the maker's listings in Dublin commercial directories. The serial numbers on Egan harps do not reflect the actual numbers of harps made. Harp makers often begin numbering instruments with a high number, for instance Lyon & Healy started pedal harp numbering with 'no. 500' in 1889.[1] Although Egan assigned no. 1 to his first dital harp prototype in 1819, it appears he abandoned the low numbering and perhaps started a new numbering sequence with no. 1821, as it was the momentous year in which he was granted the royal warrant. Serials on surviving harps skip from no. 4 to no. 1831.

Years	Serial numbers	Annual harp production	Harps per month
1821–3	1821 to 1858	18	1.5
1823–5	1858 to 1961	51	4
1825–9	1961 to 2081	30	2.5
1829–35	2081 to 2119	6	1 every 2 months

Table A.I. Serial numbers on Egan harps, their estimated dates and the numbers of harps produced, based on the theory that numbering began with no. 1821 in that year.

In the combined years of the two harp firms, John Egan and John Egan & Son, an estimated 300 harps may have been produced between 1821 and 1835. Another 200 harps were possibly made in the firm's early years of 1804–21. The most productive period for the firm appears to have been from 1823 to 1825, which may correspond to increased sales after the award of the royal warrant. In striking contrast, Nex has determined that the London Erard factory manufactured as many as seventeen pedal harps in a single month in 1812.[2] A general estimate of the total number of Egan harps produced overall

1 Samuel O. Pratt, *Affairs of the harp* (New York, 1964), p. 188. 2 Jennifer Susan Nex, 'The

271

might be around 500, concluding that harps by the Egan firm are relatively rare.[3]

Dates of inscriptions

1807   John Egan No. 25 Dawson St. Dublin

1817   John Egan 30 Dawson St. Dublin

1819   John Egan ~ Inventor 30 Dawson St. Dublin

1821   John Egan ~ 30 Dawson St. Dublin/ Maker by Special Appointment to His
         Most Gracious Majesty George IV

*c.*1822 John Egan ~ 30 Dawson St. Dublin/ Maker by Special Appointment to His
         Most Gracious Majesty George IV & the Royal Family

*c.*1825 J. Egan 30 Dawson St. Dublin/ Harp Maker by Authority of the ROYAL
         WARRANT To His Most Gracious Majesty George IV & the Royal Family

1829   J. Egan & Son 30 Dawson St. Dublin/ Harp Makers by Authority of the
         ROYAL WARRANT To His Most Gracious Majesty George IV & the Royal
         Family

1835   Egan, Read & Taylor/ Makers to His Majesty/ 21 Aungier St. Dublin

CATALOGUE KEY

Models, design stages and decorative features

phı   pedal harp, capital style 1: Grecian figures playing lyres, *c.*1817–25

ph2   pedal harp, capital style 2: stylized winged caryatids, *c.*1825–35

s-a   single-action pedal harp

d-a   double-action pedal harp

phs   pedal harp 'special' prototype

PIH   Portable Irish Harp

RPIH   Royal Portable Irish Harp

PIHı   Portable Irish Harp, style 1: slender bowed pillar and high extended head,
             pre-1819

PIH2   Portable Irish Harp, style 2: thicker pillar and oval head, *c.*1819–21

RPIH2   Royal Portable Irish Harp, style 2: thicker pillar and oval head, *c.*1821–3

RPIH3   Royal Portable Irish Harp, style 3: straighter pillar and rounded head,
             *c.*1823–35

PIHs   Portable Irish Harp, 'special' prototype

s/p   gilt sculptural acanthus piece attached to pillar front

h/h   hawk-head painted in gold on knee block

w/h   wolfhound head in gold on knee block

srt   shamrocks, roses and thistles in gold

business of musical instrument making in early industrial London' (PhD, University of London, 2013), p. 115.   3 These figures are based on an assumption that once Egan adopted serial numbers, all subsequent harps were numbered.

| IIH | Improved Irish Harp: conical soundbox, high head and wire strings |
| Ihs | Irish 'special' one-of-a-kind harp with projecting block |

Other notes

height	greatest height from the bottom of the harp to the top of the pillar
depth	greatest width from the front of the pillar to the back of the soundbox or knee block
n/a	information not currently available
n/k	details/present location not known

Location

BC	Boston College
BYU	Brigham Young University
DC	Dean Castle, Kilmarnock, Scotland
EC	Enniskillen Castle, Fermanagh County Museum, Northern Ireland
FH	Fenton House, London
FM	Fitzwilliam Museum, Cambridge, England
HHSI	Historical Harp Society of Ireland, Kilkenny
HM	Horniman Museum, London
HMM	Hamamatsu Museum of Musical Instruments, Japan
HU	Harvard University, Cambridge
ILC	Irish Linen Centre and Lisburn Museum, Lisburn, Northern Ireland
IRE	Republic of Ireland
IU	Indiana University, Bloomington, Indiana
MFA	Museum of Fine Arts, Boston
MG HAMI	MG House of Antique Musical Instruments, Nagoya, Japan
MMA	Metropolitan Museum of Art, New York
MIMB	Musical Instruments Museum, Brussels, Belgium
MMI	Museum of Musical Instruments, Osaka College of Music, Japan
NMI	National Museum of Ireland, Collins Barracks, Dublin
NT	National Trust, UK
NI	Northern Ireland
p/c	private collection
RAM	Royal Academy of Music Museum, London
RCM	Royal College of Music Museum, London
RIA	Royal Irish Academy, Dublin
ROM	Royal Ontario Museum
SM	Smithsonian Museum, Washington, DC
TCC	Treasures of the Camac Collection, Ancenis, France
V&A	Victoria & Albert Museum, London
WT	Waterford Treasures, Waterford, Ireland
YU	Yale University Collection of Musical Instruments

Serial No.	Date	Model/ Mechanism	Location	Colour	Design	Height	Depth	Strings	Inscription
	1807	pedal, s-a/*fourchette*	Howard Bryan, Virginia	varnish	phi	166cm	n/a	34	John Egan 25 Dawson St. Dublin 1807
	1809	wire-strung harp	n/k [E.W. Hennell esq,1904]	n/k	lhs	135.8cm	n/k	36	John Egan No.25 Dawson Street 1809
		pedal, s-a/*fourchette*	Bill and Vicky Bodine, Connecticut	varnish	phs	173cm	77cm	41	John Egan No.25 Dawson St. Dublin
		pedal, s-a/*fourchette*	NMI, Avondale House, Ireland	varnish	phs	167cm	80cm	43	John Egan 30 Dawson St. Dublin
		Portable Irish Harp, ring stops	NT, Snowshill Manor, Worcs., England	green	PIH1, h/h	82.5cm	43cm	29	None
		Portable Irish Harp, ring stops	O'Brien Collection, Chicago	green	PIH1, h/h	81cm	44cm	29	None
		pedal, s-a/*fourchette*	Audrey Gilmer, Belfast	blue	phs	166cm	86cm	43	John Egan 30 Dawson St. Dublin
		Portable Irish Harp,	Stroud District Museum, England	blue	PIH1, s/p	84.5cm	n/a	32	None
		Portable Irish Harp, ring stops	p/c, Dublin	blue	PIH1, s/p, w/h	85cm	40cm	29	[On paper label inside harp, handwritten in ink]; John Egan, Maker/ No. 30 Dawson Street/ Dublin
		Portable Irish Harp, ring stops	NT, Snowshill Manor, Worcs., England	blue	PIH1, s/p, w/h	91.4cm	50cm	36	None
		Portable Irish Harp, ring stops	n/k, Mildred Dilling Photo, BYU	blue	PIH1, s/p, w/h	n/k	n/k	36	n/k
		Portable Irish Harp, ring stops	Nancy Hurrell, Braintree, Massachusetts	blue	PIH1, s/p	84cm	40cm	29	John Egan 30 Dawson St. Dublin
		pedal, s-a/*fourchette*	p/c, England	blue	phi	168cm	n/a	n/a	John Egan 30 Dawson St. Dublin
		pedal, s-a/*fourchette*	Newbridge House, Dublin	blue	phi	166cm	80cm	43	John Egan 30 Dawson St. Dublin
		pedal, d-a/*fourchette*	n/k, auction sale	blue	phi	168cm	n/k	43	John Egan 30 Dawson St. Dublin [and plain brass banner on back plate]
		Charlemont portable, ring stops	F. Oster, Philadelphia	green	PIHs	104.5cm	49cm	27	None
no.1	1819	Portable Irish Harp, ditals	MMA, New York	green	PIH2	78cm	48cm	34	John Egan, Inventer [*sic*]/No. 1/ 30 Dawson St./ Dublin/1819
no.4	1819	Portable Irish Harp, ditals	n/k [Armstrong]	n/k	PIH2	n/k	n/k	34	n/k
		pedal, d-a/*fourchette*	p/c, England	black	phi	n/a	n/a	43	J. Egan 30 Dawson St. Dublin [and brass banner attached; corroded and unreadable]
	1819	pedal, d-a/*fourchette*	p/c, Las Vegas	natural	phi	169.5cm	78.7cm	43	J Egan 30 Dawson St. Dublin Harp Maker/ To the REGENTS Harmonic Institution Argyle Rooms London
		Portable Irish Harp, ditals	Scenkonstmuseet, Sweden	blue	PIH2	92cm	54cm	33	Manufactured by J.Egan Inventer[*sic*] 30 Dawson St. Dublin/ For the Regents Harmonic Institution Argyle Rooms London
		Portable Irish Harp, ditals	V&A, London	blue	PIH2, srt	90cm	46.9cm	34	Manufactured by J. Egan Inventor/ 30 Dawson St./ Dublin

Serial No. Date *continued*	Model/ Mechanism	Location	Colour	Design	Height	Depth	Strings	Inscription
	Portable Irish Harp, ditals	n/k [Hayward]	black?	PIH2, srt	n/k	n/k	34	n/k
	Portable Irish Harp, ring stops	Museo dell'Arpa Victor Salvi, Italy	black	PIH2	89cm	47.5cm	30	John Egan~30 Dawson St. Dublin
1820	Royal Portable Irish Harp, ring stops	Castle Leslie, Co. Monaghan, IRE	green	RPIH2	88cm	39cm	29	J Egan~ 30 Dawson St. Dublin/ Harp Maker to His Majesty. [brass plate replaced; not original inscription]
	Portable Irish Harp, ditals	HM, London	green	PIH2	90cm	49.5cm	30	John Egan/ Inventor/ 30 Dawson St./ Dublin/ 1820
1821	Portable Irish Harp, ditals	Birr Castle, Co. Offaly, IRE	green	PIH2, srt	93cm	43cm	30	Manufactured by John Egan Inventor./ 30 Dawson St./ Dublin [brass plate on back of neck]: J Egan. Dublin.-1821.-
	Portable Irish Harp, ditals	HU, Cambridge, Massachusetts	green	PIH2	87cm	41cm	30	Manufactured by John Egan Inventor./ 30 Dawson St./ Dublin
	Portable Irish Harp, ditals	p/c, Vancouver Island, Canada	green	PIH2	106cm	48cm	31	Egan. Maker, Dublin [brass plate replaced; not original inscription]
	Portable Irish Harp, ring stops	Lorcan Otway, New York	blue	PIH2	88cm	45.7cm	30	John Egan ~ Inventor/ 30 Dawson St./ Dublin
	Portable Irish Harp, ditals	NMI, Dublin	black	PIH2	103cm	47.5cm	32	John Egan ~ Inventor/ 30 Dawson St./ Dublin
	Portable Irish Harp, ditals	p/c, Prague	green	PIH2	n/a	n/a	30	John Egan Inventor/ 30 Dawson St./ Dublin
	Portable Irish Harp, ditals	HU, Cambridge, Massachusetts	blue	PIH2	83cm	41cm	30	J Egan Inventor/ 30 Dawson St./ Dublin
	Portable Irish Harp, ditals	F. Oster, Philadelphia	green	PIH2	88cm	41cm	30	John Egan Inventor./ 30 Dawson St./ Dublin
	Portable Irish Harp, ditals	ROM, Toronto	black	PIH2	87.6cm	n/a	29	John Egan Inventor./ 30 Dawson St./ Dublin
	Portable Irish Harp, ditals	Burns Library, BC	blue	PIH2	87.6cm	42cm	30	John Egan ~ Inventor./ Dawson St./ Dublin
	Portable Irish Harp, ditals	TCC, Ancenis, France	green	PIH2	88cm	35cm	30	John Egan Inventor./ 30 Dawson St./ Dublin
c.1820	winged-maiden ditals	RPIH, RAM, London	green	RPIHs	103.9cm	44cm	29	[Left:] J Egan/ Inventor/ 30 Dawson St./ Dublin [rt]: Maker/ by Special Appointment/ To His Most Gracious/ Majesty/ George IV; [above kb]: JOHN EGAN /INVENTOR /DUBLIN
1820	winged-maiden PIH, ditals	Museo dell'Arpa Victor Salvi, Italy	green	PIHs	102cm	45cm	28	[Gold shield on top of neck]: This improved Irish harp was invented & made by JOHN EGAN, DUBLIN, & HIS TWO SONS JOHN & CHARLES EGAN, 1820.
	Royal Portable Irish Harp, ditals	MMI, Osaka College of Music, Japan	black	RPIH2	88cm	49cm	30	John Egan Inventor./ 30 Dawson St./ Dublin/ Maker by Special Appointment/ To his most gracious Majesty George IV

Serial No. Date *continued*	Model/ Mechanism	Location	Colour	Design	Height	Depth	Strings	Inscription
1821	Royal Portable Irish Harp, ditals	p/c, New York	green	RPIH2	88cm	42cm	30	John Egan Inventor./ 30 Dawson St./ Dublin/ 1821/ Maker by Special Appointment to His Most/ Gracious Majesty George the IV
	pedal, d-a/*fourchette*	p/c, Connecticut	natural	phi	167cm	81cm	43	John Egan DUBLIN, MAKER/ To his most Gracious MAJESTY George IVth
	pedal, s-a/*fourchette*	Isherwood Antiques, Australia	blue	phi	n/a	n/a	?43	John Egan~ 30 Dawson St. Dublin/ Harp Maker by Special Appointment to His Most Gracious Majesty George IVth & the Royal Family
	pedal, s-a/*fourchette*	ILC, Lisburn, NI	blue	phi	170cm	80cm	43	John Egan~ 30 Dawson St. Dublin/ Maker by Special Appointment to His Most Gracious Majesty George IVth
	pedal s-a/*fourchette*	p/c, California	black	phi	n/a	n/a	?43	John Egan 30 Dawson St. Dublin/ Maker By Special Appointment To His Most Gracious Majesty George IVth
no.1831	pedal harp/*fourchette*	n/k, auction sale	natural	phi	170cm	85cm	43	John Egan, 30 Dawson St., Dublin, Harp Maker by Special Appointment.../ No. 1831 [complete inscription not given]
no.1832	pedal, s-a/*fourchette*	p/c, Delaware	natural	phi	170cm	n/a	43	John Egan 30 Dawson St. Dublin/ Harp Maker By Special Appointment To His Most Gracious Majesty George IVth and to the Royal Family/ No.1832
	Royal Portable Irish Harp, ditals	n/k, auction sale	black	RPIH2	88.3cm	n/k	30	John Egan, Inventor/ 30 Dawson St. Dublin/ Maker by Special Appointment To His Most Gracious Majesty George IVth
	Royal Portable Irish Harp, ditals	SM, Washington DC	green	RPIH2	102cm	n/a	32	John Egan, Inventor/ 30 Dawson St. Dublin/ Maker by Special Appointment To His Most Gracious Majesty George IVth
	Royal Portable Irish Harp, ditals	n/k, auction sale	green	RPIH2	n/k	n/k	n/a	n/k
1821	Royal Portable Irish Harp, ditals	DC, Kilmarnock, Scotland	green	RPIH2	86cm	43cm	30	J. Egan Inventor/ 30 Dawson St./ Dublin/ 1821/ Maker by Special Appointment to His Most Gracious Majesty George the IV
	Royal Portable Irish Harp, ditals	n/k, auction sale	green	RPIH2	97.7cm	n/k	32	John Egan, 30 Dawson St. Dublin/ Harp Maker to his Most Gracious Majesty George IV
no.1841	Royal Portable Irish Harp, ditals	n/k, auction sale	green	RPIH2	89cm	n/k	30	J. Egan, 30 Dawson St. Dublin, Harp Maker by Special Appointment to his Most Gracious Majesty George IV & to the Royal Family, No. 1841

Serial No. *continued*	Date	Model/ Mechanism	Location	Colour	Design	Height	Depth	Strings	Inscription
no.1845		Royal Portable Irish Harp, ditals	O'Brien Collection, Chicago	green	RPIH2	82.5cm	44cm	30	J. Egan-30 Dawson St. Dublin/ Harp Maker by Special Appointment/To His Most Gracios Majesty George IVth/ & to the Royal Family/ No. 1845
no.1858	1823	Royal Portable Irish Harp, ditals	RIA, Dublin	green	RPIH2	87.6cm	n/a	30	J. Egan. 30 Dawson St. Dublin/ Harp Maker by Special Appointment To His Most Gracious Majesty George IV & the Royal Family/ No.1858
no.1864?		small Royal Portable Irish Harp	n/k [George W. Childs,1930s]	green	RPIHs	40.6cm	n/k	15	J. Egan ~30 Dawson St. Dublin/ HARP MAKER/ By Special Appointment to His Majesty George IV & the Royal Family
	1823	small Royal Portable Irish	p/c, Bristol Harp/case	orig. blue	RPIHs	40.6cm	26cm	15	JOHN EGAN HARP MAKER/ TO THE KING/ AND ROYAL FAMILY/ No. 30 Dawson St. DUBLIN/ 1823 / 1823 [in mirror image]
no.1860		Royal Portable Irish Harp, ditals	University of Illinois	black	RPIH2	89cm	n/a	30	J. Egan 30 Dawson St. Dublin/Harp Maker by Special Appointment/To His Most Gracious Majesty George IVth & to the Royal Family/No. 1860
no.1861		pedal, d-a/*fourchette*	Thurau Harps, Germany	natural	ph1	171.5cm	101cm	43	John Egan 30 Dawson St. Dublin/ Harp Maker by Special Appointment/ To His Most Gracious Majesty George IVth and to the /Royal Family /No.1861
no.1863		pedal, s-a/*fourchette*	p/c, England	blue	ph1	n/a	n/a	43	John Egan 30 Dawson St. Dublin/ Harp Maker by Special Appointment/ To His Most Gracious Majesty George Ivth and Royal Family/ No.1863
		Portable Irish Harp, ditals (Royal?)	Westport House, Co. Mayo, IRE	green	RPIH3	n/a	n/a	32	n/a
no.1880		Royal Portable Irish Harp, ditals	MIMB, Brussels	green	RPIH3	90cm	46cm	32	J. Egan 30 Dawson St. Dublin/ Harp Maker by Special Appointment To His Most Gracious Majesty George IV & to the Royal Family/No.1880
no.1885		Royal Portable Irish Harp, d-a ditals	FM, Cambridge, England	green	RPIH3	90cm	54cm	31	J. Egan. 30 Dawson St. Dublin. Harp Maker by Special Appointment To His Most Gracious Majesty George IVth./ & the Royal Family./ No.1885
no.1886		Royal Portable Irish Harp, ditals	NMI, Dublin	black	RPIH3	89cm	52cm	33	J Egan~ 30 Dawson St Dublin/ Harp Maker by Special Appointment To His Most Gracious Majesty George IVth/ & the Royal Family/ No.1886
no.1890		Portable Irish Harp, ditals (Royal?)	Temple Newsam House, England	green	RPIH3	n/a	n/a	n/a	n/a
no.1898		Royal Portable Irish Harp, d-a ditals	Munich Stadmuseum, Germany	green	RPIH3	91cm	52cm	31	J. Egan~ 30 Dawson St Dublin/ Harp Maker by Special Appointment To His Most Gracious Majesty George IVth & the Royal Family
no.1904		Royal Portable Irish Harp, ditals	RCM, London	green	RPIH3	91.4cm	52cm	33	J. Egan 30 Dawson St. Dublin/ Harp Maker by Special Appointment To His Most Gracious Majesty George IVth & the Royal Family/ No.1904

Serial No. continued	Date	Model/ Mechanism	Location	Colour	Design	Height	Depth	Strings	Inscription
no.1913		pedal, d-a/*fourchette*	p/c, Newport, Rhode Island	natural	ph1	170cm	84cm	43	John Egan 30 Dawson St. Dublin/ Harp Maker by Special Appointment ~/To His Most Gracious Majesty George IVth and the /Royal Family
no.1918		pedal, d-a/*fourchette*	NMI, Dublin	black	ph1	170cm	80cm	43	John Egan 30 Dawson St. Dublin/ Harp Maker by Special Appointment to His Most Gracious Majesty George IVth & the Royal Family/No.1918
no.1920		Royal Portable Irish Harp, ditals	YU, Connecticut	green	RPIH3	90cm	51cm	33	J. Egan~ 30 Dawson St. Dublin/ Harp Maker by Special Appointment To His Most Gracious Majesty William IVth & the Royal Family/ No.1920
n/a		wire-strung Belfast school harp	NMI, Dublin	natural	IIH	153cm	64cm	37	[Left]: Ceol. bin./ nA. herion./ Lamh. DeArg. eirion [Rt]: YeArc. Coel[*sic*]/ Clan. MileAd./ QUI. SEPERABIT/ M.DC.CLXXXIII
n/a		wire-strung Belfast school harp	EC, Co. Fermanagh, NI	natural	IIH	155cm	62cm	37	[Inscription area on lower sb is covered by paper ads for Egan's 'New Improved Portable Irish Harp'.]
no.1933		wire-strung, Belfast school harp	NMI, Dublin	natural	IIH	153cm	64cm	37	[Left]:MANUFACTURED FOR/ THE BELFAST/ IRISH-HARP/ SOCIETY./ No.1933 [rt]:By J.EGAN,/DUBLIN./ HARP MAKER,/ to His MAJESTY/ GEORGE IV/ AND THE ROYAL FAMILY
n/a	?1822	wire-strung, Belfast school harp	p/c, Ohio	natural	IIH	155cm	64.5cm	37	[Left]: JOHN EGAN/ HARP MAKER TO HIS MAJESTY[? AND THE ROYAL FAMILY] [No address] [rt: SAME in mirror image]
n/a		pedal, s-a/*fourchette*	n/k, auction sale	black	ph2	168cm	n/k	43	J. Egan, 30 Dawson St. Dublin [inscription is on back brass plate]
no.1938		Royal Portable Irish Harp, ring stops	MFA, Boston	black	RPIH3, srt	89cm	55cm	33	JOHN EGAN/ 30, Dawson St. DUBLIN. HARP MAKER to his Majesty GEORGE the 4th,~and~the ROYAL FAMILY. No. 1938/ No. 1938 [in mirror image]
no.1940		pedal, d-a/*fourchette*	p/c, Cork city, IRE	natural	ph1	168cm	81cm	43	No.1940 John Egan 30 Dawson St. Dublin/ Harp Maker by Authority of the ROYAL WARRANT To His Most Gracious Majesty/ George IVth & the Royal Family
no.1943		Royal Portable Irish Harp, ditals	Alec Cobbe, Hatchlands Park, England	green	RPIH3	90cm	52cm	33	No.1943 J. Egan ~ 30 Dawson St. Dublin/ Harp Maker by Special Appointment To His Most Gracious Majesty/ George IVth & the Royal Family

Serial No. *continued*	Date	Model/ Mechanism	Location	Colour	Design	Height	Depth	Strings	Inscription
no.1943		Royal Portable Irish Harp, ditals	MG HAMI, Nagoya, Japan	green	RPIH3	90cm	55cm	33	No.1943 J. Egan 30 Dawson St. Dublin/ *Harp Maker by Authority of the ROYAL WARRANT To His Most Gracious Majesty/ George IVth & the Royal Family*
no.1953		Royal Portable Irish Harp, ditals	F. Oster, Philadelphia	green	RPIH3	91cm	54cm	33	No.1953 J. Egan 30 Dawson St. Dublin/ Harp Maker by Authority of the ROYAL WARRANT To His Most Gracious Majesty/ George IVth & the Royal Family
no.1961	1825	pedal, d-a/*fourchette*	p/c, Dublin	natural	ph1	168cm	81cm	43	No.1961 John Egan 30 Dawson St. Dublin/ Harp Maker *by Authority of the* ROYAL WARRANT *To His Most Gracious Majesty*/ George IVth & the Royal Family
no.1986		pedal, d-a/*fourchette*	Laura Zaerr, US	blue	ph1	168cm	81cm	43	No.1986 John Egan 30 Dawson St. Dublin/ Harp Maker *by Authority of the* ROYAL WARRANT *To His Most Gracious Majesty*/ George IVth & the Royal Family
no.1991		pedal, d-a/*fourchette*	Alec Cobbe, Hatchlands Park, England	blue	ph1	168cm	81cm	43	No.1991 John Egan 30 Dawson St. Dublin/ Harp Maker *by Authority of the* ROYAL WARRANT *to His Most Gracious Majesty*/ George IVth & the Royal Family
no.1994		Royal Portable Irish Harp, ditals	NML, Dublin	green	RPIH3	91cm	n/a	33	No.1994 J. Egan 30 Dawson St. Dublin/ Harp Maker by Authority of the Royal Warrant To His Most Gracious Majesty George IVth & the Royal Family
no.2006		pedal, d-a/*fourchette*	p/c, Australia	natural	ph2	170cm	n/a	n/a	John Egan by appointment to His Majesty King George 4 and Royal Family
no.2009		pedal, s-a/*fourchette*	n/k, auction sale	natural	ph1	167.6cm	90cm	n/k	No.2009 John Egan 30 Dawson St. Dublin/ Harp Maker by Authority of the ROYAL WARRANT *To His Most Gracious Majesty*/ George IVth & the Royal Family
no.2014		pedal, d-a/*fourchette*	TCC, Ancenis, France	natural	ph2	168cm	90cm	43	No.2014 John Egan 30 Dawson St. Dublin /Harp Maker *by Authority of the* ROYAL WARRANT to his Most Gracious Majesty/ George IVth & the Royal Family
no.2015		pedal, s-a/*fourchette*	n/k [Morley Catalogue, 1894]	blue	n/k	n/k	n/k	43	n/k
no.2029		Royal Portable Irish Harp, ditals	Thurau Harps, Germany	blue	RPIH3	90cm	54cm	33	I (J)-EGAN/ 30 DAWSON St./ DUBLIN/ HARP/ MAKER/ To His/ Majesty./ No. 2029 [in mirror image]
no.2036		Royal Portable Irish Harp, ditals	Burns Library, BC	green	RPIH3	89cm	55.8cm	33	No.2036 J. Egan 30 Dawson St. Dublin/ Harp Maker by Authority of the Royal Warrant to His Most Gracious Majesty George IVth & the Royal Family

Serial No. Date *continued*	Model/ Mechanism	Location	Colour	Design	Height	Depth	Strings	Inscription
no.2040	pedal, d-a/*fourchette*	Alec Cobbe, Hatchlands, England	blue	ph2	168cm	81cm	43	No. 2040 John Egan 30 Dawson St. Dublin /harp Maker *by Authority of the* ROYAL WARRANT to His Most Gracious Majesty/ George IVth & the Royal Family
no.2044	wire-strung Belfast school harp	FM, Cambridge, England	natural	IIH	153cm	67cm	37	J.EGAN & SON,/ 30 DAWSON ST./ DUBLIN,/ HARPMAKERS/ TO HIS/MAJESTY/ & the ROYAL FAMILY/ NO. 2044
no.?	wire-strung Belfast school harp	p/c, France	natural	IIH	157cm	67cm	37	J.EGAN & SON,/ 30 DAWSON ST./ DUBLIN,/ HARPMAKERS/ TO HIS/MAJESTY/ & the ROYAL FAMILY EGAN. DUBLIN
	Royal Portable Irish Harp, ditals	IU, Indiana	natural	RPIH3	95cm	45cm	33	J Egan…Dawson St. Dublin [full inscription not available]
	pedal, s-a/*fourchette*	p/c, Iowa	green	ph2	n/a	n/a	n/a	
	pedal, d-a/*fourchette*	n/k, auction sale	natural	ph2	170cm	n/a	n/a	John Egan, 30 Dawson Street, Dublin, Harp Maker to his Majesty George IV and the Royal Family (from auction catalogue)
no.2058	pedal, d-a/*fourchette*	WT, Waterford, IRE	natural	ph2	175cm	81cm	43	No. 2058 John Egan & Son, 30 Dawson St. Dublin/ harp Makers *by Authority of the* ROYAL WARRANT *to His Most Gracious Majesty*/ George IVth & the Royal Family
no.2063	pedal, d-a/*fourchette*	Castletown House, IRE	natural	ph2	168cm	81cm	43	No. 2063 John Egan & Son 30 Dawson St. Dublin/ harp Makers *by Authority of the* ROYAL WARRANT *to His Most Gracious Majesty*/ George IVth & the Royal Family
no.2066	pedal, d-a/*fourchette*	NMI, Dublin	natural	ph2	180cm	n/a	43	No. 2066 John Egan & Son 30 Dawson St. Dublin/harp Makers *by Authority of the* ROYAL WARRANT *to His Most Gracious Majesty* George IVth & the Royal Family
no.2076	pedal, d-a/*fourchette*	Robert Pacey, Lincolnshire, England	green	ph2	170cm	80cm	43	No. 2076 John Egan & Son 30 Dawson St. Dublin/ Makers by Authority of the ROYAL WARRANT to His Most Gracious Majesty/ George IV & the Royal Family
no.2078	pedal, s-a/*fourchette*	FH, London	blue	ph2	168cm	80cm	43	No. 2078 John Egan & Son 30 Dawson St. Dublin/ Makers *by Authority of the* ROYAL WARRANT *to His Most Gracious Majesty*/ George IV & the Royal Family

Serial No. *continued*	Date	Model/ Mechanism	Location	Colour	Design	Height	Depth	Strings	Inscription
no.2081	1829	pedal, s-a/*fourchette*	Emily Laurance, Ohio	blue	ph2	n/a	n/a	n/a	No. 2081 John Egan & Son 30 Dawson St. Dublin/ Makers by Authority of the Royal Warrant to His Most Gracious Majesty George IVth and the Royal Family
no.2082		pedal, d-a/*fourchette*	Clive Morley Harps, Ltd., England	green	ph2	170cm	n/a	43	No. 2082 John Egan & Son 30 Dawson St. Dublin/ Makers by Authority of the ROYAL WARRANT to HIS Most Gracious Majesty/ George 4th AND ROYAL FAMILY
no.2083		pedal, d-a/*fourchette*	WT, Waterford, IRE	natural	ph2	170cm	80cm	43	No. 2083 John Egan & Son 30 Dawson St. Dublin/ Makers by Authority of the ROYAL WARRANT to His Most Gracious Majesty/ George the IV & the Royal Family
no.2085		Royal Portable Irish Harp, ditals	HMM, Japan	natural	RPIH3	90.5cm	54cm	33	No.2085 John Egan & Son 30 Dawson St. Dublin Makers by Authority/ to his Majesty George the 4th & ROYAL FAMILY
no.2098		Royal Portable Irish Harp, ditals	HHSI	natural	RPIH3	89.5cm	53.9cm	33	No.2098 John Egan & Son 30 Dawson St. Dublin/ Makers by Authority of the Royal Warrant to His Most Gracious Majesty/ George the IVth & the Royal Family
no.2119	1835	pedal, d-a/*fourchette*	p/c, Cork city, IRE	natural	ph2	182cm	80cm	43	No.2119 John Egan & Co. 30 Dawson St. Dublin/ Makers by Authority of the Royal Warrant to his Majesty &/ the Royal Family
no.2120		pedal, d-a/*fourchette*	n/k, auction sale	n/k	ph2	170cm	n/k	n/a	No. 2120 J Egan 30 Dawson St. Dublin/ Harp Maker by Authority of the Royal Warrant to His Most Gracious Majesty George IV and the Royal Family
	1835	Egan, Read &Taylor Royal Portable Irish Harp, ring stops	NMI, Dublin	natural	RPIH3	90cm	n/a	33	EGAN, READ & TAYLOR/ MAKERS TO HIS MAJESTY./ 21 AUNGIER ST. DUBLIN
		Egan, Read & Compy, d-a/*fourchettes*	Railway House, Cape Town, South Africa	natural	ph2	n/a	n/a	n/a	Egan, Read & Compy/ DUBLIN

Bibliography

ARCHIVES

Cobbe, Charles, 'General accounts' 1835–43, Cobbe Papers: Ce4–3ii, Alec Cobbe, Newbridge, Ireland

Conroy Collection, Sir Edward Conroy, 2nd Baronet: catalogue 60–83, Balliol College Archives and Manuscripts, University of Oxford

Hanover Royal Music Archive: OSB MSS 146, Beinecke Rare Book & Manuscript Library, Yale University

Irish Traditional Music Archive, Dublin

Library of Congress, Music Division

Thomas Moore collection, Irish Music Archives, John J. Burns Library, Boston College

National Archives, Kew, Richmond, Surrey

National Archives of Ireland

The Rosse Papers: Lady Alicia's music books, Oxmantown Settlement Trust, Birr Castle

Royal Archives, Windsor Castle, Windsor

NEWSPAPERS AND PERIODICALS

American Review: a Whig journal devoted to politics, literature, art and science
Bath Chronicle and Weekly Gazette
Belfast Commercial Chronicle
Belfast News-Letter
Boston Evening Transcript
Chester Chronicle
Dublin Correspondent
Dublin Evening Post
Dublin Morning Register
Dublin Penny Journal
Dublin Satirist
Dublin Weekly Register
English Mechanic and World of Science
Flag of Ireland
Freeman's Journal
Galignani's Messenger
Greenock Advertiser
Hibernia Magazine
Hibernian Journal
Irish Times
London Courier and Evening Gazette
Morning Post
Nation
New York Times
Norfolk Chronicle
Quarterly Musical Magazine and Review
Saunders's Newsletter
Statesman and Dublin Christian Record
Times

DIRECTORIES

Kent's Original London Directory: 1823 (London, 1823).

Pettigrew & Oulton, Dublin Almanac & General Register of Ireland (Dublin, 1838, 1845).

Pigot & Co.'s City of Dublin and Hibernian Provincial Directory (Dublin, 1824).

Post Office Annual Directory and Calendar (Dublin, 1843).

Thom's Irish Almanac and Official Directory of Ireland (Dublin, 1848, 1850, 1868)

Treble Almanack . . . containing Wilson's Dublin Directory (Dublin, 1804–31).

Watson's or the Gentleman's and Citizen's Almanack (Dublin, 1832–44)

OTHER PRINTED SOURCES

Adelson, Robert, Alain Roudier, Jennifer Nex, Laure Barthel and Michel Foussard (eds), *The history of the Erard piano and harp in letters and documents, 1785–1959*, 2 vols (Cambridge, 2015).

Alexander, Angela, 'The post-union cabinetmaking trade in Ireland, 1800–40: a time of transition', *Irish Architectural & Decorative Studies: Journal of the Irish Georgian Society*, 17 (2014), 50–69.

Ambrose, Tom, *The king and the vice queen: George IV's last scandalous affair* (Stroud, 2005).

Anonymous, *Ierne: or, anecdotes and incidents during a life chiefly in Ireland: with notices of people and places* (London, 1861).

Anonymous, 'The harp of the last minstrel of County Louth', *Journal of the County Louth Archaeological Society*, 1:4 (Oct. 1907), 104.

Anonymous, *The royal visit, containing a full and circumstantial account of everything connected with the king's visit to Ireland* (Dublin, 1821).

Appendix to the thirtieth report of the deputy keeper of the public records and keeper of the state papers in Ireland: an index to the act or grant books and original wills of the diocese of Dublin from 1800 to 1858 (Dublin, 1899).

Armstrong, R.B., *Musical instruments*, i: *The Irish and Highland harps* (Edinburgh, 1904; repr. Shannon, 1969).

—, *Musical instruments*, ii: *English and Irish instruments* (Edinburgh, 1908).

Austen, Jane, *Mansfield Park* (London, 1814).

Bennett, John, *Letters to a young lady, on a variety of useful and interesting subjects*, 2 vols (Warrington, England, 1789; repr. Philadelphia, 1793).

Berlioz, Hector, *A treatise on modern instrumentation and orchestration*, trans. Mary Cowden Clark (London, 1844).

Billinge, Michael and Bonnie Shaljean, 'The Dalway or Fitzgerald harp (1621)', *Early Music*, 15:2 (May 1987), 175–87.

Bjorneberg, Bart, 'Renovation, restoration, preservation, conservation', *Conservation and Design International* (May/June 2017), conservation-design.com/newsletter1_BA.html.

Bochsa, N.C., *A new and improved method of instruction for the harp* (London, 1819).

—, *Bochsa's explanations of his new harp effects and passages* (London, 1832).

—, *Les plaisirs de la memoire: select melodies in various styles from the works of the most popular composers* (London, 1838).

—, *Bochsa's history of the harp*, ed. Patricia John (Houston, 1990).

—, *Nouvelle méthode de harpe* (Paris, 1814), trans. and ed. Patricia John (Houston, 1993).

Boydell, Barra, 'The female harp: the Irish harp in 18th- and early 19th-century romantic nationalism', *RIdIM/RCMI Newsletter*, 20:1 (1995), 10–17.

—, 'The iconography of the Irish harp as a national symbol' in Patrick F. Devine and Harry White (eds), *The Maynooth International Musicological Conference 1995: selected proceedings part III*, Irish Musical Studies 5 (Dublin, 1996), pp 131–45.

—, 'The United Irishmen, music, harps, and national identity', *Eighteenth-Century Ireland/Iris an dá chultúr*, 13 (1998), pp 44–51.

—, 'Constructs of nationality: the literary and visual politics of Irish music in the nineteenth century' in Michael Murphy and Jan Smaczny (eds), *Music in nineteenth-century Ireland*, Irish Musical Studies 9 (Dublin, 2007), pp 52–73.

Boydell, Brian, 'Egan, John' in Stanley Sadie (ed.), *New Grove dictionary of musical instruments* (London, 1997), p. 645.

Breathnach, Brendán, *Folk music and dances of Ireland* (Cork, 1996).

Brown, David, 'Some notes on extant chromatic harps' in Heidrun Rosenzweig (ed.), *Historical harps* (Dornach, Switzerland, 1991), pp 165–76.

Brown, William N., *Handbook on japanning* (London, 1913).

Bunting, Edward, *A general collection of the ancient Irish music* (Dublin, 1796).

—, *A general collection of the ancient music of Ireland* (Dublin, 1809).

—, *The ancient music of Ireland* (Dublin, 1840; New York, 2000).

Burke, S. Hubert, *Ireland sixty years ago: being an account of a visit to Ireland by H.M. George IV in the year 1821* (London, 1885).

Campbell, Mary, *Lady Morgan, the life and times of Sydney Owenson* (London, 1988).

Carolan, Nicholas, 'Two Irish harps in Co. Dublin', *Ceol: A Journal of Irish Music*, 7:1 (Dec. 1984), 41–5.

—, 'Egan of Dublin, an 18th-century maker of Irish pipes', *An Píobaire* 13:3 (Aug. 2017), 32–8.

Chadwick, Simon, 'The early Irish harp', *Early Music*, 36:4 (2008), 521–31.

—, *Progressive lessons for early Gaelic harp* (St Andrews, 2009).

Clark, Nora Joan, *The story of the Irish harp: its history and influence* (Lynnwood, WA, 2003).

Clifford, Helen, 'The printed illustrated catalogue' in Snodin and Styles (eds), *Design & the decorative arts* (London, 2004), pp 140–5.

Cobbe, Frances Power, *Essays on the pursuits of women* (London, 1863).

—, *The life of Frances Power Cobbe by herself*, 2 vols (Boston, 1894).

Cooney, Patrick L., 'Drogheda Harp Society', *Journal of the Old Drogheda Society*, 1 (1976), 38–40.

Cooper, David, '"'Twas one of those dreams that by music are brought": the development of the piano and the preservation of Irish traditional music' in Michael Murphy and Jan Smaczny (eds), *Music in nineteenth-century Ireland*, Irish Musical Studies 9 (Dublin, 2007), pp 74–93.

Cousineau fils, Jacques-Georges, *Méthode de harpe* (Paris, 1772).

Croker, John Wilson, *The Croker papers: the correspondence and diaries of the late right honourable John Wilson Croker … secretary to the admiralty from 1809 to 1830*, ed. Louis J. Jennings (New York, 1884).

Cullen, Emily, 'From the Comerford Crown to the Repeal Cap: fusing the Irish harp symbol with Eastern promise in the nineteenth century' in Ciara Breathnach and Catherine Lawless (eds), *Visual, material and print culture in nineteenth-century Ireland* (Dublin, 2010), pp 59–72.

—, 'Tempering the stereotypes of Irishness abroad: the Irish harp as golden lever of temperance and respectability' in Joyce and Lawlor, *Harp studies* (Dublin, 2016), pp 105–20.

Cuthbert, Sheila Larchet, *The Irish harp book: a tutor and companion* (Cork, 1975).

Dickson, David, 'Death of a capital? Dublin and the consequences of union' in Peter Clark and Raymond Gillespie (eds), *Two capitals: London and Dublin, 1500–1840* (Oxford, 2001), pp 113–15.

Donnelly, Seán, 'Lord Edward Fitzgerald's pipes', *Ceol: A Journal of Irish Music* (Apr. 1983), 7–11.

Donovan, Julie, *Sydney Owenson, Lady Morgan and the politics of style* (Bethesda, 2009).

Dooley, Ann and Harry Roe, *Tales of the elders of Ireland* (New York, 1999).

Dowden, Wilfred S. (ed.), *The journal of Thomas Moore*, 2 vols (East Brunswick, NJ, 1983).

Dunne, Tom, 'The Irish harp: political symbolism and romantic revival, 1534–1854', *Irish Architectural & Decorative Studies: Journal of the Irish Georgian Society*, 17 (2014), 14–39.

Edgeworth, Maria, *The Absentee* (London, 1812).

—, and Richard Lovell, *Practical education*, 2 vols (New York, 1801).

Egan, Charles, *A new series of instructions arranged expressly for the Royal Portable Irish Harp invented by Mr John Egan* (Dublin, 1822).

—, *A selection of ancient Irish melodies arranged for J. Egan's newly invented Royal Portable Irish Harp* (Dublin, c.1822).

—, *A selection of favourite airs, with variations arranged for J. Egan's newly invented Royal Portable Irish Harp* (London, n.d.), Hanover Royal Music Archive (OSB MSS 146, Box 33, Folder 169), James Marshall and Marie-Louise Osborn Collection, Beinecke Rare Book & Manuscript Library, Yale University.

—, *A selection of preludes and airs arranged for the Royal Portable Irish Harp invented by J. Egan, harp maker*, Hanover Royal Music Archive (OSB MSS 146, Box 33, Folder 169), James Marshall and Marie-Louise Osborn Collection, Beinecke Rare Book & Manuscript Library, Yale University.

—, *Ancient Irish melodies: as performed by express command before His Most Gracious Majesty George the Fourth during his memorable visit to Ireland* (London, 1822), Hanover Royal Music Archive, James Marshall and Marie-Louise Osborn Collection, Beinecke Rare Book & Manuscript Library, Yale University.

—, *A selection of national lyrics, the poetry by Edward Dowling esq. the melodies arranged with accompaniments for the harp, piano forte or Royal Portable Irish Harp* (Dublin, 1826).

—, *The royal harp director, being a new and improved treatise on the single, double & triple movement harps* (London, 1827).

—, *The harp primer, being a familiar introduction to the study of the harp* (London, 1829).

—, *Brillantes courtes et faciles: preludes for the harp in various major & minor keys* (London, c.1830).

Ellis, Ossian, *The story of the harp in Wales* (Cardiff, Wales, 1991).

Erard, Pierre, *The harp in its present improved state compared with the original pedal harp* (London, 1821).

Farmer, Henry George, 'Some notes on the Irish harp', *Music and Letters*, 24:2 (Apr. 1943), 100–7.

Federal Writers' Project, *Philadelphia: a guide to the nation's birthplace* (Harrisburg, 1937).

FitzGerald, Maureen, Richard FitzGerald and Robert Phelan, *William Vincent Wallace, composer and musician, 1812–1865* (Waterford, 2012).

Fitzpatrick, Siobhán (ed.), *My gentle harp: Moore's Irish melodies, 1808–2008* (Dublin, 2008).

Fitzpatrick, W.J., *Lady Morgan, her career, literary and personal* (London, 1860).

Flood, William Henry Grattan, *A history of Irish music* (Dublin, 1906).

Foley, Catherine, 'Egan, John' in Harry White and Barra Boydell (eds), *The encyclopaedia of music in Ireland* (Dublin, 2013).

Fox, Charlotte Milligan, *Annals of the Irish harpers* (New York, 1912).

Fraser, Flora, *Princesses: the six daughters of George III* (London, 2004).

Galilei, Vincenzo, *Dialogo della musica antica et moderna* [Florence, 1581], trans. Claude V. Palisca (New Haven, 2003).

Govea, Wenonah Milton, *Nineteenth- and twentieth-century harpists: a bio-critical sourcebook* (Westport, CT, 1995).

Gregory, William, *Mr Gregory's letter-box, 1813–1830*, ed. Lady Gregory (London, 1898).

Guinness, Desmond and William Ryan, *Irish houses and castles* (London, 1971).

Hall, Samuel Carter, *A memory of Thomas Moore* (Dublin, 1879).

—, (ed.), *The Art Journal*, 41 (1879), 255.

—, letter repr. in *The American Bookseller*, 15:5 (Mar. 1884), 227.

Hallo, Rosemary Margaret, 'Erard, Bochsa and their impact on harp music-making in Australia (1830–1866): an early history from documents' (PhD, University of Adelaide, 2014).

Halvey, Margaret M., 'American reliques of Tom Moore', *Donahoe's Magazine*, 34:5 (Nov. 1895), 1185.

Hayward, Richard, *The story of the Irish harp* (Dublin, 1954).

Hemlow, Joyce (ed.), *The journals and letters of Fanny Burney (Madame d'Arblay)*, vol. II (Oxford, 1984).

Hibbert, Christopher, *George IV, the rebel who would be king* (New York, 2007).

Hogan, Ita Margaret, *Anglo-Irish music, 1780–1830* (Cork, 1966).

Horton, William Ellis, *Driftwood of the stage* (Detroit, 1904).

Hudson, Katherine, *A royal conflict* (London, 1994).

Hunt, Una, *Sources and style in Moore's Irish melodies* (London and New York, 2017).

Hurrell, Nancy, 'The Royal Portable Harp' in *Journal of the Historical Harp Society*, 13:2 (2003), 19–21.

—, 'Historical harps: shamrocks, roses, and thistles', *Folk Harp Journal*, 129 (Fall 2005), 54–6.

—, 'Historical harps: a harp of Erin rediscovered in the Horniman Museum', *Folk Harp Journal*, 130 (Winter 2005–6), 45–7.

—, 'The Horniman Museum harps', *Bulletin of the Historical Harp Society*, 16:1 (Apr. 2006), 7–10.

—, 'Harps in the Royal College of Music Museum of Instruments', *Bulletin of the Historical Harp Society*, 18:1 (Dec. 2007), 3–9.

—, 'A Drogheda harp: instrument and icon', *History Ireland*, 21:1 (Jan./Feb. 2013), 34–7.

—, 'The "Brian Boru" harp', *History Ireland*, 22:2 (Mar./Apr. 2014), 49.

—, 'Egan, John' in Lawrence Libin (ed.), *The Grove dictionary of musical instruments* (New York, 2014), p. 134.

—, and Mary McMaster, 'The Celtic revival', in 'Harp', *New Grove dictionary of musical instruments* (New York, 2014), pp 582–3.

—, 'The 100th anniversary of the Boston MFA musical instrument collection', *Bulletin of the Historical Harp Society*, 27:2 (Winter 2018), 11–18.

Irish Harp Society, *Rules and regulations of the Irish-Harp Society: instituted in Dublin, July 13, 1809, with a list of the officers and subscribers* (Dublin, 1810).

Jones, Howard Mumford, *The harp that once: a chronicle of the life of Thomas Moore* (New York, 1937).

Joyce, Sandra and Helen Lawlor (eds), *Harp studies: perspectives on the Irish harp* (Dublin, 2016).

Kaiser, Linda Pembroke, *Pulling strings: the legacy of Melville A. Clark* (Syracuse, 2010).

Kelly, Ronan, *Bard of Erin: the life of Thomas Moore* (Dublin, 2008).

Knoke, Paul, 'An overview of the development of the pedal harp', *Historical Harp Society Bulletin*, 8:3 (Spring 1998), 2–11.

Krummel, Donald William and Stanley Sadie, *Music printing and publishing* (New York, 1990).

Kuronen, Darcy, *Musical instruments: MFA Highlights* (Boston, 2004).

——, 'The earliest upright piano? An instrument by Robert Woffington of Dublin', *Newsletter of the American Musical Instrument Society*, 37:3 (Fall 2008), 11–12.

Laffan, William, Christopher Monkhouse and Leslie Fitzpatrick (eds), *Ireland: crossroads of art and design, 1690–1840* (Chicago, 2015).

Langley, Leanne, 'A place for music: John Nash, Regent Street and the Philharmonic Society of London', quoting 'English literary intelligence', *English Musical Gazette*, Feb. 1819, *Electronic British Library Journal* (2013).

Lanier, Sara C., '"It is new-strung and shan't be heard": nationalism and memory in the Irish harp tradition', *British Journal of Ethnomusicology*, 8 (London, 1999), 1–26.

Larchet Cuthbert, Sheila, *The Irish harp book* (Dublin, 1975).

Lawlor, Helen, *Irish harping, 1900–2010* (Dublin, 2012).

Ledwich, Edward, *The antiquities of Ireland* (Dublin, 1804).

Leerssen, Joep, *Remembrance and imagination: patterns in the historical and literary representation of Ireland in the nineteenth century* (Cork, 1996).

—, 'Last bard or first virtuoso? Carolan, conviviality and the need for an audience' in Liam P. Ó Murchú (ed.), *Amhráin Chearbhalláin/The poems of Carolan: reassessments* (London, 2007), pp 30–42.

Leppert, Richard D., *Music and image: domesticity, ideology, and socio-cultural formation in eighteenth-century England* (Cambridge, 1988).

Libin, Laurence, *American musical instruments in the Metropolitan Museum of Art* (New York, 1985).

Light, Edward, *A new and complete directory to the art of playing on the patent British lute-harp, with suitable lessons, &c* (London, c.1819).

Loesser, Arthur, *Men, women and pianos: a social history* (New York, 1954; repr. 1990).

Loughlin, James, *The British monarchy and Ireland: 1800 to the present* (Cambridge, 2007).

Malcomson, A.P.W., *The pursuit of the heiress: aristocratic marriage in Ireland, 1740–1840* (Belfast, 2006).

Marson, John, *The book of the harp: the techniques, history and lore of a unique musical instrument* (Buxhall, 2005).

Mayer, J.B., *Complete instructions for the harp* (London, 1800).

Mayes, Elizabeth (ed.), *Áras an Uachtaráin: a history of the president's house* (Dublin, 2013).

McBride, Lawrence W. (ed.), *Images, icons and the Irish nationalist imagination, 1870–1925* (Dublin, 1999).

McClelland, Aiken, 'The Irish harp society', *Ulster Folklife*, 21 (1975), 15–24.

Mitchell, Sally, *Frances Power Cobbe: Victorian feminist, journalist, reformer* (Charlottesville, VA, 2004).

Moloney, Colette, *The Irish music manuscripts of Edward Bunting (1773–1843): introduction and catalogue* (Dublin, 2000).

Moore, Thomas, *Memoirs, journal, and correspondence*, vol. 5 (London, 1854).

—, *Moore's Irish melodies: the illustrated 1846 edition* (New York, 2000).

Moran, Seán Farrell, 'Images, icons and the practice of Irish history' in Lawrence W. McBride (ed.), *Images, icons and the Irish nationalist imagination, 1870–1925* (Dublin, 1999).

Morgan, Lady; see Owenson, Sydney

Morgan, Maud, 'The harp: historical paper', *Brainard's Musical World* (1885), 366.

Morley, J.G., *A simple method of learning to play the old Irish harp* (London, c.1898).

Morris, F.O., *A series of picturesque views of seats of the noblemen and gentlemen of Great Britain and Ireland* (London, 1840).

Moynihan, Colin, 'For a rare discarded harp, a chance to sing again', *New York Times*, 9 Aug. 2009.

Nex, Jennifer Susan, 'Gut string makers in nineteenth-century London', *Galpin Society Journal*, 65 (Mar. 2012), 131–60.

—, 'The business of musical instrument making in early industrial London' (PhD, University of London, 2013).

Ó Brógáin, Séamus, *The Wolfhound guide to the Irish harp emblem* (Dublin, 1998).

O'Connell, Brian, 'A fairytale in New York', *Irish Times*, 15 Aug. 2009.

O'Curry, Eugene, *On the manners and customs of the ancient Irish*, vol. 3 (London, 1873).

O'Donnell, Mary Louise, 'Owen Lloyd and the de-Anglicization of the Irish harp', *Éire-Ireland*, 48:3 (2013), 155–75.

—, *Ireland's harp: the shaping of Ireland's identity, c.1770–1880* (Dublin, 2014).

O'Farrell, Anne-Marie, 'The chromatic development of the lever harp: mechanism, resulting technique and repertoire' in Joyce and Lawlor, *Harp studies* (2016), pp 209–38.

O'Neill, Capt. Francis, *Irish minstrels and musicians, with numerous dissertations on related subjects* [1913] (Cork and Dublin, 1987).

O'Sullivan, Donal, *Carolan: the life times and music of an Irish harper* (London, 1958).

Owenson, Sydney, Lady Morgan, *St Clair, or the heiress of Desmond* (Dublin, 1803).

—, *The novice of Saint Dominick*, 4 vols (London, 1805).

—, *Twelve original Hibernian melodies, with English words, imitated and translated, from the works of the ancient Irish bards* (London, 1805).

—, *The wild Irish girl: a national tale*, 3 vols (London, 1806).

—, *The wild Irish girl: a national tale* (London, 1846).

—, *Patriotic sketches of Ireland*, vol. 1 (London, 1807).

—, *The missionary: an Indian tale*, 3 vols (London, 1811).

—, *The O'Briens and the O'Flahertys* (London, 1827).

—, *The book of the boudoir*, 2 vols (London, 1829).

—, *Passages from my autobiography* (London, 1859).

—, *Lady Morgan's memoirs: autobiography, diaries and correspondence*, ed. W. Hepworth Dixon, 2 vols (London, 1862).

Parfett, Michael, 'The death and life of an Egan harp', *Conservation News* (Nov. 2003/July 2004/July 2005).

Parker, Mike, *Child of pure harmony: a sourcebook for the single-action harp* (lulu.com, 2005).

Pratt, Samuel O., *Affairs of the harp* (New York, 1964).

Priestley, J.B., *The prince of pleasure and his regency, 1811–20* (London, 1969).

Reilly, Eileen, 'Beyond gilt shamrock' in Lawrence W. McBride (ed.), *Images, icons and the Irish nationalist imagination, 1870–1925* (Dublin, 1999), pp 99–100.

Rennie, Elizabeth, *Traits of character: being twenty-five years' literary and personal recollections*, 2 vols (London, 1860).

Rensch, Roslyn, *The harp: its history, technique and repertoire* (New York, 1969).

—, *Three centuries of harpmaking* (2002).

—, *Harps & harpists* (Bloomington, 1989; 2nd ed. 2007).

Rimmer, Joan, 'The morphology of the Irish harp', *Galpin Society Journal*, 17 (Feb. 1964), 39–49.

—, *The Irish harp* (Cork, 1969; 2nd ed. 1977).

Rules and regulations of the Irish-harp society: instituted in Dublin, July 13, 1809: with a list of the officers and subscribers (Dublin, 1810).

Russell, Lord John (ed.), *Journal and correspondence of Thomas Moore*, 8 vols (London, 1853–6).

Sheehy, Jeanne, *The rediscovery of Ireland's past: the Celtic revival, 1830–1930* (London, 1980).

Sanger, Keith and Alison Kinnaird, *Tree of strings* (Midlothian, Scotland, 1992).

Snodin, Michael and John Styles (eds), *Design & the decorative arts: Georgian Britain, 1714–1837* (London, 2004).

Speltz, Alexander, *The styles of ornament* [1904] (New York, 1959).

Sugimoto, Hayato, 'The harp lute in Britain, 1800–1830: a study of the inventor Edward Light and his instruments' (PhD, University of Edinburgh, 2014).

Swanson, Carl, *A guide for harpists: care, maintenance and repair of the pedal harp* (Boston, 1984).

Teahan, John, 'A list of Irish instrument makers', *Galpin Society Journal*, 16 (May 1963), 28–32.

Thuente, Mary Helen, *The harp restrung: the United Irishmen and the rise of literary nationalism* (Syracuse, 1994).

Vallancey, Charles, *Collectanea de rebus Hibernicis* (Dublin, 1786).

Vincent, Ian, 'New life for an Egan harp', *Lisburn Historical Society Journal*, 10 (2005–6), 1–5.

Walker, Joseph Cooper, *Historical memoirs of the Irish bards* (Dublin, 1786).

Walton, Russell, *A harp of fishbones* (Belfast, 1992).

Warburton, John, Revd J. Whitelaw and Revd Robert Walsh, *History of the city of Dublin: from the earliest accounts to the present time* (London, 1818).

Warren, Chris, 'Some notes on the Egan "Royal Portable" harp', *Folk Harp Journal*, 24 (Mar. 1979), 10–11.

Wells, Elizabeth and Chris Nobbs, *European stringed instruments: Royal College of Music Museum of Instruments catalogue, part III* (London, 2007).

White, Harry and Barra Boydell (eds), *The encyclopaedia of music in Ireland* (Dublin, 2013).

Wright, Revd G.N., *An historical guide to ancient and modern Dublin* (London, 1821).

Yeats, Gráinne, *The harp of Ireland* (Belfast, 1992).

Young, Hilary, 'Rococo style' and 'Neoclassicism' in Snodin and Styles (eds), *Design & the decorative arts* (2004), pp 46–61.

Zingel, Hans Joachim, *Harp music in the nineteenth century*, trans. and ed. Mark Palkovic (Bloomington, 1992).

DISCOGRAPHY

Hunt, Una (producer), Nancy Hurrell, Claire Connolly and Julie Donovan, 'The wild Irish girl and her harp' (RTÉ Radio Lyric FM, Lyric Feature, 25 July 2014).

Hurrell, Nancy, *The Egan Irish Harp* (Boston, 2011).

INTERNET SOURCES

archive.org
britishnewspaperarchive.co.uk
broadwood.co.uk/history.html
camac-harps.com
douglasharpco.com
dublinmusictrade.ie
earlygaelicharp.info

futuremuseum.co.uk

harpspectrum.org/historical/historical.shtml

horniman.ac.uk/about/museum-history

info.music.indiana.edu/news/page/normal/7032.html

morleyharps.co.uk

nationaltrust.org.uk/snowshill-manor-and-garden

posteurop.org/StampCollections?selectedStampYear=2014

royal.gov.uk

vam.ac.uk/content/articles/h/musical-instruments-collection-history

vam.ac.uk/content/articles/s/style-guide-regency-classicism

wirestrungharp.com/

Index